CW00952163

Paul Mason was just 18 years old when India stirred in him. In order to find m̶o̶ began selling off his possessions, but n̶o̶t̶ ̶b̶e̶i̶n̶g̶ ̶a̶b̶l̶e̶ ̶t̶o̶ enough ready cash for the flight, he decided instead to hitchhike there, and in this seemingly hare-brained scheme he was accompanied by Yolanda, his Italian girlfriend.

Their journey wasn't envisaged simply as a vacation or an adventure, but as a quest, an exploration of both inner and outer life, even as a pilgrimage of sorts, one which, totally unexpectedly, resulted in the discovery and exploration of authentic Yoga Meditation.

Paul Mason on a return visit to Swargashram, Rishikesh

Titles by Paul Mason:

Via Rishikesh: En Route to Chittavrittinirodha

The Knack of Meditation:
The No-Nonsense Guide to Successful Meditation

Mala: A String of Unexpected Meetings

Kathy's Story

Maharishi Mahesh Yogi: The Biography of the Man Who Gave
Transcendental Meditation to the World

The Beatles, Drugs, Mysticism & India:
Maharishi Mahesh Yogi - Transcendental Meditation - Jai Guru Deva OM

Roots of TM: The Transcendental Meditation of Guru Dev
& Maharishi Mahesh Yogi
^
Den Transcendentala Meditationens Ursprung - Turning Pages
Swedish edition 2017

108 Discourses of Guru Dev:
The Life and Teachings of Swami Brahmananda Saraswati,
Shankaracharya of Jyotirmath (1941-53) - Volume I
~
The Biography of Guru Dev:
The Life and Teachings of Swami Brahmananda Saraswati,
Shankaracharya of Jyotirmath (1941-53) - Volume II
~
Guru Dev as Presented by Maharishi Mahesh Yogi:
The Life and Teachings of Swami Brahmananda Saraswati,
Shankaracharya of Jyotirmath (1941-53) - Volume III

Dandi Swami: The Story of the Guru's Will, Maharishi Mahesh Yogi, the
Shankaracharyas of Jyotir Math & Meetings with Dandi Swami Narayananand Saraswati

The Maharishi: The Biography of the Man Who Gave
Transcendental Meditation to the World
Element Books - First English edition 1994
Evolution Books - Revised English edition 2005
Maharishi Mahesh Yogi - Aquamarin - German edition 1995
O Maharishi - Nova Era - Portuguese edition 1997

VIA RISHIKESH

- EN ROUTE TO CHITTAVRITTINIRODHA

The real life chronicle of a crazy quest, an epic hitchhiking trip, from England, through Europe, North Africa, and the Middle East, to India.

by

Paul Mason

PREMANAND
www.paulmason.info
premanandpaul@yahoo.co.uk

ISBN 978-0-9562228-7-9

A Few Words

*I realise that most of that which has been published in my name is
simply the fruit of my research, presented for public consumption,
and that I haven't actually written much that is personal,
about my past or why I did the research.*

*So I took a fresh look at the rough draft of the chronicles of my hitchhiking
trip, a journey undertaken without preparation or proper funds
(and with no insurance),
leaving from England, with my Italian girlfriend,
and travelling through Europe, North Africa, and the Middle East, to
India.*

*Whilst coaxing the manuscript into shape
I found myself undecided about what else to do with it,
other than try to correct the grammar and improve the writing style,
perhaps.*

*I thought about maps and photographs, but as the reader will discover,
we had no map or camera when we embarked on our journey,
just our passports, a change of clothes, and little else.*

*The thing is, I want to take you, the reader, into my confidence,
not in an attempt at self-promotion,
nor from a feeling of self-importance,
but out of a genuine desire to level with you.*

*I not only wish to tell the haphazard tale of my journey,
but to impart something of the inner quest.*

*I have long suspected that somewhere back in time
mankind lost something,
something of value.*

*I feel we should attempt to rediscover
whatever it was that was lost.*

*It's my belief that gaining a greater feeling of connectedness
and a deeper sense of peace within ourselves
would go a long way towards making all our lives more satisfying.*

Acknowledgements

— ★ —

Dedicated to
Gabriel Paul Roberto Mason
(son of Paul & Yolanda)

I would like to extend my grateful thanks to all the many people who helped Yolanda and myself on the trip, and to those who have encouraged me to set down my recollections and make them available. Firstly to my Dad's friend, J.V., John Vaughan, who I encountered shortly after arriving back from my journey, who first suggested I write the tale, and lastly to Dr Jessie Mercay who, after hearing of the imminent publication of this account, said she hoped that it would include some description of the meditation I practice, which gives one access to a peaceful state of mind not usually attainable by other means and thereby gives one a chance to replenish one's energy and become refreshed, enabling one to live life to the full.

Gratitude to Kathy for tea, support and invaluable feedback, who managed to persuade me to re-read the final text immediately prior to publication, prompting my decision to pop in more illustrations towards the end of the book, and make small tweaks and other necessary improvements, including adding the signatures on this page from documents of the trip. And for her help at copy-editing and proofreading. And my appreciation to Richard for tech help, especially for his patience in explaining techy terms, e.g. 'same as previous' = 'header/footer break'! And to Ben for his support, and I'm touched to discover that an entire section of his bookshelf unit has been set aside for the purpose of displaying my books.

Big thanks to friend Jonathan Miller, author of *'My Journey in 1970 to Maharishi's India'* (Boulder, Colorado: Shickshana Partika Press, 2014) who kindly sent me several of his photographs taken within months of my visit to India, and granted me permission to use those images in this book. And thanks to Ullie for permission to use any images from Frank Papentin's *'Darshan'* photo book.

Thanks also to George Wolfe for alerting me to the existence of the quote from Fr. Thomas Keating, and to all those lovely people I have not mentioned, whose assistance I would love to acknowledge, if there were only more space here!

CONTENTS

	PREAMBLE	1
Chapter 1	THE LION & THE UNICORN	23
Chapter 2	A GOOD OMEN	38
Chapter 3	PARADISE LOST	54
Chapter 4	SNAKES AND LADDERS	66
Chapter 5	A CLOSE THING	77
Chapter 6	A SPELL OF FAIRY TALE	88
Chapter 7	FORTY FIVE IN THE SHADE	97
Chapter 8	GETTING TO KNOW THE CUSTOMS	110
Chapter 9	DOWNTOWN GINGERPOPOLI	123
Chapter 10	PORPOISES OUT OF NOWHERE	136
Chapter 11	OF BAZAARS AND BATHS	149
Chapter 12	UP IN THE CLOUDS	161
Chapter 13	OUT OF THE STERLING BELT	171
Chapter 14	UNLIKELY PROPOSITIONS	188
Chapter 15	WHAT DID I SAY?	206
Chapter 16	PROPER - IN PYJAMAS	224
Chapter 17	AT THE ROOTS OF THE MOUNTAINS	240
Chapter 18	WELL BEYOND THE WORLD	256
Chapter 19	RENEWED	266
Chapter 20	MONKS AND MONKEYS	274
Chapter 21	MAD DOGS AND ENGLISHMEN	291
Chapter 22	YOGA MEDITATION	305

The author at about 2 ½ years of age

PREAMBLE

Hovering about in a state of indecision, drained of all energy, I'd begun to feel that I was cracking up. I couldn't recollect a time when decisions were so hard to make, or a time of such deep anguish. In fact, until recently I had been going through one of the happiest periods of my life.

From being confidant, outgoing and carefree, I'd become muddled, introverted and quietly desperate, a shadow of my former self. However, in the notion that through travel I might re-discover myself, a ray of light suddenly appeared, and I hoped that same light would now probe the otherwise gloomy reaches of my mind.

* * *

As a child (the youngest of four), cherished by my parents, I had enjoyed myself immensely, indulging in the normal games and pursuits of my years. I looked forward to the summer holidays; I valued attending the Wolf Cubs (a club for boys still too young to join the Boy Scouts) and visits to the swimming baths, all being my favourite treats - not to mention eating sweets, of course. Through bus-spotting and train-spotting (going around taking the numbers of buses and railway engines) I got to know my way around London whilst still attending primary school.

Ours was a Christian family with both my parents attending church regularly, so of course I sometimes puzzled about who or what God is? Indeed, on entering the Holy Trinity Church, Roehampton, sited adjacent to my primary school, I got to thinking about how I might actually make contact with God.

I sat down on a hard wooden pew and looked around me, at the grand stone building, up at the massively high roof, the stained glass windows over the altar, and the sunlight streaming in down onto the tiled floor. Since I was told that God watches over us and listens to us, I imagined that prayer must be a direct way to contact Him, and that praying was rather like making a long distance telephone call, but without the need of the phone. So I closed my eyes and sat for a while without thinking, hoping that just by sitting very attentively I would get God's attention. I waited and waited and waited, but when I got no response I opened my eyes again.

I used to like spending time outside in our garden, studying the flowers and the bushes, lifting the occasional stone to spy out the life underneath, the insects with their eggs. On one occasion, walking the crazy paving pathway I got to wondering just who I was, and stood stock still and tried to see myself from within. It was then that I noticed that my inner self was in fact a bear. But I didn't tell anyone.

Although I would have been much happier to stay at home and not go to school, I was an obedient child; that is until a little incident that suggested another way to behave. I was going from one part of the school to another, which involved going a distance uphill past the church, when I heard someone shout, *'Don't run!'* I looked around, only to see my brother Raymond, who is a couple of years older than me, and a Prefect in the school. I pondered that he would never have been able to push me about at home, and here he was laying down the law. Hurrumph!!

I loved reading comics, my favourites being the *Dandy*, *Beezer*, *Topper* and the *Beano*. What wonderful rebellious mischievous colourful characters there were, always up to crazy antics, Dennis the Menace, with his shock of black curly hair, The Bash Street Kids, Roger the Dodger and Minnie the Minx, and all the rest, my constant companions.

Academically I showed some potential, though I suspect it was my distaste for school's imprisoning atmosphere that prevented me from realising it. I seem to remember that much of my time at primary school was spent in daydreams that I wove to entertain myself, to distract myself from the tedium. My lack of enthusiasm for schooling did not go unnoticed, and I gradually became something of a rebel! Indeed, I recall Mr Whitacker, the headmaster of Roehampton Church School, phoning my mother to tell her what was in store, *'That boy will be a juvenile delinquent. Just you wait and see!'* Simply, that he had discovered I'd torn up my 'Dental Check' form, on account of my fearing a trip to the dentist!

Anyway, on returning home for lunch that day, my mother told me, *'I was making marmalade at the time, and his phoning made it stick to the pan. It all got burnt, I was very annoyed else I would have been behind the front door waiting for you with a copper stick.'* She smiled at me indulgently, for we had no such item in the house. I didn't know what a delinquent was, though I doubted this was the time to ask.

The headmaster made another prediction, that I would fail my 'Eleven Plus' exam, and he seemed really put out when proved wrong! Mind you, after finding out what grammar school was like, I felt mine to be a hollow victory. The facilities at Westminster City School, an elitist single-sex school, proved to be truly desperate, resulting in most of the teaching coming from the blackboard. Formidable masters in black gowns taught at us. I was routinely exposed to jibes and insults, and all-too-frequently subjected to humiliation. With opportunities to express myself being severely limited, I began to loathe going to school intensely.

Somehow I got curious to know about meditation, and there was a boy in my form called Bashir, who I took to be an Indian, and whom I thought might know how to do it. He replied quite willingly, telling me that it involved closing ones eyes and thinking about something, a cow perhaps. His answer puzzled me, as I couldn't understand why I should think about a cow, or how it would be of any benefit.

As with most adolescents, image meant a lot to me, and with the trend towards wearing long hair, I was determined to let mine grow, at least over my collar. Encouragement to do this was offered from an unlikely quarter - an oil painting that hung in the school's main hall. Of immense size it portrayed the school's founder, King Charles II, draped in fantastic finery, rich and colourful raiment, shoes of white satin, his hair, his crowning glory, flowing over his shoulders in a cascade of tightly wound black curls, majestically framing his face. Himself a local boy, the 17th century king presided over morning assembly each and every day.

Seated on the stage and flanked by his cohorts - a sea of black mortar boards - the tall stooped figure of the headmaster would rise, step up to the lectern, make his address, and on occasion would pause dramatically, a pained expression pinching his grey features, his eyes staring icily:

'Will the following boys see me after assembly... Brooks, Mason....' He reeled off other names too, that I don't recall.

Sitting in the wood-panelled vestibule, I pondered on what the Head might want with me. I could think of nothing I had done of late to warrant being summoned like this, so I took the opportunity to relish these moments of calm, pleased at having a valid reason for being late for first lesson. At length the ancient hardwood door to the Head's study opened, and Brooks (a somewhat older pupil) emerged, and fixing me with a conspiratorial grin he then gestured for me to go inside the office.

I stood alone in front of the Head, my hands clasped, waiting for him to speak. Springing from his seat he surprised me by ordering me to put on my cap. Slowly, obediently, I removed the tattered object from my blazer pocket and proceeded to perch it on my head.

'Ahh, just as I thought,' he snapped, *'I can't **see** it! Get your hair cut immediately or I will suspend you! Do you understand? Return here for my approval. Now **go** boy!'*

Back in the form room I found a pair of scissors, blunt as I discovered, and gave my curly locks a quick trim. Actually, I wasn't really thinking straight else I should have just let him suspend me, but then I wasn't looking for trouble, it just happened.

Having been cast in the role of the 'black sheep' it became increasingly difficult to take my schooling seriously. Cooped up and listless, I didn't apply myself; *'has the ability'*, *'must try harder'* and *'could do much better'* were phrases I became very familiar with. So I had to find a way to deal with my incarceration, and ironically I found hope in the usually joyless lessons of chemistry, which provided me the ingredient for a most enduring fantasy. When the rest of the class left the room, I would extract a large piece of phosphorous from its stoppered bottle and leave it smouldering on one of the wooden bench tops. Eventually the classroom would catch fire and the resulting conflagration would rid me of this hated institution forever. But I didn't even get as far as procuring a bottle of phosphorous…

Outside of school I was allowed a lot of freedom, and when only just turned 13 years old I arranged a camping trip with my friend, Martin Durban. Together we caught a train out of London to a village in lovely leafy Surrey, tramped the country lanes, and stayed in the grounds of a Youth Hostel, using the facilities there, and in return helped out with the chores. Martin and I were both in the Wolf Cubs together, the highlight of the year being the Bob-a-Job week, when all cubs were expected to go around and find odd jobs for which they were paid, in order to boost the funds of the organisation.

I recall something else about Martin, that both his sisters were Beatle mad! They collected their records and were excited to tell us about going to see the group, up in Liverpool. There was a lot of crazy Beatle mania in those days; and to me it seemed something that mainly girls got involved in. The music sounded good though, songs like *Twist and Shout* and *She Loves You.* Yeah, Yeah, Yeah!

I always got the impression that being a little older than Martin he looked up to me, and on hearing the lyrics of *I'm Alive*, The Hollies' hit, he told me that it put him in mind of being with me.

I used to think I was living, baby I was wrong
No I never knew a thing about living 'til you came along

Nice of him to say; I was really touched.

From an early age I attended Christian Science Sunday school, and I enjoyed going there as the people there were extremely friendly, but the lessons concerning the nature and existence of God puzzled me greatly. And as time wore on, I began to acknowledge my incapacity to benefit from this tuition. This crisis of faith in the church forced upon me a need for self-reliance and independence, which soon caused me to question and dismiss the disciplines imposed on me, lock, stock and barrel. I rejected the establishment and openly rebelled against authority and convention. I flaunted well-intentioned guidance.

I confess, when I would normally have been attending Sunday school, I found myself strolling down towards the river, and walking into a Public House, the Bricklayers Arms, where I ordered myself a half pint of brown ale. In order to be allowed into a pub one needed to be at least 16 years of age, so I was glad to be able to pass myself off as being some three years older than I was. I really loved the old world charm of the place, and the warming, cheering effect of the drink. I made a snap decision to visit there again. It was a spiritual experience all right, albeit one that required no belief or good deed from my side, just the spending of a few coins.

Just as it was inevitable that I would get around to sampling the enjoyment of alcohol, it was just a matter of time before I would become curious concerning the pleasures of sex, for it appeared, from the way people spoke about it, that sexual gratification was **the** most enjoyable experience one could have in life. But the subject appeared wholly mysterious to me, that is until a friend clued me up and explained how he pleasured himself. I admit that at the time it seemed like a most important and wonderful discovery.

Sex was a subject that absolutely no one, especially not my family nor my schoolteachers, ever seemed to want to talk about. If the topic ever arose during a television programme, there would suddenly be a lot of coughing, and immediately the other channel was selected, or the set was turned off. So most of what I knew about sex came from studying the walls of the Gentlemen's toilets at railway stations, the crude images of genitalia, male and female, drawn in pencil or biro pen, and the torrents of words scrawled across the walls of the cubicles.

Then there was the occasion I bought a magazine, called *Weekend*, which featured an illustrated article on The Beatles. The magazine also contained pictures of scantily clad women, and though it was not overtly a sex magazine my mother must have seen it as a 'dirty' magazine, for she summarily confiscated it with no discussion; it just disappeared without a trace. Let's face it, those pictures were in no way pornographic, in fact the most revealing images I ever got to see in those days were seen through the window of a garage workshop down the road from my primary school - calendar girls - and even those pictures had all hair below the waistline airbrushed out. Oh, but occasionally, in my role of newspaper delivery boy, I got to see the odd copy of a naturist magazine called *Health & Efficiency*.

My mother's censorious action rather surprised me. I suppose her attitude of prudish disapproval had been passed down over generations. Indeed, a disapproval of nudity or semi-nudity, and the desire to avoid showing or seeing 'private' parts, were all-too-common. Nobody talked about sex, leaving youngsters uninformed and vulnerable.

I recall an incident, which occurred during my early adolescence, when a much older boy punched me in the face, seemingly just out of spite. I was given permission to leave school early that day, so I set off on my way home, via Victoria Station, a large railway terminus in central London. I was sitting in a railway carriage waiting for the train to depart, when shortly before the train was due to leave, a middle-aged gent suddenly swung open the door and got into the empty compartment. I was sitting minding my own business on the long seat opposite him, when after a while, out of the corner of my eye I glanced in his direction, and thought I caught him looking back at me. I assumed he'd noticed my injury, the evidence of the mighty wallop I'd received that left my face bruised and bloodied. Anyway, after the train started, he struck up a conversation with me, asking me whether or not I had a girlfriend. Huh? What on earth was he thinking? I was but a lad, only 13 or 14 years old, not long out of short trousers, and looking every inch the typical schoolboy, dressed in school uniform, with white cotton shirt and tie, black blazer with badge emblazoned with the school motto (*'Unitate Fortior'* 'Stronger by Union'), long grey trousers and black shiny leather shoes (probably my pair of stylish Cuban-heeled, elastic-sided, Beatle boots, which I'd hankered after buying for so long and eventually scraped enough money together to buy from *Ravel's*, a trendy high street shoe shop).

Out of the blue, my travelling companion tells me he'd like to see what I have tucked away inside the bulge of my tight trousers. I was surprised… but I confess to feeling no shyness or shame at unfastening my trousers, tugging down the zipper and pulling out the object of interest for him to see. Then, quick as a flash, before I'd time to tuck myself back in, he had his wallet out and was offering me a crisp ten-shilling note to let him handle it.

In a bid for personal freedom I absorbed myself in my hobbies, my interests, and in my growing social life.

My father disapproved of drinking alcohol, but I was headstrong and intent on enjoying myself. Though I only drank occasionally, I enjoyed feeling uninhibited and it felt okay to go a little crazy sometimes…

I loved listening to the radio, which led me to purchase my own record player, a veneered wood-cased affair, when I was barely 13 years old. I found it in a second hand furniture shop in Barnes, a nearby village, and paid just 30 shillings for it, but I had no records to play on it, so the shop owner directed me to choose one from a pile of old second-hand 78rpm records. I sifted through them and chose *Tutti Frutti*, by Little Richard; as I liked the title. But, as there was no electricity supply at the furniture cave, I had to wait until later to hear it. It was a long two-mile walk back home, and carrying the weighty appliance made me feel every step of the way. When I got back I wired a 2-pin plug on the player and placed my thick 10" 78rpm record on the turntable. Dropping the stylus onto the groove, Little Richard blasted out his goodtime sound, an astonishingly infectious rhythm and beat:

'Whop bop ba-luma ba-lop bamm boom, Tutti frutti, Oh Rudy!'

The Beatles were the most popular group around, along with The Rolling Stones, but for me Bob Dylan was the artist whose music evoked the kind of world I was interested in. The first brand new record I bought was Bob Dylan's *Like A Rolling Stone* with *Gates of Eden* on the flip side:

'Of war and peace the truth just twists its curfew gull just glides
Upon four-legged forest clouds the cowboy angel rides'

Next I bought The Who's *Anyway, Anyhow, Anywhere*, and *My Generation*.

Coincidentally, after a pleasure trip up to West End, looking in the shops of Oxford Street, I caught a bus back from Marble Arch down Park Lane, and as I looked out the window I saw a series of faces staring back at me.

Immediately I knew those four faces - Roger, Pete, John, and Keith, of THE WHO - all standing there on the kerb ….

The words of their first hit record ran through my head:

'I can go anyway, way I choose, I can live anyhow, win or lose'

* * *

I was about 14 or 15 when I joined the local amateur drama group and was given a principal role in a production of *The Bald Prima Donna,* an absurdist play by Romanian-French playwright Eugène Ionesco, about people in low states of awareness. I really enjoyed the dressing up and the make up, but my enthusiasm lessened when faced with the hollowness of the accompanying socialising.

Hey, yes I already knew I enjoyed dressing up… there was the fancy dress event at primary school when I was about 10 years old, when my mum took me to a hire company, and I chose a period costume with doublet and hose, of velvet and lace, like Sir Francis Drake. There was this special slinky sensation when pulling on the canary-yellow sheer stretch-tights, the sort of stockings a ballet dancer wears, I suppose. It was such a fabulous thrill when a draught of air touched my otherwise bare legs. Kinky or what?

I suspect that most parents want their sons to be 100% boys. Likewise that their daughters be 100% girls (and not tomboys, happy to learn how to cook, sew, knit, and want to have babies). Whereas perhaps no child is 100% boy or 100% girl, so maybe it's just a toss of the dice as to which numbers come up, and how you wear your genes? Actually, I noticed how so many boys, and men, are frantic to declare how masculine they are, so, perhaps they fear exposing a tender, feminine side. I also noticed that people are quick to compartmentalise, and consider those with any obvious sign of femininity as a 'kink', and assume them to be 'pansies', 'pooves' or 'fairies'. Why can't people just accept people as they are, without pigeonholing them and classifying them, it's not as if there's some sort of audit being undertaken, on behalf of eugenicists?

One way or the other, though it was clear in just about everything I did, that I was clearly all boy, yet I sensed my mother wouldn't have minded my being a daughter, - so I guess I would have then been Paula, or Pauline.

I recall Nicholas Mills, who used to go to the same primary school as myself and he was so nice and pleasant and kind to everyone, and yet, at school, he seemed only to play with the girls. But outside of school, he was also a member of the Cubs, and was very easily accepted by all the other boys. So what were the numbers on his dice? Six of one and half a dozen of the other, I guess. What does that add up to?

Kinks? Love 'em, especially Ray Davies's *Sunny Afternoon*!

> ♫ ♪ ♫ *'Lay-zing on a sun-ny after-noon, in the summer-time…*
> *In the summer-time…'* ♪ ♫ ♪

* * *

Lucky with friends, I enjoyed the reassurance that I could be valued, and in a climate of changing social values there was considerable scope for me to pursue my whims and desires. And almost by accident, I was introduced to the world of recreational drugs. I was walking along a corridor at school, chatting with Brooks, when all of a sudden we were both forced into a form room, and told to turn out our pockets. Afterwards I asked Brooksie for an explanation. *'Doobs,'* he said, *'Blues. Pills.'* I had never had anything to do with drugs, but after this encounter I began wondering if what I get suspected of I might very well enjoy!

From what I understand, Donovan had at one time been living in a bohemian setup just along the road from where I lived in Putney. Anyway, my friend Corrine bought tickets to see Donovan playing his *Sunshine Superman* music with a jazz quartet behind him at the grand Saville Theatre in London's Piccadilly (a venue owned by The Beatle's manager, Brian Epstein). That evening I met a friend of Corrine's, Chris, who asked me *'Have you got straight'*. I answered *'No'*, and then he asked for *'skins'*, and *'boards'*, and again, in truth, I had no idea what he meant. But coincidentally I met Chris again the very next day, at the house of a mutual friend, and immediately Chris seized upon the fact that I had in my hand a packet of 10 *Olivier* cigarettes.

'Can I have one of those straights?' he asked, staring directly at the packet.

I plucked a cigarette out of the pack for him and gave him a light. Instead of getting on and smoking it he let the cigarette rest in a saucer for a few moments before raising it and taking a long drag from it. He repeated the process, and when I took a closer look I found he was pressing the smouldering tip of the cigarette into some light coloured pollen that lay in the saucer, before drawing on the cigarette. He repeated this dipping, dabbing, and smoking a few times more before I thought to light myself a cigarette and join him. So we both sat and dipped, dabbed and smoked until very soon I started to feel a change occurring, a lift, and gradually I realised I was becoming elated. It was great! Such a wonderful feeling of warmth and easiness coursing through my body, and my mind felt fresh and relaxed too.

We chatted together, drank coffee, laughed and listened to some music, and as the record continued to play I found myself wandering off into the garden and beginning to dance in step with the music. The recording was superb, something new to me, with sumptuous exotic strings and beats, the *Indo-Jazz Suite*, a quintet of jazz players accompanied by a quintet of Indian musicians. The music was really cooking, and that afternoon became etched in my memory, becoming one of the most memorable of my life. Wonderful.

I left 10 shillings with Chris, for him to get some hashish for me, and a week later, when I looked him up, he told me he had none. So I pressed him, and after all sorts of delaying tactics he then offered to give me a joint of opium instead, explaining that though there wasn't much of it, it was much stronger. And he was right! It was a very different experience - rather overpowering - altogether too strong for one person to smoke alone. Mind you, when I got over the initial overwhelment, I had a **really** memorable day.

And soon after my getting stoned, the 'Summer of Love' began, and The Beatles voiced their message of *'All You Need Is Love'* to an estimated 400 million television viewers. But, for me, what I yearned for couldn't be summed up in some over-simplistic catch phrase. I wanted to know what I would have been like had I been born in another family, in another society, indeed, what I was like beyond the programming I received from an early age. What I wanted was to get an impression of who I really was, beyond my role in the society in which I found myself. Yes, like The Beatles, I wanted love, but more than that, I needed to know myself.

Somehow we got to hear that certain stimulants gave people heightened perceptions, insights and realisations. When pills were available I sometimes popped them, I liked 'speed' (amphetamine) as it kept me awake, which got me through late night art projects; it also got me buzzing. It was extraordinary how one's confidence and self-esteem rose whilst on speed, but then I discovered that too much of the stuff and you were off your food and a bit off your head, so occasionally I'd take half a tablet or so of a barbiturate, such a 'mandy' or a 'mogadon', as well, just to smooth out the jaggedness when I got too buzzed out.

When I was offered a piece of blotting paper wrapped in aluminium foil I wondered whether I wanted to take the risk. My curiosity got the better of me; I took a big leap of faith, chewed and swallowed the few square inches of blotter, and within a few minutes found myself experiencing an astonishing feeling of elation, it was as if I had been lit up from within. Soon I was tripping the light fantastic on a totally unspecified, unquantified amount of potent LSD (Lysergic acid diethylamide), a much talked about modern discovery, a controversial substance, a hallucinogen, which though still legal in the USA was illegal in Britain. There was a lot being spoken about this drug, and its extraordinary effects, why there were even claims that it could expand one's consciousness, that it was a direct way to experience God!

The 'trip' was absolutely extraordinary, my senses lit up, and my sense of being in the now was magnified. I can't find words to describe how wonderful it was to be shimmering in bliss, so intensely, and in the company of friends too. That said, I made the startling discovery that I really liked my own company too, and that, at the end of the day, I found myself listening to records on my own, and feeling no lack of company. It was like I'd made a really important discovery on that trip, that I liked and trusted myself more than others! That said, I still enjoyed being sociable, and there were occasions when marvellous powers of empathy, telepathy, and even wizardry appeared to manifest through me.

Though I was very reluctant to take LSD again, as it was an incredibly challenging experience, physically, and mentally, in that one traversed the whole spectrum of emotions, intense love and fears too, but I did try it again. And each and every time I took it I was surprised how much I enjoyed tripping. What struck me most significant was that each time, in the initial minutes between ingesting the chemical, and the full-on experience of tripping, there was a transition period wherein my awareness increased perceptibly, almost by the minute. It was as if I was rising up in an inner elevator, and was getting progressively higher, finding my sense of awareness becoming less mundane, and no longer constrained by a sense of limitation and inhibition. I found myself becoming more confident, and intimately connected with everything about me, totally at ease with myself. It was as if my entire being was being refurbished, regenerated and made whole again. Then after is prelude the trip began, taking me on a roller coaster journey of many hours, which often left me exhausted, due to the sheer intensity of the experiences.

Many young people in London - the capital of the world - appeared to be sharing and participating in a mood of easy going optimism, and for many Londoners, even acquiring work during this period, presented no real problems, though the pay was not that good. I was lucky living in London; for those who lived out in the sticks were rather sidelined when it came to being able to enjoy drug-aided cosmic experiences. I knew one thing; these 'trips' were never going to be something for the faint-hearted or the fearful, and for that matter, not for anyone who just wanted an easy life. This was purely for those who were ready for high adventure, inner personal journeys, without any safety nets or checks.

I was increasingly passionate about music and tried a variety of instruments, including violin and trombone, before finally settling on guitar; first an acoustic, then a *Hofner* Senator semi-acoustic electric bass, before getting my hands on a bright red *Watkins* Rapier solid electric guitar. The main trouble with it was that this one was that it was a left-handed model, so it took a fair amount of cutting and sanding to adapt it, though I was still stuck with the upside down head and upside-down tremolo arm and controls. This rather irregular out-of-balance guitar became my abiding companion, and I would carry it around, along with my effects - a fuzz unit and a wah-fuzz pedal - which were stashed in a carrying box along with my favourite instrumental singles - *Beck's Bolero, Beck's Boogie, Steeled Blues, Got to Hurry* and Tomorrow's *My White Bicycle*. Influenced by the flourishing music scene, I tried to find my place in it. With its commitment to innovation and experiment there was room for anyone with enthusiasm, myself included, I hoped.

The burgeoning growth of interest in the arts brought forth interesting books and magazines that were within my means and grasp, thus filling my mind with new horizons. In this new literature I discovered a rising tide of optimism of international proportion, springing from and gripping the young. To a lesser extent this openness was evident in, or at least affecting, the older generations too.

A new vocabulary was being adopted, the usage of which conferred status on its users. New terms and ideas abounded, and amongst them appeared concepts such as 'Mind Expansion' and 'Self-Realisation' - ideas that stirred me. Eagerly I sought to familiarise myself with the means of their fulfilment.

The 'Love and Peace' period were good times for many; defined by strident optimism accompanied by quaint naivety, when being sweet-natured was considered positively trendy. On us were heaped the hopes, dreams and aspirations of our elders. Could we do a better job than they were doing? We were dubbed the 'Now' generation, and we were, for better or worse, being watched and listened to with unprecedented attention.

All too soon though, many of those so eager to espouse this new cause of freethinking and adventure became sidetracked, falling prey to the degenerative effects of hedonism. It seemed that we were neither discovering new answers, nor paying much heed to the old ones. I attempted to monitor myself, and from time-to-time would even get out my mathematics books and work on some equations, just to test that my brain was still functioning okay. Then I flicked to the answers at the back of the book, just to double-check.

Initially I worked for a hip poster company in Portobello Road (and in the summer of '68, where else should I work?), then my father offered me to work for him. He had recently left his secure and relatively well-paid position in industry to become self-employed, whereupon he opened up a light engineering and electronics company.

I took the job as High Vacuum Technician, and indeed I was (high) most of the time. Working alongside a Jamaican guy, Rudi, Jimi Hendrix look-alike and good buddy, and the rest of them, I was happy in my work. Even the BBC radio disc jockey Jimmy Young, with his incessant cheerfulness, sounded pretty good on most days. I worked quite contentedly, though not because I held any great store by the work ethic, I just placed greater importance on my personal life, never thinking much further than the next pay day, basking in the belief that things would always sort themselves out.

After a year or so of happy workaday association, my father intimated to me that I might one day take over his business. Well this set me thinking. Whilst the business was prospering, he was not, and it appeared he had little time for anything other than work, a shame since he had so many other interests and a home eager for his attention. His health was suffering too; he needed time for himself. And for some unaccountable reason a thought suddenly flashed through my head, I figured I needed adventure, travel maybe, and that if I were to become ensconced in the business, I would be trapped. As fate would have it, not long after we parted ways.

My lack of enthusiasm to settle down seemed to stem from a thirst for new experiences and a wish to make my own way through life. Coasting along I soon added Pastry Cook and Epoxy Resin Caster to my list of talents. I enjoyed myself, because, after all, if you don't take life too seriously, you can always find a laugh, can't you? Besides, there's always life after work isn't there?

* * *

I'd been led to believe that not everyone is physical compatible with one another, but I found that with girlfriends there seemed to be all sorts of ways one could please and satisfy each other's desire for pleasure, so there seemed no hurry to experience everything, though I did eventually abandon all my inhibitions, with Isabel, of Greek extraction on her father's side; her mother was from India. My relationships with young women were fairly loose and accordingly I never questioned the rightness of myself or my girlfriends getting involved with others, It was at Dario's home that I first met darling Sue, and it was there also that I met the sumptuous American Michele who lived with her parents and sisters in Eton Square, a very posh area of London. I reckon her family's wealth made her feel a bit self-conscious sometimes, yet it certainly didn't stop her from getting herself a job scivvying away in the *Yankee Doodle* burger bar.

And there was Marilyn from faraway Gants Hill, who I'd met at The Royal Albert Hall, at a concert featuring a couple of blues groups, who not long ago had asked me if I wanted to join her and her friends in going round to visit John Lennon, the leader of The Beatles, at his house just outside of London, to have tea with him.

And Vickie in Richmond, and other friends I hadn't seen lately, Steve, Nico, Nino, Andy.. Andy Fraser, who'd recently become famous for playing in the pop group Free, and having the hit record, *All Right Now*. I'd glimpsed them on the television playing on *Top of the Pops*. Andy had told me he'd used some of his money to get his mum's maisonette flat in Roehampton spray-painted and completely redecorated. He seemed to come from a family of sisters; the whole family were very nice. I'd thought Andy a bit effeminate when I'd first met him at college. He said he put talcum powder in his long hair to keep it from getting greasy, and he wore pretty girlie scarves around his neck, and was always turned out nicely. Mind you, I can talk, not only was I wearing my green chiffon scarf, colourful clothes, and even girlfriends' fur coats, I would sometimes even coat my nails with shiny varnish, clear or red, depending on my mood. My mother didn't have a problem with this, in fact she kept me supplied with pots of nail varnish, but I sensed my father disapproved as he confronted me about it once, and I calmly explained to him that I needed to paint my nails in order to harden them, else they got chipped and broken when I played the guitar. He didn't appear convinced even though that was a large part of the reason I would sometimes wear the stuff. But I certainly wasn't going to tell him how much I'd enjoyed it when Harriet brushed my eyelashes with mascara, or the fact that, out of curiosity, I had found a stick of red lipstick, wound it up and applied it liberally over my lips, just to see something of what I might look like if I was made up as a woman.

* * *

One night I went with friend Dario to *Le Bataclan,* a discothèque located in a vast windowless basement at a property near Oxford Street, in London's West End, where they played a good selection of soul music records. There I encountered two attractive young women, Yolanda and Michelle, who to me looked very similar, so that at times it was difficult to tell them apart, with their long blond hair, pretty faces and good clothes sense.

On the surface, my meeting with Yolanda must have appeared ordinary enough, but at another level, within me, I sensed something extraordinary taking place. It was as though I was suddenly capable of some sort of inner vision that enabled me to see the young woman and myself drifting towards each other, meeting as spiritual entities, as spirit bodies. All time and space was irrelevant; I had nowhere to go, nowhere to hide, nothing to do but to face the feeling that I was encountering some cosmic entity wandering through the universe and right into me, blocking my way! I was at once enchanted yet devastated too – my personal space had just been challenged and my nervous system felt extremely jarred. I watched our meeting in a state of awed shock and disquiet, as I had never encountered any like situation in my life! I had no choices to make, realising I must submit, that fate had delivered this astonishing spectacle. But the intense experience of our meeting gradually dissipated as the evening wore on, and later we stood around socialising normally with others.

I left the club with Dario, and went back to his place in Wigmore Street; and after having opened the main door of the building and when we were just about to take the lift up to his floor, I suddenly thought of the young woman I had met at the discothèque.

'What's that chick's name?' I asked him.

'I know who you mean. You'll land her, man.'

'Really?' I'd responded, surprised at him. *'But what's her name?'*

'You'll land her!' he said again with grinning impatience.

I let the matter drop, though I was still puzzled as to why he wouldn't tell me her name.

After that first encounter, even though we would sometimes meet at Dario's home (the two of them having got into a relationship) and though we were friendly enough, I made no attempt to get close to her.

However, there was that time when I walked into the drawing room of Dario's flat, and found Yolanda sitting in her tights and black blouse, crossed legged on a seat. She appeared composed and at ease, and on this particular occasion she wasn't at all the 'dolly bird' in her finery, but a mystic, her eyes slightly hooded and smiling. The sight of her at once evoked in me feelings of sensuousness and spirituality, both. Deep down within me, this image of her sat sitting this way and the expression on her face, it resonated with me, it was as though there was something I recognised, an impression from… I don't know where or when.

I sensed strongly her desire for inner tranquillity and peace. Those were magical moments, in that room, as if eternity had communicated an age-old message, the spur to seek inner peace, to look for the *'kingdom of heaven within'*, the quest to find the *nirvana* of the Buddha for oneself.

One sunny afternoon, Yolanda and I were again together, both tripping and a mutual fondness seemed to blossom between us, and at some point, whilst we chatted together outside on a terrace of the flat roof, we gave one another a warm kiss on the cheek, and it was then that Yolanda felt inspired to give me the ring from her finger - the one crafted in silver with little circles of gold hammered into it.

Yolanda was leaving London that very day, and we had no contact details for one another, so, not having a pen and paper, I removed the last couple of cigarettes from my packet of 10 *Benson & Hedges*, and scratched my address and telephone number on the gold foil backed card of the back of the box.

* * *

Amongst us young people the trend was nowadays quite definitely towards indulgence, indulgence to excess! The 'Swinging Sixties', if not quite over, were definitely on the wane. And the business world was waking to the commercial possibilities of an affluent youth market, so they seized their opportunities unhesitatingly. The young for their part, myself included, proved easy targets. Any strong desire to do other than slavishly conform to new trends was not particularly evident. This is not to say these were bad times, quite the contrary in fact. As the music found a harder edge, with groups like The Jeff Beck Group and Led Zeppelin gaining prominence and showing the way; I was really in my element. I enjoyed too, the unending atmosphere of partying that for me characterised this era. Nevertheless, the excesses that were becoming the norm did sometimes cause me to wonder where we were going.

This concern seemed to be shared by a Chelsea based magazine called *Gandalf's Garden*, which bravely sought to redress the balance. The magazine pointed a rather nervous finger in the general direction of macrobiotic food, *yoga* and meditation; carrying articles on mysticism alongside interviews with the likes of Marc Bolan of Tyrannosaurus Rex and disc jockey John Peel. Personally I bought the magazine mainly on account of the attractive graphics images, contributed by John Hurford and Michael English, but having done so I necessarily cast my eyes over the text too. Though not that enamoured with the magazine over all, I did however like its direction.

One evening, sometime late in the winter of 1969, I was at my girlfriend Sue's bed-sit room, and since she needed to arise early next day she went to bed, and I was left alone but still very much awake, so I wondered what to do with my time.

On an impulse I decided to meditate. I sat myself down cross-legged and leant against a wardrobe, my back upright, my head steady and my eyes closed, instinctively I then went about clearing my mind of thoughts. It was easy enough, and I was almost free of thoughts when I noticed the sensation of my nerves jangling. Realising I could progress no further with my meditation until my nervous system was more settled, I opened my eyes again and just rested there for a while.

* * *

It was a snap decision, purchasing the old wooden armchair.

I was 17 years old, had the money spare, and on an impulse decided I wanted to buy an easy chair for myself. I got the idea of getting myself a special chair after visiting a good friend, who called himself Leo Sebastian Davis (thus giving himself the initials L.S.D.), at his place in Philbeach Gardens, Earls Court; the basement flat he shared with Lemmy, guitarist and singer with the Sam Gopal Dream. That day Leo had told me he wanted his friends to be my friends, a nice sentiment. I noticed that both Leo and Lemmy each had grand antique dark-wood high-backed chairs with armrests, which looked rather like thrones, and I laughed at their lordly pretensions.

I recall the times I hung out with Lemmy, not least the occasion when he asked to borrow my treasured pre-war semi-acoustic *Radiotone* guitar, with solid ebony fretboard and beautiful abalone inlays, which I lugged around with me at the time.

'Lemmie it, Man, just for a few days I'd really love to use it on our next recording session, on Monday?' He pleaded.

I flatly turned him down.

When the *Escalator* LP by *Sam Gopal* was released, Leo was credited with writing a track called *'Angry Faces'*, but on the day of its release, as Leo and I together listened, it was difficult for me to figure out his reaction, and only after hearing the entire album did he share with me his claim that most of the other compositions on the album were derived from music Leo had been playing whilst they lived together. I never did ask him whether or not he confronted Lemmy on the topic.

Anyway, I had never bought an item of furniture before and I enjoyed the freedom of making a choice over what I would be sitting on at home - but the second-hand furniture shop, situated about a quarter mile from my home, didn't have an antique throne, though they did have a solid enough armchair, and as it didn't cost a lot, I bought it. When it was delivered I placed it in my bedroom, in a corner near the window.

At that time I was working (at a factory), and I recall that after work, when I came home, I would, more often than not, park myself down on my armchair, get comfortable and close my eyes for a while.

It was my bit of lazy time.

I would sit, just watching my thoughts until there appeared to be no thoughts to watch. I kind of melted into myself, and found I became very still and composed. I found it most enjoyable, then I would open my eyes and look around at my bedroom, enjoying just being me and having all my stuff around me.

* * *

Whilst Yolanda was away in France and in Italy, she wrote to me frequently, and we shared our thoughts with one another, easily. And in those letters I discovered that Yolanda would sometimes use unfamiliar terms such as 'ego', 'identification', 'non-attachment', and she was fond of quoting philosophers, mainly Europeans, the names of whom I was not familiar with. Nietzsche? Voltaire? Sartre? Amongst the pages of writing she wrote to me, Yolanda once mentioned that she'd like to be more like the Maharishi. Well, I didn't know quite what she meant, as I didn't know much about him, other than I gathered that The Beatles had visited him in India in 1968, and that Bob Hite, the singer in Canned Heat, had encouraged listeners to *sit back and meditate, as the Maharishi says*. Well also there was a photograph of this Maharishi guy on the cover of one of Donovan's records, and I remember seeing this same Indian guy on a television show once, and I found his giggle rather strange, as if he had smoked something not quite right.

Anyway, in her letters Yolanda told me she planned to return to London one day, but she wouldn't put a date on it. Our correspondence had convinced me of our need to get to know each other better, so it was reassuring to know that, in time, we would meet again, in the not-too-distant future.

* * *

In the latter part of 1969, Dario's mother purchased a black sofa for her son, a sofa that doubled up as a large bed, and there was talk of Yolanda returning to London, and I got the drift that Dario and his mother believed that on Yolanda's return, she and Dario would be sleeping together. I said nothing. It really wasn't my business, I was just happy to receive the *Espresso Poste* letters from Yolanda.

Actually, when Yolanda gave me the ring she had cautioned me not to wear it in front of others, especially Dario - evidently, she didn't want him to know how close we'd become. But in private I would sometimes take the ring out and put it on, and found it was quite tight and quite a struggle to take off. Though it didn't bestow a cloak of invisibility on me, over time I began to see that it had some significance, that in some way I was the Lord of the Ring. That said, though I sensed the two of us were getting romantically closer, this didn't stop me seeing other girls.

* * *

After Yolanda's arrival back in England, on New Years Eve, December 1969, we spent the next days together amongst friends, during which time I came to understand a few things about her that related to me. One was that she looked forward to being alone with me, at my own home, and another thing, which rather surprised me, was that she seemed to want to discourage me from taking drugs (which was rather odd, bearing, in mind she also said she wanted to trip together with me). And she also made it clear she wanted to share her interest in things spiritual.

'Oh, you need to meet my friend, Steve, Steve Holland,' I told Yolanda, *'he's into all that sort of thing,'*

I said this because Steve often had a far-way look in his eyes, and I gathered from odd things he had said about vibrations, spirits and forces, that he had an interest in the supernatural. Besides, there was the hooded robe he kept hanging behind his bedroom door.

Yolanda looked disappointed at my response. Shaking her head, she made herself clearer, indicating it was my own connection with this subject that interested her, which took me by surprise, and gave me food for thought.

Though my Christian Science Church upbringing reinforced positive values, that God is Mind, Spirit, Soul, Principle, Life, Truth, and Love, it also warned against involvement in external mind-control such as hypnotism, and mesmerism (also known as 'animal magnetism'), and against summoning spirits ('necromancy'). But I had no appetite for such things anyway, so I was never tempted to try an ouija board or to attend a séance. But I do recall, on one occasion some weeks back, when Leo and myself were sat outside a cafe in Central London, and a gypsy approached us offering to give a reading. I could tell that Leo was excited, he being the one who relished singing the verses of *'Hoochie Coochie Man',* time and time again:-

> *Gypsy woman she told my mother*
> *Just a while before I was born*
> *You got a boy child comin'*

I was first to be given a reading by her, and after making sure we were completely alone the gypsy woman looked into my eyes, then stared at my ears. After this she spoke to me, but made no mention of omens and talk dark strangers, in fact there was no sense of foreboding about her, instead there was only pleasant re-assurance, in which she referred to me as a musician, and assured me that I had *'made it'*, which I took to mean that all was well with me. After my reading it was Leo's turn, and the two of them sidled off to where they could be alone. When, quite some time later, he returned, he looked very displeased... I didn't ask.

* * *

So it seemed that Yolanda and I shared a mutual fascination in each other, and we spent much of our time regaling each other with our life stories, discovering shared opinions, and sharing our love. The name Yolanda, she told me, means 'Land of Violets', how wonderfully beautiful a picture that evokes. In fact, Yolanda and I became almost inseparable, with her coming to see me each and every day. In truth I found myself thinking about her even when I was alone. I had become very involved with her, and the idea of resuming my job as a technician in a local factory just didn't seem right, so after several weeks I popped in to see them, just out of courtesy, to tell them my news, that I was leaving to form a rock group, The Superstars!

I was sure Yolanda and I had a deep abiding affinity with one another, and I convinced myself we were made for each other. Certainly there was no doubt in my mind that I was in love. She told me she was on the pill so we made love often. Though it seemed we wanted to be treated as a couple, neither of us were bothered about it being 'official'; as there was time enough for all that. *'Perhaps'*, I thought, *'but when I become rich and famous we'll be able to afford whatever we want...!'* Such was my optimistic outlook; I could see nothing but good fortune and happiness for us both. A fairy tale romance in a modern age, two souls destined to share and love each other eternally. I believed that my most treasured desires would gain fruition. My cup was running over, or so I thought.

Then it happened... the lecture on fidelity!! According to Yolanda, it was unacceptable to retain a fondness, let alone a love, for old flames or sweethearts.

'If you love somebody, you have to give them all your love, you can't share it with other girls!' she blistered.

I stared at her in disbelief and discovered to my alarm that she was not joking but in deadly earnest. On this occasion I shrugged it off, but this bone of contention was to surface time and time again.

As fun as it usually was to be with my girlfriend, this issue, of her interpretation of fidelity came to vex me greatly, an unwelcome intrusion on my emotions. Maybe this was all part of the age-old game of love, an act of courtship? Perhaps hers was a valid viewpoint? I couldn't be sure. I had no way of knowing. Whichever way I looked at the matter, I was reminded of how much she meant to me. I even began to feel guilty at not having saved myself for her (as if I could have known we would meet!). I took her rebukes as flattery, as a promise of some higher and more precious love that perhaps she alone could give. Letters and mementoes from other girls were duly jettisoned, believing as I did, that I would now be safe from further attack.

But there was more to come, and the time spent together would become punctuated with hot intellectual debate. My interest in music, clothes, and collectibles et al had to be defended and justified. I sensed a challenge in her words; I was being cross-examined and it made me uncomfortable. Beliefs, opinions and hopes; all were discussed. I found myself fighting for beliefs I didn't even know I had, defending not only my own viewpoints but those of my friends and family too. The discussions became more and more fervent, and more intense. In consequence I began to re-examine every possession, every thought, weighing up its origin, worth and function. Every vestige of my life seemed to be undergoing this treatment.

Amidst all the self-enforced introspection I made an important pact with myself, to no longer tell any lies, either out of weakness or a desire to deceive, and to be honest too. My resolve was largely born out a desire to put my relationship with Yolanda on the best possible basis.

It was during this period of re-evaluation that I also made the monumental decision to abandon the use of 'artificial' stimulants - drink and drugs, for I had convinced myself that I could reach a higher level of happiness without that sort of help, that merely by being more aware I would stay happy.

I was soon to discover that this decision wasn't going to go down too well, for most of my friends and acquaintances still indulged. My late father, with his commitment to the Christian Science faith, would have been happy with my change of attitude.

The only immediate threat to my resolve to avoid stimulants came from Leo, a guitarist friend and good buddy from way back. His visits would be characterised by his repeated wish to play on our upright piano. Thumping out the chords to The Beatles' *'Let it Be'* and crooning its hymn-like lyrics extremely loudly; he would give a serviceable rendition of the song and usually raise a laugh. On these occasions he would attempt to challenge me, saying: *'Go on Man. Join me in a drink Man. Just one glass.'*

'No. I've already told you,' I said, *'told you repeatedly in fact. No.. No... No!!!'*

'Well, maybe a smoke then. It's really good stuff, really strong.'

'Look, I don't want to. Thank you but No!'

'Huh,' he said, turning to Yolanda, *'I remember when young Paul here would never have refused a joint. What's up with you, Man?'*

Yolanda looked annoyed. She was no longer smoking (hashish) either or drinking herself anymore, and I think she found Leo's manner over-bearing.

'Yes, Yes, I know. I was there too, you know,' she answered him somewhat dismissively.

Silenced, he wandered out of the room - a trip to the bathroom being in order.

Emerging some minutes later he asserted his wish to play his favourite tune of the day *'just one more time'*. Seated at the piano his fingers plunged at the keys as he embarked on yet another rendition.

'When I find myself in times of trouble Mother Mary comes to me, whispering words of wisdom, let it be. Let it be, let it be, let it be, let it be. Whispering words of wisdom....'

Other friends showed surprise at my decision to stop the partying, looking upon me with curiosity, concern, suspicion even, since I had now become something of a recluse. Stepping out of line, I guess I had to pay the price. Stubborn and wilful I stuck to my guns and was rewarded by all but a few of my friends giving me a wide berth, or so it seemed, but the truth is I didn't go out visiting them either!

After a few weeks' abstinence from stimulants I still felt no ill effect or deficiency, quite the opposite in fact. But thereafter I perceived a gradual deterioration of my normally cheery mood, and I didn't know why.

I realised I still had my share of good fortune; I knew that I had a particularly loving, caring mother, a large circle of friends and many absorbing interests. Obsessed with music I still found a fountain of pleasure in listening to records and playing guitar. Then of course there was Yolanda; who still seemed to think the world of me.

Somehow though, all this did not prevent me from falling prey to an intense feeling of vacuousness and melancholy. Unfamiliar as I was with this mood, I fought long and hard to cast away these feelings and rediscover my former identity. Fitfully I regained some semblance of the joyfulness that for so long I took for granted, only to return repeatedly to a well of despondency. Happily it was not a permanent condition, though my changes of mood were quite unnerving.

Many reasons could be offered for the condition I found myself in.

Were these the effects of reckless indulgence, wreaking their vengeance, finally catching up with me?

Or maybe, as an incurable romantic and unswerving idealist, I had pinned too much hope on the fruits of true love. Whilst this road promised much in the way of fulfilment, it seems it can also be a source of psychological unrest. More likely, it was a combination of these things.

Importantly, I knew of no one else who was in such an extremely close relationship, though I knew that John Lennon of The Beatles had taken up with an *avant garde* artist called Yoko Ono, and the two of them seemed to have a similarly intense relationship as the one I was going through with Yolanda, and he too was becoming distant from his former friends and becoming more intense and quirky.

I felt certain that no one would understand my predicament; particularly since I had so recently been dabbling with LSD, a substance very few had much understanding of. So I therefore sought my own solution, and it felt like I was looking for an antidote to some disabling disease. I wracked my brain for an answer.

* * *

As I re-assessed I also looked to reconcile myself with my possessions. I had accumulated quite a lot of clutter over the years. In a cupboard I discovered old toys, long discarded, hidden away. My toy garage with *Dinky* cars, the hand-made model of a shop beautifully crafted for me by my father, *Minibrix* (those small brown rubber building bricks, which come with white window fittings and green rubber roofs), plasticine and old tea cards and the like. Happy recollections of my childhood came flooding back.

Marc Bolan of Tyrannosaurus Rex once reminisced about his favourite playthings and it seems that he too played with *Minibrix*. He kept something of his childhood in that his imagination remained active. When he appeared at a festival I attended, Marc announced that we were all going to listen to the music that elves play in the glades of the forest. He was unique, a really curious guy, who was actually quite local; his bongo player, Steve Peregrine Took, told me that at one time Marc used to be known as the 'King of the Pillheads' in Shepherd's Bush.

Whilst going through my belongings, with a view to clearing some of the stuff out, I came to opinion that I should avoid being sentimental, for what does *The Bible* say; *'When we were young we played with childish things, now we are grown we cast aside those things'*? So, ruthlessly I pursued a vigorous, thorough purge. So many possessions, such as records, clothes, guitars, books, and comics, were given to friends, whilst other items, which were not mine, I attempted to return to their rightful owners. On presenting one particular friend, Steve Holland, with goodies, he commented, with poetic licence, that I resembled a snake shedding its skin.

* * *

I recall the previous year I had made a rather half-hearted attempt to re-decorate the room after my father and I had visited a shop in Hammersmith, in West London.

'Have you any purple paint?' I had asked the old gent in a brown coat, who gave me a 'knowing' look, which I didn't know the meaning of.

'No, just the colours on the chart over there,' he had answered, pointing. But I found no purple on the swatch of colours, no snazzy colours at all in fact.

'What about other shops, would they have purple?' I persisted.

'Doubt it,' he grunted, *'Never seen it myself, that is.'*

So I had settled on buying a can of sky blue and one of dark blue, the darker being for the woodwork, with the lighter colour being for the walls.

Back in my father's estate car, I discussed my purchase, commenting I'd been unable to buy purple paint; and he too gave me a 'knowing' look and raised his eyebrows. *'He's probably right. They know their job, Paul. That's a very good shop.*

If they haven't got any, you probably won't get that colour paint anywhere else.'

This being the first time I had tackled any decorating, I was determined not to overdo it, besides, no one would look behind the brown hardwood bureau (a relic from my schooldays), or behind the cupboards and shelves.

Why should I get fussed about them the? I had asked myself. So I hadn't, and had instead contented myself with merely painting around the furniture, around the pictures and around the posters too.

So I redecorated my bedroom, the walls of which used to be covered in doodles, messages, and a series of story-telling cartoons neatly executed by Robina, a friend. The ceiling had been the most in need of attention, being in a dreadful state, as many moons ago I drew smoke pictures on it with a lighted candle. There were also the splattered remains of flies I'd swatted, each one circled in pencil. I remember my father having been particularly disapproving about that.

Having recently given away my brightly coloured psychedelic posters, the walls of my room looked naked. And worse, that where they hung, the former lemon yellow decor stood revealed, and there was my abstract painting, my masterpiece entitled *'Train Drivers Cufflink'*, in bright red oil paint on the bedroom wall beside the window, painted whilst listening to Jimi Hendrix's *'Stone Free'* playing repeatedly on my mono record player.

No, I couldn't bring myself to cover up that painting.

* * *

So, what of my various friends? I wondered if they missed me? Not just the close friends but others too. Ingrid, April, John and Larry, Dave, Richard, and Nick. Dear old Nick, he must have been puzzled why I'd not been going around to see him, and why he never heard from me anymore? The truth of the matter was that the size of my world had shrunk to a point where I hardly socialised at all, I didn't even think of getting in contact with anyone.

I began to realise that, unless I re-adopted my former values, I was destined to an isolation of my own making. Though it didn't show in any obvious way in my behaviour, I think that I was actually going through a crisis - a big shake-up within myself, and nothing helped calm me down or made me feel satisfied with life.

In an effort to clear my head I took to visiting Hyde Park, in the hope that contact with nature would bring me some peace of mind. Surrounded by the wide expanse of grass and trees I wondered if by simple contemplation I might settle down and resolve my feelings of discomfort. But I couldn't seem to do it, I couldn't free myself from my thoughts and feelings long enough to really relax for long.

I would wander about the park, and sometimes sit on one of the benches near Marble Arch, watching the comings and goings of the visitors and pigeons there.

On one such occasion, I saw a band of *Hare Krishnas* - those shaven headed monks and nuns attired in orange cloth - chanting their dirge-like hymn or *mantra*. They approached the area where I was sitting, and seeing a group of tourists sitting on a nearby bench, they set about apprising this captive audience of their beliefs, whilst zealously brandishing their brightly coloured magazines aloft.

I just sat and watched them, half-hoping they would sense my unrest and come over, but though they glanced at me, they passed me by, only to badger bystanders, regardless as to whether anyone was interested or not; and after having gained the coins they so eagerly sought, they resumed their cymbal crashing, head shaking and general hullabaloo. Evidently I was not a suitable target for their attentions, as in all likelihood I didn't look wealthy enough to bother about.

Long I toiled with the problem of inner strain, the days of inner turmoil turning into weeks, many weeks. Yet still I drew a blank. But how was I to resign myself to accepting the situation? Was this the Higher Consciousness I was seeking? Hardly! More like over-exposure. Perhaps there was some sort of exercise or mental technique that could alter my state of mind?

Yolanda had mentioned her interest in *yoga*, but after watching a demonstration on TV by Richard Hittleman, I'd figured it must just be some kind of genteel keep-fit discipline, little more than a sort of contemplative gymnastics routine. But I did wonder if I might benefit from some sort of visualisation technique, that that such a practice might provide a way to experience a higher reality. So I sat and deliberately looked into the flame of a candle for quite some time, but despite repeating the process I came to the conclusion that nothing special was occurring. So I figured I ought to find a special pattern and stare at that instead. And I tried staring at all sorts of images, but nothing out of the ordinary occurred, if anything it left me feeling worse and decidedly vacant.

Having been raised in an environment strongly inclined towards religion, I had been primed to try to discover the truths of Christian literature and attempt to find God. So I couldn't help thinking that I must respond, as a matter of urgency, to the spiritual questions that arose in me, else were they forever to be ignored and unanswered? I cogitated long and hard, hoping to regain a sense of purpose, and fulfilment, but the questions kept coming at me...

Who am I?

Why do we live?

What should I do with my life?

Is there more to me than just the body, mind and ego?

Is God really watching me, watching over me?

In truth I was feeling very gloomy, on the edge of a breakdown, and very close to breaking point.

Things got so bad that I went the bathroom and started swallowing a load of paracetamol tablets, until I paused a few moments, screwed the cap back on the container, returned it to the shelf, and immediately put the incident out of my mind.

Chapter 1

THE LION & THE UNICORN

One afternoon I find myself doing something I don't recall ever doing before; I go and look at the ornamental globe near the window in the sitting room, then after seizing it and perching it on the dining table, I give it a spin. The world is spinning at thousands of miles per second, with continents and seas a grey indistinguishable blur; then, as it slows down I start to contemplate it.

Does our world really look like this? I ask myself.

In geography lessons at school I remember being tasked with drawing the coastline of Norway, with all its fjords, and also being force-fed information about escarpments, alluvial soil and igneous rock, and about rainfall in India, but I was left lamentably ignorant about the shape of the world we live in.

Peering closely at the globe I ascertain the whereabouts of South America, and find myself muttering the names of the countries I find there, scrutinising their shape and size. Moving my attention I discover other countries, Finland, Denmark, Sweden, Greenland and the U.S. of A. It is then that I discover the Soviet territories.

'Wow, they take up about half of the world!' I exclaim to myself.

Now, playing with this orb, I rapidly absorb the positions of the continents in relation to the Polar Regions.

*Now, I wonder where **we** are? Ah, here's Britain!*

I note that according to the globe, Great Britain is very small indeed.

My eyes then scan across Europe, the Middle East and further eastwards, homing in on India!

'Ah!' I say aloud.

Then I feel the faint glimmer of an idea enter my mind. It takes some time before it actually gets a firm hold on me and captures my imagination.

Maybe I should go see the world, and find out how the other half live? Perhaps people in other countries have got a few answers?

But how can I travel? I ask myself. *How can I possibly afford to jet around the world with only a few pounds in my Post Office account?* And this is not the only doubt that besets me.

Why should I have to journey to find my peace of mind? Surely, I argue, *I'm as likely to find it right here at home, which has given me security and comfort for so many years.*

Since I haven't much money I soon realise that if I'm intent on travelling I will have to resort to hitchhiking, and I begin to plot a route to India that would entail the minimum amount of sea travel. The direct route - cutting straight through Europe - seems the most obvious. However, since the world is, at least for the moment, my oyster, I start to contemplate the alternatives.

I recall, when I was very much younger, my father had once asked me a question related to travel. *'Supposing you could travel back in time Paul, where would you go and what would you like to see?'*

Hesitating only for a moment, I soon found an answer. *'That's easy,'* I confidently replied, *'America, to see the cowboys and Indians. What about you, where would you go?'*

My father looked at me in a thoughtful and serious manner, then answered in a quietened voice and with evident emotion, *'To the Holy Land in the time of our Lord.'*

I felt ashamed of myself as I recognised just how devout a Christian my father was; it humbled me. And me with my dreams of the Wild West!

Now I consider the options of the hitchhiking trip, and I find that planning the route is fun.

After popping over to France, I think it might be good to cross into Spain - Spain sounds exciting - then over that little bit of water into Morocco, a country that sounds quite mysterious and alluring.

By nipping along the coast of Africa I'd come to Egypt, that land of archaeological dreams. One of my childhood interests was in following the footsteps of Leonard Wooley and Sir Mortimer Wheeler, and going on local 'digs' when I got the chance.

'Egypt. Now that's a place I'd like to see,' I murmur to myself.

After Egypt, next stop would be Israel; I'd heard that a friend, John, had stayed on a commune there, a *kibbutz*.

But after Israel, where to then?

Okay, by turning right, and crossing this area here, going in that direction would eventually get me to India!

A wave of exhilaration casts aside my anguish.

Perhaps Yolanda would like to come with me, I wonder.

* * *

After Yolanda arrives to see me the next day, I cautiously broach the topic of hitching to India; and she listens with visible eagerness as I explain my intentions. Apparently, she too has harboured an interest and desire to visit the East, and recognising the possibility of fulfilling this wish she readily agrees to join me. Which is great! But what spoils the idea is that even by pooling our resources we figure that we can only scrape together but about a hundred pounds. This sum is fine for a short holiday, but I doubt it's enough to get the two of us to India.

'Have you got a passport then?' Yolanda asks, fixing me with her large deep brown eyes.

'No, I've not needed one before,' I reply, surprised at the question, then ask. *'Do I really need one then?'*

'Of course you do, you idiot. You couldn't get through all those borders without one,' she points out exasperatedly.

'I'm sure I could!' I retort somewhat petulantly.

Apparently, after her schooling at a Roman Catholic convent boarding school in Siena, Yolanda left Italy and gained employment in France as an *au pair*. Since then she has ventured back and forth between Italy, France and England. So, when she speaks of travelling abroad she speaks from experience, therefore I decide not to argue.

* * *

Living in Putney, in suburban South London, there are plenty of parks and commons to wander around in at leisure and contemplate my innermost thoughts. When I think about this hitchhiking trip that we're talking about, the problem is that I don't see myself as a traveller. No, much more a Bilbo Baggins figure, preferring to be within easy reach of a kettle and, of course, the 'biccie barrel'. J. R. R. Tolkien, in his creation of *The Hobbit,* depicted this character as having the very conflicts that I'm feeling. The desire to see new lands, to witness wonders there and experience the thrill of adventure, versus the craving for the reassurance that home, family and friends can offer. Unlike Bilbo however, I receive no visit from a personable wizard coming to offer me direction and advice.

I've done a certain amount of hitchhiking on my own, oft-times going to see my sister Margaret in Brighton, where she attended Sussex University, and travelling elsewhere; even a trip to North Wales, and with my good friend Henderson visiting places like Oxfordshire, Gloucestershire and Cornwall. But travelling to foreign parts, now that's a different kettle of fish altogether.

And how can I front this notion of international travel to anyone else either? Nobody just takes off on the spur of moment to visit distant lands!

Loyalties are another issue I have to consider. How can I tell my mother I'm entertaining such an idea? I haven't even any proper plans or destination yet. Actually, I'm not at all sure how she would take the news, my father having only recently passed away. She dotes on me, all the more so now that I'm the only other resident family member.

My mind is in turmoil, for other than in flights of fancy, I have never been interested in the idea of travel, not even faintly, and now it looks like I'm about to embark on a journey of epic proportions.

My system collapses under the pressure. Though gradually reviving, I am thrust back again and again into an enfeebled condition. The choice, quite surprisingly, is made the easier **because** of this predicament. Stated clearly the decision is now markedly between going on the road, or off the rails!

Recognising the severity of the situation I realise that to procrastinate further could well lead to my entire undoing. So, since I still have a streak of self-preservation, I elect to GO!!

* * *

Notwithstanding Oxfam's ubiquitous advertising campaign to gain funds for charitable work, utilising as it does the photograph of an emaciated tearful child, I still feel inexplicably drawn to India. So, it looks as though this trip is going to be a test of Biblical proportions, a sort of modern pilgrimage to the Holy Land, Egypt and India. I recall mention in one of the *New Testament* stories of Jesus, of his 40 days and nights in the desert, and the hunger and temptations he faced. Though I'm not going into a wilderness, I wonder what tests and temptations I'm likely to encounter.

The truth is that I sense this journey to be some 'calling' of sorts. Yes, there is definitely the feeling that the God of the *The New Testament* is involved in this in some way, that I'm being summoned to fulfil a mission. And to an extent I'm okay with this, but as I have no particular sense of self-importance or specialness, I can't help but wonder; *Why me?*

* * *

After going to the Post Office and obtaining the necessary forms to apply for a passport, I return home and set about completing them. Numerous though the questions are, most of them I can answer without much difficulty.

But even after repeated attempts to determine my height by means of a tape measure, I meet with little success. Then, resorting to the time-honoured convention of marking the wall with a pencil, the task is made much easier, and I duly record the result, namely, 5 feet, 10 inches (though I feel sure I'm taller). Scrutinising my reflection in the bathroom mirror, I am able to reveal the colour of my hair and eyes, being brown (well I have to be sure!) and green respectively.

Portrait photographs are also required, thus prompting an excursion into town.

Making use of a *Photo-Me* cubicle in the ticket hall at Earls Court underground station, I position myself according to the instructions, and press the coins (2/- shilling bits) into the slot. The flashlight immediately blasts away; leaving me momentarily blinded. Then I stand outside the booth awhile, waiting for some many minutes before retrieving the somewhat clammy prize from within the chrome grilled delivery chute.

The pictures are simply awful; particularly as they bear very little resemblance to the image I have of myself. My long sharp face appears gaunt, positively haggard, but what I find really disquieting is the look in my eyes, an expression of fragile openness and anxiety. Something tells me I'm really not the man I was, and yet I'm barely 18 years old!

But at least my hair has recovered from the rather crazy impulsive cut it received some six months before, though it's still considerably shorter than it was previously. However it frames my face comfortably, loose fuzzy curls sprouting out healthily and placing me over six feet. A flicker of a smile involuntarily tightens my lips. Should I write on the passport form, in the section marked height, 'with hair, six foot two'?

* * *

I have to get the photos countersigned by an authority figure of some kind, a person holding some status within the community, someone who has known me some years.

'That's impossible,' I complain to my mother. *'How can they expect everybody to know a judge, or even a solicitor for that matter?'*

'Why not get the vicar to do it for you?' my mum suggests.

'But I don't even know him,' I reply uncertainly.

'Never mind. He knows you and he often asks after you. Juergen Simonson is his name.'

'He doesn't sound very English. What's he like?'

'It'll be all right. He'd love to see you. Now you know where the vicarage is, don't you?'

'Sure, I used to deliver papers up that way. Top of Luttrell Avenue, on the right.'

'That's it. Well see you later, good luck.'

I arrive at the vicarage feeling somewhat resentful. After all, why should the lack of a signature prevent me from going wherever I please? It's as if I am seeking this man's approval to travel.

The reverend opens the door, greets me warmly, and ushers me inside. Bidding me take a seat in his study, he asks the purpose of my visit and readily accedes to my request, and is soon signing the relevant paperwork and endorsing the back of each photograph. Formalities over, we enjoy a good old English cup of tea, thoughtfully provided by his housekeeper, and we sit for a while exchanging pleasantries. Languishing in the comfort of an easy chair, a distinct mood of calm and serenity pervades the room; I feel quite at ease.

Realising that we have been chatting for quite some time, I begin to get up, indicating my intention to leave, and the vicar stands and vigorously shakes me by the hand, wishing me well on my journey.

I walk quite briskly towards home, feeling refreshed by the visit, and I ponder on just where this trip is going to take me.

* * *

All the relevant bits and bobs (including my birth certificate, which I've discovered amongst our family papers) are now dispatched to the Passport Office.

With little to do other than wait and fret, I set myself to gather any necessary items for the trip, like sleeping bags and a rucksack. Common sense suggests that it's best to ask around before deciding to buy new.

Trekking off to High Street Kensington one day, Yolanda and I make our way to French Michelle's flat in Hornton Street. I haven't seen Michelle Sampieri for a while, and it's nice to share some time with her. I've always liked Michelle, a lot, ever since we met on the same fateful evening as I first encountered Yolanda, at *Le Bataclan* club.

Michelle appears to be in high spirits.

'Paul! How are you, Man? What's all this about going with Yolanda to India? It sounds great!! I'm sorry Paul I haven't got a pack, a bag. What do you call it, Man? But I've got some sleeping bags, you're welcome to them, Man, I don't need them.'

As Yolanda and I sit and drink our tea, Michelle slips off to find the sleeping bags, and soon returns; *'Sorry they're not better, love, but ...there you go Man!'* The way she pronounces the word 'love' as *'loov'* - is a delight in itself. I can't restrain my laughter. She really cracks me up.

'That's fine Michelle, don't get hung up about it, they're groovy. We'll get the rucksack somewhere. Don't worry. By the way they're sometimes called knapsacks. Have you heard the song? "... How I love to go a wandering with a knapsack on my back".'

'Oh cool it,' Yolanda admonishes me, impatient to catch up with her friend.

I keep my own company while the Yolanda and Michelle chat.

28

As I'm still affected by pendulum-like swings of mood, Michelle's support for the idea of going travelling is very welcome. Her healthy interestedness, along with a general improvement in the weather does much to better my mood; I'm beginning to see our journey differently now, as something vaguely trendy, and definitely desirable.

* * *

So we have to buy the rucksack new, and I find myself sourcing and purchasing it at a camping centre in central London, in Leicester Square, where I'm tempted to buy a small tent too. But I end up emerging from the store holding just a rucksack, bluey-grey in colour, with space enough for a fair amount of stuff, and with two separate pockets, clasps and leather straps. The bag, though not overly spacious, is affordable and I'm confidant it will do the job.

* * *

At last a telephone call comes from the Passport Office: -

'Hello? Mr. Mason? Paul Mason? Yes? Petty France here. Your passport is ready, Sir. Would you like to come in and collect it? Yes? Well come to reception and they will deal with you'.

I find I like being addressed as 'Sir'!

At the Passport Offices, in Petty France near St. James's Park Underground Station, I endure the formality of a long wait, and am then shown to a room where an official plies me with questions concerning which countries I intend to visit. I've already decided it's unnecessary to present myself as anything but a run-of-the-mill tourist getting ready for a Continental break, therefore I omit any mention of my hope to travel to India. At length the official hands me my passport and wishes me a good holiday.

On my way back home by tube train, I sit and study my passport, with its black leatherwork cover from which issues an odour similar to that found in antique shops. Embossed in gold leaf are the words 'BRITISH PASSPORT UNITED KINGDOM OF GREAT BRITAIN AND NORTHERN IRELAND', and images of a lion and a unicorn which hold twixt paw and hoof a shield wrapped in ribbon, on which the words 'HONI SOIT QUI MAL Y PENSE, DIEU ET MON DROIT' are written. *But surely, that's French, and this a British passport?*

Near the top of the front cover, in a lozenge shaped window, is my name, 'MR. P. MASON' written in blue fountain pen ink on fresh white paper, and appearing in a similar window near the bottom, is a number, '355468'.

Adhered to one of the inner pages I find the smallest of the forms I filled in, the one that reveals my most personal details. For profession I'd written 'MUSICIAN', born in 'LONDON', additionally, I am detailed as being '5ft 10ins' tall with hair 'Green' and eyes 'Brown'.

'Oh, no!'

29

But, at a second glance, I see it is written correctly, hair 'Brown' and eyes 'Green'.

On the reverse of the front cover, in old-fashioned copperplate handwriting, and printed on what looked like a high denomination banknote, is a message:

Her Britannic Majesty's
Principal Secretary of State
for Foreign Affairs
Requests and requires
in the Name of Her Majesty
all those who it may concern
to allow the bearer to pass freely
without let or hindrance,
and to afford the bearer
such assistance and protection
as may be necessary.

I smile to myself.

Let's hope everyone reads this or I will be in trouble!

* * *

Recognising that now there's nothing holding us back from leaving for India, Yolanda begins to show her first signs of doubt, earnestly seeking my reassurance that I really want to travel. During the last few months Yolanda has been working part-time in a gift shop, trading as *Admiral's Eye*, near Trafalgar Square, selling souvenirs and jewellery. She mentions that her boss at the shop, Mr Lyons, on hearing she's hoping to travel to India, has mentioned that he once stayed at some sort of retreat for businessmen there, at the same place where The Beatles stayed.

Yolanda gives her notice to her employer, and to her digs in Earl's Court where she has been living in a cupboard (well, it barely qualifies to be called a room) in a house situated on the corner of Nevern Road and the busy Cromwell Road.

The days drag by as Yolanda works out her notice, and during this time an uneasy stillness descends on the basement flat in which I live, and I have nothing with which to express my pent-up feelings since my guitars, amplifier and effects pedals are all gone - sold to raise money for our journey.

Sitting in my bedroom, day after day, I have so much time to reflect, far too much time in fact. I'm getting really fed up.

* * *

The light is fading as the weather becomes suddenly overcast, and turning on both of my table lamps - the one with the brown bear carved in hard wood and the effort I made in woodwork at school - does little to dispel the gloom.

I reflect that rightfully, I shouldn't be hanging about the house having a gloomy afternoon, that at my age I should be in my prime - staying out all night, enjoying a good social life, footloose and fancy-free.

But I've already been through all that.

What's in store for me in the future? I wonder.

I'd never really given much thought to growing up, though once, as a child, I'd puzzled over a packet of *Kellogg's* cornflakes on which there was an artist's impression of a normal average family outside their dream house. Casually dressed and well groomed, there was the man of the house with his 'Cindy Doll' wife and two kids, all getting into their new car, parked in the forecourt of their home. It didn't resonate with me at all, and I had no desire to have a stereotypical life!

Maybe my mother realised this, for she sometimes addressed me as Peter Pan; I guess I just didn't want to lose out on the fun of being a child. After all, what's the point of 'growing up' if all one can look forward to is the chance of earning money and getting married?

Actually, as a child, the very idea of my parents seeing me get married filled me with acute embarrassment, but now I would love them to be there and see me get wed to Yolanda. Unfortunately this cannot happen, for he died in hospital shortly before her return to England. Being a Christian Scientist he delayed in getting medical help; and it was only on account of my dear mother that a doctor was ever called, but it seems it was rather too late. From what Yolanda says, it seems she once spoke to my father on the phone, which I'm glad about, but what with Yolanda being foreign, and a bit of a glamour puss, it's likely she might have been a bit much for him? Perhaps though, in time, they would have clicked; I suspect so, in fact I'm certain of it.

I light a perfumed incense stick and position it in a holder on the shelf, watching the smoke spiralling upwards. I have quite a few packets of incense, my favourite being *Sugandha Shringar Aravinda Agarbatti*. I buy them in bulk from the local Indian grocers, next door to the *Taj Mahal* restaurant in East Putney. I also have some of those very short sticks of the slightly peppery exotic variety, which I buy from the local Japanese food shop, which come with a little ceramic holder. I guess my sister Margaret set off my interest in incense, as when she lived at home she would sometimes burn a 'joss stick' in her room. In addition to being air freshener, incense is also handy in masking the smell of cigarette smoke.

I stare at the wooden shelves that stand beside my bed, which are painted in the same two-tone blue emulsion paints as the rest of the room, a colour combination similar to that of the *Wedgwood* blue china cheese dish, in the front room. I ponder over my assortment of treasures, spread about on the shelves, my collection of nick-knacks; the silver boot hook, the antique china cream pot (that I salvaged from some nearby road works) and the miniature statues my uncle gave me.

I pick up the Indian-looking bronze image, of a seated figure with what looks like a child beside it, and another little statuette stood beside it, also given to me by my Uncle Jack.

I wonder where they're from? I puzzle.

I am also minded of the little black painted wooden box covered with Indian postage stamps that my father used to keep old coins in. I wonder whether or not my uncle visited India, but I don't recall anyone mentioning it. And all those things in the trunk in the workshop, amongst them the decorated parasol, which belonged to my dad's mother, I imagine that comes from India too.

Right now I want to DO something, but I didn't know quite what. In former times I would have given vent to my feelings on the fretboards of my instruments, but now I can't, as they're all gone. So instead I turn to my depleted record collection, a collection that once spanned the breadth of the fireplace, but now numbers barely a dozen. The immediate choice is between Syd Barrett's *'Golden Hair'* and Sonny Boy Williamson's *'Peach Tree Blues'*, songs that have become abiding companions of late. I choose the latter, and find the track with practised alacrity, casually dropping the worn stylus into the groove. The rich and deeply soulful tones of Sonny Boy once more break out full throttle, and re-awaken me to their beauty.

'Oh look at that honey ooh ooh eee, way over down by the pe-eeach-a tree'.

The temptation to join in again possesses me; I utter the words with impassioned force, keeping time by slapping my knees. *'Oh look at that honey, ooh ooh eee, way over down by the pe-eeach-a tree'* … and that harmonica!! Wow!

On an impulse, I decide the time is right to talk to my mother about my plan to go travelling. I find her and explain that I intend to journey to the Holy Land, after which I'm hoping to get to India. It isn't easy telling her, but as I break the news to her I feel better for it. She listens patiently and endures my attempts to explain my plans with a concerned expression that fails to conceal her disappointment. It feels as though I'm betraying her in some way. I feel awful. But I steel myself against the emotions I feel, realising that I can't afford to pass up this chance to try and sort myself out by means of taking to the road.

* * *

Accompanying Yolanda up the ill-lit stairway to the excuse for a room that she has been renting, is a depressing experience. We are here to pick up her belongings; her suitcase and anything else she has here. The roar of the traffic outside causes us to have to shout to one another as we scoop the last of her belongings into a paper carrier bag. Perhaps to rid ourselves of the depressing effect of visiting the place, or perhaps just for the hell of it, we hail a black cab taxi to take us back to Putney. Blow the expense!

The idea is this that Yolanda will stay overnight at my place, and in the morning we'll leave together for our travels. I do hope that my mother doesn't mind Yolanda stopping over for the night. But soon the two of us will be on the road, and will be spending our entire time together, day and night, so what difference can this one night make?

This evening, after supper is finished, Yolanda and I go to my bedroom and we start to pack. We've already decided that we'll take only the minimum of bulk, and I begin collecting what I'll need, plucking socks, underwear and a T-shirt from my chest of drawers. We make a pile of clothes to put in the rucksack, and add a couple of Yolanda's towels,

'I won't bother with any spare jeans or extra shoes,' I tell Yolanda.

'Well, I'll take some spare things, they won't take up much room,' she replies, placing a couple of blouses and a dress on the pile.

Guessing that sometimes the weather might get a bit parky, I add a woollen sweater, one that was hand-knitted by my mother.

'Well, we're almost finished then,' I announce.

'I don't believe it!' Yolanda replies. *'Surely we need more than that, there's the toilet things and my make-up yet.'*

Those items are also added, and then I scour my brain for anything else to take.

Those years in the Wolf Cubs; I really enjoyed those times, and they've left their mark. Our motto, 'Be Prepared', is stamped on the buckle of my belt that I've got laying around somewhere.

'I'll also take a penknife as well', I suggest, *'it could come in useful.'*

'Yes, and a needle and cotton too,' Yolanda responds.

'A biro, some paper too, and where's your passport?' I ask. *'We'd better get them together as well.'*

I've put mine in a grey plastic passport wallet issued by *Sabena Airlines* that I've found in the flat, which is handy in that it protects the passport and there's also space to put our money in too.

After rummaging around in her suitcase Yolanda hands me her passport, which I flick open, and check over.

Her name - Iolande Baldi - date and place of birth, 26th June 1949, Siena, Repubblica Italiana, and the photo; Yolanda's appearance has been likened to Mona Lisa, but perhaps she looks a little more like Sophia Loren with a beautiful aquiline nose.

'Wow! You look really different here! It doesn't look like you at all,' I laugh; Yolanda returns me an embarrassed, soulful look.

'What does 'Casalinga' mean?' I ask her.

'Housewife,' she replies, her face reddening considerably.

'Oh!'

This reminds me of a declaration Yolanda made to me some while back: *'I don't want to be like every other Italian woman, tied to the kitchen sink. My life will be different from that'.* But here it is in black and white, her declared occupation, *'Casalinga',* 'Housewife'.

'Shall we take something to read?' I ask, *'I thought of The Bible.'*

Rummaging about in her suitcase she produces an old green hardback.

'Oh yes. I'll take this book,' she replies, looking at me expectantly.

I recall how she'd shown me this book before, and I remember browsing the pages at Dario's flat. Opening Yolanda's *Voice of Isis* book again, I notice the drawing she made in it with coloured pencils, of a sunset on the sea's horizon, and I recall how she'd written to me telling me about this drawing, just after she left England, when she was on vacation in France with French Michelle.

This book is no ordinary book for it seeks to direct the reader along 'The Path' and contains numerous references to Egyptian beliefs. I know this because Yolanda sometimes quotes from it whilst attempting to add weight to an opinion she holds. For instance, on the subject of stimulants, the writers are categorical in their condemnation of them, stating that those who use them *'can never achieve the Goal in this lifetime'.* Personally, I believe the book to have been written by a couple of oddballs, though I keep this opinion to myself since Yolanda obviously derives solace from its pages, and I believe that is important.

Another book she's been reading lately emanates from the *Hare Krishna* people, a commentary on an Indian Scripture called the *Bhagavad Gita* - which Yolanda refers to as *'The Jeeta'.* Personally, I don't take to this sect, and anyway, Yolanda indicates no wish to take the *Hare Krishna* book with us, which is a relief, if for no other reason than it weighs a ton.

As preparations for our travels seem to be finished, we decide to go and clean our teeth before bidding my mother *'good night'.*

I've offered Yolanda to sleep in my single bed, with its veneered wooden headboard etched with a former girlfriend's message, *'Don't cross out my name, Harriet!',* and I'm intending to sleep on the floor.

Though I used to be a sound sleeper, I no longer enjoy the thought of going to bed; in fact I've begun to harbour an unhealthy dread of the night.

Long I lie here in the gloom, my chest tight, my breathing overactive, reviewing the events of the day.

I hear Yolanda sigh deeply and roll over.

'See you in the morning, Landa. Night night.' I whisper.

'Uh what? Oh yeah. Night, night Paulikin.'

* * *

As I open my eyes I realise that it's morning; and I'm surprised to find myself lying on the floor. Then I remember that last night Yolanda stayed the night so I gave up my bed, giving it over to her

Yolanda opens her eyes and looks over at me; she's still a bit dozy.

'Oh, hi ya,' she murmurs.

'Would you like a cup of tea, some breakfast?' I ask.

'Oh, I'll get up,' she responds.

When ablutions and breakfast are over, I pack some last things in the bag, toothbrushes, hairbrushes and a couple of handkerchiefs.

Everything looks ready, but there's one problem though.

'How are we going to carry the sleeping bags?' Yolanda asks.

'What we need is a strap,' I point out.

Unable to find one, I rummage through the chest of drawers.

'I could use these,' I suggest, holding up a bunch of neckties.

Yolanda eyes me in apparent disbelief, but doesn't offer any alternative.

'They'll do, if I tie them together,' I say, trying to convince myself.

The packing done, I figure Yolanda and I now need to have a pow-wow.

'Are we really going to go, still, going this very day?' I ask, clumsily. *'No time like the present,'*

But, right now, she doesn't seem to want to chat.

'Would you like to leave it a while then?' I ask.

'No, today's fine by me. Have you told your mother yet?'

'Yes, but not that we're leaving today. But she must have noticed us packing. I'll go and tell her now.'

I go in search of my mother.

'Whereabouts are you going?' my mother asks apprehensively, her expression appears uncomfortably grave. She tilts her face a little, as if looking over an invisible pair of glasses, *'Do you still want to go to India?'* she asks.

'That's right, and we hope to go to lots of other places too. Around Europe, Morocco, even the Holy Land.'

I gaze at her ashen expression, and at her greying hair, noting for what seems like the first time that her beautiful copper curls are losing their engaging colour.

'Lunch will be ready soon. You'll want some before you go?'

'Thanks. Yeah, we'll leave after lunch.'

Wandering into the front room, I encounter my brother Raymond who's arrived to stay for the duration of his summer break from studies at Leeds University. He's got a holiday job to earn himself some money, as a bus conductor for London Transport.

Though Raymond is the younger of my two brothers, and only slightly older than me, I think he views me as his 'little' brother. I find that attitude only slightly annoying; as usually it just amuses me to observe the power play. After all, his social life is only just beginning whereas mine has been in swing for some years. He's aware of this, of course, nonetheless, as he seems to relish the role of him as the older, wiser, brother, he continues to play it out with well-seasoned practice.

We exchange pleasantries.

'So,' he says, *'Mum tells me you're off to India.'*

'Yes, that's right.'

'Do you know people there, then?'

'Yolanda's got a few addresses. Yes,' This is true to a point, but actually they're not people that she actually **knows**. And what's more we've actually decided **not** to take the addresses. But I don't need to tell him that!

'How much money have you got?' he queries, *'You'll need at least a hundred and twenty quid each for the fare.'*

'I don't need that much,' I answer hesitantly.

'Yes you do, that's how much the airfare is! Have you got enough for it?' he demands, his voice taking on a faintly menacing tone.

He appears surprisingly well informed about the cost of air tickets to India, so I wonder that perhaps he's been aware for some time of our intentions to go travelling.

'Well, that's as much as you know,' I respond defensively, *'Actually, we're going to hitch-hike, you twit.'*

'That's a bit dodgy isn't it?' he queries, *'that could be really dangerous!'*

Raymond looks genuinely concerned. He's a good lad, in spite of our differences and all our ups and downs. I reckon his heart is in the right place. But right now it feels like he's trying to make me feel foolish and I won't have it; I tire of his tones.

'Look I've hitchhiked hundreds of miles. I've been all over the place. With Henderson, on my own, all over the place.'

'A bit different though, going to foreign countries,' he retorts, ever the 'last word Harry'.

'Not really!' I say, but wondering all the while.

My mother enters the room, and I sense that she's been hovering about whilst my brother and I have been talking. I'm glad of the interruption, for in truth he has begun to piss me off.

At the lunchtime meal, conversation is almost non-existent, limited to asking for the condiments and in vying with one another in thanking mum for cooking such nice food.

At length we disperse, and after returning to my bedroom I let out a sigh of relief, *'Phew that was **heavy**! Come on, let's go, there'll be no better time to leave.'*

Fastening the straps of the rucksack, I hoist it aloft and swing it onto my back. Then I look about, surveying my room, slowly and thoughtfully.

'Have we got everything then?' I ask, *'Do you want to carry the sleeping bags?'*

'I think so. No, you take the bags, I'll carry the backpack.'

'If you really want to,' I say, paying no particular attention to what she's saying.

As we walk from the bedroom and down the hallway, I shout out, *'We're off everybody. Bye-ee!'*

My mother and Raymond emerge and in raised voices make their farewells. Hugging my mother, we kiss each other, and then I make my way to the front door.

Will I ever see my mother again, she who has brought me up and given me such tireless devotion? Would this be my last opportunity to tell her how much I love her, how much she means to me? I can't bear it. I struggle hard not to show how torn up I am. I weep inside.

After making our last gestures and words of farewell, my throat suddenly feels completely dry. I find it difficult to speak, but I force myself.

'Bye Mum. Bye Raymond. I'll write to you when I get the chance.'

'God bless,' my mother says, *'God bless you both.'*

We leave, and as we do I hear Raymond's voice: *'See you in time for tea!'* he calls.

Chapter 2

A GOOD OMEN

Emerging from my mother's flat, Yolanda and I climb the red-bricked steps. Fine droplets of drizzle fall lightly on my upturned face, cool and refreshing.

Wrenching another last goodbye from my anguish, I make my way across the stony driveway as purposefully as my weakened legs allow. The gorgeous scent of the rose bushes wafts in the air and catches me for a brief moment as I take one last wistful look at the house where I've lived my whole life.

As Yolanda and I step out onto the pavement, I wonder if this will be the last time I'll see my home, the last time I'll walk down this road?

Countless times, I've waited at the nearby bus stop; and there, as a schoolboy, I had the opportunity to chat up girls from the local comprehensive school, where I would talk to Mimi and Corrine. As we near the bus stop Yolanda looks at me enquiringly.

'Well, we could go by Underground or by British Railways, the big trains,' I tell her.

'What's the easiest?' she asks.

'The Underground's further, and we could manage the walk to the other railway station easily, without taking the bus.'

My words came back to me, as they sometimes do, and at once I realise how confusing my answers sound, but this isn't the best time to launch upon a dissertation about suburban travel.

Yolanda appears confused; she really isn't very *au fait* with the transport system.

I look over my shoulder… there's still no bus in sight.

'Oh come on, let's just start walking,' I suggest, so we continue along the Upper Richmond in the direction of Putney Station.

'Why can't you explain?' Yolanda asks, catching me up and walking beside me.

'Don't worry, the station's not very far. We can easily walk it.'

We pass by the parade of local shops.

I recollect that, as a youngster, in the Christmas holidays I worked at Godfrey's the greengrocers, and at the florists with old Mr Len Dando, he of the relaxed and friendly country manner. Amazingly, I never once saw him grumpy or cross.

Onwards we trudge, the drizzle slowly turning to rain. *But this is the summer*, I protest, *it's already late July!*

Yolanda has chosen to wear her glossy black fur coat, a black chiffon blouse, purple velvet trousers and open-toed wooden-soled *Scholl* sandals. Discovering that she was going to wear her fur coat made me decide to out dig mine, a tattered vintage brown one, a relic from the time they were fashionable back in '68. I remember seeing Stevie Winwood wearing one on Top of the Pops, in the height of summer performing *'I'm a Man'*, sweating profusely and grinning as if he was really 'out of it'. I like to wear fur, as somehow it makes me feel closer to nature.

I'm wearing a purple polo-neck sweatshirt, and jeans that a girl friend altered for me, sewing in extra denim to make them flare out like sailors trousers. I've even bought myself new shoes; sandy coloured desert boots, just for this trip.

But neither of us has brought along any rainwear. How absurd is it to be wandering off like this in a downpour of rain. I'm really tempted to turn back, but my brother's words echo in my ears.

We walk on.

'Only a few minutes more and we'll be there,' I assure.

Yolanda stares at me with an air of disbelief, but stays silent.

We're approaching an ornate building that was originally the Globe Cinema, where on its re-opening our entire family had gone to see a vintage comedy, the 1953 film entitled *Titfield Thunderbolt* starring Stanley Holloway, about the threatened closure of a railway branch line. Since then the place has changed ownership and name, and is now the Cinecenta showing offbeat films with titles like *Les Biches* and *Charlie Bubbles*.

'I saw Wonderwall at this cinema,' I enthuse, *'George Harrison did the music. Brilliant it was,'*

'Are we almost at the station?' Yolanda asks, *'I'm getting soaked.'*

As we go to cross the road I answer her, *'Yup! The station's right here.'* I announce.

After purchasing two single tickets to Victoria I show them to Keith, the West Indian ticket collector, who recognises me, and nods agreeably. I can hear our train pulling in to the station, so I hurry down the stairs to the platform and together we enter a carriage where we find a pair of unoccupied seats on which we plonk down our bags.

'This is the route I used to take to school,' I tell Yolanda.

'Oh really?' she answers, sounding decidedly disinterested.

*'Yes, I went this way **every** day. My friend Henderson went there too, actually it was quite a good school, you know.'*

'Really?' she asks, apparently warming to the subject.

The train moves very fast and soon I notice we are nearing Clapham Junction, where we have to change trains, so I get up and start to pick up our baggage.

'Quick, we're at Clapham Junction, we have to change here.'

'Oh I've been to Clapham, before, when I went to see someone in Peckham.'

'Peckham? That's on the 37 bus route,' I say in reflex response.

Taking our time now, we descend a steep flight of stairs and make our way along the gloomy damp-smelling subway.

'Our train might come in on platform 12, or it might come on 14. Fast trains on 12, locals on 14,' I explain.

Yolanda looks at me, a touch bewildered.

'Quick, run! It's on 14,' I call out to her.

We hurry up the stairs and clamber onto the train with only moments to spare. Once inside, and in close proximity with others, I try to avoid the eyes of my fellow passengers and so I take to gazing out of the window.

Clapham Junction, the biggest rail junction in the world!

How many times as a keen young train spotter I had stood around on the ends of the platforms of railway stations, a thr'penny notebook and a blue *Scripto* biro pen in my hand, fortified by *Branston* pickle sandwiches and an orange drink, which mum had packed, carried in the duffel bag hung over my shoulder?

Our train now passes over a viaduct, taking us through bleak Battersea, and continues its way onto and over a bridge across the river.

In my collection at home I still have a very old ticket related to this bridge, a 3rd Class ticket, issued by the London, Chatham and Dover Railway (L.C.&D.R.) for travel from Clapham Road to Grosvenor Road, a station built around 1860, that's been closed since way back in 1911, which used to stand here by Grosvenor Bridge, just outside of Victoria Station. The ticket is also very old, dated round about 1890.

The train rattles on and into the vast terminus of Victoria Station, where we alight and make our way towards the ticket barrier; the collector snatches our tickets.

Officious sod, I think to myself, *'I won't be sorry to miss your kind!'* I mutter under my breath.

This incident reminds me of a recent exchange with an official at the unemployment exchange:

'Right,' he had said, *'Next week, when you come in, I want to see you looking smart. We're going to find you a job!'*

'I won't be coming in next week, I'm off to India,' I had replied.

'Well .. Just you come in smart, that's all,' he stuttered, trying to sound self-assured but not making a convincing job of it.

Yolanda and I now move across the concourse of the station.

We need to get our tickets for the next part of our journey, so first I check with Yolanda where we are actually going on the train.

'We book to Dover, then get a ticket for the boat at the other end,' she informs me.

I've never travelled from this side of the station before. This is where the 'specials' depart from, the Golden Arrow and the Orient Express

'Shall we change some money?' I ask. *'We've got time; according to the timetable the train leaves in about twenty minutes. How many francs do we get for the pound? A franc's about one and six (one shilling and sixpence) isn't it?'*

'I'm not sure,' Yolanda replies.

'Well you ought to; after all you've been there before. I haven't.'

Yolanda becomes embarrassed. I think it's possible that she actually looks more attractive when she gets embarrassed.

Once we have our tickets and foreign currency we go to the departure board to see which platform our train is leaving from. There's a group of youngsters gathered there waiting, with baggage, suitcases, holdalls, and backpacks strewn about their feet and a clump of bicycles too.

We negotiate a passage past all the people waiting around, and approach the train.

The carriages appear crammed full; faces peer back out the windows at us as we search for a couple of available seats.

'It's packed full,' I exclaim.

We continue searching, walking further up the long line of coaches, and are halfway up the platform before we find some vacant seats. After chucking all our belongings up on the netted-string luggage rack, I settle down and study the currency notes and coins we obtained from the bank. The French notes are really very attractive, much more so than their British equivalents, which are dull by comparison. I really don't like the decimalisation that's happening, with the Bank of England withdrawing the ten-shilling note, and replacing it with a silly looking seven-sided 50 new pence coin. The first old coin to go was the farthing (a quarter of a penny), and last year it was the ha'penny (half penny) and then around Christmas the dear old half-crown (two shillings and sixpence) was taken away. It looks as though they'll eventually even drop the sixpence and the shilling. In truth I still haven't forgiven them for withdrawing all those lovely early Victorian 'bun' pennies (probably a reference to the image on the back of the coins of Queen Victoria with her hair tied into a bun), those large solid copper coins, which are scarce these days. I know I'm not alone in being concerned about these changes; I reckon there are many who find the changeover to decimal coinage unpleasant and unwelcome. I suspect the French currency is undergoing such changes too, as all the coins and notes are new, and marked *'nouveau' francs.*

'I wonder who this chick is with the funny hairdo, on the banknotes?' I ask myself

aloud.

The carriage gives a jerk.

'We're off!' I say.

'Y-e-e-s-s,' Yolanda responds, as if to herself.

So, after weeks of indecision, prevarication and listless waiting - time spent in seemingly futile soul-searching - we are finally OFF!

Wiping the back of my hand across the glass, trying to remove the mist of condensation - my rings scratch against the glass, making my teeth grate - I settle down to enjoy the view out of the window.

The train makes good progress and it seems but a few minutes before we are out of London and well on our way.

The swaying motion of the train and the sound of the rattling of the wheels along the track make it difficult to make ourselves heard, so for the most part we stay silent.

Outside, it's raining hard again and it's virtually impossible to discern much out there, but I figure we are by now in Kent, the countryside here being known as the 'Garden of England'.

At length I notice that some passengers are starting to get up from their seats and are reaching up for their luggage. By the distinctive taste and smell of the air, I just know we are near the sea. Quite why people rush to the sea in droves to get their lungs full of ozone is a mystery to me, even though, as a child, I liked being taken to the seaside. Now, I don't like the smell, it reminds me too much of the chemistry lessons I endured whilst undergoing compulsory education.

Being a Boat Train I had assumed that our train (with us in it) would be transported across the Channel. But I figure we must now get off and then transfer to the ferry.

Before walking down to the quay, we go and purchase our ferry tickets, and then I make for the sign marked 'UK PASSPORT HOLDERS', where I hold out my passport and ticket. An official, wearing a peaked cap and naval style jacket, casts his eyes over me, and then at my passport and gestures for me to pass.

As a 'FOREIGN NATIONAL' Yolanda goes through a different gate, but we soon rejoin one another, and together make our way up the gangway of the vessel.

Once on deck I stand and watch as carloads of holidaymakers slowly inch forward making their way into the hold.

For years I've heard about getting things 'duty free', so with time on our hands I look about for a shop. We stand outside waiting for it to open, and as I stand there, I stare at my girlfriend's hair, studying with interest the fine jewelled droplets of drizzle sparkling there. It looks quite magical.

The huge ferryboat starts to commence its voyage across the Channel, and it soon gathers speed and is putting some distance to the shore.

'I do hope the crossing won't be too choppy.' I pray.

I catch the sound of a door being unlocked, so we now shuffle inside the Duty Free Shop, where on display are perfumes, spirits and a selection of electrical gadgets.

Spotting the shelves of cigarettes I pick up a carton of Benson and Hedges King Size, and after paying for our duty-frees we wander off to check out the many wooden benches fixed to the deck, but all the seats appear to be taken.

'Yolanda how long does it take to get across?'

'I can't remember. Two or three hours maybe?'

'It's a bit of a drag isn't it?' I respond.

We watch as some young guys cavort about, seemingly trying to impress their girlfriends. Yolanda seems to find their antics annoying.

'Pitiful aren't they? Why can't they act their age?' she sneers. *'I wish they'd cool it,'* she adds haughtily.

But, with the roar of the waves Yolanda's comment must be lost to them.

One of the youngsters, who's mucking about, stares in our direction, a belligerent look of scorn written across his face. I suppose he disapproves of our appearance, we probably look like hippies to him.

We ignore them and at length the young couples move away. They were possibly hoping get a reaction to their stupid behaviour, and when they didn't get one, thought to go elsewhere in search of a fresh audience. Perhaps they tired of their childish games or maybe we freaked them out. Whatever the reason, they've gone.

'Good!' Yolanda remarks, making her way across to the vacated seats.

Instead of joining her, I choose to wander across the slippery deck and lean on the white tubular steel railings, and as I do I observe the coast of France coming into view.

As a happy little boy on summer holidays, I remember standing on the Dorsetshire cliffs, near Weymouth, straining my eyes to see the French coastline. Now, sighting France for the first time, I marvel at its resemblance to our own South Coast, the chalky white cliffs look so similar.

Surely, if one could push them together, we'd be joined to France!

* * *

We disembark, and unsurprisingly there's no reception committee waiting for us. We make for the *'Douane'* where the French customs officials check and return our passports, after which, and at a distance, I inspect my travel document, in order to discover what has been stamped in it.

Trudging through the dockyard here at Calais, with its cranes and railway trucks, we eventually reach the railway station, which bristles with activity. Trains are waiting here, ready to whisk travellers off to their holiday paradises. Gazing at a signboard I try to decode the name of the organisation, SNCF, *Societe Nationale Chemin de Fer*. *'National Society of the Iron Horse'*, that's a nice idea, then I realise my mistake, not the *'Iron Horse'* but the *'Iron **Path'***.

With the intention of finding the main road and getting a lift, Yolanda and I make our way out of the station yard. But when we get to the road it's immediately apparent that the majority of the traffic comprises of families travelling in cars, many of them having caravans in tow. Unsurprisingly we find no one is willing to offer us a lift, but I guess that for the most part they are unable, packed as their cars are with children and luggage.

Over the course of the next few hours not a single vehicle stops for us, so it becomes increasingly obvious that we're only going to become further demoralised by waiting here, so we walk.

When evening comes we have ourselves a *tête-à-tête* and decide it's best to give up hitching for today, and instead we go and look for a place to lie down and rest. After gaining access to an adjacent field, we unroll the sleeping bags, and bed down for the night.

* * *

Wiping the sleep from my eyes, I stir and take in the new morning.

I don't know how long it's been daylight before I awoke, but clearly we've slept soundly beneath the open sky, and I'm now wide awake and feeling refreshed and renewed.

I gaze about me, and my eyes light on a dark shape between our sleeping bags. I look closer to discover it's a young kitten lying asleep, seemingly warm and secure. This furry little creature looks adorable and when it awakes it becomes the focus of our attention. It's great that he's joined us. A good omen,

We linger awhile playing with and cuddling the kitten, then breakfast on the remains of our packed food from yesterday, some bread and fruit.

We fret that we have nothing for kitty, *le petit chat*, the little cat.

After rolling up and putting away our sleeping bags, we fasten the rucksack and bid a fond farewell to our little kitty friend, then head off to resume our journey.

After our disappointing wait the day before, today we resolve to walk further along the road and get right out of the port, figuring we'll have a better chance of getting a lift once we're out of Calais.

But as we walk we find the friendly kitten soon catches up with us.

We're really not sure what to do for the best… We figure that he probably belongs to one of the many caravans or bungalows dotted around about so we try telling him to get back and go home. But no matter how much we discourage him from following us, he continues to trail after us and follows for about two miles or so.

In desperation we hatch a plan to deter him from staying with us. We decide to totally ignore him, and only cast the occasional glance just to check he is no longer there.

But alas, the plan fails, as just like that cartoon superstar, Felix, he just *'keeps on walking'* with us.

It seems fate has ordained the kitten to be our travelling companion, so we start to discuss how we're going to get him through passport controls, and how we're going to feed him.

But then, when I look around again, he has vanished. He's nowhere to be seen. Though it's obvious it's for the best, we feel a sense of loss now he's gone, we both grew so attached to him so quickly.

Though we keep sticking out our thumbs, the traffic just whizzes by us, but again, it has to be said, most of the cars seem full up, holidaymakers most likely.

So we continue walking onward, and for several miles we walk, by which time we develop quite a thirst. With no shops or cafes in sight, I decide to knock at the door of the next house we come upon.

On hearing our request for a glass of water, the occupant slams shut the door in our faces.

'Some people!' Yolanda exclaims.

We continue on our way, and as we do I notice that most of the local men seem pretty true to the stereotypes, in that they sport big bushy moustaches, wear broad striped sweatshirts and black berets. Many of them are riding about on bicycles, and all with long French loaves protruding from their persons.

Pleasant as it is to observe the locals going about their business I am getting rather impatient to get on the move. How long are we going to have to keep on walking?

'Are we ever going to get a lift?' I lament, *'At this rate we'll take years to get anywhere at all.'*

Just as I say this, a lorry (or *camion* as Yolanda calls it) pulls into a lay-by a little way up ahead. I guess the lorry driver is answering the call of nature, and when he reappears and walks slowly back to his vehicle, he finds us waiting for him.

Yolanda does the talking for it seems she's able to speak French well.

'*On va aller aux Indes,*' she says.

The man looks concerned.

'*What does that mean?*' I whisper.

'*Oh, that we're going to India,*' she replies airily.

But this information seems to panic the poor man, and even when he's reassured that a lift to Paris will do, he still seems nervous about taking us with him.

But we badger him and at last he agrees to take us along.

Jubilant, we climb into the cab.

As we motor along, I realise that this is my first experience of motoring on the 'wrong' side of the road, this being the right side of the road, whereas in Britain the correct side is the left side.

I'm surprised to find that the French countryside looks remarkably similar to the British landscape, and that the buildings here are not markedly different either. My attention drifts from noting the different makes of cars, to reading the advertising hoardings that line the road. Though written in French, the posters communicate clearly through their images. Predominantly the products being advertised are brands of coffee and soft cheeses. Pictures of long-horned cows are used, but as I've never seen a cow before with horns, I conjecture that, on this basis, on our travels we might even chance upon horses with horns, unicorns!

Very little conversation falls between the three of us in the cab, and after about 6 miles or so - about 10 kilometres - the driver indicates that he's turning off the main road and so the *camion* comes to a stop.

'*Merci beaucoup Monsieur.*' we thank him. It feels good to use a little of the schoolboy French I learned.

It's by now mid-morning, and seeing there's a *café* a few yards away, we decide go in for some coffee and *croissants*.

I set about mine enthusiastically as I eye with interest the advertisements covering the walls; there was a time I'd wanted to become a commercial artist.

As we sit here relaxing, I think of my mother back home. I can picture her sitting at the table, with a cup of coffee and a biscuit or two, a concerned look on her face. She seemed so apprehensive about our leaving, so saddened. I do hope she isn't worrying about us. Then it dawns on me that we're one hour forward here in France, so maybe she hasn't even started her morning coffee.

In an attempt to fraternise with the locals, we strike up a chat with the staff of the *café* and mention we are going to India. But it's just as it was with the lorry driver, they become full of concern; they just can't understand why we want to travel there.

So, getting up and strapping on the rucksack and sleeping bags, we go over to the manageress to pay for our snacks. Converting backwards and forwards the *centimes* to pence, and the pence to *centimes,* I try to familiarise myself with the worth of French money.

Then with a hurried '*Bonjour*' we're off.

As we walk along the road, I enjoy the warmth of the sun as it emerges from a screen of clouds. The sound of any approaching vehicle from behind us, going our way, causes us to put out a thumb in the hope of getting a ride.

Almost immediately a car pulls up and stops just by us. It's quite a long vehicle, an estate car, and is displaying British registration plates. I notice too there's a large bulky object projecting from rear, yet, as it turns out, there's still ample space for us, so we bundle inside.

The driver is a genteel man by the name of Henry, who explains he's coming from England on his way to Paris to deliver a harpsichord. When he hears of our plans to travel to India he gets really excited. His enthusiasm is timely, and we become absorbed in conversation, he's great company.

And though we spend much of the journey chatting, I keep an eye open, watching out for the signposts, and after a long while there are indications that we're approaching the outskirts of Paris.

Henry talks rather less now, focussed as he is on negotiating the radial roads here, and as I look about me I start catching glimpses of landmarks and in particular the Eiffel Tower (referred to here as *La Tour Eiffel*).

Actually, it seems that Henry is not only busy finding a specific *café* but is pre-occupied with a certain young lady, Steph, that he's repeatedly mentioned in conversation on our way here.

Henry swiftly locates the *café* and after we all pile out, he ushers us to a table outside of the café on the wide pavement. From here we have an imposing view of a vast and classically proportioned archway, which I take to be the *Arc de Triomphe*; looking similar to one of those imposing monuments dotted about London, such as Marble Arch. We're so close to it that it feels like we are actually sitting inside a picture postcard. Henry treats us both to a coffee and a warm savoury slice topped with melted cheese and a slice of tomato. It's so scrumptious I'd like to eat more, and I make a note for future reference, that it's something called '*pizza*'.

A young woman sits down next to Henry, who I immediately realise must be his *rendezvous,* and after introductions the four of us chat for a while. I realise though that I should watch for an opportunity to make our excuses, so as to leave the two of them together. After we finish our snacks and drinks, and there's a pause in the conversation, I make as if to get up to go, and soon Yolanda and I are making our exit.

Alone again, we take to strolling along the quiet Parisian *boulevards,* where I find myself peering in at the lavish displays of the ostentatious shop fronts. One store proffers heaps of dark chocolate and rich *gateaux*, whilst another, selling clothing, displays luxurious long gowns and expensive looking accessories.

Now here's an opportunity for me to discover *'Gay Paree'*, to see the sights and maybe get a taste of its glamour, why we could even visit the Moulin Rouge and maybe get to see some *cancan* dancers?

Yolanda has been to Paris before, so she knows her way about, but she shows no inclination at all to explore the city, so, instead we look to find a way out.

According to Yolanda the best way to travel across Paris is by 'Le Metro', the metropolitan underground train. So the plan is to cross Paris by rail, then find a good point to hitchhike from, such as a major crossroads or the start of a motorway.

Descending into the Metro, we buy our tickets and board a train. The carriage is already packed with passengers standing shoulder to shoulder, but I'm relieved to find there's space for us to sit on one of the slatted wooden benches. The pungent smoke of French cigarettes, *Gauloises* and *Gitanes,* soon becomes a bit overpowering, and the pervasive smell of garlic and body odour too. But for all that, it's nice to be travelling together with French people, and I enjoy the ride.

Arriving at our destination we emerge from the dimly lit station into bright daylight on to a busy street, with cars and buses moving at a frantic and dangerous pace. On seeing some young people, we ask them where we can find a good hitching spot nearby. Not only are they able to point to where we should make for, they also offer to take us there. It's quite some distance, and as we walk the young girls offer us fizzy *limonade*, which to my surprise actually tastes of real lemons, and as luck has it, as we walk along together, I find some coins on the pavement, so I purchase another bottle of *limonade* at the next *magazin* (shop). After this we walk some more, and I find more coins, so more fizzy lemon, and then, yet more coins, and yet more of this thirst quenching delight. Providence! Seems to be that we're being looked after!

The straps of the rucksack and the ties around the sleeping bags cut into our shoulders. I ache for release from the discomfort.

Finally, arriving at a large road junction, we make ready to break company with our newfound friends, however, we discover that one of the girls, Josette, has decided to stay on, and plans to hitchhike alongside of us on the *autoroute*.

Josette's companions all make their farewells.

'Bonjour to you too,' I shout.

From Josette we discover she lives in Lyon (a far distant city), and when she realises we might be persuaded to go via that route, she presses us to travel with her and to stay at her home. We agree, but I wonder that the three of us together will be able to get a lift!

There are other hitchhikers already here, holding their thumbs aloft, and there's some sort of queue, so we get in line, and when someone gets a lift we gradually move up. Those waiting keep their distance from each other, so that drivers get to choose who they pick up.

It's tempting to shout out after those cars unwilling to give a lift, and sometimes we make a gesture of our disapproval, a way to keep ourselves amused.

I sing snatches of songs, including the hit from the Los Angeles' blues band, Canned Heat, *'On the Road Again'*.

> *'The first time I travelled,*
> *out in the rain and snow,*
> *I didn't have no fare oh,*
> *oh I didn't have no place to go,*
> *I'm on the road again... '*

Gradually the queue lessens until we find ourselves at the head of it, after which it's not long before it's our turn to run towards a waiting vehicle.

It's a large articulated lorry, a truck, a *camion,* and only with difficulty do we manage to hoist ourselves up into the cab. This involves climbing up a set of steep metal steps to quite a height, the girls first and then myself, hurling our baggage into the cab.

Once we're all in and on the move, the girls make conversation with the truck driver, and as I understand very little of what is being said, I settle back and listen to popular French songs on the radio, trying to drink in the meaning of the words. I enjoy immersing myself in the feel of unfamiliar styles of music. The driver, a powerfully built, swarthy dark skinned man, seems contented to sing along to the radio and shoot comments across the cabin to the girls.

The tarmac whizzes by, blurring and disappearing beneath us. We continue in this way for quite a time before I notice the sunlight gently dimming as the evening approaches.

I really wish the driver would pull up for a break as I'd really like to empty my bladder sometime soon, but I think better than to ask our driver to stop, and he just keeps driving on.

Eventually, after what seems like about another half-hour at least, the vehicle quite suddenly pulls off the road and comes to an abrupt halt, whereupon the driver opens his cab door, leaps out, and disappears into the darkness.

I gather that we've stopped at a roadside *café*, so I jump down and look for a loo.

I find a door marked *'Hommes'* but as I open it, unspeakably foul odours emerge. Nothing has prepared me for the stench nor for the lack of normal amenities either. There is just a shallow dip, set into the filthy tiled floor where I presume one is meant to stand or squat, and a bowl with a tap over it that passes for a washing basin. The floor is awash with a layer of ominous looking liquid. It's really quite disgusting. As the door closes itself behind me I find myself all but retching for the lack of fresh air. So, stretching out my leg, I attempt to keep the door wide open, that I might be able to have a pee, but in vain, so I go back outside and search for somewhere else to go, but to no avail. So, hurriedly I again open the loo door, and again attempt to use the facility, and gain only slight relief before becoming overwhelmed by intense discomfort again. My eyes burn fiercely. I actually become panicked that as a consequence of exposure to this vile chemistry I might even damage my eyes.

I rush outside and as I gradually regain my sight I glimpse what I take to be our driver returning to the lorry, so, not wanting to delay him, I hasten back to the truck.

The driver has bought back a bottle of *Tizer* drink, some snacks and a supply of cigarettes, which he shares about, only they're not the normal *Gauloises* but full strength yellow ones, which really get me coughing. I make a mental note not to accept another.

We motor on for another hour or two, during which time I feel increasingly uncomfortable; I worry that my bladder will suffer, as I remember my father, by way of warning, once telling me of someone who held out so long before they had a pee, that when they did get to a toilet they couldn't pass water, and that it required surgical intervention. I really hope, wish and pray, that the driver will stop soon; else I fear it might turn into a medical emergency.

Suddenly the *camion* grinds to a halt, and the driver explains that if we wish to go to Lyon then this is where we should get off. We climb down and the girls offer him their thanks for the lift.

Shouting out a hurried '*Merci*' to the driver I disappear off into some bushes to have a pee. Oh, what a relief, what a great welcome relief!

I notice my eyes still weep from the acid attack at the *café*, but mercifully the fresh air starts to soothe them.

The street lamps shed a strange glow, which results in everyone's skin being bathed in orange light, making us appear like apparitions or extras from a science fiction film set. After sitting for so long in the cab we are in dire need of exercise, so we spend some time walking about and rubbing our limbs. As evening draws on, we become increasingly chilled and hungry, and rummage through our bags to fetch out any tit-bits of food. We walk to a nearby service station emblazoned with signs promoting *Chevron*, and obtain a bottle of fizzy orange.

I chat easily with Josette but I notice that Yolanda seldom joins in the conversation. Hitch hiking, which Josette calls '*autostop*', can be very tedious when you have to wait for hours before getting moving again. For far too long we stand about hoping to hitch a lift, up and down the wide pavement we pace, desperately trying to keep ourselves warm.

For the first time since leaving London, I feel a strong desire to be home.

It's not until the wee, wee hours of the morning that we eventually get a lift and are on the road again, speeding swiftly towards the outskirts of the city of Lyon. It really has to be said that this all-night trip with Josette has been really tiring, and because it's still early in the morning there are no cars about, so we must complete the remainder of our journey on foot.

By the time we arrive at the apartment building where Josette lives, the sun has risen and has become particularly hot, taking its toll on us as we struggle on towards her home.

Josette lives in a modest apartment that she shares with her mother, the front room of which is sparsely furnished and has a tiled floor. The place contrasts greatly to my mother's flat in London with its homely atmosphere, where books and curiosities line the shelves in happy disarray. Back at my mothers, one might recline in an easy chair or lounge on the comfy sofa, but here, function and formality hold sway, though there are some few ornaments and nick-knacks around the place.

On our way here, Josette mentioned that she and her mother sometimes go hitchhiking together, and that they recently went to Spain, so it appears they enjoy an unusually close relationship. Shortly after our arrival, Josette's mum appears and greets us warmly. Seeing them together, it really wouldn't surprise me if Josette's mother were sometimes mistaken for being her older sister; with her shoulder length blond hair tied back, her casual tasteful attire of neutral colours, and no make-up on her suntanned round face.

We must look a sight to behold, bedraggled and weary, our clothes crushed and misshapen, our hair matted, our feet and shoes covered with dust. We aren't exactly dressed for a garden party at Buckingham Palace or a day out at Ascot!

After being shown the bedroom Yolanda and I are to stay in, we drop off our baggage on the floor and return to the sitting room. The room is now deserted but the television set is on so I idle through the channels, chancing first on a news report and then on a game show. I find the French language attractive, but I don't enjoy this my first exposure to the daytime television here, it looks so very dull.

Josette's mother thoughtfully provides us all with coffee and some food - bread, soft cheese and *gateaux* - and we all settle down to enjoy the breakfast she has set, leaving no more than cake crumbs and coffee dregs as evidence of our meal.

A wash and brush-up is now in order, and one by one we lock ourselves in the bathroom and bathe ourselves, and each of us returns looking just a little more presentable. But nothing can disguise the fact that we're all definitely the worse for wear, not having slept last night

The day passes uneventfully, and when evening comes a simple supper of soup (*consommé*), bread and tinned fruit is served. When the meal's finished, we bid our hosts '*bon nuit*' and retire to our room, but, strangely, I find I can't actually face the idea of settling down and going to sleep, as I've been feeling rather cooped up and over-exposed. So I open the rucksack and take out *The Bible*, in the hope that by reading it my feelings will lighten. Flicking over the thin, seemingly brittle, pages I scan the chapter headings; *Kings, Corinthians, Thessalonians, Acts...* then I dip into it, reading passages at random, but it's all about doom and gloom. I carry on though, flicking over the pages in search of solace, but the readings only result in a deepening of my unsettled mood. It's quite a shock to realise that I can't depend on *The Bible* to help restore my flagging spirits.

I sense hot teardrops forming so I close my eyes for a while.

'Could we be on the move early tomorrow?' I ask Yolanda, *'I really want to get on with our journey.'*

But clearly she's tired too, perhaps even a bit moody. Initially it proves difficult to get a conversation going with her, but she brightens up somewhat, and expresses agreement about getting an early start. Then we stop talking

* * *

The next morning we awaken, and I feel somewhat refreshed, and over late breakfast of black coffee *croissants* and *comme pot* (chilled stewed apple), we tell Josette and her mother of our intention to move on today.

Before we go we kiss each other cheek-to-cheek and hug one another. Then Yolanda and I set ourselves to walk across the sprawling suburbia of Lyon to find a suitable hitching point.

So much for the early start, it's now past midday, but we get a lift.

Carrying no map, and relying only on signposts and our driver's advice, we speed on our way, the travel bug still exerting its influence as strongly as ever. Motoring along, punctuated by spells of waiting and walking, we find ourselves travelling to the town of Perpignan and then onwards to Montpelier.

When our next lift presents itself, I climb in the back of the van, sit myself down on the floor, then hold on as best that I can when the vehicle starts to lurch and turn. Yolanda sits in the front and converses with the driver, while I give my full-hearted attention to the radio, listening to one French ballad after another. Then comes a record by British folk-singer Donovan, Jennifer *Juniper,* not a recent release but the radio station is probably playing it because some of the lyrics are in French.

'Qu'est-ce tu fais, Jenny mon amour?'

What are you doing, Jennifer my love?

After a few minutes of listening to Donovan, I notice that the easy-going chatting in the front has given way to an abrupt exchange of words, so naturally I ask Yolanda if everything is all right - she responds with affirmative nods and so I get back to listening to the radio.

Suddenly the van swerves and screeches to a halt, whereupon Yolanda opens the door and clambers out. The driver turns and indicates for me to follow after her example. Confused, I look at the driver enquiringly. He gestures angrily so I scramble out, dragging our baggage behind me. Then there's the sound of the van door slamming shut and the grind of rapid acceleration, and I turn to see the van tearing away off up the road.

I look to Yolanda for an explanation of what's happened, but she's unwilling to talk. I wait for her to gather her thoughts.

Yolanda stands on the side of the road, not saying a word, and then, after a long while, begins slowly and hesitantly to tell me what happened. It seems the top button of her gauzy black blouse had, of it's own volition, become unfastened, and the driver noticed and got rather interested in looking at her breasts. Then he urged her to undo more buttons and when he realised she wasn't going to do his bidding he threatened to stop the van and leave us on the roadside.

So, now we're in the middle of a motorway with no lay-bys or crossroads to hitch from, and it's likely we'll have to walk many miles before we can get another lift. It's a long, long, walk, and for the most part it's one that is spent in silence.

Long after nightfall, as we stand hitching at an intersection of a motorway, a tall uniformed individual, wearing a peaked black hat decorated with a badge and white band around it, approaches us and hustles us into an office further up the road. There he questions us and pressures us to submit to a thorough search of all our belongings.

I keep an eye on the *gendarme* as he checks very methodically through our possessions, and I notice how he pays particular attention to Yolanda's black suede fringed shoulder bag and the silver pillbox he finds in it. Obviously he suspects us of carrying drugs but on completion of his search he finds nothing incriminating or illegal. There's nothing for him to do but to let us go, but as he dismisses us, he informs us that it's against the law to hitchhike on an *autoroute*.

Before putting back the contents of our rucksack, I point out to him that we're carrying a copy of *The Bible*.

'*Il etait le premier,*' he shouts, the meaning of which is '*He was the first!*'

I recoil as he lambastes me with a stream of abuse.

I stare at him agape; for this is the first time I have ever encountered open hostility towards Christianity. Hitherto, I have never witnessed anything other than awe and reverence towards Jesus.

Well that's not strictly true, for there was the jokey 'Wanted' poster I had once seen in London, one of those outlaw posters, like those from the days of the Wild West, but this one was for Jesus Christ, portraying him as an anti-social with left-wing leanings! And now he is being depicted as the first undesirable to make his way along the roads of civilised society, to upset the likes of this here *gendarme*.

But I'm grateful for this telescoping of time, in that it not only presents Jesus in a new light for me, as a dropout hitchhiker, and also, what's more is it's a timely reminder that we are on a spiritual quest. Unexpectedly, I am totally re-energised, and all feelings of tiredness are gone.

Chapter 3

PARADISE LOST

Eventually we get another lift, which whisks us away from the police checkpoint and takes us onwards a good distance, well on the way to Montpelier.

As the new day breaks, we find ourselves travelling even further still, taking us ever closer to Spain, with the surrounding countryside looking particularly well-managed and productive, and dotted with villas and grand residences that almost resemble castles. Evidently, we have entered the grape-growing region of Southern France and are in sight of the French Pyrenees.

Low walled vineyards stretch out in all directions, with stepped terraces where dusty pale green clusters of ripening grapes bask in the warmth of the sun. Birds hop and bop about peacefully, seemingly unperturbed by our compact *Citroën* car, as it noisily complains against the steep hilly terrain.

When the road evens out, and we can again hear ourselves speak, Yolanda and I recount some of our recent adventures for our driver, a middle-aged English woman who listens to us with apparent eagerness.

Upwards we rise, the countryside becoming ever more rugged and mountainous.

When at last a village comes into view I surmise we are almost at our destination.

We park up outside an imposing white villa, and it's not long before we are all sitting relaxing in the kitchen, enjoying a snack and a cup of tea.

At length I enquire of our host about the local bus services to the border; and not knowing the timetable the lady offers to go out on our behalf in order to find out more. Whilst she's out, Yolanda and I spend our time in idle chitchat, sometimes glancing at a magazine and occasionally gazing out of the window. It's such a pleasant change for us to sit in the quiet awhile, and it's quite some while before we hear the car returning.

'No buses, none at all,' the lady announces ruefully, *'But don't worry I will take you to the border myself.'*

Almost without delay, we are all back in the car and travelling ever deeper and higher into the Pyrenees. As she drives, the kindly lady asks us to tell her more about our journey, so we share with her something of our hopes and plans, to which she responds with genuine enthusiasm.

A castellated wall comes into view, and it seems we are drawing close to the border point as the car slows and halts. Waving our lady friend goodbye, we turn to face the two officials standing there in front of the road barrier.

We proffer up our passports for inspection, and the guards return them telling us we cannot pass through the border.

Met with similar circumstances, some would give up and turn back, I guess, but despite the gravity of the situation, or perhaps because of it, I'm determined not to take their decision seriously but to treat it as a joke.

Smilingly, I ask them to buck up and stamp our passports.

But they are not to be won over that easily, so I think to mention that we have no intention of staying in Spain, that we are merely travelling through, on our way to Morocco.

Hearing this they stamp our passports and obligingly raise the barrier for us to pass through.

I suppress my urge to dance a jig. Instead I pull out a blue and white £5 note and take it to the *bureau de change* where I obtain its equivalent in *pesetas*, the currency of Spain, before taking off down the steep winding road, and only once we are safely out of earshot of the guards do we fume and rant about the incident back at the border. It seems so unfair that they refused us, even though they eventually relented. As day follows day, it feels like our trip is becoming ever more challenging.

As we walk we find ourselves cooking in the extreme warmth of the late afternoon, though soon it becomes obvious that the sun is beginning to set, albeit very slowly. Despite putting in some real effort and walking as fast as possible, it looks increasingly unlikely that we'll find somewhere to stay before nightfall.

My spirits pick up as a *laubergio* (inn) come into view, but it looks pretty expensive so we hesitate a little before going in. But both of us are in such dire need of sustenance we enter and order a cheese roll and coffee each.

If the cost of our snack is anything to go by then we won't be able to afford to stay here, so after finishing our snack we press on in search of more modestly priced lodgings.

Along the way we discover the trees, hedgerows and surroundings to be abundantly alive with nature, in fact it's no exaggeration to say that the sound of grasshoppers hopping about in the grass is so loud that we struggle to hear each other speak, and we stop to watch as several lizards scuttle across the road, so well camouflaged as to make them barely distinguishable from the trail of dust they stir.

We discuss our options and agree that, come what may, we're likely better off sleeping rough if we can find somewhere soon. The light is failing fast as we make our way along further down the road, hunting out somewhere, anywhere, to sleep. With the aid of the glow from the sky we convince ourselves that we've found a good spot.

'At last!' I exclaim, *'I was beginning to think we wouldn't find anywhere.'*

I heave myself up onto an old iron gate and attempt to climb over it.

Once over we find ourselves in a large meadow, and to avoid unwanted attention from anyone passing by, we decide to sleep behind the clump of bushes that grow adjacent to the road, thinking that we'll be screened from view.

Mercifully there appears to be no grasshoppers or lizards here. All is peaceful.

We set about preparing our bedding for the night and I make myself a pillow by slipping my jeans and sweater into the flap of my sleeping bag, and there I secrete our passports and cash reserve inside. I then take a leak in the bushes before crawling down into my sleeping bag.

It's wonderful to have a place to stretch and relax, a chance for us to get over the strain and worries of the day. I gaze up at the sky, and although it's cloudy I find I am able to see a multitude of stars. I think about how far we've come.

Winding my wristwatch I murmur goodnight to Yolanda.

'Have you got the passports and the money safely?' she asks.

'Safe and sound,' I reply.

Making myself as comfortable as possible, and closing my eyes, I offer a quiet prayer for our welfare, and for that of my mother.

* * *

I awaken and open my eyes but I can't seem to figure where I am, or more importantly, who I am! I sit up and take a quick *shufti* about me; I seem to have been asleep in a field somewhere.

Suddenly a shot of pain disturbs my train of thought.

'Ah my face. Ow, Ow, Ow,' I yell.

'What is it?' comes a bleary voice.

'My face! It's really painful, take a look at it, would you?'

Yolanda stares at my face, studying it for a few moments.

'Oh! You've been bitten, they look bad,' she solemnly announces.

I look at the ground and my eyes light upon some insects swarming over Yolanda's footwear, I guess it was them that bit my face.

'Now that's hardly a fair deal', I complain, rubbing and massaging my face, actions I regret as unfortunately they only makes the pain worse.

Then I notice my sleeping bag is damp, probably on account of the morning dew, so I peel it off me, get dressed and pack.

Shaking the red insects off Yolanda's sandals, I offer them to her, the sandals that is, not the insects.

As I stand waiting for her, I brush my fingers over my cheeks and again feel my skin, which is swollen and very sore.

Back on the road we walk the distance to the local town, Port Bou, a picturesque little place of pleasant appearance, the houses and shops all having shuttered windows.

At the cobbled market square we discover a water point, so, making sure to be discreet, we go about our ablutions, brushing our teeth and generally freshening ourselves up.

As I brush my hair I discover that it's become matted and unmanageable, but I do my best to spruce myself up before entering a *café*, where we breakfast on orange juice and a roll, at no great cost.

Then, at a distance, we spot the presence of an officer of the *guardia*, a handgun at his hip and on his head a devilish looking black hat. His appearance has Yolanda cowering, from which I get the impression that she's heard something about these police at some time. Spain is a complete mystery to me, other than knowing that a General Franco, whose face is stamped on every coin, runs the county.

Interestingly, Yolanda assumed that the Spanish language would be similar to Italian, but since being here she has found it difficult communicating with local people. I am secretly glad of this, since it's not much fun being translated for, and it's oddly preferable to both be on a level, the two of us.

It's lovely to take in the panoramic Pyrenean views from Port Bou; the verdant rounded hills and the wooded slopes etched with paths roads and streams just beg to be explored. But we've no strong inclination to stay in the area, as we're itching to get on with our journey.

Finding a signpost, which reads 'Barcelona' we stand by it, in readiness of a car appearing. But the morning is still young and there are few vehicles on the road yet.

While we wait I scrutinise the house in front of us, staring at its several stories with their large green painted shuttered windows, and at the little houses in the distance, on the cliff top, high above the level of the sea, upon which, only with difficulty can I make out the distant shapes of vessels floating upon it.

I ponder too looking at the weathered faces of passers-by, the parents and their dark-eyed children who eye us curiously as they pass, and all the while I mechanically raise my thumb at the sound of any approaching car.

Of a sudden I hear raised voices.

A van has stopped and its occupants, young people, are waving and shouting at us.

'Come on, hop in!' one of them calls.

So we pick up our stuff and bundle in.

The van is coming from Britain, and has seats, benches really, which have been fixed to the sides of the interior of the vehicle on which a band of travellers sit around on, smiling. Our fellow travellers are curious about us, and appear impressed when we tell them we are headed for India. They are coming just to visit Spain and Majorca, an island off the mainland. There is an openness about these people that attracts me. Before long they start to encourage us to join them.

Surprisingly, I feel a stirring to drop our plans and share a holiday with these young people with whom I have so quickly developed a strong sense of friendship. It's such a long time since I had anything like a social life, and meeting with these travellers plunges me right back into the world I once knew, of easy conversation and getting interested in one another. But Yolanda seems to want to keep herself aloof and distant from them, even as I continue chatting, charmed by their camaraderie and enthusiasm. Eventually the penny drops, that she's not drawn towards their company. For a moment I think I detect a faint air of jealousy... then I realise Yolanda actually appears to be scowling!

After a few more miles we arrive at a big town, the van pulls up, the doors are flung open and we all pile out.

Apparently our companions want to stock up on provisions, and they also need to find somewhere to freshen up.

Yolanda uses body language and facial expressions to tell me that she wants us to break company with them, and though I'm inclined to try and persuade her otherwise, it's obvious from her attitude that I better not chance it.

So it's soon the two of us again.

We just keep trudging on, and by the time someone else stops to offer us a lift we are exhausted. The driver is Spanish, a businessman who has a pretty good command of English and proves pleasant company.

For what feels like many hours, we motor along the coastal road.

Necessarily I spend much of the time idly peering out through the windows, and whilst doing so it occurs to me the Spanish have a thing about fortifications, for there are turrets and castellated walls popping up everywhere we go.

Our lift runs its course without incident, and the driver drops us near to a beach on the edge of a major town.

'*Multo gracias*,' we call out to him as he speeds off.

As we're really hungry, we spend about 50 *pesetas* on some groceries, bread, cheese, oranges, and a carton of milk, which we figure is much better value for money than going to eat in a *café*. Then we make our way along the sandy beach to find somewhere to sit down and eat. On the way we discover a hut someone has constructed from branches and leaves from the palm trees. I'm puzzled that there's no one else about though. It's as if we've stumbled on some idyllic South Sea paradise.

What a wonderful place to settle down to rest, such utterly idyllic surroundings, complemented by the tranquil sound of the gentle rippling waves, which gently and repeatedly lap on the shore. We set about eating our *al fresco* meal.

To our relief, no one comes to stake their claim over the hut, and as the light begins to fade we watch the splendour of the setting sun. The sky is shot with gorgeous reds, oranges and pinks - we marvel at the fading afterglow - and in the distance we see beach fires, which send sparks shooting upward into the firmament of stars.

Just along the beach is a standing pipe where we wash ourselves and brush our teeth, and after doing so we return to our paradise shelter, intent on getting an early night.

We lay ourselves down and enjoy the simple natural charm of our leafy hut, the pleasant scene enhanced by the dancing flickering candlelight.

* * *

We sleep so soundly that neither of us stirs before at least eight o'clock next morning.

In the bright light of day our paradise looks even better than it did last night.

We breakfast on the remainder of our milk and bread, then lie about basking in the beauty of our surroundings, realising we'd be crazy not to stay longer. We figure on staying at least a few more days.

What with the warmth and a general feeling of well-being, rather self-indulgently we take to lazing about, and quite spontaneously our thoughts turn to other things. Returning to our tropical paradise hut, we peel off our clothes and yield to our passions. Sexual intercourse can be such a deeply satisfying way of showing one's desire and love for someone that you care deeply about. It can also be an incredibly wonderful indulgence, affording spectacular satisfaction and thrills, before finally giving a fantastic sense of release, bringing one to a state of restfulness and satisfaction.

I realise I don't think that often about sex, but when the call to indulge in primeval acts of self-indulgence come, I respond with lust and enthusiasm. I thank God we have our sexual organs to do with as we wish.

Having re-affirmed our feelings for one another again, we lie entwined in each other's arms without a care in the world. But then, oddly in the circumstances, as we have no plans on leaving just yet, I feel a sudden urge to get up and put my clothes on. Yolanda gets up too, and pulls on her dress.

As we re-emerge into the bright sunlight, we happen on a sight that immediately chills me and dissipates any sensation of ardour I still feel. For there, walking at a pace along the beach, and fast approaching us, is a dark uniformed figure, pushing a bicycle. He's got to be a policeman, a *guardia* most like!

I avert my gaze and sit myself down, pretending not to notice him.

As he draws close to our paradise shelter, he halts, and stares at us in tight-lipped muteness, all the while leaning against his bicycle.

Suddenly and harshly, he snarls a question in broken English - and then another, followed with more questions, as to our citizenship, and about how long we have been here.

Sensing danger in his manner, I tell him that we've only just arrived.

His dark mood softens perceptibly, and he looks less angry, less threatening.

He stands awhile, pondering the situation, looking from one to the other of us.

'Pass-e-Ports!' he suddenly demands, thrusting out a rigid hand towards us.

He studies the passports long before looking up again.

'Oooh kaay!' he says, fixing me with his steely eyes, *'Now **go**!'*

As he spits out his command he gestures to us to go back up the beach.

We stare back at him defiantly, but not for long, as instinctively I realise he's not one to mess about with. So, we retreat inside the hut and silently gather up our baggage before making our way back up the beach.

All the while he stands there, leaning on his bicycle, giving us the evil eye.

In silence we walk, and I wonder to myself; *What would have befallen us if we hadn't been dressed? What if he'd arrived just a few minutes earlier?* It seems we were *'listening to the small still voice within'*, as recommended in Yolanda's book.

But I confess I'm more than a little annoyed to have been cast out of our beach hut paradise in this way, and when we are well out of earshot of the policeman we let our feelings rip. But my over-riding emotion is not one of anger but of relief that we are out of the clutches of the law. And in truth, it might be that we only narrowly avoided finding out what the inside of a Spanish jail looks like!

* * *

The facial sores caused by the bites of the red ants still irritate me a lot, and wandering towards town, I sense that everybody I pass is staring at them. We continue walking until we come to a railway station, and there we stop and hang out for a while.

I gaze about at the crowds of tourists milling around and notice a middle-aged gent in a white short-sleeved shirt, baggy trousers and sandals, heading for the newspaper stand, where a quantity of English newspapers are spread out for sale such as *The Daily Mirror* and *The Daily Telegraph*. I scan the headlines and the photographs of two former Prime Ministers, Alec Douglas-Home and Harold Wilson.

'Oh who cares?' I ask myself.

I recall, that whilst still at school, one of my schoolmasters attempted to give us all the habit of reading newspapers, though, in my case he was unsuccessful. I wonder, in this sun drenched holiday resort on the Costa Brava, who on earth needs to be kept up-to-date with the news - especially from these out-of-date papers?

This question prompts me to start singing the lyrics of one of the lesser-known songs of *The Rolling Stones'*, just to entertain myself:

'Who wants yesterday's papers? Nobody in the world!'

Actually, I sing the song repeatedly, that is until I get into a chat with an English tourist who's about my own age, togged out in shorts, with a camera swinging from his neck and grasping a bulging holdall. He explains he has the Spanish equivalent of a 'Rail Rover', which affords him cheap unlimited travel around Spain. Before our chat, I had actually been musing on the possibility of catching a train down the coast.

I go back and find Yolanda and tell her I want a few minutes to myself, and then I go off to consult the railway map and timetable, reasoning that rail travel might make a nice a change from hitching.

At first glance the idea appears a good one, but after finding out how much the tickets cost, I do wonder if it's wise to fritter away our precious funds, after all we only have about £40 each, and that has to last. Though I'm still tempted to buy us tickets I do not yield, and eventually, when the train pulls away from the station I try to convince myself that we wouldn't have enjoyed the trip anyway.

So, with no other realistic options, Yolanda and I return to the main road and stick out our thumbs. Our next lift whisks us off down the coast to the next major town, which turns out to be a vast holiday resort with numerous high-rise hotels, a veritable concrete jungle.

Amongst the various shops here I notice a supermarket - a self-service shop - something of a novelty back in England, and since neither of us knows the language, self-service seems a good way for us to shop, as we'll be free to browse and choose our groceries at leisure.

Whether the manageress hasn't quite adjusted to the ethos of supermarket shopping yet, or she's just suspicious of foreigners, but as soon as we enter the store, the severe faced woman in attendance becomes completely over-attentive to us, babbling in what appears to be her native tongue, she shadows our every move. Actually, she proves such an utter pest that we opt to buy nothing at all.

As the intense heat is making us both very weary, it's seems reasonable that we take a break from travelling, and so make our way down to the glorious sandy beach and lie down. There are already hordes of sunbathers stretching themselves out, lazing about and browning themselves.

Yolanda produces her one-piece bathing suit and my pair of swimming trunks from the rucksack, and in the time-honoured tradition, we shuffle about uncomfortably beneath our towels getting changed. After considerable exertions we emerge in our swimsuits self-conscious at revealing our pale un-holidayed skin.

It's not long before we take to the inviting blue waters though I'm careful to look back from time to time, to keep an eye on our belongings, as we certainly can't afford to lose our money or our passports. I wade in and submerge myself whilst Yolanda has a brief swim, and soon we are back on the beach, towelling ourselves down and getting on with the serious task of tanning ourselves. Having applied suntan oil liberally over our faces, limbs and bodies, we now submit to the scorching hot sunshine, which is hotter than I have ever before experienced it.

In order to make the most of this coveted opportunity to get a decent tan, we lie here for a long while, patiently absorbing the sun's rays. Occasionally we shift about, roll over, and turn our faces this way and that. But the severe overheating and the mind-numbing boredom of just lying here, and for so long, really tests my patience.

'I'm going to get a drink, what about if I get some oranges as well?' Yolanda suggests.

'Good idea, I'll look after the stuff.'

Yolanda slips on her pretty purple dress, and is off.

As the minutes slip by, I can't help fretting that perhaps something has happened to her. All too often the mind seems to do that, that it looks for something to worry about, it's as if it needs to find something to agitate about.

Yolanda returns, and we tuck into the oranges, which taste really good. Then we settle back down again to the serious matter of browning ourselves. We stay for a good while longer, but eventually I have to admit to myself I've really had enough and am feeling woozy. I figure it would be a really nice to be like the other visitors here and have the luxury of being able to pop back to a hotel room. Anyway, it isn't difficult to persuade Yolanda that we should leave, that it's time to get off the beach and back on the road.

We're standing on the main coastal road, waiting for a lift, but I'm not feeling right in myself. Actually I'm beginning to feel slightly faint and even a bit sick. It's likely I've become extremely de-hydrated.

Soon we both of us start to get desperate; we're getting so--o-o-o- hot, and getting so desperate in fact that we make a pact that we'll go in either direction so long as we can get a lift, just to get out of the intense heat.

Standing on opposite sides of the road, we raise our thumbs to each and every approaching vehicle.

A car stops, and I'm relieved to see that it's pointing in the right direction, headed down the coast.

A breeze blows in through the open window, and though the air that's blowing is warm, it's nonetheless a vast improvement to standing in direct sunlight. As I peer out through the windscreen I'm surprised to see that the road appears to have vast pools of water gathered here and there, yet I hear no splashes as we go through them - and as we approach them they disappear, only to be replaced by others in the distance.

Yolanda dons her sunglasses to counteract the glare of the sun. Dust is everywhere, inside, outside, on the road and in the air.

From the other direction a steady stream of vehicles flow - oil tankers, lorries and cars, and they're all belching forth exhaust, filling our nostrils with foul fumes. Telegraph poles, signposts and houses flash by us. Horns resound in my head as again and again we overtake and are overtaken by other vehicles.

As the day wears on, the glare and the heat begin to subside and the draught from the open window blows cooler. Neon advertisements glow in the twilight sky, and I become aware that oncoming vehicles are now showing their lights.

Stopping only for traffic signals, our driver drives on, relentlessly.

It's well into the evening before our driver pulls the car over to the side of the road and stops, telling us he needs to sleep. Instinctively I feel cautious, and though I'm grateful of the chance to have a bit of peace and quiet, I resolve however, not to go to sleep. As I chew a piece of gum I watch as first our driver and then Yolanda fall asleep.

The unearthly glow of the streetlights colours the air.

I light a cigarette, but as I smoke it I find it difficult to ascertain how much remains unsmoked, so I take to feeling the length of the cigarette and in consequence get rather sore burned fingers.

My girlfriend awakens first, and we speak together in hushed whispers so as not to disturb the driver.

Eventually, from out of the gloom come other sounds of life - yawns, grunts and a long sigh - then finally, our driver's head bobs up.

Opening the car door he lets his feet fall to the ground outside then leans forward to rub his legs. Turning, he indicates that he's leaving us for a while and we should await his return. Without any further ado he makes off and disappears into a nearby building.

Yolanda and I glance at one another, exchanging questioning looks.

Opening a fresh pack of cigarettes, one we'd bought earlier, I discover this Spanish brand to be even stronger than the French ones; and the smoke tears the back of my throat. Coughing savagely I realise I'm in desperate need of a drink.

Too much heat, too much smoking; I'm feeling decidedly unreal and uncomfortable, made all the worse by the severe sunburn we brought upon ourselves by our stint on the beach.

Around the street lamps outside, night moths dizzily fly.

I tire of waiting. *Where's our driver? What is he up to?*

As if by way of an answer I notice a stooped figure emerging from a nearby building, it appears to be that a man and that he's carrying something and he seems to be heading towards the car. I only recognise it's our driver when, with the back of his hand, he knocks on the window Catching the gist I lower the window and take hold of the bag he's holding out to me.

I take a quick peek inside, to find it contains filled-rolls, bottles of juice and cigarettes.

The driver seats himself back down, leaving his door slightly open, triggering a tiny light within the car, by which we can now see each other better.

I catch the smell of aftershave, which now wafts about the car, and the face of our driver is now beaming, he looks totally refreshed and wide-awake. It's so kind of him to have to have brought us the juice and the food. It works wonders on my system, and when we are almost done with our snack, he takes to handing out other fancies, such as biscuits and sweet bars.

Now it's our turn to freshen up, and stumbling out of the car we go for a much-needed walk about. It's so wonderful to stretch my legs again.

Soon we are back in the car, fully awake and ready for the road again.

In contrast to before, the driver is now quite chatty, which makes for a pleasanter, easier journey. Traversing kilometre after kilometre, with our headlights lighting all the twists and turns of the way, we hurtle on.

Reading the road signs, first it's Valencia, then it's Alicante, and onwards towards to Almeria, keeping mainly to the coastal route.

We're doing well, very well. My geography isn't good but quite good enough for me to realise that any chances of our seeing Madrid - which is in Central Spain, or Granada - are slowly dissolving.

As the day progresses, the time comes when we must bid our driver goodbye. We continue, one lift giving way to another, each driver accepting our companionship in exchange for their generosity.

* * *

We've already come a long way away from London, along unfamiliar roads, speeding forth on our way, crossing bridges and catching sight of mountains, vineyards, tollhouses, windmills and watermills. And now we are making a short detour, a trip through the desert, where, according to our driver, cowboy films are made - where the ghost town of a movie set stands, useless and surreal - the area now deserted by all but wild animals.

The journey, so falteringly begun, is gradually gathering momentum. As the miles flash by, my spirits rise; I'm pleasantly surprised how well we're taking to life on the road. I enjoy observing, seeing how the people are living, looking all the time for some inspiration, something to show me how to live a better life.

It's mid-afternoon, and the car pulls up in a small village, high in the hills, and our driver disappears off to visit a local shop.

Taking this opportunity, we go in search of a toilet, and at a nearby bar we try a variety of words that might convey our need - loo, toilet, *toilette, cabinito, and lavatorie* - we even try using mimes and gestures, but to no avail. I guess that if we waited for our driver's help things might be a lot easier for us, but as I'm growing rather desperate I take my chances and wander into the back of the kitchen, and locate the toilet for myself.

Afterwards I re-appear back inside the bar, and Yolanda then goes to use the facility.

The locals grin and nod at me, signalling that they've now understood what we were asking them. And now our driver appears, and the woman in charge of the bar explains the situation to him, amidst explosions of laughter all round.

Back in the car we discover he has bought some bread, which he hands to me. To our surprise the bread tastes sweet, and of that loaf of bread, not a precious crumb gets wasted!

We resume our journey, and come evening time, our lift ends, so again we find ourselves standing on the side of a road in the fading light.

Since it's late, and we've travelled far today, it seems a good idea to find somewhere to sleep for the night, so we climb the verge to find a comfortable spot to lay ourselves down out of sight of the traffic, where we figure we'll most likely be safe for the night.

We arrange our coats and sleeping bags and try to get reasonably comfortable, but as for settling down to sleep, I find I must first try to shut out the sound of the traffic, which sweeps up from the busy nearby motorway, so I stay awake much longer than I would wish to.

Chapter 4

SNAKES AND LADDERS

It's daybreak, and sleepily I look about and take in our new location. Close by, behind a fence, there's a plantation of some kind with tomato plants growing, and just within my reach there's a cluster of tomatoes, so I take the opportunity to pick some of the ripe fruits for our breakfast.

Once we are fully awake, we lower ourselves down onto the hard shoulder of the motorway and make our way to the next crossroads to start the new day's hitching.

After several hours waiting with no sign of a lift we become despondent and set off on foot, trudging up the highway to the next town and through it.

Taking only short rests from time to time; we march on in grim determination, until we come in sight of a roadside bar.

There's something rather enticing about the place, so we venture inside and are immediately befriended by a crowd of fellow countrymen, who demonstrate how they enjoy their stay here in Spain - through an alcoholic haze! And seeing two new visitors arrive, the barman presses free drinks on us. Unfortunately it appears the drinks here are only alcoholic, so after a diplomatic pause we pass our drinks on to the revellers and make our exit.

On the other side of the road to the bar I notice there are fruits growing on the trees, so I cross over to take a *recce*. I've never seen fresh oranges growing before, but oranges they definitely are. I assume they're probably the remnants of the crop; so I feel free to glean them, and am delighted at the taste of the warm slightly over-ripe juice of the blood oranges. When I depart the grove I carry with me a few of the fruits clasped against my chest, and sit with my girlfriend eating them.

As we're lacking the energy to walk right now, we don't even try, preferring instead to conserve our strength.

But when a car slows and stops, we are not slow to react.

'At last,' I cry out.

The driver seems a happy sort of guy, wreathed in smiles. It's a small car, and for a change I sit in the front beside the driver, who immediately points to the car record player and offers to put on some music. From the pile of singles scattered on the floor he selects a disc and inserts it in the slot of the player. Crackles, scratches and pops provide a fanfare to a multitude of violins that burst through the speakers, energetically bowing a strange and beautiful melody. Rich patterns are woven with the help of a variety of wind instruments that come floating in and out of my awareness.

'Brilliant! Amazing...! Spanish?' I ask, enthralled.

'Maroc,' he answers, grinning.

'Huh?'

'Moroccan, he's Moroccan,' Yolanda explains.

Immediately I know I am going to like Morocco, and I can't wait to get there.

This is very stoned music, so it makes me wonder if the driver himself indulges. He's certainly a very chatty fellow, though much of what he's saying is lost on me, as I understand so little French.

We're a merry throng, driving along.

We coast along, listening to music, chatting and eating fruit, for what seems like hours before eventually arriving at a very large town, the city of Malaga in fact. Along the seafront is an unending line of palm trees and I look up in the hope of finding coconuts, but I cannot see even one, so perhaps they're dates palms instead?

Once the car is parked up, we all tumble out, then Yolanda explains to me what our driver is saying to her, *'This man has to go and do some business in town,'* she says, *'If things go well, he will then be driving on further down the coast to somewhere called Algeciras. From there he will be going to Morocco.'*

Yolanda continues to interpret for him, saying; *'He comes from Marrakech, and he wants to know whether we would like to go there with him?'*

I look at him enthusiastically and he beams his smile back at me. Of course we want to go! So, after agreeing to meet him later on at a central point, in the main square, the Plaza Aduana, the Moroccan goes off to deal with his business here in Malaga.

Now, with time on our hands, we go off looking around the shops, nosing through the windows of cafes and restaurants, and I'm surprised to find they cater for the tourist market, selling typically English fare like steak and chips, mixed grill, egg, chips and bacon etc, so we set off elsewhere in search of fresh food.

We are fortunate in coming across an indoor market, an immense imposing place with incredibly high ceilings giving an overall impression of cleanness and coolness, which provides a temporary respite and contrast to the scorching heat outside. Here we buy some provisions, some fruit, bread and cheese.

It's such a huge relief to eat again after becoming so very hungry, yet we don't gorge ourselves, and put the remainder of the uneaten food in our rucksack, saving it for later.

Refuelled we continue on our stroll around the city. Life in Malaga seems to move at a gentle pace and since we have rather a lot of time to kill, we decide to indulge ourselves in a little sightseeing. There are stately columns to see, and some astonishingly high buildings and a vast and imposing cathedral too, that all jostle for our attention. But we soon tire of being tourists and make for the Plaza Aduana.

We arrive early, far too early for our *rendezvous* with our Moroccan friend and find we have a long, long time to wait for him.

As we hang around the Square, I notice the shadows stretch themselves ever longer and longer.

When at last I catch sight of our new friend, I can hardly contain my pleasure at seeing him. I greet him earnestly.

'Oui, nous allons a Marrakech,' he exclaims, grinning widely.

He's such a good ambassador for his country.

We are soon back in the car, and heading towards the port of Algeciras.

Tucking into the food supplies, drawing on our cigarettes and listening to music, we while away the time.

I find Moroccan music so enticing, it sends me messages of freedom and excitements, which bathe my senses, feed my imagination, and please me in a way I'm not used to. Onwards we travel, the twilight giving way to the night, and losing yet another night's sleep will be worth it, knowing we are assured of a lift all the way to Marrakech.

Before dawn, the car pulls into the city of Algeciras.

We stay seated, watching the first powerful rays of sunshine thrusting forth into the morning sky.

Then, opening the car doors, Yolanda and I together wander off along the quayside, and we gaze out at the vast waters of the Mediterranean.

After finding the local conveniences, we make ourselves ready for the new day, and a little later, when the foreign currency office opens, we change more of our precious funds, in order to buy tickets for a boat trip to the Moroccan port of Tangiers. After we return to the car, our friend goes off to buy his ticket.

It's quite a while before he breezes back again, and now he looks very different, for he's put on a different set of clothes, shaved his face and trimmed his moustache too.

He restarts the car and drives a short distance to where there stands a queue of vehicles, all waiting their turn to drive aboard the ferryboat to Tangiers.

I'm really getting excited now; it feels like a truly momentous occasion, leaving Spain and sailing to Morocco, how wonderful!

In fits and starts the queue of cars advances, moving slowly forward along the quay, and drawing ever closer to the vast hold of the boat.

Down the ramp we descend and soon it's our turn to drive onboard.

Then we pass through passport control.

All at once the light of the sun is behind us, and virtual darkness ahead, with but a string of naked light bulbs to illuminate the hold, I struggle hard to see about us.

In single file the cars move forward past a figure seated at a desk.

Suddenly an official pokes his head in at the window of our car whereupon our driver responds by handing him his passport, and we do likewise. Whilst the official takes the passports to the man at the desk I turn to chat with Yolanda, but am soon interrupted by our driver who directs my attention to the seated official, who I now notice is motioning for me to go over to see him. I assume he means for me to collect the passports so I set about retrieving them.

The official sits impassive, gazing steadily at me for several long moments and then he gets up from his chair.

'Nice suit ..?' he asks me, pointing to his clothes. *'Yes .? Nice? Good shoes, Yes? Yes!'* he answers himself

'Uh? Excuse me?' I enquire.

'N-i-i-ce hair? Yes?' he says, preening himself. I start to feel uneasy.

'When you come to my country, you wear nice suit, nice hair, Yes?' he continues.

I stare back at him, trying to conceal my growing disgust at his behaviour.

Then he hands me back the passports and I return to the car, closing the door behind me.

'What a jumped up little shit,' I grumble.

'What did he say?' Yolanda asks.

A shout interrupts me before I can reply.

I can see the first official gesturing at me again. And though it's clear he wants me to get out of the car again, I don't move, as my senses are swamped with anger and frustration.

Our driver looks over at me uneasily and points to the official at the desk.

Grudgingly I get out again, and am treated to another display of theatrics from the customs official, but the words he utters are totally incomprehensible to me, so I look back beseechingly at our driver, who shrugs, and then again at the official at the desk, who points back to the ramp.

Clearly, we are being thrown off the boat, and not wishing to cause our well-intentioned Moroccan friend any hardship, I think it best to comply and curb my tongue. So, pulling our baggage out of the car, I smile weakly at our driver, and thank him for having given us the lift.

He looks back at us sadly.

Mister Suit watches all the while and grins across at me, a smug look on his face.

'When you come to Morocco you come nice, look like me,' he calls.

'You've got problems!' I counter, hardly appreciating the irony of the remark.

'What a cretin,' Yolanda murmurs, *'Who does he think he is?'*

I had almost forgotten how unpleasant officials could be. The *gendarme* on the *autoroute,* the border guard refusing our entry to Spain, then the *Guardia,* and now this!

They're clearly not interested in the message conveyed in my passport, *'To afford the bearer without let or hindrance...'*

'Balls,' I say.

Though there's nothing we can do about the situation, it doesn't stop us talking about it. For the next half-hour or so we rage, keeping up an ongoing volley of insults directed towards the power-mad conceited official back on the ferry.

'How are we going to get to Morocco now?' Yolanda asks at length.

'First let's go and see if we can get the money back on these tickets,' I suggest.

Returning to the ticket office I have no difficulty getting a refund, which surprises me. Then I hover around an information board, positioned on the quayside, close to the ticket office, where I find a sketch map showing the local shipping routes to and from Algeciras.

As I study the map I figure we actually have several options, the most obvious being that we can go back to France and make our way through Italy. Otherwise, we could take a boat to the port of Tangiers in Morocco, or failing that, a boat to the neighbouring country of Algeria, both of which voyages might well be costly, the latter being the most expensive option, but one that would ensure we don't miss out on North Africa altogether.

Whilst we're poring over the map some fellow foreigners join us, and we tell them of our predicament, about my run-in with the Moroccan official.

'They're in the pay of the Yanks,' comes the confidant reply.

'What?' I gasp.

'Yeah, a ploy to keep Heads out of the place. America's bribed them to keep out all longhairs.'

I stand there digesting this information, which I have no reason to disbelieve, in a state of shock.

'To hell with them! They're not going to keep me out, Fascist bastards!' I snort indignantly.

'Yeah,' he nods, *'But how you gonna get in then? Go to Algeria and come back over the border into Morocco? That's how it's usually done.'*

Well, it's starting to look like dealing with officials and getting on with travelling is like some sort of game of snakes and ladders.

I'm concerned not to spend too much money on a short sea crossing, especially as it's so early on our journey, and besides… I've just had another idea of how we might get to Morocco, but first I need to ask our new friends where Ceuta is, it being one of the destinations I've seen listed at the ticket office.

'Oh it's a part of Spain,' comes the reply.

'But it's over the water and a part of Morocco? Really?'

'Yes.'

'So there's nothing to stop us going there? No passport checks or anything?'

'I suppose not, but you're better to go travel to Tangiers.'

Checking at the ticket booth I find that a ticket for Ceuta is much cheaper than it would cost for us to go to Tangiers, so I see this as a very persuasive argument for going to Ceuta.

'Shall we try it?' I ask Yolanda, pleased at having figured out what looks like a solution to our problem. She agrees and we book our tickets, but we're disappointed that the boat's not due to leave for several hours yet, though there's nothing for us to do now but wait, so I lean on a fence near the ticket kiosk and stare about me. Nearby are some public conveniences, and outside them I see a large family, dressed in brightly coloured clothes, washing themselves and cleaning some unusual shaped brass cooking pots, and I figure, that like us they're probably foreigners, and Moroccans most like. They seem such a happy lot, cheerfully splashing about amidst the wash of bubbles swirling about their ankles.

Eventually, after observing several families do their washing, I wander off along the quay in the hope of finding out where our ferry's going to depart from. As it happens, our boat has already arrived, and for a while I become engrossed in watching the comings and goings of the crew.

We're the first passengers to arrive and there's still about an hour to go before departure, but we board the vessel and take a good look around it. We sit ourselves down on one of the many well-constructed long wooden benches arrayed over the vast deck.

We make no further mention of the incident with the customs man, for having given vent to our feelings, there is little more to say; it seems we're just pawns caught up in a game beyond our control. As I'm feeling sapped of humour, I keep my own company, as does Yolanda, who has little to say for herself.

In truth I'm feeling rather vacuous and uneasy again, a reminder of how my mood had sometimes been back in London, just prior to our departure. Aware of this I'm determined not to let the mood take hold, but I realise I am powerless to do much about it. I sense a feeling of apathy coming from Yolanda too; perhaps the trip isn't working out so well for her either? Perhaps the Moroccan official was right after all? Perhaps it's my fault? Maybe I've let her down, let myself down?

I'd been feeling a bit more carefree of late, but now that feeling's gone. Confused and devoid of *joi de vivre* I have little of value to give out to anyone.

As we sit here waiting, the weather takes a turn for the worse and becomes overcast. I get the impression that there's impending rain.

After sitting alone wrapped in thought, I've hardly noticed that others have been boarding the boat, and before long quite a few passengers come to sit on the benches.

I surmise that we must soon be leaving, and in that I am correct.

After a few perfunctory shouts, and some interaction between members of the crew, we cast adrift and float very slowly away from the quayside. And as we move away I sense my spirits lift, just a fraction.

The craft comes abruptly to a halt, and there are more shouts, and I hear machinery springing into action, and then the boat begins to move again and gets up some speed, and before long we're cutting through choppy waters on our way across the strait which separates Spain from North Africa.

I look round about me, hoping to amuse or distract myself; I contemplate the vast funnels and survey the various sorts of deck fittings. Then I notice some Japanese looking people sitting close by to us, with unsmiling expressionless faces, which unsettles me a little. The strangers talk amongst themselves in a language I do not understand. The blank expressions on the faces of the Japanese tourists puzzle me, as they seem unnatural.

I ask myself what brings them all this way, to travel on this dull boat ride? But perhaps they are actually enjoying the trip; I have no way of knowing. I eye their expensive looking luggage and ask myself why it is that Americans and Japanese tourists always seem to carry cameras around their necks, a craze that has certainly not taken off with the British.

One of the tourists leans across and asks Yolanda a question, but she doesn't understand, and it soon transpires the strangers speak no English. In turn, they discover we know not a single word of Japanese. We have a total *impasse*, but for some reason this does not stop them from wanting to talk to us, and one of them slips off from his seat to undo his luggage, and takes out a small bag. Opening it, he excitedly shakes out the contents into my outstretched hands. There are coins of different shapes and sizes, all with strange symbols and markings, and some with holes in them. I nod appreciatively and hand them on to Yolanda, who in turn passes them back to the excited little chap. Grinning from ear to ear and showing the many gaps in his teeth, he presents us with a few of the little coins, as mementoes of our meeting. As he packs away his moneybag he produces some postage stamps. We look at them, but they are of limited interest, and soon the 'conversation' lulls. Moved by this spirit of sharing, however, I offer the Japanese people to share some of our food and they open up theirs for us to share too, and I find myself warming to these folks, realising that, like us, they are just lonely travellers, a long way from home.

Happily, as we finish our *al fresco* meal, I notice our ferry is fast approaching land. We all get up and walk over to the railings to watch the landing, whereupon the boat came to a dead halt, and suddenly the crew - who during the trip have not revealed themselves - are here, there and everywhere about us. The boat manoeuvres and it seems that quite a long time slips by before the vessel comes to rest. Then we make for the gangway where the crew are lined up, all muscular and sailor-like to give us a send-off. I hold out our passports ready for any awaiting officials, but put them away again, remembering that we are still in Spain.

We have no idea where to go so we tag along with the other passengers and venture into the town of Ceuta, where I notice the shopkeepers all seem to wear colourful clothes, and straw hats even, with coloured ribbons attached. An atmosphere of suppressed gaiety prevails - a full-time round-the-clock fun city - and the idea has a certain appeal. But where are the revellers? Most surely not us lot!

Passing slowly through the town we come first to a square, which a sign tells me is the Plaza de Africa, and after walking along flagstoned alleyways, we come to an imposing cathedral, and we cross more squares, thus do we explore the holiday city of Ceuta.

As we pass by the cafes, restaurants, gift stalls and the like, my attention focuses on a barber's shop, outside which I linger for a few seconds as an idea stirs in my head. Yolanda eyes me curiously, questioningly.

Catching the attention of the owner, I stride in, chuck down my baggage and collapse in the chair. Without a word but with a glint in his eye, he leans across, picks up a pair of scissors, and begins hacking at my hair, carelessly lopping off large clumps. This causes me a good deal of pain, though with knitted brow and gritted teeth I endure the discomfort in silence. The barber of Ceuta deploys none of the niceties usually associated with hairdressers - no careful trimming, no prolonged attention to microscopic rogue hairs that have escaped the scissors - and within 3 minutes, and without so much as a squirt of the spray of smelly stuff (which usually signals the end of this kind of job), he lays down his scissors.

Surveying the damage in the mirror, I lean forward and help myself to a hairbrush, trying to coax the remaining hair into a shape that appears at least half-reasonable. Standing ankle deep in brown curls I give the barber a withering look. Decidedly un-withered by my scowl, the barber greedily demands the sum of 50 *pesetas* from me, and I pay the money without a fuss.

Yolanda looks really annoyed.

That's all I need!! I think to myself, but I keep my silence and press on, attempting to catch sight of our fellow passengers, hoping that we're going the right way.

'Why did you do it?' Yolanda demands.

'Oh balls', I retort, *'we want to get into Morocco don't we?'*

I'm surprised to find we've come adrift from the rest of the passengers that were on the ferry, and we now have to get through Ceuta with nothing but intuition and guesswork to guide us.

We come to a bus station, and here I spot some young hippie-looking Europeans, and wander over to chat with them. Apparently they've just come from Morocco and have only good to say about it. As I eye their leather shoulder bags, embroidered with beautiful colourful stitch work, they tell us they got these in Marrakech. Then the conversation turns.

'How did you get here?' one of them asks.

'Huh, that's a story! Actually we already had a lift that was going all the way to Marrakech, but we couldn't get past the customs in Algeciras.'

And soon we are regaling them with an account of all our recent misfortunes.

'Paid by the Americans,' comes the explanation from one of them.

'Well they owe me 50 pesetas then,' I quip.

I marvel at the Jungle Telegraph system that operates, keeping all but me informed.

'Fascists!' I say for the second time this day. *'But how did you get into Morocco then?'* I ask, eyeing his waist-length hair.

'Oh, you gotta fly in. It's alright that way, they want your bread, you see, it's as simple as that.'

'Too late for that now. I've had my hair cut so we shouldn't have any trouble getting over the border.'

'Good luck! You shouldn't have any problem, you're fine!'

It appears we don't need to catch a bus as we are within walking distance of the border, but we must get a move on for darkness is closing in fast.

As we draw closer to the border post, I figure we should spend the last of our Spanish money so I buy some biscuits and fruit.

Then we head for the Moroccan customs building - but not without a sense of trepidation - and nervously we approach near to where a uniformed official stands.

He appears pleasant enough, and smiles at us both as we give him our passports. Slowly and deliberately he peruses them, whilst intermittently looking over at us. Then he catches my eye and makes a motion with his head - the message is clear enough, he wishes to see if I am concealing some of my hair.

As I give him a whirl he looks back at me with a look of surprise writ large on his face, but nods approvingly, and sets about stamping our passports.

I resist the urge to express my delight at getting through the border, and instead set about changing some money; getting a fiver's worth of *dirhams* - another £5 note from our precious stash - but I'm so-o-o-o looking forward to discovering Morocco!

I re-open my passport and take a closer look at the custom's stamp.

Light of step we now make our way down the narrow road from the border point. Ten days out of London and already we're here in Morocco - not bad!

We venture into the nearby town, with the curious name of Fnideq, and from out of the shadowy gloom figures come and go. Amusingly, most of them appear to be dressed in nightgowns, going out for a stroll in the warm evening. It all seems rather odd, decidedly surreal in fact.

Amongst the cluster of low buildings we locate a *café*, the owner of which appears in the doorway. A well-built middle-aged man, he sports a vast moustache. As celebratory drinks are definitely in order, I go in and order two cups of tea before rejoining Yolanda. I note that Yolanda now seems much more relaxed, in fact she looks positively radiant, and she thanks me for what I did back in Ceuta.

The genial proprietor appears again, holding out and setting down two drinking vessels, clear glasses with chrome surrounds and handles, each containing a green liquid, a potion containing a mass of foliage.

I nudge Yolanda. *'Maybe it's marijuana?'* I suggest under my breath.

'Maybe it is!' she replies, full of curiosity.

But before we have a chance to sample the beverage, somebody else appears, someone who appears to be a policeman, who comes and joins us. He seems to be a friend of the proprietor - and I become suspicious that this is a put-up job, that the

75

owner gives us the marijuana tea, and afterwards the friendly Mister Policeman joins us, then it's *I've got you two, now come along quietly!*

Nevertheless I can't resist having a slight sip of my drink, and I almost choke laughing. *'It's mint, mint tea, wow!'*

The policeman, who positively bristles with tokens of his office, wearing as he does his badges, buttons and braiding, smiles over at us, completely oblivious as to why we're falling about laughing.

We sit comfortably in the half-light and enjoy a cigarette with our over-sweet mint tea. It's great to be here in Morocco, taking the evening air; it's a thrill, it's unbelievable.

At length the policeman gets up, and we wave him a cheery goodbye.

As I go to pay for our drinks I study the 5-*dirham* note; and observe that the face that's printed on it looks not unlike the officious customs man back in Algeciras. When the friendly proprietor brings me our change I notice that some of the coins have stars struck on them, whilst others have relief designs reminiscent of art nouveau; all the coins are dated from between 1370 and 1390! Wow, it seems we've slipped into a time warp, and arrived in another reality. Although it feels like that, the date is probably related to another calendar, an Arabic one most like.

We now realise it's time we looked for lodgings, and I worry that we didn't consider this need a bit earlier, back in Ceuta. Anyway, we go searching the local streets for a place to stay, but without success, and when we find ourselves on the outskirts of town we despair of ever finding any lodgings.

It seems a bit dangerous for us to start hitchhiking in the dark, so we decide instead to find somewhere comfortable to unroll our sleeping bags. Veering off the road we walk for some minutes, with stones beneath our feet scrunching noisily, with but the faintest light to guide us we make our way, but as it's a moonless night the darkness soon becomes total, and we cannot see each other properly, hardly a shape even.

I stoop down to touch the ground, hoping to find somewhere comfortable enough to lay ourselves down. Repeatedly I do this, feeling for a patch of ground that's a bit less stony. I call out to Yolanda, and getting no response I shout to her again.

When I hear her voice calling back to me she sounds to be some way off, so I keep calling her, in order to give her a fix on where I am, and before long I hear a scuffling sound, and then she bumps into me.

'We can't keep walking on like this, all night.' I say, as we stumble along together.

I keep on touching the ground until I find a patch that is reasonably thick with vegetation.

'I think we ought to stop here,' I say, *'it's the best I can find so far.'*

We unroll our sleeping bags and slip into them, murmuring our last thoughts of the day, wishing each other good night before settling down to sleep.

Chapter 5

A CLOSE THING

The sun shines brightly making it difficult to open my eyes. I have had such a great sleep, a really comfortable night, quite the best in a long time. Rather than jump up, I lie for a while enjoying the warmth of the sun bearing down on me. I rub at the sores on my faces, which are still very painful, but as I stroke my jaw I notice with a certain pleasure that I am starting something of a beard. I have never tried to grow one before. Out of habit, my hands go to push my bushy hair into shape and I give a gasp as I remember how recently I have come to lose it.

'Fascists!' I mutter to myself.

Stirring a little, I lean on one arm and look about me to survey the scene, Yolanda is still asleep, though I think I notice her stirring briefly. Looking down, I notice that the ground's apparent softness is nothing but a few straggly weeds growing in the cracks of solid rock. It's hard to believe I have slept so well as I have, sleeping on solid stone. Again I look about me.

On turning my head just a little, a feeling of panic seizes me - I let out a sort of choking sound and then, after a moment or two's reflection, I call quietly but firmly over to my girlfriend:

'Yo- Yol- Yolanda!'

She opens her eyes, blinking and startled.

*'Yolanda, sorry to wake you, but it's important. Please do **not** move. You will not be in any danger if you don't move. When you are ready, crawl over towards where I am lying, bringing your sleeping bag too.'*

She can tell I am serious and she does what I say.

Now she looks about.

'Oh-h my-y-y God-d-d-d,' she exclaims.

Approximately a foot from where she was laying, the hard rock floor comes to an abrupt end, and beyond it is only empty space.

Gradually we both sit up and cautiously position ourselves in order to peer over the edge. Far, far, far below, at the foot of a sheer drop, the frothing sea crashes.

With difficulty, I clear my throat.

'Just as well we didn't go any further last night eh?' I offer, weakly.

We stare at each other.

'It must be destiny that we were not meant to die,' Yolanda declares soulfully.

I now drag myself back to safety and Yolanda follows soon after.

We are both badly shaken by the realisation of the near catastrophe, our brush with death, and it's some while before we able to compose ourselves enough to get up and set off in search of the road.

Gradually though, we get into gear and become enthusiastic for the new day. We're hopeful that we'll get the chance to travel to Marrakech, or perhaps even get to Tangiers.

Over the years I have marvelled at the music of Davy Graham, especially his LP *Folk, Blues & Beyond*, and his guitar style marks him out as a true original, though I would think that some of his material is influenced by North African music.

The circumstances of my first meeting Davy were quite singular, insofar as I was visiting my friend Patrick, who lived with his mother, June, off the Portobello Road, over a launderette. Anyway, Patrick was at home, and I knew someone else was there because I could strange sounds playing, a recording of the *Hare Krishna* chant. For some reason which I don't recall now - I was probably looking for a box of matches - I opened a door in the flat and there was a man there, stark naked, and there was June too. I reckoned they were both tripping, as it wasn't unknown for an eyedropper bottle of LSD to be kept in the fridge there. Well, I didn't hang about staring at Davy and June, but U-turned back and closed the door behind me.

'Taste of Tangiers' is an instrumental composition by singer songwriter guitarist Davy Graham and is one of my all-time favourite tunes, the images and emotions it engenders just makes me long to go be there.

Cheated of our lift to Marrakech, by the customs official in Algeciras, I still hope that by hook or by crook we will to get to some or all of those places I have heard of here, such as Marrakech, Casablanca and Tangiers.

I spy a lorry coming along the road, making it's way slowly towards where we are standing. The driver eyes us with evident curiosity and pulls his vehicle to a halt beside us. Throwing open the door on the passenger side of the cab, he beckons us over to speak with him.

'Where's he going?' I ask Yolanda.

Yolanda then says something to the driver in French.

'*Tet won*,' the man answers her, enthusiastically.

'Let's get in,' I suggest, *'He seems like a nice enough bloke.'*

After throwing our baggage in ahead of us, we clamber into the cab. The driver whistles a cheery tune as he sets the lorry in motion and drives off down the road. We haven't been in a vehicle going this slowly since we left from Calais, it really makes a change; it's quite relaxing in fact.

I listen to the conversation between my girlfriend and the driver, though I don't understand much, but I get the impression they're getting on well enough, which is all I need to know.

Through the dust-caked windscreen I view the scrubland around us, and espy a signpost for a place called Tetouan.

'I do hope we're going the right way for Tangiers,' I say hopefully. Yolanda asks the driver, who looks back at her blankly but nods his head vigorously.

As the lorry negotiates the many twists and turns of the road, it lurches about, every which way. Though I don't know much about vehicles, I suspect the suspension of this one may be in bad shape.

Then I notice the driver craning his neck as if he is suddenly interested in something; perhaps he too is concerned about the vehicle.

I look, but what with the billowing dust clouds being churned up from beneath the lorry, I can't see much beyond the low wall along the roadside. Then, of a sudden, I see a huge stack of melons, perhaps twenty foot high, piled by the road, an impressive sight. The lorry makes a horrible grinding noise as it comes to a halt, there's a huge lurch, which throws us forward, and then all is silent.

'Wow,' I exclaim, *'That was a bit heavy.'*

The driver bounces out of the cab and makes his way off into the field where he is lost from sight around a corner. Beside the mountain of melons there are people gathered and all appear to be wearing robes similar to the 'night-gowns' that I'd seen the previous night. Some of the men are seated whilst others lay down there, the hoods of their gowns tightly pulled over their heads; their faces completely covered.

Our driver is gone some minutes before I catch sight of him again, as he returns to the lorry accompanied by some of the men, carrying green melons of immense size. I assume they are loading them up in the back of the truck, for I hear all sorts of thumping noises coming from that direction.

When our driver gets back in the cab, he pulls out a very dangerous looking knife and proceeds to slice a melon into pieces, offering us to share them with him. Yolanda seizes a slice and bites into it hungrily. Unaccustomed as I am to such fruit, I don't wish to appear ungrateful so I too accept a piece and take a bite of the deep red flesh, and then another bite, and then another. In truth we all gorge ourselves, cheerfully spitting the masses of shiny black pips out of the window.

Having finished his business, the driver turns on the ignition and revs the engine wildly before steering the truck back onto the road. Again the vehicle heaves and lurches and there's a constant need to hold on tight. But even though this is much less comfortable than travelling by car, it's in some ways preferable, as we are higher off the ground, and it's fresher too. Cars are almost invariably stuffy, I find.

Cigarettes are passed around, and almost immediately there's an outbreak of coughing and spluttering as these Moroccan cigarettes pack a mighty punch.

The openness and unquestioning generosity of those that offer us lifts does much to restore my faith in human nature, and, it's clear that at least some of the people we meet also value our company. I'm relieved to find the world revolves around deeper values than just money and status, an important discovery that!

It's great to be on the road, never knowing where we'll be at anytime, never knowing who we might meet on the way. Sure, we've had a few hassles, but then perhaps that's all part of it? Anyway, I feel like I'm in pretty good shape, considering - the trip is definitely working out as far as I'm concerned.

A town is coming into view, with whitewashed low dwellings now lining the way, some with tiled roofs but mostly they're flat. Wet clothes are hanging out to dry on the roofs. And I catch sight of the odd woman who comes out of her home and stares across at us. The scene is like something from out of *The Bible*, it's as if we're caught in a time warp, back to a world some centuries back in time.

What was the date on the coins? Sometime in the 14th Century? It figures!

According to our driver this is Tetuan and he indicates to us that this is the end of our ride. With warm smiles all round, we climb out of the truck and bid him farewell and a big thank you.

We walk on, making for the town centre, and as we go I can't help noticing the happy expressions on all the faces that look towards us, there's a brightness in their eyes, and their faces are wreathed in smiles, the like of which I haven't seen before. It's certainly looks like the first real sign of the deep happiness and contentment I am seeking.

Quite suddenly we are surrounded by a group of young children who block our way.

'Kif, kiff, you want kiff?' a boy offers, *'Kiff? I get for you.'*

I glance at Yolanda, and smirk.

It's obvious she likes the children, for though she shakes her head at them, she smiles into their sparkling eyes. But this only encourages them to keep on with their hassling!

'My uncle he has much kiff,' calls one child, of no more than eight years old.

I wave my hand and tell them all to go away, and they get the message and buzz off, but almost immediately there are others who crowd in around us, and adults too, some holding business cards, which they thrust into our faces.

'Good hotel, mister, cheap hotel, come here,' they tell us, all the while pulling at our clothes.

Yolanda's patience doesn't hold, and soon she's giving them a mouthful, but they don't go away. Whilst keeping their distance they keep on chanting their well-rehearsed sales pitches. But beyond showing our disapproval, we feel no animosity towards them; they're too nice for that. What concerns me though, is that they appear overly interested in our baggage.

Unable to rid ourselves of those around us, we move away and continue our walk through the streets of the city.

Of the many whitewashed walls we pass, I catch sight of one which is yellow coloured, and notice that men are milling about it; then it dawns on me that this particular wall might be the public urinal. How very basic!

Oh dear, oh dear, no matter where we go, we're followed everywhere, even when we quicken our pace and make our way at speed. But after crossing the main square, and then moving from street to street, we eventually escape the badgering hordes.

'They're such hustlers, aren't they? Such a mischievous looking lot! They'd have your socks off your feet without you feeling a thing,' I tell Yolanda, who answers me with a smile and a nod. She looks great; I haven't seen her looking so happy in quite a while.

'By the way, you look all right without your make-up you know. All that money, why did you bother? You look great without it,'

She looks at me bashfully, obviously lapping up the compliment.

'It's all this sun and fresh air. Do I look different then?' Yolanda asks.

'No! Mmmmm... that's why I said it!' I say, teasing...

We chance on a *café*, a European styled affair with a *Coca-Cola* sign dominating the front of the place, and order two bottles of aforementioned drink, but recoil as we reckon up its cost, about twice that which would be charged back in England!

We take it in turns to go to the loo here, and then settle down to relax awhile with our drinks in this air-conditioned haven. It appears almost all of the clientele here are foreigners, and I strike up a conversion with a fellow Englisher.

When I enquire about the route to Tangiers he gets out his map, and together we pore over it, but it soon becomes obvious that if Yolanda and I want to visit Tangiers we'll have to retrace our journey and double back. Oh that's disappointing!

Though the guy with the map is casually dressed in jeans and T-shirt, he is nonetheless appears smart, in fact he's a bit of a smoothie, with shades, bracelet and wrist bag. It's not easy talking with this guy; in fact it proves more difficult than opening a can of beans with a penknife. So, I give up on him and turn my attention back to Yolanda who's been observing him.

'What a cretin!' she remarks of him, rather loudly.

'I tend to agree.' I tell her, *' Let's get going.'*

We notice more of his ilk posing at the tables outside the *café*.

In the glare of the hot sun, I realise, as I have on many occasions since we left England, that I'm over-dressed, and I curse the decision to bring the fur coats, as we have either to wear them, carry them, or tie them to our baggage.

Not only are we over hot, we are also hungry, for apart from the melon this morning we've had nothing to eat all day, so we go in search of a suitable shop, and we find somewhere that looks promising, so Yolanda selects some groceries, and asks how much we have to pay.

'*Trente dirhams*,' the shopkeeper responds coolly. Yolanda turns to me for support, as it seems to her that 30 *dirhams* sounds like too much to pay.

'*Give him five and see what happens,*' I suggest.

Accepting the 5-*dirham* note, the shopkeeper searches for some coins and gives us our change.

When we're out of earshot of the shopkeeper, we yack on and on about the situation back at the shop, chuffed that we tuned into the situation correctly and avoided getting burned. He was asking six times the proper price! Imagine that. What a cheek!

Finding a shaded spot, we settle down for a bite to eat, taking turns to get up and stick out a thumb whenever a car approaches. And it's not so very long before a car does stop for us.

The driver is friendly and tries to engage us in conversation. He speaks French, so Yolanda answers him but I can tell she isn't very chatty, and I notice that whilst he's talking to her she gives a big yawn, though she tries hard to stifle it.

The heat is unbearable, so I open my window, which helps, just a bit.

But I notice Yolanda is yawning again, then she yawns some more, and her eyes start to hood over. The driver is still talking to her; and she nods and grunts her responses, so I lean over and give her a nudge, and though I can see she tries to pay attention to him, she quickly falls asleep.

The fact that the driver has no one to talk to is bad enough, but for us **both** to nod off in a car of a complete stranger would be like inviting trouble. So in an attempt to keep myself awake, I light up a cigarette. It works for a while, but all too soon I find my attention drifting and my eyes closing, I fight to stay awake.

I awaken and open my eyes to find Yolanda is shaking my arm and I hear her telling me we have to get out of the car, so I shift myself, still half-dreaming and mumble my thanks to the driver.

Moments later we are both wide-awake, and seemingly our normal selves again.

Thankfully another car stops for us, and this driver too is chatty and tries to engage us in conversation, and again both of us become sleepy. We no longer seem able to control ourselves, what with the heat, being tired and the motion of the car.

I'm the first to wake and as I struggle to sit up I make some sort of apology to the driver, but I can't quite work out whether he's annoyed with us or not.

After Yolanda awakens he offers us both some boiled sweets and tells us that the area we're passing through is similar to Lourdes in France - a place where ill people go in the hope of relief. I wonder why he is telling us this; perhaps we look as though we need to be healed?

Anyway, we tell him of our journey so far, and of our problems in getting into Morocco, and he sympathises with us, telling us of his own travels abroad, that he has recently returned from a business trip to Paris.

His manner suddenly becomes very serious, and I wonder why.

Hesitantly he directs a question to Yolanda, and I stare, waiting to get a hint as to what is going on.

When Yolanda tells me what he's saying, I'm s-s-so so relieved to find it's nothing problematic! It seems he just wants to know whether we would like to meet his family!

We nod our heads, yet he continues to look serious, and goes on to tell Yolanda that his family are currently in the country and that he's due to go there to meet them to pick them up, and suggests to her it would be a good chance for us to see what rural life in Morocco is like.

'Great. Let's go! Oui Monsieur, tres bien!' I answer, with enthusiasm.

From his expression it appears he's mightily relieved.

A little way on I notice we depart the main road, taking to a narrow country lane. Although the surface is generally in good repair, the car lurches from time to time, for, in places, the tarmac has split, probably on account of so much sunshine. I notice too that many of the riverbeds here have all but dried out; leaving crazed criss-cross fractures in the grey clay.

Afore long I notice that the road runs adjacent to a massive vineyard where bunches of dark grapes ripen in the sun. Our driver, on noticing my interest in the grapes, asks if we would like some. He stops the car, and armed with a sharp knife he trundles off between the vines, and severs a couple of large bunches, then washes them under a standing pipe before returning to the car and passing clusters of the ripe fruits to us.

'Gorgeous, unbelievable,' I exclaim. The fruits are truly amazing; they look like grapes yet they taste more of strawberries, perhaps they're a rare crossbreed grown here specifically for a certain wine?

The pace of the journey is now getting more sedate, and Yolanda and I are by now thoroughly and properly wide-awake. We understand from the driver there are only another few kilometres to go.

The car eventually slows and comes to a halt. From all directions adults, youths and children come racing towards us, all smiling and craning their necks, eager to get a look at us. They greet our host with kisses and embraces, and in turn we too are received with warmth and friendliness.

We are now guided between some primitively built dwellings and outhouses around which chickens cluck about around our feet, and our host stops outside a small low dwelling where we are asked to remove our shoes.

After stepping inside the building, it takes a while for my eyes to adjust to the sudden lessening of light. There is little in the way of furnishings here; just a *pouf* and some patterned cushions strewn about the dried mud floor, around a little inlaid ornamented table. I notice the room is illuminated solely by a shaft of sunlight streaming through an aperture in the wall; I hesitate to call it a window, more like a wind hole, for it has no glass. An unlit oil lantern hangs against one wall.

Our driver now enters the room, accompanied by his attractive wife and another lady, who appears to be a relative. The ladies are dressed in what appears to be traditional costume; they both wear long loose fitting dresses that stretch way down to their ankles; their hair being tied up in scarves.

They ask us if we will take tea, and when we say *'mais oui'* (*'yes please'*), they smile and disappear.

When the ladies return, they carry with them a patterned brass tray spread with tea things, and taking up a tall fluted metal pot, a light green brew is poured into clear glasses, which appear to already contain quantities of sugar. The ladies offer us cake too, and as we all settle down to sample the refreshments our driver explains to the womenfolk what little he knows about us. The ladies listen attentively. They seem a very happy lot here; and seldom do many moments go by before someone breaks into peels of laughter.

Our driver turns to us and asks if we might like to go out for a walk soon, to meet the rest of his family, suggesting that before doing so we might like to change into Moroccan clothes. Although the idea is voiced as a question it appears that only one answer is acceptable!

Once we have drained the pot of all the delicious mint tea, our host leaves us, and the ladies set off on their self-appointed task of finding us suitable clothes. They bring back a long robe for me - which they tell me is called a *djellaba* - it's a vast and ancient garment, which I slip over my head, only to be greeted by laughter, smiles and gestures of approval from the ladies.

'Now it's her turn,' I laugh, pointing to my girlfriend.

First the ladies strip Yolanda down to her underwear, and then they drape her in a long flowing dress, to which they add pins, bracelets and jewellery. I watch as the women stroke, touch and fuss over her. To finish off the outfit, a pair of finely tooled leather sandals has been brought in to adorn her feet.

The expressions of glee on the ladies' kindly faces radiate good humour, and they go off in search of our host to bring him back to judge their handiwork. Then, once they get the voice of approval we are set to go. But in order to leave the building we have first to fight our way out through the plastic tassel strips that hang in the doorway before emerging into the still brilliant sunshine.

Yolanda finds the *kaftan* dress way too long for her, so she hoists her skirts to prevent them dragging along the ground. Perhaps the ladies anticipated this, for they have laid on transport especially for her; a donkey awaits her, and the ladies lay some blankets on its back for Yolanda to sit upon it sidesaddle.

I, on the other hand, am expected to walk, and we all make our way gently and slowly across the sandy tract.

Oh, it's so good not to be carrying our luggage for a while! I tell myself.

We shuffle along for a while, and I notice that the sandy path is gradually veering round in another direction, and soon we turn the corner a ravine comes into view.

A group of people are already gathered there, and to them the ladies present us with our change of attire, which causes much merriment, and from the ladies expressions it appears they are very pleased with themselves.

I help the star of the show off her ass, and tether the animal in the shade of a nearby tree, before joining the others and sitting alongside them on the mats we've brought from the village. I gaze out over the river at the children swimming there, and look up at the bank high up on the other side of the river, which must be some hundred feet high at least.

We watch as figures climb up the cliff, and having made it to the top, proceed to hurl themselves off into the water far below, after which they swim a little way upstream, and then scale the sheer bank once again.

They jump, dive, and even turn the occasional somersault, and one little chap, who can't be more than 5 or 6 years old, competes and eagerly matches the achievements of the older boys. Then our host joins them. He has already changed into his swimming trunks, and he shows himself to be a man of broad and muscular build, and from his confident appearance he's certainly no stranger to this pastime of leaping off the cliff. Time and time again they all dive off the ridge and into the water, then swim and clamber back up, putting themselves though the process again and again. None of them seems to tire of the sport, and it's not until the sun sinks low in the sky that our host rejoins us. He rubs himself down with a large towel and quenches his thirst from a bottle of fruit juice. Then on goes the white shirt and suit, but not the lace-up shoes; he chooses instead to walk barefoot when we all straggle back towards the little village.

The scent of wood smoke wafts on the cooling breeze and on our return to the village we find the inhabitants milling around purposefully, some of them grouped around a fire apparently preparing a meal. The light of the day has by now all but disappeared, so lanterns are lighted and affixed around the general area where everyone is congregating. Yolanda sits herself on the ground and contemplates the scene. I too sit down and get so caught up with gazing at the fire, at the flames peeking out from underneath the cooking pot, that it takes me by surprise when our host and his wife try to catch my attention. They get us to hold out our hands, and then, from the long spout of a metal pot, they pour water over my fingers, after which they pass me a towel to dry myself with. Everyone performs this ritual.

It's explained to us that we should eat with our right hands, an idea I'm unfamiliar with, and I get to wonder why my left-hand mustn't touch the food. I don't ask.

'*Khus-khus*,' our hosts announce, as they serve us portions of chickpeas and vegetables.

Like anyone else who is ignorant of the customs of a people, I'm a bit apprehensive about what we might be offered; I even fear that we might be served a dish with sheep's eyes staring back at us.

In fact the meal is exceedingly tasty and we do good justice to it.

'*Kool*, *kooli*,' the gathered circle of villagers shout to us.

Our hosts tell us that '*kool*' and '*kooli*' both mean '*eat*'; that *kool* applies to men and *kooli* to women.

It's obvious that these simple people interpret our enjoyment of their food as a compliment, and our host's wife, in particular, keeps telling us to eat more. She confides to us that a chicken has been killed especially for the meal.

'*I don't think I can eat anymore,*' I whisper to Yolanda, and I sense that she too is upset, though needless to say we conceal our feelings from the villagers.

I was raised on a mainly vegetarian diet, which probably renders me particularly sensitive to the issue of killing. My father was a vegetarian, as was his mother too. I myself haven't adopted any particular diet, I've been a social eater, usually eating what is set before me, but seldom choosing to eat fish or meat.

With gestures and a smattering of limited French I tell our hosts how good it feels to be here with them, and Yolanda also makes a little speech.

From the reactions we get as we are led away from the gathering, we did the right thing in making our speeches, for we receive a loud round of applause.

We are led back to the room where earlier we took tea, and by the light of a hurricane lamp we change back into our own clothes. Now the plan is for us to accompany our host and his wife back to their home in town, leaving their son with the folks in the village.

I sense Yolanda is relieved to be getting back into her own clothes, and we now pick up our baggage and make ready to leave.

Like tiny perforations in a blanket held over a bright light, thousands upon thousands of shining points of light shine brightly above our heads, a canopy of stars in a dark blue velvet Moroccan sky.

Amidst much shouting and waving we make our departure.

We find that there's barely enough room for us in the car now, joined as we are by our host's wife and sister-in-law.

On account of the moonless sky, there is little for us to see on our way, just whatever the headlights light upon, mainly hedgerows and trees. The ladies chatter on non-stop; and it falls to Yolanda to remain sociable on behalf of both of us, as she can speak with them in French.

Eventually, after the car weaves its way through the long winding country lanes, we reach a built up area, and after taking a sharp turn the car comes to a sudden halt on a steep incline. The ladies pile out, with us tailing after them, and walk across a narrow street, through an alleyway and into a house where we are led to an inner chamber lined with ottomans strewn over with cushions. Here we are urged to put down our bags and make ourselves comfortable.

We are not here long before a trolley is wheeled in, on which is displayed pomegranates, white melon, cake and a pot of mint tea, all of which we're encouraged to partake of.

A television crackles into life and the chatting subsides as everyone stares over at the contraption. The picture flickers and is off again.

Our host asks something of me, and points to the wall behind me. Momentarily confused I stare uncomprehendingly, and then I notice two wires dangling there. I understand; the wires need to be joined together in order for the television to work.

'A bit dangerous,' I muse whilst hooking the wires together, 'Somebody could get shocktrecuted!'

The monochrome picture re-appears, rolling on the screen, settling only after some minutes. I am very cautious to avoid touching the bare wires behind me again lest I interrupt the programme, or worse still, get an electric shock.

It's a French film; so I understand very little of what is being said, let alone what is happening. I ache to be back where we have just come from, back in the country, back to basics, wonderful.

When the movie is finished, our hosts suggest it's time to turn in for the night.

Checking first that we're happy to sleep in this room, rugs and blankets are then pulled out of low cupboards and ottoman boxes, after which our hosts retire to another part of the house, leaving us to use the bathroom down the corridor (an utter luxury for us) and to get ourselves ready for sleep.

Left alone we fall to chatting about our day. After turning off the light I make my way back across the room, and after slipping into my sleeping bag I try to get comfortable, but the carpet and the blankets itch. I wonder if I'll ever get to sleep.

Chapter 6

A SPELL OF FAIRY TALE

We awaken naturally to find the air humming with activity. The room is still dark and remains so, as the heavily curtained windows are located high up out of reach.

The room has two double doors, and opening one of them I wander off in search of the bathroom and in so doing make my way past an area where people are engaged in making flat breads. They are evidently servants, for they have a certain look in their eyes, as though they are not free.

I locate the bathroom and set about my ablutions accompanied by the sound of birdsong, and I open the blind, whereupon the brilliant morning sunshine floods the bathroom with radiant light, purging every last vestige of darkness. After brushing my teeth and washing, I feel refreshed and eager for the new day.

Returning back up the corridor, I smile an easy greeting at the cowering figures in the kitchen. When I re-enter the room we slept in I notice the curtains are now open, and the lady of the house is there.

'*Bonjour Madam, comment ca va?*' I greet her.

Answering gaily, she asks if we have slept well.

Yolanda and I help by folding the blankets and stowing them in their rightful places in a trunk, and as we busy ourselves tidying the room, a trolley is pushed in weighed down with coffee, croissants, fresh bread and fruit, all invitingly arrayed.

After breakfast, Yolanda and I are again left alone. I occupy myself by taking a closer look at our room, finding the walls are all adorned with velvet hangings, fabric pictures with fussy fringes, vivid colours printed deep into the weave; images of lions and camels clamour for my attention, and pictures of mysterious looking locations with palm trees and exotically architectured buildings, the like I've never seen before. They're executed in an unusual, almost childish, style without any great attempt at realism. Lacking shadow they have a flat appearance though this does not detract from their charm, no, not one iota. My attention now turns to a little bookshelf on which I find a radio, a clock, a calendar, a framed photograph of the couple's little boy, and a few small toys. I also find a few magazines, paperbacks, and a dictionary, all of which are in French.

Yolanda explains to me that Morocco was formerly a French colony.

Our hostess returns and asks us if we would like to join her and her sister in visiting the *Souk*, the local market, and of course we accept with some enthusiasm.

On leaving the house we discover that the family lives in an area of the town that is quite European in appearance, but on this walk we penetrate further into Sidi Kacem and I notice a marked change of style. Traversing quaint alleyways we peek into the more traditional, crudely built dwellings and shops, all of which appear simple and clean. I halt outside one of the buildings after catching sight of a large group of small children at their lessons, the kids look such a happy bunch, all with shaved heads, sitting crossed-legged, eagerly reciting their lessons in front of their teacher; chanting words written on their wood-framed slate boards:

'The *Koran*,' our host informs us.

'That's like the Arab Bible,' Yolanda explains to me, *'Arabs pray to Allah.'*

We pass by various tradesmen, such as tailors and carpenters, most of whom sport moustaches and beards, and all of them garbed in *djellabas* and wearing semi-spherical skullcaps of embroidered cloth upon their heads. Many of the traders grin at us and lean out to greet us as we pass. As we stop to watch them at their labours, there's no glimpse or any sound of a modern machine; we might as well be taking a walk, way back in time, back in the Middle Ages.

Madame and her sister both wear long *kaftans*, which in addition to appearing comfortable serve additional purposes too, in that they cover the flesh of their limbs and conceal the contours of their bodies from prying eyes. They also have hoods, light blue in colour, that cover their hair, similar to the head coverings that nuns wear, but these are much more attractive. Additionally, Madame's sister also wears a veil over the lower portion of her face, and with a sparkle in her eye Madame explains to us that whilst in public an unmarried woman should keep her face veiled.

Personally, I'm unconvinced that the veil conceals that much, as it's of such thin gauze. So it seems to me that, paradoxically, that it might serve quite a different purpose, as it could be a lure, to indicate her availability to prospective suitors.

Entering a large spacious cobbled area with stalls selling a variety of goods, it's evident we have arrived at the *souk*. The place is choc-a-bloc with merchandise, with tables arrayed with richly coloured fabrics, garments, accessories and other finery. Hand-made sandals, shoes and other leather goods are also on display, whilst the neighbouring stalls offer fruits, vegetables and sweetmeats. I spy an exceptionally tall man carrying a bulging leather sack slung over his shoulder, tied with a cord, with a small metal cup clasped in his hand. Our guide confirms my suspicion that this man is actually selling water. The very idea seems preposterous! Coming as we do, from a country where water is on tap, and freely available, it's difficult to understand how something as basic and essential as water could anywhere be sold as if it were a luxury.

As we explore the market, Madame encourages us to buy something for ourselves, and as we follow the ladies about they show me a stall heaped with *djellabas*, patterned, striped and plain. Certainly, I had enjoyed dressing up in a *djellaba*, and this would be an ideal opportunity to choose one of these garments for myself. I light on a plain off-white one, with broad silvery stripes down it; the seams joined with a chord striped with white and silver. Loose fitting, it's a good deal better fit than the one I wore in the country village yesterday. I love that where one might expect to find side pockets, there are slits through which I can reach through, to the pockets of my jeans. Surprisingly, though this garment is made of wool, it's light and cool to wear, and having tried it on, I'm now reluctant to take it off again.

After my purchase Yolanda mentions that she would really like to get a straw hat and we find there are many here to pick from. She chooses a *sombrero*, a wide brimmed hat of natural neutral colour, patterned in pastel green and pink. Our purchases have not been costly, about 17 *dirhams* for the *djellaba* and 3 *dirhams* for the hat.

We continue to stroll around the *souk*; and watch as the ladies shop for clothing fabrics and buy fresh fruit and vegetables, placing their goods in a capacious shopping basket made of straw. Our shopping all done, we leave the relative cool of the indoor market and step back out into the sunshine.

The sun is now burning fiercely so we do not linger on our way back, and as we near our house I suddenly remember that we've finished our cigarettes, so I excuse myself and slip into a local tobacconist to purchase a packet of *Casa Sports* and a box of waxed matches.

Rejoining the ladies, who are waiting for me, we cross the courtyard and re-enter the dark interior of our host's well kept home. Once Yolanda and I are back in our room, I take off my jeans and top, as I feel so comfortable in just my underwear and *djellaba*, I decide that whilst we're in Morocco I'm going to keep wearing the robe.

Monsieur returns home from work (I get the impression he owns a garage close by), and the rest of the day is mainly spent between idle chatting, and responding to repeated visits of the trolley laden with cooked dishes delicacies and fruits. Indeed, so many times do I hear the cry of *'Kool, kooli'*, that I gradually become fearful that before long I'll become unable to stand up properly.

It's certainly quite a change from the frugal existence we've become used to on the road, and I certainly don't want to overdo it and become overindulgent.

We ask our host questions about Morocco, about its culture, its history, and we ask about the use of *kiff* in his country, telling him of our experience in Tetuan with the kids trying to sell us *kiff*. The expression on our host's face clouds.

'Yes, some smoke it,' he admits, *'But they're mad.'*

Well, that's how Yolanda's translates his words. Anyway, I ask him why he thinks they're mad.

'They don't want reality, just dreams,' he says.

I change the subject, asking him about the cities, of Casablanca and Marrakech.

And I think also to ask him what he knows of Algeria, and he surprises me, in that he is emphatic that Algeria is just like Morocco, no difference at all.

I wonder, that if the two countries are so similar, why we are thinking of going out of our way to visit Casablanca or Marrakech, which would mean making a massive detour, when we could just as well move directly along the coast of North Africa, as I had at first envisaged.

Our host suddenly asks what we have in order to defend ourselves, specifically whether we carry a handgun.

'*Rien*,' Yolanda answers, emphatically telling him we have no gun.

The family reacts with surprise, urgently trying to convince us of the need to arm ourselves. After I show them the penknife that I carry in the rucksack, they are anything but reassured, so I try to change the subject.

Since our discussions have brought the subject of our travels into prominence, I take the opportunity to ask whereabouts we might hitch from locally. Obligingly, Monsieur draws a sketch map indicating our proximity to the rest of town. Pressing him further, he tells me of a nearby street where we might obtain a lift, and impresses on us that we should travel at night, for apparently this is the custom in Morocco. After our experience of falling asleep in the intense heat, I can see the sense in this idea. So we start to hatch a plan, aiming to take the road leading east and complete the 450 km distance to the border with Algeria, the next country along the coast of North Africa. Monsieur indicates it's about 50 kilometres from Sidi Kacem to the town of Meknes, and from there we must go on to the next big town, Fes, and then keep going until the border.

Not wishing to become a burden on our hosts we resolve to leave this very night. Cautiously apprising our hosts of this decision, we impress upon them how much we've been enjoying our stay, but remind them of our intent to reach India, pointing out that we still have far to go. Our hostess makes a promise to keep in contact with us, telling Yolanda that she will make a white *kaftan* for her, for when we marry.

Though we are already over-satiated with food we receive yet more visitations from the food trolley before the sun sets, and when the time comes for us to leave our kind hosts I find I have difficulty in getting up and moving.

Outside the house we make our last farewells, and we're presented with food for the journey. I feel very emotional about leaving them for they have been such attentive and kind hosts. But, that said, I look forward to there being just the two of us again, on the road.

The few electric lights strung aloft above the streets afford little assistance in lighting our way through the darkened town. But following Monsieur's directions we find the allotted place where we are likely to be able to get a lift and there we encounter several bands of individuals waiting around on the pavement, whose attention seems focussed on each and every passing vehicle. The waiting

Moroccans don't appear to take any notice of us, but perhaps in the half-light they don't see us as foreigners, after all I am now shorthaired and heavily tanned, and I'm also afforded additional anonymity by the hooded gown I'm wearing.

I'm gradually discovering some hidden bonuses to wearing a *djellaba*, in that I find that by billowing the gown one can create an updraught of cool air, and by wrapping it tightly about one's body one becomes much warmer. Then there's the hood, which, in addition to being a shield to screen one from excessive sunshine, also acts as a filter when the air is dusty. Now I see that whilst resting, those who are wearing *djellabas* pull the hood down over their faces.

Touching my face I can still feel the marks of my encounter with the killer ants back in Spain.

A large truck comes bouncing and swaggering along the road, churning up clouds of choking dust, and our fellow hopefuls raise their arms and rush forwards the moment it comes into view. With a volley of shouted exchanges, men climb on, throwing on their curious bundles too. Lorry after lorry turns up and gradually the numbers of those of us waiting for lifts reduces. Hoping that in time our turn will come, we stare impassively at the goings on. Sounds from a radio swirl about us, the dramatic music blending easily with the noise of the street life.

I begin to notice that the flow of trucks is lessening, and I become anxious lest there will be no lift for us tonight.

When another truck comes along, bucking its way along the rutted road, I stand at the vanguard of the remaining hikers, with Yolanda close behind me. As soon as the truck draws to a halt we open the cab door and drag our luggage inside, whilst others just as eager, and more experienced, force their way past us. With the heat, the dust and the clamour, it's hard to handle the situation.

The driver of the truck seems completely unmoved by the pandemonium and commotion. Soon it becomes obvious to me that there are way too many people inside the cab, with the most obvious solution being for us to offer to get out. But we're not in genteel England now, no, this is Morocco, so everyone stays put and endures the discomfort. The vehicle pulls away and here we all are, crushed tightly against one another. It's really uncomfortable; for as the truck moves my hips bash and grind against those seated either side of me. Then the truck jerks and bounces mightily, serving only to create greater havoc and discomfort. I'm really tempted to give up on this absurd situation and get off, but there's such a jolly atmosphere here, with passengers laughing and chatting gaily, so because of this good naturedness I feel like seeing this through.

Everyone is smoking each other's cigarettes and the comradely warmth that forms between us all has the effect of lessening the discomfort, making the uneven road feel just a little smoother. Actually, in spite of the obvious drawbacks, the lift is a good one, for the truck is going all the way to the border with Algeria. Mind you, this also means we have a long, long night ahead of us.

Quite without warning, the truck comes to a sudden halt and the headlights are extinguished, throwing us all into a darkened silence. Yolanda and I gaze out of the dust encrusted smeary window, looking for a cause for the delay. No road works or toll station are in sight, so there's no apparent reason for our stopping. We sit in silence for several minutes before the driver lets out a loud whoop and sets the truck rolling onward again.

We speed through the warm dark night, and from time-to-time it seems to me I see lights hanging in the sky without any visible means of support, and neon signs too, which burn with a curious haze surrounding them.

With no discernible moon the few lights there are along the roadside gain disproportionate importance. The brilliance of their colour both fascinating yet overwhelming.

Once more our driver brings the vehicle to a halt and silences the engine, and this time I look at him enquiringly. He gestures to the road ahead.

'There's something fishy going on.' I whisper to Yolanda

'Why have we stopped?' she asks.

'I reckon there's a police check up ahead, what else could it be?'

'I haven't seen any police,' Yolanda responds.

I keep my eyes peeled, and when a truck approaches us from the opposite direction I put my attention on the row of lights studded across the roof of the driver's cab. Up until now I've not taken much notice of these lights, assuming them to be merely decorations. But now, in a moment of inspiration, I begin to wonder if the blue, red, orange, green, yellow and white lamps might contain coded messages. I convince myself they do. Then, as another truck approaches, I notice our driver's mood change; he becomes very animated and gestures enthusiastically to the driver of the other vehicle who grins broadly at us as he drives by.

Without delay we swerve back onto the main road, and are soon going at a good speed again, and, even though visibility is dim, I can see faint outlines of tall buildings in a built up area, so it looks like we have reached a city, Meknes perhaps. But we seem to be taking a route that bypasses the main city, for there is little for us to see, though in the half-light I can just about make out more indistinct silhouettes of clusters of buildings embellished with the sparkle of tiny lights, then we are out of town, hurtling onwards. It's extremely hot now; my clothes are sodden with sweat.

We stop again; and again we wait in silence, and in time I glimpse a truck appearing from the other direction, and seeing this our driver turns the ignition pulls away. I don't understand the reason for the delays, but I'm totally convinced now that the cab lights hold the key to the mystery of our stopping and starting.

After galvanising back into action and speeding on for a while, we are all but shaken off our seats by the suddenness of the driver braking.

'Oh here we go again,' I announce. *'**Now, what are they up to?**'* I ask, as the other occupants of the cab clamber out, carrying coiled lengths of rope.

Speaking to the driver in French, Yolanda asks what's going on, and he explains it's now so hot that they are going to try and tie the cab doors open. It seems an odd and potentially dangerous idea, but as I'm sweating from head to toe I understand all too well why they would want to do this. The men struggle for some time before successfully securing the doors, and we're off again, with air conditioning. But I worry that there's now nothing separating us from the tarmac below; danger lurks at every jolt and twist… this lift is turning into quite a drama. Despite everything done to tie the doors open, the measures do little to lower the raging heat inside the cabin, but there's nothing to do other than grimace and bear it.

I find, as we tear on through the darkness, that there's nothing to occupy my mind. As a child, on long journeys, I was given an *'I-Spy'* booklet to record any sights. Unusual signs, old-fashioned pillar-boxes, windmills, watermills, Elizabethan architecture, oast houses, traction engines and steam rollers, were just some of the things I was alerted to be on the look-out for. Perhaps that's what I still do? Maybe my memory is rather like a collection of personalised *'I-Spy'* books?

As we approach the city of Fes I wonder if perhaps this could be where the funny Fez hats come from; those curious flat-topped comical red hats with tassels on, like the one comedian Tommy Cooper wears? I recall that a friend of my father, John Vaughan, presented dad with a Fez. I wonder if I'll see someone wearing one here.

When approached in the nighttime, densely inhabited places tend to emanate a perceptible glow, visible from some distance, and as such I know we have reached the city. The truck brakes and quite a few of our fellow passengers descend from the cab clutching their belongings, and disappear into the night. With space now to stretch and readjust our squashed limbs, we sit and gaze.

From where we sit we can see the comings and goings of the city, the people passing through a gate of the inner wall of the old city. I convince myself I can recognise our former fellow travellers passing through the gateway and becoming absorbed by the crowds. I see a concentration of buildings, rich in variety and shape, scored with alleys and stairways hung with lights, where people move about, seemingly oblivious of the late hour of the day. Transfixed, my senses drink in the fabulous vista of this mediaeval city, and I become spellbound staring at the spectacle arrayed before me, which so resembles those illustrations in fairy-tale books, which portray the magical splendour of life within such ancient habitations. It's been worth all the journeying so far just to see this enchanting sight.

As our driver sets the truck in motion again I take one last wistful longing look at the city, and am repaid by catching sight of a man striding near the gate wearing the venerable Fez!

Straining up the hill we pull away from the city and continue on our way again, and there's no more stopping now, until it's time to refuel the tank.

At the petrol station our driver brews up, offering us all mint tea and food too. For our part we contribute the bag of food we were given back in Sidi Kacem. This brief letup in the incessant endless travelling does us a power of good.

We resume our journey, and as hour follows hour we just keep moving, but I find myself more asleep than awake, though I try to keep my eyes open I can't help wishing I were tucked up in bed between cotton sheets. I fight to stay awake, but there's so little to focus my attention on. The beams of the headlights pick up and light up the tufts of scrubland on both sides of the road, and from out of nowhere insects fly towards the vehicle, and impact on the windscreen. It's really quite depressing, but my spirits rise a little at the first signs of the new day that start to brighten up the sky.

'How are you?' I ask my girlfriend quietly.

Yolanda looks at me gloomily.

'Alright, I suppose,' she murmurs.

What a joyless pair we are right now, of no use to each other or ourselves. What a big mistake we've made coming on this journey, how futile are our hopes and dreams. The harsh reality of life on the road is overwhelming me; it might well be better to think of going back? But even this idea brings little consolation as we're now so far away from England, and besides, what can we hope for on our return?

'Fuck it, I hate travelling,' I suddenly announce.

Yolanda looks at me with a blank expression, which I see as her being quietly contemptuous.

Though the sun has not yet arisen, the sky is becoming brighter at every moment; and the strong light shining in my eyes makes me squint; it's all too much.

A town comes into view, just up ahead; I stare out at the ramshackle inhospitable looking buildings without interest, the bleak view deepening my dark mood. Again I close my eyes.

I feel a tug at my sleeve - sluggishly I respond, for it seems I've been asleep.

I find it impossible to open my eyes wide. To say I've been rudely awakened is rather too accurate, for I had slipped into a pleasant sexual reverie that I feel disinclined to return from.

'We're here,' Yolanda announces, nudging me.

Opening my eyes I see the truck is now stationary and the driver and his mate have got out and are leaning against the bonnet, talking with one another.

Though not fully awake, I force myself to get up - a painful process, as I have become fairly welded to the seat.

Lowering ourselves to the ground, we stand staring blankly about us. We probably resemble victims of hypnotism as we stumble and sway unsteadily.

I try to attract our driver's attention but in vain, as he too seems a bit spaced out.

'Which way is the border?' I enquire. Yolanda asks too but gets no reply. She moves closer to the driver, and asks again, this time a good deal louder.

Slowly he turns and offers directions, which amount to a bit of pointing and a certain amount of muttering.

Involuntarily I begin rendering a version of The Beatles' *'Hard Days Night'* delivered in a theatrical Shakespearian fashion, the style made famous by Peter Sellers:

'It's been a hard day's night, and I should have been sleeping, like a log'.

I take stock of where we are, looking at the lumps of concrete, the barbed wire and the snarling mongrel dogs, and there's a rank odour too, emanating from God knows where, or what.

'What a bring down!' I grumble.

'Oh shut up,' Yolanda rebukes.

'Shut up yourself,' I retort mechanically.

I do wonder if we're going in the right direction but there's no one here to ask. No one else seems to be about at this time of day; the place is totally desolate.

Wearily we trudge on.

As the sun peeps over the horizon, I cringe.

'Sorry about back then, Yolanda,' I mutter.

'It's all right, don't worry,' she reassures me. *'How much further is it to the border?'*

"I think it's that building up ahead, it appears we've been going the right direction after all.'

At the Moroccan customs checkpoint, a sleepy eyed official stamps the passports of two tired and very dispirited travellers.

As our passports are returned to us, a bolt of agony hits me as pleasant recollections of our times in Morocco tug at me. I am already missing the family back in Sidi Kacem.

Inhaling the fresh air of dawn my spirits rise, and with confidant stride I make my way over to what must be the Algerian side of the border, with Yolanda by me.

Chapter 7

FORTY-FIVE IN THE SHADE

The notice above the door reads '*DOUANE*'.

I knock and await a response. The handle turns and a uniformed official strides out, to whom we dutifully offer up our passports to, and he takes them back inside the office, sits down at his desk and performs the ritual application of the rubber stamp, before returning the green (Italian) passport to Yolanda, and the black (United Kingdom) passport to me. I relish the growing collection of quaint marks that are accumulating within my once unwanted and formerly pristine travel document. I have a quick look at this new one.

Thanking him and bidding him '*Au revoir*' we stroll away.

We walk no more than a few paces before the Customs Officer calls us back.

His mood is altered; he's now agitated and indicates to us he wants us to return to his office.

He demands to see our passports once more, and returning to his desk he proceeds to stamp the passports again.

I watch him, puzzled, as he rises from his chair and stands framed in the doorway, staring, thrusting our travel documents out in front of him, before breaking into a stream of abuse, directed at Yolanda and myself!

We withdraw and move to a safe distance where we cannot be overheard.

'*Wow! That was heavy, very heavy,*' I complain.

'*Yeah! He's really screwed up! What's wrong with what I'm wearing, anyway?*' fumes Yolanda. '*What a creep!*'

'*Mmmm, the guy's nuts, but what can we do about it?*' I reply.

I check our passports.

'*You do know that he's cancelled our entry stamps?*' I tell Yolanda.

Yolanda winces.

'*We'd better keep our cool.*' I say. '*Ohhh, do you reckon he understands English?*'

'*I don't think so, but you never know,*' answers Yolanda.

It's difficult to understand why the guy got so het up about our clothes.

'Strange, he seems to hate Morocco?' I observe, *'He really doesn't like my djellaba! How odd!'*

We rummage about through our rucksack, spilling the contents onto the ground as we dig about trying to find alternate clothes to wear. Then I open the door to the washroom and go in and slip on my jeans and a T-shirt. I freshen up too and brush my hair.

As I look myself in the mirror, I grit my teeth angrily.

'What a creep! Creep! Fuckin' creep!' I hiss, remembering why I had my hair cut.

Now that I've changed my clothes I feel taller, more assertive.

Now it's Yolanda's turn to change, and from a distance I watch her as she sheds her velvet trousers and embroidered Rumanian blouse, and puts on her violet Victorian dress.

'How do I look?' Yolanda asks.

'Pissed off, actually!' I reply rather curtly.

It's a while since I last saw Yolanda in a long dress.

'Fine,' I add quickly, *'you look nice in that dress.'*

Yolanda is clearly annoyed.

'He's just on an ego-trip,' Yolanda mutters angrily, *'wants to have a bit of power. What a **pig**!'*

'You can change out of your dress later, as soon as we're out of sight. Now, let's go see Supercreep!' I suggest.

So we return to the office where we stand for our demented persecutor to inspect us, and I half expect another outburst from him, but instead he smiles approvingly.

Then he asks for our passports and stamps them again, and indicates we are free to enter into Algeria now.

Under the previous stamp, which was crossed with *'ANNULE'*, is another: -

FORTY-FIVE IN THE SHADE

As we now need some Algerian currency, I hand over some of our precious pounds in exchange for what I take to be the equivalent in Algerian *dinar*. It seems to me that all the while he's eyeing Yolanda rather lasciviously.

When we're finished he gives us directions, and we traipse off up the road.

Out of sight of the customs house, we continue walking and as we do we complain to each other about the way we've been treated, and whilst we're grousing we feel the effects of the incredibly scorching hot weather here.

My footsteps become more difficult, it's as if the asphalt is melting under my feet. Then I think to look down and I'm shocked to find my desert boots are sticking to the road. I stand in mute amazement and try to move my feet, discovering that the melting tarmac is becoming fused to the soles of my shoes. After wrenching them free, I share this discovery with Yolanda, who merely raises her eyebrows.

'Forty-five degrees in the shade, that's what it is here,' she announces.

'I don't know anything about temperatures, you know that! But I do know it's bloody hot. Anyway who told you that it's forty-five?'

She doesn't answer me. How rude!

I can't understand why she is being so offhand with me, and moments later we start our first quarrel since leaving Britain, our first hammer and tongs argument erupts, Soon we are both screaming, swearing, and being as unpleasant as we possibly can to each other. We give each other hell! It's horrible, ghastly!!

And then I figure what's going on; it's the extreme heat that's frying our brains and I point this out to Yolanda.

Only with great effort do we refrain from further antagonism, however, the maddening fury is quelled, though I do wonder how long the truce will last.

As the raging madness leaves us, we sit apologising to one another. Then after we tire of repeatedly saying sorry we resist any further exchanges. We've been totally out of our minds - a frightening experience - it's left me feeling very shaky.

'We're very near the equator you know?' Yolanda remarks airily.

I look across at her, but keep my peace.

My boots are still bothering me, and I discover that one of them has cracked across the sole and it pinches me quite painfully as I walk along the sand strewn desert road. They really are quite useless.

'Desert boots,' I snort, *'That's a joke.'*

I'm not sure who first hears the approaching vehicle, but together we spring out of the shadows where we have taken refuge, and frantically wave our arms, panic stricken that we might miss this opportunity of a lift.

A jet-black limousine comes sliding alongside us; almost soundlessly it slows and comes to a halt just ahead of us. To my mind the car is like something out of a gangster movie; sleek and flashy with blackened windows, chrome fittings and highly polished black paint.

I notice the bumper plate of the car bears a CD plate - so I take this to mean that the vehicle belongs to a diplomat, that it's a *Corps Diplomatique* car.

Grappling with our burdens we run to the waiting vehicle and I grasp hold of the handle of the passenger door but immediately let go again, releasing it and vigorously shaking my hand. Although I can see no sign of injury, it sure feels like I've been burned.

The passenger door swings open and sympathetic comments are offered to me as we ease ourselves into the spacious interior.

The car moves off at a sedate pace and the two be-suited gents in the back strike up a conversation with us.

The interior is undoubtedly luxurious and has been built for comfort, but the air-conditioning proves quite ineffective at dealing with these adverse conditions. We all swelter in the heat.

After some minutes driving along through the desert I spot a building ahead, which, from its style and the advertising signs, I take to be a wayside *café*. The sharp suited diplomats sitting with us notice the *café* too, and one of them gives a sharp command to his chauffeur, whereupon the purr of the engine is immediately silenced, and then, in an atmosphere of pomp and occasion, we are ushered out of the car and accompanied into the nearby building.

The *café* is a grand colonial looking place with very high ceilings, the *café* space itself being embellished by ornate wrought ironwork features. We seat ourselves down around a circular wooden table, and as if by magic, bottles of fizzy drink are brought to our table by a waiter and placed before us.

As we sip our chilled refreshments I look about and notice several large propeller-like rotating blades, mounted at intervals across the ceiling, to cool the place. So wide they are as to make it appear they might even have been manufactured for an aircraft.

As I gaze about me I notice the room is gradually becoming extremely crowded, in fact there are no longer any vacant tables in sight. There's a stillness, a silence, as though everyone were waiting for something to happen. The expressions on the faces of the hunched overheated men sat about us appear set and motionless. No sound proceeds from their lips; in fact nothing stirs in the room other than the occasional fly. On a high up shelf a television flickers, with ghosted fuzzy monochrome images bending out of shape, snapping into focus, disappearing and reappearing. The sound of the TV is barely audible. No one appears to be paying it any attention.

'Freaky isn't it?' I whisper to Yolanda.

Though my remark is spoken very quietly, I am all too aware that many eyes are now homed in on me. The silence challenges. I clear my throat.

'Excuse me, why is everyone so quiet?' I ask one of our companions.

Initially he seems deaf to my remark, but then he asks me to repeat myself.

I am unused to diplomatic exchanges, yet I think to rephrase my question.

'Is this the custom in Algeria, to stop everything when it gets this hot?'

He nods slowly, mops his brow with a handkerchief, and turns away again.

I find the silence of the *café* unsettling, disconcerting.

At length our diplomat friend resumes eye contact, and after making sure we are both paying total attention to him, he speaks.

'Where are you travelling to?' he asks, enunciating each word of his question very precisely, in perfect BBC English.

Oh no! How I hate formality!

I take another sip of *Fanta* as I tug at my uncomfortable brain cells, trying to summon up a suitable response.

'Mmmm we don't quite know yet, Egypt perhaps? If we're lucky, India even.'

Another long wait ensues, during which his face holds an expression of utmost seriousness, as if weighing up my answer.

'Why do you wish to go to these places?' he asks, frowning.

'I want to know how the people live. Besides, it makes a change from being in London, do you know what I mean?'

There is now another long pause! I really wonder why he is taking so terribly long to respond to my comments. It could be the heat I suppose, but I wonder nonetheless.

At long last he answers me; *'I think so. You are students?'*

'No, no!' I protest.

As it happens, since leaving Britain, we have all too frequently been asked if we are students.

*'No, we're **not** students,'* I hear myself say, as calmly as I can.

The atmosphere in this *café* is really super strange. I reckon that if a life-form from another galaxy were observing us all here, it's likely it would assume we had all been slipped some kind of experimental drug to keep us from intelligent interaction, since the flow of life energy within us appears to have been arrested. Lamentably, during the hour or so we sit here, at no time do things get any better.

And then I think I hear someone speak…

'Are you ready to leave?' the voice says gently.

It might as well have added *'.. to join us on our quest and return to our own galaxy.'*

I grin as I drain my glass, thinking through a variety of answers to this most welcome question about our being ready to leave.

'Yes, we're ready,' I reply simply.

Oblivious to my mischievous mood, our diplomatic acquaintance courteously holds the back of Yolanda's chair firmly whilst she gets up.

So, our party at last extricates itself from this experiment in suspended animation, and with a polite exchange of *'After you!'* and *'No, after you!'* we resume our seats in the limo. The tense unnatural quietness back at the *café* has left me exhausted so I now close my eyes and daydream myself away, far, far away.

Other than the strangeness of the *café*, the lift in the limousine is a really good one, in that it has taken us from the border and into Algeria proper, so when we are eventually dropped off, we are fairly optimistic about being able to continue onwards without much hassle.

Apparently, according to Yolanda, Algeria, like Morocco, was a French colony until fairly recently.

But it seems that Monsieur, back in Sidi Kacem, was very wrong when he told us that Algeria is just like Morocco.

'Algeria seems such a dismal place, not a bit like Morocco,' Yolanda moans.

'Yes, how could we have been so misinformed?' I add. *'Everyone seems depressed and boring here. Added to which they all seem to shop at C&A's.'*

'What do you mean?' Yolanda asks.

'You know, all the same synthetic shirts and trousers, and lace-up shoes. It doesn't matter though; they'd be the same however they dressed.'

A car comes to a stop nearby, and a friendly moustachioed face leans out of the window, offering us a lift.

Our new driver asks us our names and where we come from, and whether we like Algeria? And we reply to him good-naturedly.

We haven't been travelling very long before we arrive at the next town, which looks pleasant enough, though not as obviously picturesque as the towns in Morocco.

The driver asks us if we would like something to eat. Not a bad idea, not a bad idea at all! So he parks, and disappears into a shopping area, before soon returning laden with foodstuffs, which he passes through the window for me to look after. His tone now becomes pleading as he asks if we can all go to the local beach for a picnic.

After the previous events of the day it seems almost too good to be true. Things are certainly looking up again, so we agree, and I sit right back and enjoy the breeze blowing through the open window onto my face. Yolanda seems relaxed too as she sits chatting happily in the front. With some eagerness I look forward to the meal, as we've had nothing to eat all day, and it's by now late afternoon.

Our driver hands around his cigarettes, *Sports*, a local brand, and I discover that like Moroccan cigarettes they're rather harsh to my taste.

The road that we're currently motoring along gives us a good view out to sea, and it's not long before we slow, pull off the road and park up close to the beach. Our driver stalls the car, springs out and opens all the doors wide open. Then Yolanda and I help him carry the food from the car to the beach and lay out some matting.

Soon enough we are sitting around tucking into plates of tasty food, a great *au fresco* meal, though when some fried chicken is produced, the topic of killing jumps back into my mind; and I suddenly, possibly for the first time, feel I understand something of my father's aversion to eating meat.

After our meal we lounge about, and nibble on some fruit. Then the water is put on the stove to boil, for a nice cup of coffee. Our new friend is so thoughtful; it's so nice of him to arrange this treat.

Absent-mindedly I'd assumed that after the picnic we would soon be leaving, and be back on the road again. Yet, even though the light of day starts to slip away, our host appears in no hurry to go anywhere. And when he does get up, instead of packing up the picnic things he paces over to his car, turns on the interior lights, and whacks up the volume of the radio.

It's good to hear the music louder, but I sense something about his manner that feels odd… and then, instead of sitting back down again, he approaches Yolanda, and asks her to dance with him. She just frowns.

Then he pleads with her and his manner becomes increasingly intense until it appears that he's actually ordering her to do his bidding.

But, in spite of his pushiness, I wonder at Yolanda, as it's not as though she doesn't like dancing.

In a low whisper I ask her what the problem is, but she doesn't answer me and she doesn't budge.

So I try explaining to him that Yolanda and I have had no sleep of late that she just isn't in the mood to dance. I make it clear to him that she means no offence. That it's nothing personal. He stands immobile staring at Yolanda, but she avoids his gaze and stays silent and self-absorbed, smoking a cigarette, staring out to sea.

Since the guy is causing us to feel uncomfortable, my immediate response is for us to break company with him, and when I suggest this to Yolanda she readily agrees. So together we try and explain to him our situation, that we need to find a place to sleep. To my surprise he accepts the situation easily, and walks away back to his car.

Well, I hadn't expected it to be this easy!

But no sooner do we start to breathe easy than I see a figure walking towards us; it's the all too frustrated dancer, carrying with him a cushion and blankets and explaining that he too is tired and plans to sleep on the beach.

We attempt to dissuade him but it's clear his mind is set.

So, without further conversation, Yolanda and I set out our sleeping bags ready for the night, then we lie in silence for a long while, until darkness falls, at which time I whisper my plan, that after a suitable wait, to give our driver time to fall asleep, we'll pick up our belongings and make a break for it.

But the minutes pass slowly, so very slowly.

Eventually though, after convincing myself that sufficient time has elapsed, I lean over, touch Yolanda lightly, and motion for her to get ready.

Hearts pumping and adrenaline flowing we noiselessly make our escape.

Stooped double and on red alert, we slink across the dunes.

I crane my neck to see that the guy is not stirring, hoping that our absence has not been noticed, then I hasten my pace, with Yolanda shadowing my every movement, and gradually we break into a trot and run across the sands.

After I become breathless and am on the verge of collapse, I slacken my pace and call over to Yolanda:-

'I reckon we're safe now. What do you think?'

'I can't go any further,' she groans.

So we lie down again, in a hollow in the sand, fairly close to the waters edge.

The mutual need for reassurance and affection soon has us cuddling and caressing each other, and making love. It seems so long since we last slept underneath the stars. The sea laps quietly as we lie in each other's arms and slowly fall asleep.

* * *

Of a sudden I'm awoken by the sound of an engine revving wildly. I force open my eyes, and to my alarm I see beams of light flashing across the sand. It appears that someone is driving a car along the beach, so I reason it can only be the guy who we had the picnic with, trying to seek us out. The car spins about furiously, headlights bouncing, slicing and slashing the dark night sky. Up and down the beach it races. We don't move an inch from where we are, but we are panicked so we clutch each other close. I lie there waiting, listening, hoping he will go away.

* * *

The very first light of day brings me to my senses, and getting to my feet I cast my eyes all around the sandy cove. Memories of our tussle with the midnight dancer are still fresh in my mind, so I am impatient to be up and away from the scene, as I figure he might return. Yolanda needs no persuasion, and soon we're on our way, getting off the beach and walking briskly along the road.

With a total absence of shops or cafes there's no possibility of obtaining any breakfast here. But as we're both gasping for a drink we approach the gate of what looks like a smallholding or farm, and catching sight of the inhabitants, Yolanda gets their attention and calls out to them in French. Surprisingly, they don't respond, but Yolanda asks them for some water anyway.

'Aqua, aqua,' she repeats loudly.

But they just look at each other, seemingly confused, and then wander off.

'That's ripe. Things have got really bad, haven't they?' I mutter.

'They just walked away!' Yolanda groans, *'They don't even have the decency to answer me!'*

'I'm going to stand here until they do.' I tell her, *'I'm not going to put up with that kind of nonsense. I've got my self-respect you know.'*

'Oh come on, let's go,' Yolanda responds dejectedly.

'No, I'm just going to stay put. They can't do anything about it and anyway....'

Whilst we're talking, some people emerge from out of the shack, and one of them walks towards us holding a tray on which there's a jug of water and two transparent plastic tumblers.

Greedily we reach out and fill, and refill, the tumblers with the cool, cool water.

As we quench our thirsts the group disappears back into the shack, but almost immediately re-appear with their arms and hands full; they are holding plums and small melons, which they pass to us over the fence. Soon Yolanda's Moroccan straw hat is brim full and overflowing with ripe fruits.

I recognise that these folks just want to please, to make us happy.

We pour out our thanks, as best we can, and our benefactors stand there beaming at us as we bid them farewell before shuffling off along the road.

'It's great to be alive, isn't it?' I exclaim.

'Simple people... You know, I don't think they know a word of French.' Yolanda concludes. *'Hey! What shall we do with all this fruit?'* she asks; now struggling with her hat.

'Eat them?' I suggest, biting into another plum.

Turning a corner in the road we find ourselves facing a broad range of verdant hills.

'Let's climb up there,' I suggest.

'The Atlas Mountains,' Yolanda responds, thoughtfully.

How does she know? I ask myself. Perhaps she receives communications from the mother ship hovering above us in a cloak of invisibility, more likely though she merely paid attention to her studies at school.

Climbing the mountain slope is just the exercise needed for us to counteract and deal with the nervous tension brought on by the previous night's dramatic episode.

The view here is impressive, endless peaks and dips as far as the eye can see.

'We are not alone!' Yolanda announces, somewhat ominously.

I glance about, and a few hundred yards away I catch sight of a small group of hikers, kitted out with all the gear, packs, shorts, cameras and knobbly knees. They hail us in a foreign language, and I figure they are possibly Austrians.

'Hi there!' I shout.

'Good day to you,' comes their hearty response.

After making small talk with them for a short while they continue on their way.

I turn to Yolanda; *'Quite amazing how well organised they are. God, Yolanda, we don't even have a map, but it's more fun this way, don't you agree?'*

'They're Germans! Too efficient by far, too much for my liking.'

Wandering back down the slope, we sit by the road and eat some more of the fruit, whilst all the while looking out for a lift. After we've had our fill of food, we force the remaining fruits into our rucksack.

Sometimes we stand, and sometimes we sit, and sometimes we wander about. But no matter what we do, there's still no sign of any traffic.

'Ohhh, come on-n-n-n,' Yolanda moans.

'Something will come along, eventually,' I reassure her.

On such occasions as this, a great deal of patience is required in order to hitch hike from one place to the next, and the way we usually deal with the monotony is just to start walking, and hope for the best that we'll get offered a lift before too long.

We set off but suddenly stop walking and face each other to speak.

'I wonder if he....?' I say.

'I wonder if he....?' Yolanda says in unison.

We look at one another intently, for clearly we've both have been dwelling on the selfsame topic, at the same time.

'We're both still at it then,' I observe.

'What?' Yolanda asks, thus disproving my assertion.

There are times when I feel as though my mind has somehow become subsumed, that my thoughts are no longer entirely my own. About this I have mixed reactions, for though a part of me likes the adventure, another part of me feels resentment that my most private thoughts are apparently being traced. However, I convince myself it's all on account of a predestined connection between us. But I can't always be sure whether this is the paranormal, the supernatural or simply paranoia?

I hear a vehicle coming our way, so I turn about.

'It's stopped!' Yolanda yells jubilantly.

Again, as on the previous day, the driver turns out to be young, friendly and glad of our company. Yolanda seems happy in his company, eagerly gabbling away to him in French as we head for the next town, called Oran, and at our driver's invitation we stop at a roadside restaurant and dine with him.

As we eat I watch Yolanda as she chats easily with this young man, and I pray that no trouble is brewing.

Yolanda turns to me: *'He says we can stay in his flat.'*

I stare at her; my thoughts are on open transmission.

'Wait. Before you speak, let me explain. He says he will drop us off at his home, then he is going off elsewhere tonight, and he won't be returning until tomorrow. We can use his flat until he returns. What do you say?'

'And pigs have wings?' I retort.

The extraordinary heat of the day is lessening, and the shadows are growing long. It's evening before we catch sight of a city on the distant horizon, and night descends before we actually arrive.

As we drive into the city, opulent grandiose buildings rise up on either side of the streets as we pass through, white stone fronts boasting porticoes and luxurious verandas. I note that everyone here is dressed in European clothes, there's not a *djellaba* or *kaftan* in sight. People's faces all seem grimly set, with no trace of the cheeriness we found to be so abundant in Morocco. In short they look to be an oppressed people.

Yolanda mentions to me that Algeria has only recently been granted its independence, so I reflect that perhaps it's too early for them to have re-discovered, or re-established, a homespun culture again?

Now we're in the city we have two options - 1. To break company with our driver, or, 2. To take up his offer of letting us stay at his home.

Being trusting souls we naturally choose to take him at face value, so, after telling us the number of the flat and giving us the key, he leaves us to make our own way upstairs.

Thankfully there appears to be no catch to our good fortune, and we marvel at the way this somehow compensates us for the tension brought on by Mr. Rave-up the previous night, and after convincing ourselves that we are quite alone, we help ourselves to some cereal and make ourselves a hot drink before turning in to get a good night's sleep.

I lie mulling over recent events; I can't rid myself of the feeling that the guy who wanted to dance only had good intentions towards us. But then why did he get so upset about Yolanda not wanting to dance? Perhaps he was a weirdo after all and Yolanda had done the best thing in the circumstances? Turning these thoughts backwards and forwards in my mind, I close my eyes and hope for sleep.

* * *

Morning time finds us fast asleep, and when I wake I pull back the sheet and bounce out of bed, letting out an enthusiastic whoop.

Yolanda stirs and props herself up in bed, looking decidedly sexy with her tousled hair tumbling over her naked breasts. Leaping upon her and gripping her wildly, I roll her about the bed in mock frenzy.

'What's wrong with you?' Yolanda gasps as I withdraw my lips from hers; she fights to get her breath back, her chest heaving and her face flushed.

'I can't resist you!' I joke, before again wrestling with her.

'You're mad Paul. You know something? You're over-sexed or something like that, you're not normal.'

'More than likely, but aren't you the lucky one? Wanna cup of coffee daaarlin'?' I ask her, adopting a cockney accent and flashing her a leering grin.

'Yes please. I like you playing the fool!' Yolanda laughs.

'Yeah, I was only joking.... make your own coffee!' I retort.

When she appears in the kitchen she seems relieved to find there are two steaming cups waiting on the sideboard.

We breakfast, and then loaf about for a while, before eventually deciding it must be time to leave. Making sure the place is as tidy as when we arrived; we place the door key on the table (as requested) and leave the flat, slamming the front door closed behind us.

'Thanks for the flat,' I say out loud as we make our way down the stairs. *'You really did your country proud,'* I announce in a pompous upper-crust accent.

So-o, here starts a new day, a new road, and new adventures.

From Oran we are fortunate in getting a steady succession of lifts, taking us ever closer towards the capital city, Algiers.

For the most part of the day we travel in the cab of a lorry, taking a route along seemingly endless desert roads, the journey being unspectacular, dull even. Quite why pipelines are so prevalent here I can't begin to understand?

As we trundle along, the heat intensifies and eventually becomes quite intolerable. I reckon the heat and the obvious lack of water must constitute a serious problem for the local inhabitants, who resort to a very primitive means of irrigating their land here. Attaching an ox or a camel, a wooden apparatus is turned, which results in a chain of pots or buckets bringing water up from underground.

As I watch the brightly clad peasant folk at their labours I am transported back to my childhood, when I studied a working model of such a mechanism, located in the children's section of the Science Museum. With the exception of the arresting skeleton of the diplodocus and the other dinosaurs there, that model always captured my imagination more than anything else there at the museums.

I think the mechanism is called an Archimedes' screw. Anyway, I had always assumed that such devices for raising water had long since been superseded in all parts of the world, and that everyone used mechanical pumps.

Fortunately for us, our driver stops at fairly regular intervals along the route, providing frequent opportunities for us all quench our thirsts from the standing pipes - I find myself drinking pint upon pint of cooling water at every stop.

On one of the stop offs we discover a freshwater stream, so we all douse ourselves with the fresh *aqua*, and for a while I even hold my face under the surface of the water, in an attempt to cool myself and at the same time slake my insatiable thirst.

Soon after this stop, I start to feel a bit groggy, but this is not entirely surprising considering the sudden changes of temperature brought about by this alternating between the cooling and the overheating. But sadly, before long I develop a high temperature and a streaming cold, a real ripsnorter, which soon overwhelms me in full. All I want to do is to go to bed and rest up.

By the time we finally arrive in the capital, Algiers, I am hardly capable of walking or doing anything other than feel self-pity.

As we need a place to stay, we wander the city in search of somewhere suitable, and the problem is eventually resolved when we meet with a priest who tells us he offers accommodation to foreign travellers.

In the outer courtyard of his home is a spacious elegant marble and alabaster veranda close by to a balustrade, on which hangs a trellis with spreading sprawling tendrils of a grapevine hanging laden with fruit.

Unrolling my sleeping bag I lie down to rest, but my congestion is bad and my head is pounding, and it aches so much that I can only sleep for short periods.

At those times when I cannot sleep, I stare about me in the half-light, my brain besieged by crazy confusions brought on by the fever.

Chapter 8

GETTING TO KNOW THE CUSTOMS

T he worst symptoms of my cold have passed by morning, however the headache persists, as does the extreme congestion.

We take to the road again, though a handkerchief is never far from my face, and my head is really muzzy. Over the next two days we gradually move across Algeria, finding that folks here are friendly enough to us, giving lifts, sharing their food and sometimes showing us what lies off the beaten track. When we accept a lift from someone driving a *Morris Minor* car, I immediately note the poor state of repair of the vehicle, with the door handles so broken that the driver has to tie the doors closed after we get inside, and as we bounce our way up a rock-strewn incline we're witness to some of the abuse this old machine gets subjected to.

But against all the odds we arrive without incident, and the driver is unexpectedly generous and hospitable, insofar as he and his wife invite us to stay at their home. They are especially considerate and sweet to us, watching over our every move and response (especially whilst showing us their photograph albums), and when the time comes to sleep, they show us to a double bed made up with crisp fresh white sheets. What absolute luxury!

When morning comes we are awake at first light and eager to resume our journey.

Bidding farewell and thanks to our hosts, we strike out on foot for the main road, passing along a rough lane where stand dwellings, which look relatively comfortable, luxurious even, though the walls appear to be made of mud. As we pass through the village, small children peep out from behind darkened windows and doorways, their little faces intense and full of curiosity.

We notice too that to the sides of the roads grow many cactus bushes, and Yolanda shows great interest in these odd specimens that she refers to as *figs d'Indes* ('figs of India'), which bristle with lethal looking spikes, and a local man kindly stops to demonstrate the art of picking and skinning these fruits without getting hurt.

Today we are fortunate with lifts, getting one lift after another, and as we motor our way through the heartlands of Algeria, I realise something; that virtually everywhere that we've travelled through up until now, the people seem to have had black hair, whereas here in Algeria many of the native folk seem to have ginger hair, and some of them even have bright orange frizzy hair, which certainly has me puzzled.

Another thing I notice is that football seems to be extremely popular amongst the youth in these parts, and on the outskirts of one town we pass through I notice a sports facility with teams of tall muscular young chaps running about in their bare feet, kicking a football about.

Curiously, the rural shops seldom have formal signs, such as printed or painted name boards, as vendors seem satisfied just to display their wares openly, with, for example, a butcher displaying the head of a bull or cow over the entrance to his shop. Macabre and gruesome it is, and the sight saddens and nauseates us, its only defence being it's brutal honesty. The pieces of meat hanging outside such places attract vast swarms of flies, and when we discuss this with someone, he tells us that some is horsemeat, a normal component of the diet here. We make an instant decision to avoid eating any meat for the remainder of our stay here in Algeria.

After really enjoying the little we got to see of Morocco, we are not forming a very favourable impression of Algeria, and we yearn to move on.

Eventually we reach the very last town before the border with Tunisia, and we think to spend our remaining local currency on some oranges and cigarettes, before striking out across a bleak and seemingly endless tract of uninhabited scrubland, a no-man's-land. If the walk weren't bad enough, the sores inflicted by the continued chaffing of the straps of our luggage cause me further misery. But our spirits rise as we come in sight of several buildings, which constitute the border point.

Finding the office, we dump our bags on the floor and settle down to the tedious chore of filling out the required forms, a task made easier at each border we pass through, as I gradually begin to memorise all the required information about us both, the passport numbers, dates of birth, and so forth.

'How are you travelling?' the official asks.

'Autostop! We are hitchhiking.'

'So, how did you get here?' he continues.

'We walked from the last town. It's a long way.'

'Yes, also long way to next,' he informs us.

In truth, it's already late, and since it's also starting to get dark the idea of wandering off into the wilderness has no appeal at all. In fact after a chat with Yolanda it's decided that we'll stay put here until daylight.

As darkness sets in the lights here attract the insects of the night.

I note there appears to be three men working at the border post, the main official and his two assistants.

When the young men understand that we're going to be around for a while they show themselves to be very hospitable, and offer us to share an evening meal with them. They even offer us wine, which we politely refuse. This friendliness is such a welcome change from some of the heaviness we've encountered so far, both at borders and elsewhere.

Later, as we start to unfurl our sleeping bags, one of the officials appears and offers us to sleep on a camp bed inside the office. When I discover there's only the one single bed available, I willingly give it over to Yolanda, before settling myself on the floor and getting relatively comfortable, as comfortable as one can lying on bare boards.

I lie for a time unable to sleep, and in the stillness I become aware of the shapes of several people slinking about. Silently they pad their way about, this way and that, then they come close by me, lighting their way by a torch, with the bright beam subdued and partially covered within a wrap of cloth.

They both appear pretty shaken when I sit up and demand an explanation from them for their intrusion. Startled, they initially give no reply, and then, in a nervous voice, one of them mumbles something unintelligible and then they leave.

By now Yolanda is also awake and receives news of the guards' nocturnal behaviour uneasily.

'It's okay,' I tell her, *'You sleep there, I will close the door and sleep across it.'*

Comforting myself with the thought that any attempt to enter the room will automatically arouse my attention, I pull my sleeping bag up as far as it will go and close my eyes, hoping there will be no more interruptions.

* * *

'Why are you here?' a voice storms.

It's now well into the night and one of the border guards - I think it's the most senior one - stands menacingly, staring down at me with a dark scowl spread across his dark features.

Since the reason for my being here is self-evident, I don't trouble myself to answer him, instead I ask him what he wants.

'Get out of the doorway,' he orders.

'No,' I reply firmly.

Three more times that night I am awoken by movement and footsteps, so by the time dawn breaks I have clocked up precious little sleep.

Yet again an official appears, wanting access to the office, and this time I lean over, knock on the double doors, and call to Yolanda.

Once we're both wide-awake we take stock of our situation and determine that henceforth we'll keep out of their way, and make the most of the day, enjoying a bit of exercise and doing some chores. After locating a nearby stream we settle down to washing our hair and cleaning our clothes, which we leave to dry out in the sun.

But as hours drift by, without any prospect of a lift, we become increasingly apprehensive and uncomfortable at the idea of another night on the border. In the event, it's already nightfall before we hear the sound of an approaching vehicle coming from the Algerian side, and all at once everyone is on their feet.

I can see it's a family car - jam-packed full - why even the roof is laden down with suitcases and bundles! I reckon that even if these people wanted to help us out that there would be no way they'd be able to find room for us.

We don't even approach the driver or his family, but wait and watch them as they show their passports and have the car checked over. Words are spoken - the driver looks our way and then back at the officials.

Perhaps the official has been intimidating him, or maybe he's just naturally friendly (I prefer to think it's the latter), but for whatever the reason it is, the driver has agreed to give us a ride, and is setting about making sufficient space for us to squeeze in.

Though the driver appears amiable enough it feels like he's being a touch too polite, so I sense that he's a little wary of us, maybe even frightened perhaps?

Anyway, as soon as the car starts we have to hold onto our seats to stop ourselves bouncing about and being thrown around on account of the rough uneven road. Notwithstanding the discomfort, the trip from the border post is unexpectedly pleasant, jolly even, as the family pass around sweets and snacks for everyone to share.

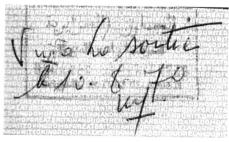 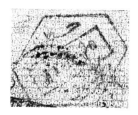

By the time we are clear of the border zone and properly into Tunisia, the sky is starting to brighten, and after exhausting all possible topics of conversation we lapse into a sleepy silence. As I sit there thinking, I take stock of the situation, and figure that these people have saved us from spending another night on the border, and have got us well into Tunisia, so they shouldn't feel they have to take us any further. Bearing this in mind I call out to the driver.

'This will do. Thanks, merci!'

We now have a fair amount of hanging about to do before we're offered another lift, but it's worth the wait, for our next trip promises to be very different, as we are now being offered an express trip to Tunis in a gleaming flashy *Lamborghini* sports car!

Clearly, we are now hob-knobbing with the jet-set and I lean back comfortably, thoroughly determined to enjoy it. I notice Yolanda too seems particularly at ease, possibly on account of discovering that the driver has recently returned from a visit to Italy, her home country. Apparently he'd gone there just to arrange the car's routine maintenance. How the other half live!

On hearing of our plans to continue travelling further across North Africa, our driver offers us some advice, telling us that when we get to Tunis we should go to the Libyan embassy, for he's sure we'll need visas to enter Libya, and he warns us the visas might be costly.

Well, all good lifts have to end sometime, and this is no exception, and after we part company with our driver I think I notice a far away look in my girlfriend's eyes.

'He's your sort of guy, isn't he?' I ask gently. Yolanda face now flushes and as she focuses her eyes on me, she answers quite defensively. *'What do you mean? What a lot of rubbish, I'm not impressed by wealth!'*

I keep silent.

Now we're in Tunis we decide it best not put off our trek to the Libyan embassy, and we discover, on our arrival there, that Signor Lamborghini is pinpoint correct about our needing visas, and also about them being expensive, as mine alone is going to cost over £2 of our British money. Relative to the amount of funds we have this is a very large sum indeed and it worries me. Also, it's going to take a couple of days for the visas to be processed, so we have lots of time on our hands.

Finding ourselves on the main street of Tunis, the Avenue de France, we all too quickly realise how expensive the restaurants are here, and we begin fretting over our financial situation.

'We could always take to begging,' I suggest in all seriousness. *'There seems to be a lot of very wealthy people in this part of town.'*

So, after sitting ourselves down in a doorway we throw ourselves into the part, and since a job worth doing is a job worth doing well, I decide to make an effort to stop looking happy and appear uncomfortably hungry. In the circumstances it's all too easy, as I'm uncomfortable about begging **and** I'm very hungry for a square meal.

Yolanda's *sombrero* hat is soon chinking and tinkling with the sound of both large and small denomination coins being thrown into it. I convince myself this is conscience money, that these people are loaded and are only ridding themselves of their loose change, so, as such; I feel no real gratitude towards our benefactors. Mind you, my lack of gratitude does nothing to help rid me of my sense of guilt or my embarrassment.

Twenty minutes of begging is a very long time, and we are done with it!

'Never again,' announces my accomplice, *'I really pity those who don't have a choice.'*

With pockets full of cash, we leave the main street and begin exploring the alleyways, wherein we come across a stall selling freshly squeezed fruit juice. I watch as the vendor crushes lemons to extract the juice, and then adds sugar and ice before setting them whirling in a blender. The resultant frothy liquid turns out to be so deliciously cool, refreshing and extremely moreish.

We just have to have another juice, so we try orange this time, and as I sip my drink I figure it tastes all the better for not costing us any of our foreign currency.

And now we are in search of food, and to this end we wander far, and eventually find ourselves in the Arab Quarter. There's not a white face to be seen here, and there's not one person here wearing European clothes; instead the men go around in long gowns and they sport funny little hats, all of which looks pretty good to my eyes.

But the atmosphere feels tense; and in all probability we are being looked upon as intruders, so I reckon we would best be careful about how we behave.

Down the narrow rambling lanes we wander, until a familiar sign grabs my attention, the red and white one, which advertises the popular drink that *'things go better with'*. We step inside.

The dark eyes of the *café* owner peer at me inquisitively, challenging and fierce.

'What shall we have?' I ask Yolanda.

But she doesn't answer me; she just looks vacant.

I know nothing about the local dishes, so I order something simple for us both.

'Egg, chips and two Cokes.'

The man looks at me, confused, so I repeat myself, loudly and slowly.

'Eggs, potatoes, in oil,' I explain, gesturing as best I can the process of frying.

We sit and wait, and soon the waiter reappears clutching our drinks.

'Do you think he understands?' Yolanda asks uncertainly.

'We'll probably get a plate of sheep's eyes or roasted horse.' I retort.

At length the waiter reappears, bearing two frying pans, which he places on our table. Each pan contains one raw egg and some slices of partly cooked potato swimming in warm oil. Beside the pans are lengths of French bread, which are spread with chilli paste.

What can I do?

I have nothing else I can do other than resort to the default indignant Englishman routine, and the staff gaze uncomprehending at me as I rant and rave at them.

We have consumed no more than a few gulps of *Coca-Cola* and a bite of bread, yet I still feel acutely embarrassed as we get up and leave without paying.

Luck, fate, or providence, seems to be running in our favour today, as no threats are made against us, and no lethal looking knives produced.

Back out on the street, we scurry off as fast as we can to the relative safety of the westernised part of town, where we find something more suitable to eat.

The problem of finding accommodation is always a concern, but today, after explaining our circumstance to a stranger who stops to talk with us, we are offered an unusual solution. He suggests we camp in his van that is parked nearby.

So, after um-ing and ah-ing over the topic for some time eventually we decide to take him up on his offer, and later, when it's dark, we find the car, let ourselves into it and lay ourselves down in the back on the rusty slatted floor. It isn't exactly comfortable, but would be a pretty good answer to our needs if it weren't for the light from the streetlamps shining in, which long delays us from getting any sleep.

* * *

As we need to stay around in Tunis for a few days, at least until our visas have been processed, we attempt to make the most of the visit, which isn't really so very difficult, bearing in mind the city is quite geared up to tourism.

We find people are friendly enough to us here; young people come up to us and chat. Even at a distance, from across the street or from a motorcar, comes the familiar cry of greeting, '*Ça va?*' ('How are you?').

'*Friendly lot,*' I comment.

'*I suppose so,*' replies Yolanda dismissively.

Looking up I see high above us what appears to be an overhead railway. But it appears very ancient, so I'm intrigued to find out more about it.

'*Far out,*' I blurt, '*That looks like an aqueduct.*'

We stand and gaze at it. Yes, it **is** an aqueduct.

'*It must be almost two thousand years old maybe. Imagine that!*' I add enthusiastically.

I suppose some people would buy a guidebook and explore the sights properly, but we just wander around, chancing on the remains of interesting structures, and occasionally refreshing ourselves at a fresh fruit juice stall.

In the evening we're invited by some Frenchy-type Tunisians to go to their apartment for a party.

It's not a good decision we make, us being teetotallers! And we end up having to spend the passing hours watching two-dozen or so students getting pissed. Then I spend the rest of night hunched in the corner fighting off tiredness in order to keep a watchful eye over my sleeping girlfriend. A voice in my head tells me that these students, though friendly enough, cannot be trusted, as they wander around carrying bottles of wine clutched tight in their hands and keep coming back into the room where we are, checking to see what we're doing.

'*Ça va?*' they ask again.

'*Ça va pas,*' I retort, with growing impatience.

With the new light of day Yolanda awakes, and after strapping on our baggage we leave the party. Although I've barely had any sleep, it's strangely comforting for me to be back on the streets again.

Whilst traipsing about the city we meet with a local Tunisian lad who offers to take us home for a meal, to the ramshackle terraced house where he lives with his folks up on the third floor. When lunch is ready, frying pans are placed on the table, and from the pans are served eggs, tomatoes and undercooked oily vegetables. But all in all the food is much appreciated and does a great job in satisfying our hunger. Then another course is served up, some meat and salad stuffs, but I give the dark meat the go by, not even daring to ask which animal has provided it.

Later in the day, as he wander round the city streets, an English lad befriends us and proposes that we join him to go and sleep at the guest house he's staying at.

'*Cheap. Only 5 dinars,*' he declares.

I muse awhile thinking about the term *dinar*, which I suppose is akin to the word *dinarius*, the coin of the Romans who ruled this country in the early centuries of the Christian era.

The 5-*dinar* accommodation is safe, though nothing more. All of us 'guests' are granted space in the front yard of someone's house, a yard that is also home to some chickens and a spectacularly coloured cockerel. The property is conveniently situated for sightseeing, as immediately overhead is another portion of the aqueduct we noticed earlier.

Our English friend spends much of his time explaining to us the ancient history of the area, of Carthage and other places. I have a hunch that Tunisia has a long history of foreign domination, and like Algeria has only recently gained independence, so maybe this accounts for why there is so little evidence of local culture?

* * *

'*As the rooster calls at the break of dawn, look out your window and I'll be gone.*' I sing; a line out of a Bob Dylan song, adding, *'We're off... so long.'*

Yolanda and I are really itching to get going again but before doing so we indulge ourselves in a bus ride out of town in order to locate a suitable hitching point.

Although it's midday before we actually obtain a lift, it turns out to be a good one, a long modern truck of the articulated kind. It's so great to be on the move again, racing through the middle of nowhere, on the edge of the Sahara Desert. Suddenly my eyes light on an unexpected sight only a short distance from the road - it appears to be Roman coliseum, an amphitheatre, completely intact! Yolanda and I stare in wonder as we flash by it, whilst the others in the vehicle give it no attention at all.

The truck speeds onward, and we pass through one town after another as we make our way along the coastal road - I try to remember their names, Sousse being one of them. At Sfax our lift ends, and there we join a dense mass of sun drenched tourists, and laze around for a while, and when the sun drops over the horizon, the holiday makers return to their hotels, and we are left on the beach by ourselves.

* * *

After a good night's sleep, we take a leisurely walk along the front in the hope of finding a little breakfast. From time to time I stop to shake the sand out of my shoes, and one occasion note that ahead of us walks a young man holding a curiously shaped musical instrument.

'Can I have a go?' I ask boldly.

The instrument resembles a mandolin but with a long neck, having an extended fret board strung with thick metal strings. The sound box is a smooth hemisphere of polished wood, making the instrument difficult to position comfortably. As I lightly strum the strings they produce a wonderful rich full sound. Then I play a lead run, and the peel of notes fills me with intense delight, and I'm enraptured as colourful harmonics flutter from every fret. Apparently this is one of a family of lute-type instruments, this one being known as a *baglama*.

'Thank you, merci beaucoup!' I say, handing the magical instrument back to him, my eyes quite moist. I do miss having an instrument of my own to play.

* * *

By afternoon we have hitchhiked another hundred kilometres further on, and have arrived at a town called Gabes where we find a shaded spot to rest, out of the glare of the sun. A young man stops by and engages Yolanda in conversation. The two of them chat away in French for several minutes before she calls over to me and tells me he's inviting her to go to an oasis. She seems really enthusiastic to go there. I don't respond.

Then she's all smiles, asking me to mind the baggage while she goes off.

Gritting my teeth I acquiesce, then ask her not to be long.

After half an hour I am beginning to lose my cool, such as it is, but by the time

118

Yolanda actually reappears I am seething with anger. She stands waving a newly acquired wickerwork fan, which she repeatedly wafts across her face while she continues to nonchalantly chat with her escort. I stare morosely at the pair of them.

When Yolanda and I are alone together again she behaves as though she'd only been gone a few minutes, and refuses to acknowledge that I'm hard done by in any way.

'How the hell did I know you were all right?' I ask, *'You've been gone for ages. I didn't know what was going on,'*

'I really enjoyed myself,' she tells me, *'You're spoiling it for me.'*

It's as if I've never been angrier in my life, and I can do nothing to gain relief. For me the bright sunshine only spells out gloom and I crave respite from the light. Closing my eyes helps, but only a little.

My nervous system has become strained by the angry exchange, and as we shuffle slowly away from that place I have my work cut out just to walk along without falling over. *How could Yolanda be so unfeeling and upset me so?*

We walk on in silence and as we do so I half-heartedly look out for a suitable spot for us to settle down for the night. Seeing a building site, and a partially built block of apartments, I pin my hopes on gaining access to the building and being able to find a place to sleep there. When I'm sure nobody is watching, we sneak in though a narrow chink in the netted wire fence and enter the building under construction. At least here, out of sight, we'll be reasonably safe for the night.

* * *

Sleep is a good healer and by the morrow we're in better shape, if not exactly overflowing with lovingness towards each other.

Though there's still a bit of an atmosphere, we turn our attention to finding another lift, and meeting with success we are soon speeding along on our journey again, riding in the cab of a long articulated truck. The driver has business in a town along the way, the last before the Libyan border, and on our arrival there he thoughtfully drops us off at the local washhouse so we can use the time whilst he's away, freshening ourselves up. We take to the place like those proverbial ducks, soaping ourselves thoroughly and taking turns to wash each other's backs. Amidst the bubbles we indulge in a bit of kissing and cuddling, and it seems the upsets of yesterday are forgotten now.

As we get dressed and dry each other's hair, the door of the washhouse flies open, and there stands our driver, breathless and clearly anxious about something. He makes it clear that he wants us both to hurry up, so we grab our luggage and follow him out. Once outside, he hurriedly climbs into his cabin and gets the truck moving. I look about me and see there are hordes of people lining the street, and from their manner they seem agitated. It occurs to me this might have something to do with us, that Yolanda and I were both inside the washhouse at the same time, so perhaps they have an issue with a man and woman being together there.

Dashing across the cobbled street we swing our belongings through the open door of the cab and heave ourselves up, slamming closed the door behind us. Before we are even sat down the driver puts his foot on the accelerator and pulls away, leaving the crowd of irate locals well behind. The driver gabbles away excitedly in French, and Yolanda starts to explain what he's saying, but I interrupt her.

'Yes I heard him! We're idiots, but why does he say that?' I ask.

'He doesn't say.'

With the mob well behind us now, the lorry slows to a less manic pace.

We are outside the city limits and all about us, in all directions is sand.

'Is this the Sahara?' I ask.

'Yes I think so,' Yolanda confirms.

To all sides lie vast unending sand dunes dotted with only occasional clumps of hardy vegetation. Although the road is spread with drifting sands, the wheels of the truck seem to have no trouble gripping the hot tarmac, so we are able to maintain a decent pace. Although this is a lonely place it is not without charm; there is even the occasional bird that flies across our path, and the presence of fresh tracks in the sand, made by small animals, suggests the presence of water somewhere in the area.

At few times on our journey so far have I felt more dependent or reliant on our driver and his vehicle. If we were to breakdown here how on earth would we get help?

When again I see signs of human life, in the shape of roadside buildings and a barrier, I let out such a huge sigh of relief.

Having exited Tunisia, we show our passports to the uniformed Libyan border guard, and to my surprise he indicates that he wants to go through our bags. Slipping his arm to the bottom of the rucksack he rummages about for a few moments, satisfying himself that all is in order.

'What are you looking for,' I ask, genuinely curious.

He bends his finger and cocks his thumb, and whilst squeezing an invisible trigger he mimics the sounds of gunshots. So he was looking to see if we have a handgun.

'Oh no. Definitely not,' I exclaim.

After he stamps our passports I have a quick look at the Arabic script there to see what is written, but it's all too indecipherable for me, double-Dutch.

Once the border formalities are dealt with we drive on towards Tripoli, but stop when a cafe comes into view, and our driver gets out and slumps down at the nearest table. We join him and order ourselves a snack and a drink.

A group of *beduoin* folk, attired in robes and turbans, appear out of nowhere, leading their camels along with them.

The snack is soon ready, a chunk of French bread and pickled vegetables, which we fall upon hungrily, whilst watched by the locals. From their appearance and their manner they appear hardy people, their eyes flinty and flashing, signalling their self-respect, their pride.

'Oh God. What's in this roll Yolanda?' I cry out, prising open the bread.

'I think it's chilli sauce,' she says.

'Shit, it's burning me up,' I gasp.

I have a hefty slug of *Coke* before scraping off as much of the offending red paste as I can, after which, on account of my hunger, I force down the rest of the bread.

Then, when we're all finished, we all get back into the cab, and the driver takes us right into the centre of the city of Tripoli, and once there drives down a succession of broad avenues before dropping us off.

We sit close to where we've been dropped, on a sandy foreshore by the sea, and once there I find myself suddenly clutching my stomach and shrieking out in pain. And the pain increases and the associated symptoms of digestive disorders visit me mightily. I am violently sick and repeatedly I feel the need to empty my bowels.

Fortunately, my plight does not go unnoticed, and a stranger who speaks Italian offers his assistance, and goes and buys a tub of capsules, which he assures will solve my problems. I take the medicine and though I remain really uncomfortable the worst of the illness soon passes.

'Magic, that's what these capsules are,' I marvel.

It's a shock to have suddenly fallen ill; and thinking about it I guess that the upset must have been caused by what I ate back at the cafe. Anyway, no point in sitting about pondering on it, it's time to do something useful and go and change some money, as it's just a matter of time before we'll need to buy something else here.

There's a bank close by and, since I've run out of £5 notes, I change a precious tenner, and to my surprise I discover that here in Libya the currency, like Britain, is in pounds, and what's more, I'm shocked to find that British pounds - referred to as 'sterling' - are worth less than Libyan pounds. That's a turn up for the book, as I'd always thought a British pound was the largest monetary unit in the world. But for my £10 sterling I get only nine Libyan pounds and some loose change (the coins being various multiples of decimal units called *milliemes*).

Since we are way too tired to look about for a cheap hotel for the night, we head back to the beach, and as there's no one about we feel free to spread out our bedrolls and lay ourselves down on the sand unobserved.

I wonder how come Yolanda didn't go down with a stomach upset; after all she had much the same food? Perhaps she has a 'cast iron constitution' as had my maternal grandfather, who allegedly stated that he should drink alcohol over water so as not to rust! Yolanda has purchased some cans of *Libby's* orange juice, so we satisfy our thirst and sit and watch as the light of the sun fades and disappears, giving way to a clear starry night; the moon shines brightly above us as we settle down for some well-deserved shuteye.

Chapter 9

DOWNTOWN GINGERPOPOLI

A rising amidst the first rays of astonishingly bright morning sunshine, I take in the view, a delightful expanse of light coloured sand, and I listen to the water gently lapping some metres away on this glorious Mediterranean shore. Up above us seabirds glide and soar on the wing. And I look over at my girlfriend, Yolanda, who is gazing far out to sea, an air of contentment surrounding her.

We have time to enjoy the moment; there's no need to go anywhere as yet, and certainly no need to rush about, and we take our time rolling up our sleeping bags and sorting out our packs, before taking ourselves off along the front, vaguely in search of breakfast. There we find a cafe, an Italian style *espresso* bar that provides us with frothy *cappuccino* coffee and cake. Not an ideal breakfast, but certainly a lot better than nothing.

Afterwards we decide to walk a bit further along this road the cafe is on, a promenade, which runs parallel to the seafront. Here there are long established old-fashioned looking hotels with names such as 'Grand Hotel' and 'Uaddan', the likes of which one might find on the South coast of England in places like Hastings or Bexhill, perhaps. But, in Britain there would be lawns and rose gardens, whilst here there are paved walkways, overhung and shaded by immense ancient palm trees.

A signboard directs the way to the British Consulate, and it occurs to me it might be a good idea for me to pop in there for a chat.

On our way to the consulate we get talking with a local who shows an interest in us, a chap by the name of Dowee. He reminds me of my friend Dario, in fact Dowee is the spitting image of him.

'We'll come back after we've been to the embassy,' I tell Dowee.

'Sure. Okay. I'll wait,' Dowee assures us, leaning back against his car.

Speaking with Yolanda reveals that she too has been struck by the likeness between Dowee and Dario. The similarity is quite unnerving, for not only do they both share similar bone structure, facial appearance and hair, they also have other things in common too, such as their mannerisms and their attitude.

After opening the main door of the consulate we enter a room in which several youngish looking diplomats are seated, their names displayed upon their desks, the first is called Bull, and the next is Carrington.

'Hi. Can we ask you a few questions?' I inquire.

'Of course you may. You are English?'

'Yes I am. My girlfriend here is Italian.'

'How do you do?' he asks, politely shaking hands.

Carrington surprises us when he reveals that, at present, Yolanda and I are the only western tourists in Tripoli.

I offer him a short recap of our journey so far, and explain to him that our goal is to get to India. As we chat I notice a large-scale wall map of Libya and the surrounding regions, and I study it figuring that our best plan would be to cut across Libya and pass into Egypt. As I explain myself I sense the besuited official getting increasingly flustered until he looks quite seriously ruffled.

'Impossible,' he blurts, *'you can't go across the desert; the only traffic there is the occasional oil tanker. You had better return to England. I urge you to seriously reconsider your situation.'*

I get the message loud and clear; we have clearly encountered a prize example of the 'can't' mentality, so it seems pointless to stand about arguing. We hear him out, thank him and make for the front door.

We leave the consulate and find our newfound friend Dowee waiting for us outside; and he has a proposition for us, he wants to take us for a meal in an area of Tripoli called Downtown Gingerpopoli. The mere mention of the name creases me up with laughter as the name 'Gingerpopoli', or whatever name he's saying sounds so much like 'Ginger Pop'. When I was a kid our Christmas's weren't complete unless we had some *Idris* Ginger Pop. The cause of my mirth is lost on both Yolanda and Dowee.

Coasting through Tripoli we come to an expensive looking area, a 'new town', with a wide choice of places to eat, such as *Guy and Joe's Snack Bar, Hot Meals: Red Cat and Tavola Calda*. We draw up in the car park of the Italian sounding one.

For someone so recently released from the grips of dysentery it's difficult for me to know what best to choose. I settle on something reasonably simple.

'Cheese salad and Coke,' I request, and as Yolanda nods to me, I add, *'Twice.'*

The atmosphere of the spacious restaurant is nicely relaxed. Our order is delivered promptly and I get real enjoyment tucking into the meal.

As Dowee speaks good English the three of us are able to chat easily over our meal, and I learn from him that he has visited the United States, a fact he seems inordinately proud of. It occurs to me that there are probably many Libyans like him who are attracted to the West.

* * *

Over the ensuing days we circulate around the city, and as we make friends with various Libyans we become frequent visitors to Gingerpopoli, and sample the delights of both Uptown and Downtown Tripoli.

At nights we sleep untroubled on the beach.

One morning, after waking up drenched in mist, we lie drying off in the sun, but the heat becomes so intense that we soon feel the need run off the beach in search of some shade. Later on in the day we meet with Dowee again and he suggests we might like to join him to go for a picnic on a deserted palm beach beyond Tripoli. It sounds a great idea, so we all pile into his car and Dowee drives some distance out of town, and parks up at an idyllic stretch of deserted sandy shoreline.

It seems we'll be quite alone here, the three of us.

We set up a large parasol and share a meal together before fooling around awhile, playing some beach sport on the sands. Then I take a dip in the crystal clear sea and am delighted at seeing swarms of small exotic fishes swimming there, it's like looking into a giant aquarium, one you can walk into.

Once back on the beach, I find Dowee wants to show me his camera, a *Polaroid Land* camera that can produce 'instant' pictures - I've never seen such a camera before. Dowee then takes a whole wodge of photos of us sitting around on the beach. But the heat is so great that we need to keep returning to the shade of the umbrella, to get out of the sun. We stick it out until late afternoon, and then decide to go back to town, returning of course in Dowee's car. But as we drive closer to the city limits I get the impression that all is not right with Dowee, and I hope - hope upon hope - that he's not about to spring some unwelcome surprise on us, as we've had quite enough odd encounters on our trip so far.

Dowee stops the car, and goes to speak with someone. When he returns to the car he gets in and turns to speak with us:-

'Cholera outbreak. They've sealed the city off with roadblocks,' he tells us nervously, *'But I have an idea....'*

As we now race around the outskirts of the city, churning up sand, Dowee keeps looking about him furtively, before an expression of relief flickers across his open face. Yanking wildly at the steering wheel he races the car along a narrow lane towards a gap between some buildings and just about squeezes through, with barely inches to spare.

'We've done it!' he ejaculates, clearly mightily relieved.

Safely inside the city again, Dowee pulls up and goes to confer with some men who are standing about further down the street. Returning to the car he asks us if we'd mind going with him to the hospital to get vaccinated against cholera.

We're there in a jiffy.

It's a very modern hospital and outside stand long queues of men and women, waiting in the blistering sunshine. But to my surprise Yolanda and I are immediately shepherded past the waiting populous and given red carpet treatment, in that we are whisked to the front of the queue. The doctor uses a large tool, akin to an electric drill or gun, with a needle attached, which pierces through our clothes. It's all over in a matter of moments and I hardly feel a prick. Then we're issued with little yellow vaccination cards, medical mini-passports with details of the jabs.

Whilst we're at the hospital Dowee takes the chance to find out more about what's going on.

'The American troops are restricted to base,' Dowee informs us.

'What American troops? What are they doing here?' I ask.

'Don't drink any tap water for a while,' Dowee warns, ignoring my question.

Now he takes us back to his home and introduces us to his wife. She doesn't seem to speak much English, and doesn't have a lot to say.

Dowee has a record collection so I ask him if I can put on some music. But I'm disappointed in what I find, as the hippest record I can find is an LP by Roger Whitaker! Though *'King of the Road'* is a good cut, we have also to endure the nonsense of *'Eng-a-land swings like a pendulum do, bobbies on bicycles two-by-two.'* I get to wishing I could hear my own selection of sounds, back home.

After our visit to Dowee's, Yolanda confides me a theory she has evolved, simply that Arabs like their womenfolk plump and light-skinned. She contends that accordingly they keep their women out of the sunshine and let them eat a lot.

* * *

The cholera scare has some rather unwelcome consequences; one being that suddenly there are no fizzy drinks available (the reason given being that they might contain contaminated local water) but this lack turns out to be a blessing, as the only available alternative to carbonated soft drinks is canned pineapple juice. This comes from South East Asia, with such unlikely names such as *Telephone Brand*.

On the basis of our experience in Tunisia, we think it wise to check whether or not we might need a visa in order to enter the next country on our itinerary. So, on a whim, we decide to track down the Egyptian Embassy.

We find the embassy without difficulty and are met by a charming man who listens carefully to us and then outlines our position. He explains that no one is permitted to cross into Egypt from Libya, except that they arrive by boat or aeroplane But that if we wish to travel to Egypt we will be most welcome there.

As flying is obviously out of the question, being an unnecessary expense, my first instinct is to ignore his advice and strike out for Benghazi, the next major city along the coast, and from there try our luck at the border. But there's another option to consider, the idea of arriving by sea. So before it's decided that a trip to the docks is in order.

When we find the shipping office, we explain to the clerk there that we need to get to Egypt.

'Yes there's a boat sailing for Benghazi and Alexandria on the 31st of August,' he informs us.

'We'll have two tickets to Alexandria then.' I interrupt enthusiastically.

'I was about to say.... that; due to this cholera scare the boat will not be stopping at these ports,' he adds gloomily.

'How can it go there but not stop?' I snap.

He continues his explanation, *'No, the boat will not stop at Benghazi or Alexandria. It is bound for Istanbul but also it will stop in Athens.'*

We withdraw from the shipping office and convene a meeting outside.

As we chat about it, there appear to be three options open to us. 1. We can take our chances and just go to the Egyptian border. 2. We get a boat to Italy and take an alternative route to India (an option Yolanda warms to), or 3. Take the steamer all the way to Istanbul.

There is of course a more obvious solution, and that is to take the advice of the British embassy and give up! And frankly, at this point in time, this looks by far the most realistic course of action, but I am adamant we explore our other options first.

Well, after further discussion, Yolanda and I agree on one thing, that if we're to buy any tickets whatsoever, then we'll need some extra cash, as otherwise we'll be placing an undue strain on our resources. But how can we get ourselves some extra cash sorted out whilst here in Tripoli? The situation appears desperate, but we hit on a tempting idea, that we could present ourselves back at the embassy and tell them we have lost some of our money, maybe tell that it has been stolen. Then we might be able to borrow enough for our needs?

Unfortunately, when we show up at the consulate the official on duty shows little concern for our predicament. But as we don't wish to borrow much, his lack of apparent concern for our welfare frustrates me terribly, so I become angry and frustrated. Resolutely he remains unhelpful and after a heated exchange ensues I give his desk a huge shove, causing things on his desk to jerk forwards, and papers to fall out from the drawers and become strewn across the floor.

Having given vent to my feelings I assume an indignant air and make my exit, with Yolanda trailing behind me.

If only we had something we could sell, then we'd be only too happy to sell it, but amongst our belongings we can think of nothing that has any great value.

But, remembering Yolanda's little silver pillbox, we hit on a plan, that we might offer this up for sale, and just see what happens.

Standing on the esplanade we show it to passers-by, and time after time we are met with bemused expressions as we practice our sales pitch. And repeatedly we are faced with the same smiling reactions, that no one here has any need of a little silver box, and they prove it by showing us their wrists and hands, which gleam brightly with heavy gold bracelets and rings. Then Yolanda explains to them that we don't have enough money for the boat trip.

'*Non a biamo soldi,*' she says in Italian, as many here have some grasp of the language, since Libya was for some time controlled by the Italians.

Well, once people understand our situation, some of those we speak to open their wallets and make a contribution to our funds. Their bulging wallets usually seem to contain upwards of a hundred pounds, and seeing how much money these people carry about with them I am astonished. We persist with our sales patter and in a few hours we have almost enough to almost pay for our tickets. What a good bunch of people they are, so openhearted and generous to us travellers in need, and none would take anything in exchange for the money. So we even get to keep the little silver box.

* * *

We continue to sleep on the beach at night as no one bothers us there, though we do get the occasional visitors. One night a friend of someone we know comes to visit, his name is Steevee. He doesn't have anything much to say though; he just stands there in silence, but we take the initiative to get the conversation going, and share our worry about raising enough money to get to India. Steevee at last speaks.

'*What have you got to sell?*'

'*Silver box, a penknife, nothing more,*' I say.

He appears unimpressed.

'*You sell me something. I have lots of money,*' he tells us.

Certainly this country appears to be much more affluent than Britain, so yes, I can believe he's wealthy.

'*What do you want to buy?*' I ask him.

'*I want...*' he says, very quietly.

'*Pardon. I don't hear you.*' I tell him.

'*I want **fuck**,*' he announces.

He is neither aggressive nor offensive; he has stated an answer to my question, nothing more. But where on earth has he got this idea, that Yolanda, a female tourist, would prostitute herself because we are in need of money?

'*Okay,*' I answer him: '*you want a fuck... FUCK!! There you are, now how much will you give for that?*'

Well what can I do? At least my flip response diffuses the tension. And now, without any further ado he walks back to his car and drives away.

Surprisingly, Yolanda doesn't seem particularly bothered by what the guy has just said, but she is concerned that he might get desperate.

128

Later, when our mutual friend Dowee turns up, and he hears about the incident, he can't stop apologising; he seems really angry about it.

* * *

Now, when we count our money, we find we already have enough Libyan pounds to pay for our voyage to Turkey, so we go back to the docks intent on purchasing the cheapest tickets available, so we buy two 'deck-class' tickets to Istanbul, but the departure is not for quite a few days yet, so we resign ourselves to a wait, and try to make the most of the rest of our stay here in Tripoli.

In a city where all the street signs are written in Arabic, if you can't read Arabic script then it's not at all easy to know where you are! According to what we're told, until a few months ago the streets were all signposted in English.

Another change has been to prohibit the sale of alcohol, which is now unobtainable in bars or restaurants. But despite this, some still have access to drink.

We run into someone from another part of Africa who claims to be a foreign correspondent for the *News of the World*, a trashy Sunday paper in Britain, and he invites us back to his apartment, and when we get there he attempts to ply us with rum. After succumbing to the temptation we get involved in a rather disjointed interview, and the journalist tells us he will wire the resulting story to London.

For a teetotaller there's only one thing worse than being rather drunk, and that is being a bit worse for wear in a country where liquor is illegal, thereby running the risk of discovery. Yolanda and I are now unable to walk a straight line, though we have the good sense to keep ourselves to ourselves, and definitely not let anyone smell our breath, which is no mean task when you're walking through busy streets!

When Sunday comes we go to a newsagent to look for a copy of the newspaper and read the article. Curiously though, when we arrive there we discover the proprietor stooped over the foreign newspapers, locating and scissoring out advertisements for ladies undergarments; a censorship presumably called for by the authorities. Our search for the interview is to no avail; perhaps it has already been given the chop?

* * *

The cholera jabs have caused us a fair amount of misery, as our arms have become swollen and sore, making sleep very difficult, and we've been told to return for boosters after ten days.

At Muassat Hospital, an ultra modern institution, on payment of a few coins (200 *milliemes* for each of us) we receive injections against *variole* (smallpox) and cholera, and our inoculations are recorded in little booklets known as *'International Certificates of Vaccination'*. On the certificates are affixed red postage stamps of Tripoli Castle - I am confused that the stamps are marked *Royaume de Libye* (Kingdom of Libya) as I've been led to believe that the army's in charge?

On the main street I find a stall selling an odd assortment of items, including framed photographs and nail clippers, and I have the choice between a pair of clippers that is embellished with a green and gold bird sitting on a branch, and another with a photograph of a man in army uniform. Amongst the other items for sale are various other pictures of this man, and one, which is captioned beneath, so I am able to identify the man as Colonel Muammar Quadafi, and I wonder that perhaps it was his idea to ban alcohol and take down the English street signs?

* * *

A Libyan friend, who calls himself Rok, tells us about himself, that he works in oil and has come to Tripoli for a break. He confides that he's worried for our welfare and safety, and wants to take any available opportunity to look after us.

One evening he suggests that we all go to the cinema. A British film is showing, 'Kelly's Heroes'; and even though I'm no movie buff, I'm most especially not interested in war films, but I agree to the outing all the same. It's a bizarre experience, as the film is dubbed in Arabic with English subtitles.

Afterwards Rok announces that he wants Yolanda and myself to go and stay in a hotel at his expense, but he has his work cut out in order to convince us.

We like sleeping on the beach, and we feel moderately safe and very happy there. However, he's not convinced, and so eventually, to avoid causing offence, we reluctantly agree to his proposal.

'How can we repay you?' I ask.

'A postcard.. Send me a postcard, that's all I want from you,' he answers. He's a rock, true to his name.

Actually, in the event, I don't enjoy staying in the hotel at all, as I yearn for the open sky and the sound of the water lapping. It's **so** claustrophobic being inside, and even though there are cooling fans pushing the air about, it gets far, far too hot for us. So we stay at the hotel only the one night.

* * *

The longer we remain in Tripoli, the more we love it, we love the weather, the people (with but few exceptions), the affluence and the location; which are all really good reasons to want to stay and settle down in a place. From what we learn, the population here is low and the gross income is high, so workers are paid very high wages. The problem is only that they have too little to spend the money on. We hear that Libyans go away and holiday in resorts such as Tunis and Beirut.

Since the national economy is very prosperous, new developments flourish here. It seems that after years of foreign rule, the Italians from 1911 to 1943, and then the Allies from 1943 to 1951, the Libyans are now calling the shots. The only dissent we hear of concerns the prohibition of alcohol, which has resulted in the Italian-style nightclubs of Giorgimpopoli, which were licensed to serve alcohol, are now only selling soft drinks. I had mistakenly thought the area to be called Gingerpopoli, but in the light of the prohibition this would be quite an appropriate name.

One afternoon we get taken to visit a downtown club that's decked out with nautical trappings, and whilst there we receive an invitation to stay over at an ex-pat's house, where we are offered homemade alcohol, the results of D-I-Y distilling. But despite passing up the booze, we do get to enjoy the luxuries of sleeping between fresh sheets and having access to a proper bathroom.

When morning comes I have an urge to wash my purple sweatshirt, and having done so I hang it outside on the fence to dry. Being an impatient sort I leave it for barely a quarter of an hour before going to check its progress and am shocked to find it's completely dry already.

'Totally unbelievable,' I exclaim, *'Yolanda, look at this!'*

Not only is the shirt bone dry but it's also gone two-tone, the sun having all but bleached the top half of the front!

* * *

All the concern that's been expressed over our safety finally gets to us! We've now become infected by the irrational worries of others to the point where we really don't feel safe on our own patch of beach anymore. So when we hear that one of our friends has an acquaintance that owns a beach hut on the other side of town, we are well and truly baited.

We take ourselves off down to see the guys at the beach hut colony, and after introductions are over I raise the matter of our need for accommodation, that we have been told we could stay here.

'He said you agreed to let us stay the night,' I explain

'Oh really?' the owner asks, assuming an air of surprise, which barely masks his devious smile.

'Yes. Is it okay?' I continue.

'What's in it for me?' he asks, casting a lewd look in Yolanda's direction. His many friends stand about us, watching and waiting.

'What do you mean exactly?' I enquire suspiciously.

He explains…. So, here we are again, someone else who wants to have sex with Yolanda, but this time it feels much more threatening and dangerous, that there's the potential of this situation turning into a rape scene.

As I stand there facing the guy and his gang, I realise in a flash we're outnumbered and trapped, therefore I figure I have to assert myself, and do so right now. Quite suddenly and without warning I thump him in the face. His friends just stare, then Yolanda and I storm off, leaving him to nurse his nose and his bruised ego.

I must admit to being mightily relieved that none of his friends came to his aid, as I imagine that, had I not jumped in, Yolanda would have been raped, and possibly we'd both be killed. But, as it is, they just stand there and watch us walk away.

My hand really hurts! I cannot move my thumb, and I realise that in the heat of the moment my thumb must have got wedged within my fist, so when I thumped him, I crushed my thumb.

'It might be broken,' I moan, *'I can't move it.'*

Yolanda looks at me warmly. She seems impressed at my chivalrous deed.

A few days before, it happened that that Yolanda and I had fallen out over some trivial matter and she had threatened to go back to Italy.

'Not without a passport you don't,' I had said, patting our passports, conveniently tucked away.

After the disagreement had passed, and the dust had settled, I offered to go to the shipping office and arrange her trip back to Italy, as I didn't like to think she might only stay with me on account of my holding the passports.

'I didn't mean it,' she assures me.

'Well anyway, why don't you look after your own passport from now on?' I suggest.

'Would you mind if I said "shut up"?' says Yolanda, kind of closing the topic.

* * *

We are due to sail tomorrow, and it seems almost too good to be true when we get an invitation to go back to someone's house for supper, with the promise of overnight accommodation too. Things couldn't really be working out better, for this our last evening in Tripoli.

In the event, our host has to go out, and he leaves us in the company of his Sudanese cook-cum-housekeeper, a massive dark-skinned giant. This man seems to take a liking to us and we to him, and though he only communicates with a little pidgin Italian, we nonetheless have a reasonable idea what he's saying.

He prepares a meal for us consisting of cooked meat and vegetables.

'Manjaaree, manjaaree ' he keeps saying, cajoling us to eat and eat and eat.

By way of casual conversation, somehow the topic of our picnic with Dowee gets a mention and I we get out his *Polaroid* pictures. As soon as he sees the photos the Sudanese cook demands that we give them to him, but we don't really want to part with our mementoes. As the cook becomes quite pressing reluctantly we release our grip on the photos, but during the course of the evening he becomes increasingly oppressive and overbearing. I can't be sure whether it's because he's been drinking or if this is his normal temperament. The atmosphere has become tense and I sense that we'd do well, very well, to leave his company at the earliest opportunity. Actually, I'm in fear for our safety and in particular for that of my girlfriend. I know that if it came to a confrontation I would be pulverised, so the only answer lies in our escape, and when he disappears to do some washing up, very quietly we get up, open the front door and run for it.

With baggage swinging from our shoulders we hurtle off down the street, not even looking back to see if he's following us in pursuit.

Flustered and breathless we make a bee-line for the harbour, for it seems foolhardy to return to our place on the beach, where he would easily be able to find us.

So we spend the evening and the whole night uncomfortably sitting at a table by a cafe close to the dock. But at least we feel safe!

* * *

In the morning we think to pick up some provisions for the voyage before presenting ourselves at the dockside customs hut. We must appear a decidedly grim pair of individuals.

'I'll be glad to get away from Libya,' I remark to my girlfriend bitterly.

Our passports and medical papers are checked, then, without explanation, the officer requests for us to enter a small room just along the corridor.

I have a feeling of impending doom. The officer sits us down and tells us we have breached the terms of our visa. But in truth, I've been unable to read my visa, which is in Arabic, but it seems that somewhere, very lightly stamped, there's an order to register with the police. When this is pointed out to me I apologise for my oversight, though it occurs to me that the police must have been aware of our every move on the streets of Tripoli, after all we must have stuck out like a sore thumb, being the only tourists there.

Long we are questioned, nay, interrogated, about our stay in Tripoli and as the questioning persists, I worry that we'll miss the boat, and worse.

'You don't like Libya?' the most important looking officer asks us dramatically.

The penny drops. So this is what all the fuss is about; someone must have overheard me talking outside. Oops, me and my big mouth!

How can I explain to these officials how much we've enjoyed staying in Tripoli, but that we've had a few problems? There being the creepy guy who made sexual advances towards Yolanda, the run-in with the gang of youths, and our needing to get away from the drunken cook! But it would only complicate things for everyone if I were to mention these incidents, so instead I go for the direct approach.

'We really like your country,' I tell them, *'Really! We just had an upsetting day yesterday, and we didn't sleep at all last night,'* I answer truthfully.

The policeman looks relieved. His fellow officers also look relieved.

'Then you like Libya?' he smiles.

We nod vigorously. Grins all round and back slapping too. There are no more questions. We are free to go!

'That was amazing,' I whisper to Yolanda, after the officials disappear. *'They really*

care about what we think, don't they? I can't see that sort of thing happening back in England.'

Yolanda nods and echoes my feelings.

We pick up our bags and make our way to the gangway of the steamer.

There, the captain of the SS Kades courteously welcomes us aboard his ship, and to my deep consternation takes charge of our passports.

The captain introduces us to a member of the crew and informs us that the man is responsible for us and will show us to our 'quarters'. Now that sounds pretty grand but perhaps there's been a mix-up? I'd assumed that since we're travelling with only deck class tickets we'd be spending the entire voyage on deck, in a deck chair perhaps. Anyway, we walk with the crewmember and descend below deck where we're shown into a large space filled with bunk beds. There's just one other person here, a young European, lying in a bunk reading. He lifts up his eyes and watches us as the steward shows us about.

It transpires that Anthony, for that is his name, has sailed from Tunis with the intention of visiting Libya, though his plan has been scuppered by the cholera business. We settle down and listen to his tale, and he explains that he's undertaking a gradual *'overland'* trip to Australia, during which he intends to spend his time *'following the sun'* to secure a whole year of sunshine - a novel concept to me.

As Anthony's story unfolds, I discover his most recent job has been as a salesman in that most famous London store, *Harrods*. Now he wants to travel the world, and as a part of his plan he intends to find work in Australia. I have to hand it to him, he's certainly seizing his opportunities, and I admire him for that.

Anthony has a lot to say, perhaps as a result of his travelling alone for so long. He complains of the cockroaches and at the overheating onboard and points out to us that the vessel that we're sailing in is actually a former Nazi mine sweeper, which has been converted, and that we're staying in what used to be the equipment area.

There is some German insignia and some cast metal signs around our quarters, in *Deutsch*, all of which seem to bear out his claim.

Anthony just doesn't stop talking.

He produces a map and with his finger traces out his intended route for us.

'To Istanbul via Greece, then through Turkey by train, buses through Persia, or Iran as it's known. Afghanistan, Pakistan, India. After that I'll sail to Indonesia and maybe fly on to Australia,' he explains. I can't help but notice he has two copies of the map, one spread out on the bunk, and another lying folded by his side. I ask him why?

'Oh, one of them I use as a fly swatter,' he replies, somewhat defensively.

Well, I'm no champion of flies, but in truth I'm in half a mind to try and coax the swatter off him.

There are bunks enough for dozens of people, so it seems odd that there's only the three of us here, though I have no problem with this arrangement as it will certainly give us more than enough space to get along with one another.

'Would you like to see the rest of the boat?' Anthony offers, *'I'll show you the galley. It's a bit pricey, two dollars a meal.'*

'Yes, let's go. But I don't like the sound of the two-dollar touch though. Don't they have any snacks there?' I puzzle, there being only about $2.40 to the pound.

Up winding metal staircases and along corridors, and even though it's clearly not a luxury liner I do catch sight of some rather plush looking cabins, then we go down more winding staircases, then along more corridors and we're back in the mine sweeping area. The walk around the boat is most enjoyable.

And it now appears that we are four, for the luggage of another deck class person, which includes a cardboard crate containing a television set, lies neatly placed by a bunk on the far side. Nearby the luggage stands a heavily tanned little chap who we soon discover is charm itself. He appears such a very gentle soul and I immediately feel endeared towards him.

Yolanda, Anthony and myself get down to some intense talking, and we barely notice the ship's departure from Tripoli harbour.

We talk for ages about this and that, and the topic returns once more to bugs, and Anthony has lots to say about these. With a haunted look on his face and a great furrowing of his brow, he describes the cockroaches he's seen, really huge ones, many of which live in our quarters, he says. Yolanda sits spellbound.

'How big? Ohhh, no, I don't belie-e-e-ve it,' she coos.

'Perhaps it's the heat that attracts them. Can't you open the windows?' I suggest.

'Can't open the portholes, the Turkish guy's got the key. But if you think this is hot, then just wait! That's all I've got to say!' he splutters.

'Oh we'll open them, don't worry,' I tell him, optimistically. *'I bet there's a way. I'll try to figure it out in the morning.'*

Before turning in for some sleep, Yolanda and I have a last mosey around the vessel, and standing out on deck we find ourselves staring out at the star-studded firmament about us. It's just wonderful.

Returning below I glance over at where we met the new guy, and see a sight that shakes me.

'Hey, look you guys,' I whisper.

There on the bunk lies a mummy, an Egyptian style mummy. Neatly tucked under the feet and head, the spotless white sheet clings to a still and lifeless human form!

Deeply shocked we all stand around staring intently at it, hoping in vain to see some signs of life.

Chapter 10

PORPOISES OUT OF NOWHERE

In the clear light of day. with sunlight shining through our portholes, things look very pleasant here below deck. Certainly, the two tier bunk beds that proliferate our quarters are preferable to sitting on deckchairs, and as yet there are no fresh sightings of any giant cockroaches.

The mummified corpse is gone, and the bed where it was laid is freshly made, and there's a gentle looking man standing nearby the bunk, beaming a warm smile at me. I take a leap of faith and hazard a guess as to the identity of the corpse.

'Hi! How do you sleep all wrapped up like that?'

'Sleep? Yes! How you are?' he answers falteringly.

Though it's plain he understands very little English, I persevere and try to strike up a conversation with him.

'You sleep with a sheet over you? How do you breathe?'

'I go home Pakistan,' he replies nervously.

'Do you all sleep like that in Pakistan?'

'I television take Pakistan. Good television.'

'You buy television, Tripoli?' I ask, trying it his way!

'Tripoli. Yes. Go home Pakistan.'

'Very good. I go breakfast. I later see you.'

'Yes, later see you.'

Yolanda and I make our way through the boat in search of the galley, and once there we wait to be served.

'One breakfast please.'

'Only one?' the steward asks in surprise.

'One breakfast, yes. But can we have two cups?'

Seated at other tables are the cabin passengers; and something warns me not to strike up conversation with them, for I sense they feel superior to us. Isn't it strange how people convince themselves that they're better than others, keeping themselves in a state of separation, a kind of apartheid? Such peoples' realities co-exist with one's own but they don't necessarily have a meeting point.

But even with regards to my own reality there are many unanswered questions, here I am floating somewhere off the coast of North Africa, and in search of my identity. We are truly out at sea, but pointed in the direction of the mysterious east. Persia and India, what mysteries do they hold for us?

Our breakfast arrives, consisting of a pot of tea, a bowl of porridge and some toast and jam. We share it equally between us, 50/50. For myself it feels life saving, as I haven't had a hot drink or any sustenance in quite a while.

When we're done, we go back below deck where I poke around our quarters, nosing about.

'I've got it!' I call out to Yolanda.

'What?' she puzzles.

'I've got the answer, we'll be alright now.'

'Oh I see what you mean. It's a lot better now!' Yolanda says, relieved.

I get a glow of satisfaction.

'I can't understand why the windows were closed in the first place,' Yolanda exclaims.

Anthony has had his breakfast and is now returning, and immediately he notices a difference. *'Great. You've really done it. I just hope he doesn't find out you found the key.'*

'We sleep here, it's our business, he can stuff it!' I scoff. *'Anyway he's a creep, the opposition. Spot the opposition and you're halfway there,'* I quip, in a mood of self-congratulation.

We spend another day loafing about the boat.

Yolanda seems to want to wash anything she can lay her hands on, and soon there are knickers, bras and blouses all hanging across the network of pipes.

Anthony continues to use the spare map as a fly swatter. He really needs to realise that this is not an appropriate use for such a valuable resource, so I continue to look over at him, and at the map. I suppose I'm trying to connect with him psychically.

'You did well to get your jabs in Libya,' chirps Anthony, *'but why didn't you get them in London before you left?'*

'We didn't know we needed any,' I explain.

'Well, you probably couldn't get into some countries without them. Anyway, it's better to have them, for your own sake.'

He has a point.

'I went to Istanbul last year. It's great there, fantastic food and cheap too,' Anthony enthuses.

Since the discussion has turned to diet we tell him of the butchers we saw in Algeria. He nods, *'They eat anything. Horses even. You name it!'*

'Shall we change the subject?' I ask.

We stop talking, and everything falls silent

'Indians don't eat meat,' Anthony suddenly announces, *'the cow is sacred in India. When you buy sandals there, sometimes they have a stamp on them denoting that the cow died a natural death. I'm going to get a pair, I also want a pendant like the one John Lennon wears.'*

It seems that India holds a strong attraction for Anthony; it's strange how the three of us are being pulled there.

Anthony peers over at me, gives me a steady look and without a sound passes over the map.

Yeaahhhh! Yolanda and I now have our very own map of Turkey, Persia and Afghanistan. I open it and study it awhile, but nothing sticks, just a huge section of printed-paper with endless lines running across it. Since it doesn't cover the area that we're in right now I close it and save it for later, but not before brushing off the remains of the squashed flies.

Curiously enough, just to be in possession of the map makes me feel much more confidant that some day we'll get to India, maybe.

Treading the deck I realise that, looking in any direction, no vestige of land can be seen from the ship, and instead there lies one unending expanse of placid blue water. Undeniably a pretty sight for a picture, it's daunting to feel so cut off from dry land. Never before have I been this far out to sea and I'm stunned at the isolation here. This ship is not only our home; it's also our city, our world.

Apart from the few metal plates and insignias with German text on them, thankfully there is nothing else to remind us that the ship was once used in warfare. The crew are all Turks; which makes it difficult when it comes to making oneself understood. From time to time, when I wander around the vessel, I sometimes notice members of the crew prostrating themselves on rugs. I report my finding to Yolanda and Anthony.

'They're Moslems, they're praying,' Yolanda states confidently.

'They're doing it all the time,' adds Anthony. *'At regular intervals in the day. They pray towards Mecca in Arabia.'*

'What's the difference between Moslems and Mohammedans then?' I ask, eager to clear up a few confusions.

'Same thing,' Yolanda says.

'Same,' Anthony says.

'Buddhists?' I ask, pressing my luck.

'India, Burma, Thailand and all those countries,' Anthony explains.

'Are the cows sacred to all of them?' I puzzle.

'Oh that's in India, the Hindus,' Yolanda corrects.

'Yes. I know a bit about Hindus. I went to school with a couple of those. Bashir, and Deepak Mathur, nice quiet people, I think they were both Hindu. They seemed to me as if they were very contented, not easily put out, neither of them.'

'Buddhists pray to Buddha. He believed you should give up all desires and seek Nirvana,' explains Yolanda.

'Isn't seeking Nirvana a desire?' I ask sincerely, *'But what or where is Nirvana anyway? Is it in India?'* I suggest, my tongue deeply in my cheek.

'It's a state of peace, enlightenment,' explains Yolanda patiently.

'The Hare Krishnas are into that, aren't they? I saw some of them in Hyde Park. They didn't appeal to me. They had this magazine 'Back to Godhead'. What's all that about, never heard of Godhead before?'

'Godhead is Enlightenment. It's all about losing the ego,' explains Yolanda eagerly.

'I'm not sure about that. It seems to me that it's necessary to have an ego. Nobody would make it very far if they didn't have egos. Everyone needs a sense of identity. But isn't that what happened to Pete Green and Syd Barrett? They took so much acid that they lost their egos? I think I almost lost my ego for a time, you know? It was ghastly, I'm only just over it now, thank God!'

'You don't understand,' Yolanda states coldly.

'I try....!' I reply honestly.

* * *

It's so peaceful, sitting around on deck; mind you, we're starting to get decidedly peckish as our rations of juice, biscuits and fruit are rapidly zeroing out, but we really can't afford to buy meals in the restaurant. It's no fun getting this hungry, it's got so that when I move past any crew members I tend to stare at them; attempting to telepathise my needs. But it doesn't seem to work, and when I discuss the problem with Yolanda I find that she's been doing the self-same thing!

'Oh, roll on Greece; maybe we'll be able to buy something suitable to eat there?' I wonder.

When darkness descends again we find ourselves down in our quarters, chatting away to one another again. In these conversations we seem to be on a contact high.

139

Tonight I'm wearing my *djellaba* and both Anthony and Yolanda seem to be greatly amused when I launch into an impression of Richie Havens singing and playing *'Freedom'*. In truth I enjoy myself immensely, cavorting about until I finally collapse in a heap, exhausted, splitting my sides laughing.

* * *

Strangely, we never ever seem to see the steward who's in charge of us, but as far as we're concerned this is a good thing, since he would most likely go crazy at us for opening the portholes. But as these are well above the water level there's no danger of seawater getting in.

I stick my face out through the porthole and see a movement in the water close by.

'Look you two! Sharks!' I shout excitedly.

'Let's go up on deck, we'll get a better view,' suggests Anthony.

Hurtling up the metal staircase we're met with such a wonderful sight; a whole school of dolphins swimming and dancing about, near the ship.

'Porpoises,' Anthony states informedly. *'They're probably after food. The kitchen's probably been throwing some food out. Yes, look over there.'*

I see all sorts of debris bobbing up and down in the water. Yes, it might well be food I suppose. But why is the kitchen throwing away food?

'I'm hungry,' I say involuntarily.

Anthony does not reply. It's an open secret that he eats regularly at the restaurant and I suspect he feels a bit uncomfortable sliding off and leaving us while he fills his stomach.

I'm curious as to how the porpoises know the food is being thrown out. I wonder if telepathy really does occur?

As Yolanda and I stand about on deck, the Ship's Mate sidles up and makes himself known to us, inviting us to his cabin for a meal!

* * *

The spread is fantastic and we eagerly tuck in to the various dishes arrayed about the table. I have a thirst on me too, and so I get through glass after glass of water. But it seems to me the water has a slightly aniseed taste to it, which is pleasant enough. I don't complain, but it is a little odd.

We really enjoy the food but gradually get to a point where we can eat no more. We are well and truly stuffed!

It's a jolly gathering, and I for one am immensely grateful to be eating a square meal again.

The mate leans over and tops up our glasses again with water, and this time the water seems to go cloudy, but though I'm curious why, I make no comment.

When the time comes for us to leave I ready myself to get up from the table, and I start to stand up but I don't understand why my legs cannot support me, why I unceremoniously slump back into my seat.

Have I eaten too much food?

I try again, and again, but each time I try, I slide back into my seat. Yolanda seems to have the same problem too. The crewmembers laugh uproariously.

With difficulty we force ourselves up and make our way back out of the quarters, staggering down the corridor, and then fairly falling down the stairs, all the while giggling and laughing aloud.

The truth finally dawns on us both, that we're drunk!

We sway our way into the shower room, strip off our clothes, and take a *'douche'*, a shower, before collapsing on our bunk beds draped in towels.

On our way we meet no one, there's no one about, which is just as well as we now find ourselves entwined in each other's limbs, doing what our intoxicated bodies dictate.

* * *

It's dark when I awake.

I feel giddy and more than a little wiped out.

My self-respect takes a tumble as I feel awkward and slightly depressed.

I remain lying down awhile and only start to get up when I start to feel relatively sober. I get dressed and go to chat with Anthony. When he hears about the meal, he looks downright jealous, and doesn't look any less peeved when I tell him of the cloudy water and of our drunkenness.

'Hali raaki, Turkish whisky, a bit like Greek ouzo. Strong stuff. But you've found that out, haven't you?'

I roll my eyes.

I search for my toothbrush and go off to clean my teeth.

'No more booze for me. Never again!' I mutter to myself, still half smashed, and I get back into bed.

We must have been sleeping for quite a while longer before I have the dream. In my dream I'm lying in the rain, and the rain is falling in torrents. I stir slightly and then continue with the dream. More water is falling; but now it's falling heavily on my face.

I wake up gasping.

'Oh shit. Yolanda, Yolanda, wake up, wake up! We're being flooded!'

'Oh my God,' she panics, *'the floor is covered.'*

Whipping out of bed I slam shut first one porthole, then another, and then another in an attempt to contain the problem. Anthony comes down the gangway sloshing through the swirling storm water. I reckon he wants to help me but what can he do?

'We're gonna be for it, look who's here!' Anthony warns.

I look behind him and catch sight of one very angry Turkish steward.

Finding brooms and mops we work hard to clear the water, and it's very much later before I feel free to take a break, then I find a dry bunk to rest in and stretch out, satisfied that the problem has been dealt with. But I haven't been resting long when I become aware of someone standing by my side; it's Anthony again.

'He's looking for the key,' he confides in a hushed whisper.

'Well he can look!' I retort.

*'He's **really** angry,'* Anthony continues.

'The windows are all closed, so what's his problem? Besides, if he had come and checked down here before, he would have known that they were open. He only kept them locked so he wouldn't have to bother to check. And meantime we roasted.'

I hear Yolanda mutter her agreement.

'What a cretin he is,' she remarks, *'but we had better give him his bloody key though. He looks like he's really in a mood.'*

'Let him stew. If he's still looking for it later then, well, somehow he'll find it... Somewhere...? On the pipes maybe? Don't worry about it!'

Well after the storm is over the steward still persists in searching for the key, so I join in the search, and manage to 'find' the key somewhere behind the pipes.

He departs only after he has checked that every porthole is closed and locked tight, knowing that we'll not be able to re-open them. The temperature is already rising again, and I guess that somewhere, hidden from view, the cockroaches are getting ready to run riot again!

* * *

'What are your star signs?' Anthony asks us, out of the blue.

'I'm a Cancerian,' Yolanda obliges.

'And you Paul?'

'I'm not sure. Someone did my numbers for me; a friend of mine called Nick. He said my number is 2 and I'm a double moon.' I offer.

Anthony looks at me uncertainly and asks me on what date I was born.

'1952, on June the eleventh.'

'Ah, you're a Gemini. The sign of the twin.'

'Oh, is that good?' I wonder.

'It's an air sign.'

Fine I'm a double moon, twin air sign Gemini. No surprise in that! What a load of balls!

I don't like all this star sign claptrap. It smacks of fake stuff; I like the real hippy thing, the real people, like Jimi Hendrix, Donovan, Arthur Brown, John the Bog, anyone who doesn't fake it. Don't give me star signs, shoulder bags and brown rice; give me a guitar, a light show and some good friends. Pseuds! I don't like pseuds. Perhaps that's cos I'm a double moon Gemini or whatever.

John 'the Bog' worked at UFO, the legendary hippy hangout. When I met up with him we travelled across London in a taxi. We were drafted in to test some crystal LSD of unknown strength. We had heard of each other before. So, how did we fare with the testing of the crystals? Fine... absolutely fine, on account of the fact that, whatever the crystal was, it wasn't LSD, and thus we saved the guy who was thinking of buying the stuff a huge amount of money.

Anyway, hippies aren't only people who squat in expensive buildings on Piccadilly. Why I knew a hippie that would sometimes wear a suit. Hippiedom is a state of mind, and most hippies just want to have fun and have adventures. I would say that most people I would describe as being hippies tend to question authority, are basically straightforward, reasonably honest, joyous people, and are sometimes even a touch mystical, and generally not violent unless really riled or provoked.

We were the ones that took risks. I guess John was nuts in his own way, and I was nuts too in my own way. Risks paid off! We had a ball and that's what counted. John in fact had a veritable harem of girls following him around (lucky him).

But all that crazy stuff is over nowadays, at least for me, anyway.

We had an intense immersion in psychedelics and a great taste of the 'good life', which opened doors to a greater awareness, and now we have to find a way of making those magical experiences into a long-term thing. A permanent high perhaps, or something like that? The mission now is to find the answers. That's why I have to travel. Somewhere out there are maybe people who have it sussed, surely there are? At least maybe if I can find some little bits of suss, I could fuse them all together and get the answer. I feel I have a purpose, a man with a mission!

'We're approaching Greece,' announces the ever-informative Anthony.

Sure enough, on the horizon, though only indistinctly, I can see land.

But it's a very long time before we come anywhere close to it.

Actually, the land mass turns out to be an island without any visible signs of habitation, the first in a chain of islands we pass.

As night starts to fall the islands glisten with tiny specks of light.

Hour after hour I sit watching, until a cloak of darkness gradually gathers us in its folds. Now, only the beautiful array of sparkling lights offers any clue as to where land lies. Like clusters of precious stones they are, set in wonderful designs.

Is it all by chance I wonder - an accidental artwork for a passing ship to view?

When I return below deck again I ask Anthony about the islands.

'There are hundreds of them,' he tells me.

'I wonder how many more islands before we get to Athens?' I marvel.

Anthony looks kind of bleary.

'I'm crashing out now. Athens can wait,' he says.

We're all agreed on that.

* * *

It's a slow awakening for me this morning, then I sigh, stretch and swing myself onto the edge of the bunk.

Through the porthole I can see other ships, moored and stationary, but our ship is moving, though only very slowly.

Anthony is looking out another porthole, next to his bunk.

'This is the port of Piraeus,' he announces, *'Athens is inland, a fair distance from here.'*

'So we won't have time to visit it?' I ask him, disappointed.

'I should stick to the port. We're only stopping for an hour or so.'

Yolanda and I make ourselves ready to get off the boat.

'Anthony, we only have large notes. Have you got anything smaller?'

'Here's an American dollar. Pay me back when we get to Turkey.'

'Great!'

The ship has stopped and all the necessary nautical procedural things are now being done to secure us to the land. As we approach the gangway we catch sight of the captain, who waves to us. He returns to us our passports before we disembark.

We walk along the dockside and find somewhere we can change some money, converting the US dollar to *drachma*, the currency of Greece.

My first impressions of Piraeus are not favourable, but after having been at sea for several days, we're not about to pass up this opportunity of enjoying a change of scene, so we stay.

We make for a cafe where we find our dollar's worth of Greek *drachma* change is barely sufficient to buy us a coffee and a roll each. Greece is very famous for its coffee so I can't wait to try the real thing. Personally though, I find the coffee rather

144

strong, and after drinking a measure I discover a large deposit of what looks like mud at the bottom of the cup, so I clench my teeth to filter the thick contents of the remaining coffee. Disgusted, I beg a glass of water to wash my mouth clean of the sediment.

With the remaining Greek money I go in search of a postcard for my mother. Though she's never travelled here she's exceptionally fond of all things Greek; she just loves the music, Nana Mouskouri and all that *bazouki*.

I find some cards, and calculate that just one of them will cost us our remaining Greek coins.

'What's this?' I ask myself, looking at a selection of cards. *'The Acropolis. Ah this will do nicely. A picture of some ancient ruins. Oughtn't they to rebuild it, it's falling to pieces?'*

'Are you going to post it?' Yolanda asks.

'We haven't got any more Greek money.'

'I hope your mum's alright.'

'Do you know, we've been away nearly six weeks? Over forty days and forty nights.'

'I don't belie-e-eve it!'

'It's true, work it out for yourself,' I suggest, silently amazed myself.

When we return to the ship, things are looking very busy.

We stand and watch as a large white van is hoisted from the quay and lowered onto the deck, then a couple of the crew release the ropes that tie it to the crane.

Down below deck are a group of German youngsters, whose van it is. Anthony seems delighted they're here; he appears to relish the opportunity of meeting new people. I join Anthony in welcoming the newcomers, but it's doesn't come easy, as I have been inculcated with anti-German attitudes, with comics, films and jokes portraying the German people as being arrogant, aggressive and insensitive.

'They've come to reclaim their minesweeper,' I whisper to Yolanda.

The new visitors are pleasant enough; two young couples. Their spokesman is an engaging young man called Hans, and his girlfriend is the very attractive Monick. The other couple, Gretta and Christian, seem to have a looser connection. Whether they have fallen out with each other or were never together is unclear.

Not very much passes by way of conversation on account of mutual problems of language. There is something about Monick that I find distracting, and it's not just her long black hair, her sexy figure or her self-confidence.

I'm puzzled that these couples are travelling with us in deck class as they look far from being poor. Their clothes, their luggage, everything about them speaks loudly of they're coming from well-off families. But, regardless as to why they have chosen to slum it, I get used to the extra occupants in our quarters. No one else joins us in deck class, so there's still more than enough room for us all to spread out. The German group annexes bunks at some distance from us, whilst Anthony keeps his place in the corner and our friend from Pakistan occupies a bunk near the door.

Anthony soon recovers from the novelty of the company of the newcomers, and returns to his reading, and getting on with his writing, and from time to time we fall back to our usual occupation, with Anthony, Yolanda and myself, just the three of us, chatting.

Anthony figures that this might well be our last night on board, and thinks that we'll soon be in Turkish waters.

So it won't be so very long before we'll be in Istanbul, which Anthony tells us is the current name of the ancient city of Byzantium, which also known as Constantinople.

* * *

The commotion startles me, I don't know how long I've slept but I sit up and try to take in the situation.

In the half-light I can just about make out the scantily clad figure of Monick lying in her bunk, and beside her stands a burly official - with a revolver clipped on his belt - who with a cigarette in hand is leaning over her, and seems to be questioning her.

I haven't seen him about before, and from his over-confidant swaggering manner I suspect he's drunk. He certainly looks a bit heavy. I wonder what he wants of her, coming here in the middle of the night, but I can't tell if she's frightened of him or not, so I lie back down again and try to go back to sleep.

I sleep only fitfully and each time I wake I notice the same guy prowling around our quarters. Again he stands staring at the Germans in their bunks, his manner is intimating. He lights another cigarette and talks to an acquaintance. I hear their gruff voices but I cannot make out a word of what they're saying. It feels quite unreal, as if we are caught in a movie, but without having been told the plot. *What are these guys about? What's their game?*

When I awake again the officials have moved away from Monick and now appear to be checking the seals on the locked doors, the doors with the German insignia on.

I start to wonder what is locked behind the doors.

Yolanda is now awake, and we whisper to one another, trying to work out who the guys are. We figure they are probably customs men who must have come aboard after we left Athens.

I am so relieved when at last they leave.

* * *

I awake again, this time to the sound of shouting.

'Darda nell. Darda nell,' a voice booms.

For all I know this could well be the Turkish for 'Abandon Ship' so I waste no time delaying; I leap out of my bunk and pull on my clothes.

After making sure Yolanda is following me, I go up on deck to try to discover the cause of the commotion.

On deck there are a few people milling about in the grim dim grey light, but as nobody is wearing life jackets and all appears to be calm, I figure there is no need to panic. Yolanda joins me, and we stand about, trying to understand what is going on.

'Darda nell,' a Turk informs us, winking.

It is cold, and nothing appears to be happening so we go back down below.

'I wonder if Ant knows what's going on?' I wonder.

'Is that creep with the gun still about,' Yolanda asks, *'Did you see him waving it about? What was his scene with the German chick?'*

'Heavy guy. It seemed like he was gonna rape her!' I respond.

'He came round our side and was staring at me too. He really gave me the creeps. Has he gone?'

'I haven't seen him. There's Anthony. Hey Anthony what's going on?'

'Darda Nells.'

'What's Darda Nells? The guy woke me up shouting that.'

'D-A-R-D-A-N-E-L-L-E-S, haven't you heard of it? Really famous place. Churchill. Ancient history. Famous place.' Anthony informs us.

What with the mist, the visibility outside is approximately zero, so we can only just make out the fuzzy outline of the distant shore.

'Huh. Is this what they woke us up to see? They must be mad,' Yolanda grumbles.

After the disturbed night I really wonder if it's really worth waiting here, but we sit it out for about two hours, and then I feel we've earned the right to return down below. Though Anthony looks tired too, his eyes are glazed and staring, he stays on deck, seemingly performing some kind of vigil.

The morning drags by, but my spirits rise when a message gets passed around that we'll soon be arriving at Istanbul.

Bags are quickly packed and we make ourselves ready up on deck, but it's several more hours before we actually dock.

The little man who has been so quiet, who has the unusual habit of wrapping himself up to sleep, now joins us. He seems quite emotional.

'When you come Pakistan, you come my hotel,' he says, handing me a scrap of paper with his address - Mustapha, Crown Hotel, Gujvanwala.

'Thank you. We come see you,' I say, shaking his hand.

'What a sweet guy,' Yolanda whispers.

Anthony, who is now wide-awake asks us, *'What are you going to do now? Are you going to stay in Istanbul?'*

'Yup. I want to see the bazaar you mentioned,' I say.

'You're going to need visas for Iran, you know. Shall we join forces and look for a place together?'

'Sure, we get on well don't we?'

The ship's mate approaches me and I thank him again for the meal, which was a lifesaver; and after all, he wasn't to know that I'm teetotal.

'This is last trip,' he tells me.

'What? Your last trip?'

'For ship, this last time, kaput.'

He explains to me by gestures that the ship is to be broken up and scrapped.

As the news hits me I am aghast. It is so-o-o good that we didn't know of this any earlier else we would all have worried, as in all probability the ship is an old rust bucket, after all I don't reckon they'd be scrapping it unless it was unsafe.

Those of us who've been travelling deck class all get very emotional as we prepare to bid each other farewell and leave the SS Kades. There's lots of shaking of hands and big huggings. The scene is witnessed by the cabin passengers, who look on uncomprehending; for they keep to themselves, very right, very proper and very boring.

Our passports are returned, and I peep to see if I have any new stamps.

Chapter 11

— ★ —

OF BAZAARS AND BATHS

B ehind the mass of boats moored in the harbour lies the majestic skyline of Istanbul. The view is grand, powerful and imposing; a mass of domes and slender towers monopolise my vision, and immediately I feel a strong urge to go and explore, to become a part of the city life.

'Want to buy sexy pictures?' a voice queries.

'What?'

'You both want sexy pictures?' the man persists.

'No we don't.' I say dismissively.

Standing here on the threshold of the mysterious East, I can honestly say I have no appetite at all for a fist full of grubby photos of undressed women.

I look over at Yolanda.

'Where on earth is he coming from?' I mutter.

Now Anthony joins us, looking excited and nervous, and I wonder why? Maybe he's been looking at some of the pictures?

'I'm thinking...' he says, *'Shall we all join up together? Shall I ask the Germans too?'* he adds breathlessly.

'Maybe it would be a good idea,' I concede.

'I'll go and ask them....' He answers, clearly pleased.

He beetles off before we even have time to discuss the idea, so we stand there waiting, waiting for him to come back.

He returns flushed with success.

'Yes, fine. They're dealing with their van, and then they have to find somewhere to park it. We're all going to meet up by Galata Bridge. Before then we've got time to change some money and have a drink,' he suggests.

Clearly, Anthony revels in the thought of us all staying together and I suppose it's a good idea to make the most of one another's company.

'The Galata is a floating bridge, and we need to cross it to get to Old Stamboul. That's where the Pudding Shop is, the Sultan Ahmet and all the cheap hotels,' Anthony babbles, demonstrating his knowledge of Istanbul.

149

The subject of eggplants (aubergines) had been a constant source of amusement on board ship, as I seriously doubted the existence of such a vegetable that could resemble an egg.

'What about eggplants?' I ask him now.

'Yes. Lots of eggplants too!'

'I am the eggman, you are an eggplant, she is the walnut.' I sing, to the tune of The Beatles' *'I am the Walrus'.*

We meet up with the others at the Galata Bridge, a bridge that spans the vast expanse of water that lies between the two main areas of Istanbul. The bridge seems to have been constructed in a series of separate sections that bob and wobble up and down, gently but quite perceptibly.

Once we're over the bridge we take to the steep and busy streets of Old Stamboul, an area that exudes and projects a strong air of mystery and enchantment. Here we search for a suitably cheap looking hotel.

It starts to look like Anthony and the two German guys are taking responsibility for finding us rooms. They go from hotel to hotel until they find one with vacancies.

'A room for seven please,' says Anthony, holding up seven fingers.

'Seven? Seven room?' the manager puzzles.

'One room with seven beds,' Anthony repeats, turning and checking with us all that it's alright. I frown slightly but nod my head.

'One room? SEVEN beds?' the manager asks again.

It really is too much for the guy, and he shows us a room containing just two beds.

'This room too small!'

'No, no, no.... more bed... Yes?'

He disappears and soon returns dragging a mattress behind him. Then we help him to haul in more beds, mattresses and bedding into the tiny room.

But he's right; it can be done, though it leaves virtually zero space for anything else. So we set about stuffing our bags under our beds.

It's less than ideal, as in order to get in and out of the room we're going to have to climb over one another's beds. But as nobody voices their dissent over the bizarre arrangements, I don't question having to slum it like this. Anyway, we've not come all this way in order to sit around in a hotel room, so we all agree to leave our bags and go out to taste the delights of the street life.

After securing the room, we make a beeline for the nearby cafe, which presents another opportunity for Anthony to play out his role as The Oracle: -

'Achik chaay is weak tea without milk in a small glass, demlik chaay is really

strong. I prefer "achik chaay". Then there's coffee, they call it "kahve" here, "sade kahve" is no sugar coffee, "sutlu kahve" is white coffee and sweet coffee is "checkerli",' he advises.

'Check early? I think the sweet tea sounds best,' I decide.

Actually, we all order the sweet tea and almost immediately the light brown nectar is brought to us, served in what looks like oversized sherry glasses. The sugar comes in the form of lumpy rough large cubes placed beside our glasses.

I expect tea without milk to taste bitter, but instead it tastes smooth and refreshing.

This cafe has an all male clientele, so the girls, Monick, Gretta and Yolanda, find themselves the focus of attention, and I don't hear them complain.

After finishing our tea, we are of one mind in wanting to scout out the rest of the area.

It seems that it's the accepted norm here to buy snacks on the street, so there's no need to waste our precious Turkish *lira* ordering food in restaurants or cafes. The Turkish *lira* is roughly equivalent to about 7 pence (there are about 35 TL to the pound) and each *lira* is equal to 100 *kurus* (pronounced *kuroosh*). With the price of a tea between 25 and 50 *kurus* and the snacks being cheap too, I can see no immediate money worries looming.

Satisfied that we know whereabouts we're staying, and where the local cafes are, we all agree that it would be a good idea to turn in for the night, as none of us has had much sleep lately. Soon it's lights out in the dorm!

* * *

After breakfast Anthony's big priority is to visit the Post Office; and since he seems to think we'd enjoy ourselves there, Yolanda and I tag along with him.

Anthony is intent on explaining to us how the *Post Restante* facility works, and he tells us it's a great system for travellers; the idea being that family and friends can write to you 'care of' the main Post Office in whichever city you stay. What's more is that it's a free service with no hidden charges; in fact the system sounds ideal. So, for example, in order to get mail sent to me here, my address would be, Paul Mason, c/o Post Restante, Istanbul, Turkey.

At the Post Office I watch the queue of people who wait in line for their turn to call out their name at the little window in the hope of retrieving post. If mail is waiting to be collected, then one has first to prove ones identity, usually with a passport. Most of those waiting are heavily tanned, so it looks as though they're old hands at this game.

Two guys in particular catch my attention. Both of them look under-nourished and travelled; and one of them has a particularly faraway look in his eyes. They're both dressed in unusual getups, and appear to be returning from a long trip away somewhere. I ask them where they've come from.

'From India, we're on our way back to London,' one of them explains.

When I ask him if he has enjoyed the trip, he just smiles, rather weakly.

They can't know this, but to date these two guys are possibly the most important people I've met on our journey, not as individuals, but for what they symbolise to me. My ambition right from the start was to get us to India, and merge amongst other pilgrims there in order that we can engage in a pilgrimage of our souls, and these are the first travellers I've met coming back from India by road, the first real proof I have that this marathon trip is possible and can really be accomplished.

Istanbul, I now discover, is a crossroads to the East. Many come here just to enjoy the atmosphere of Turkey, or as a stop off point on the way to their way home from some far-flung place. But for others this is just the start of their adventures.

I now realise that by coming via North Africa we had taken a massive, and perhaps unnecessary, detour, but though it was my idea, and though we both wanted to go that way, I feel sure we could have reached Istanbul within a week or ten days had we travelled more directly. So, have we wasted our time and money dragging ourselves around the long way? Who can tell? Who knows what's been achieved? Anyway, right now I am raring to go and get on our way to Persia, and on to India!

Whilst we're here at the Post Office I mail the Acropolis to Mum and tell her that if she wants to write, she can do so, addressing the letter to me, c/o Post Restante, Main Post Office, Teheran, Iran.

* * *

We're going to have to stay in Istanbul for some days, as the formality of getting visas for our journey is going to have to be dealt with before we leave.

Whilst we're here I intend to enjoy myself, and I can't wait to make a visit to the Grand Bazaar - as I've been waiting for that treat since Anthony first told me about it on the SS Kades.

'You need to wear sunglasses there,' he had said. *'The brightness of the gold is so bright, quite unbelievable. It's the biggest bazaar in the world. You've just got to see it. There are tons of alleyways with stacks of different stalls and shops. You can buy virtually anything there.'*

Though he joked about the need for sunglasses I reckon he hasn't exaggerated too much otherwise. It's an amazing place, a labyrinth both magical and mysterious, where, in the quaint shops here, one can find curious objects, records, leatherwork, pottery, clothes, metalwork, jewellery and food, and these are just some of the items for sale. It would take days to explore the place properly. Mind you, getting about the place is not at all easy.

We go around as a group, all seven of us, and we're badgered and hassled almost continuously by the traders here, who have a surprisingly good grasp of the English language. When we turn down their offers to show us their wares we are treated to a volley of abuse. They must have learned the swear words from passing tourists; so perhaps they are unaware of quite how coarse their language is with the 'b', 'f' and 'c' words being used rather freely?

Some weeks ago, before we left for this journey, it was Yolanda's birthday, and now we have an opportunity to buy her something special. After visiting many, many of the shops we eventually find a suitable dress. It's basically white, with wide yellow and gold bands, and it's loose fitting and modest. It looks just great on her.

And I'm looking for something for myself too; my kick is a passport bag. All the ones here are made of leather and designed to be worn around the neck. I select a bag that's slightly larger than a passport and has space enough for all our travel documents as well. But it takes time to haggle down the price, and I do well as I get it down from 10 Turkish *liras* right down to 4 Turkish *liras*. So I have no hesitation when it comes to handing over the cash.

'Fuck off,' the guy mutters dismissively.

'Charming!' I counter. But clearly, he's taken offence and no long interested in making a sale; so unfortunately we'll have to look elsewhere. Shame, it's a nice pouch.

I'm mildly curious as to what the Germans have got their eyes on. It seems Christian has got it into his head to buy some leather trousers and since the place is full of leather goods, he has no end of choice. Most of the shops and stalls in the bazaar are crammed full and very busy, so it's quite a release when we're back out of bazaar and able to escape the hustle and bustle of the place.

All of us return together to our area again, to a cafe near the *'otel*, where we order up fried eggs and tomatoes followed by rice pudding with cinnamon.

'Seven tomategg, seven rice, seven tomategg, seven rice,' the owner chants.

The fried food is served up in small portion-sized frying pans, which is a brilliant way to present the food as it gets served fresh and keeps hot. And I guess it saves on washing up too.

We discuss getting visas for Iran, and since Anthony also has to get a visa we decide to travel to the embassy together. He explains to us that Istanbul has several modes of transportation, and that when walking proves too wearing one can resort to buses or taxis, as they are surprisingly cheap. *Dolmus* taxis are the cheapest, at a price of TL/2 per head one can travel wherever the taxi is heading. A *dolmus* is a bit like a bus, insofar as a ride is frequently spent in the company of other passengers. But the catch is that you cannot stipulate where the driver will take you, so when the *dolmus* goes off course you simply have to get out and go find another *dolmus* heading the right way. But the real thrill about the *dolmus* is that most of these cars are vintage 1950's American *Cadillacs, Buicks, Pontiacs* and *Chevrolets*; they're all out there. I guess, maybe the Yanks sold them a job lot way back. Smashing old cars, probably rare even back in their own country.

Anthony, Yolanda and myself take a *dolmus* to take us to the Iranian Embassy.

Actually it takes us two *dolmus* taxis followed by a long walk.

The Iranian embassy is located on the modern side of Istanbul, where the rich hang out, an area with expensive looking hotels and clubs. Turkish belly dancing can be seen here by night, though it's said that the girls are unlikely to be of Turkish origin, apparently one is more likely to find some lass from Manchester, caught up in a modern version of the white slave trade.

'How come you don't need a visa?' I ask Yolanda.

'I guess Italy's friendly with Iran,' she responds uncertainly.

After filling out the forms, we leave our passports in the hands of the embassy staff, who tell us it will be some days before they'll be ready to collect.

We meet back up with the Germans again and together decide to get around to see some of the sights. They want to go off to the Sultan Ahmet (the Blue Mosque), and I am eager too, as I have never been inside a mosque before (other than when visiting the outer precincts of one in North Africa in order to use the toilet).

Before we leave, Christian, is able to 'score', to buy himself a little piece of hashish that he wants to smoke. Out of the seven of us, he alone wishes to indulge, but he can't find any cigarette papers, as they don't seem to sell them here in Turkey.

I offer to help him out, and improvise by first removing the silver paper from a pack of cigarettes, then carefully separate the thin tissue paper backing from it. Breaking open a cigarette I empty the tobacco onto the paper, heat the sweet smelling hashish with a lighted match and crumble a little of it into the tobacco. Rolling together both paper and contents a cigarette is formed, the resultant 'joint' being sealed with pieces of gummed postage stamps. Last of all I roll a short piece of card and insert it in place of a filter tip, and with the special cigarette now prepared and ready, Christian is all set for lift off!

We all make our way off towards the mosque, and as we walk Christian smokes the joint right down to the boards. I'm intrigued to know why the others don't want to join him. Maybe, despite their hippyish appearance, they haven't 'turned on' yet? Christian giggles to himself, and producing a wooden flute from his bag he tootles fitfully on it, playing snatches of unfamiliar melodies, entertaining himself.

At last we arrive at the Sultan Ahmed, a vast building with multiple domes clinging like limpets to the main body of the structure. Some half-dozen balconied minarets pierce the surrounding aerial space like ancient prototype rockets.

As I stand gazing at the imposing and impressive structure I am struck by the uncomfortable fact that I'm not exactly sure what a mosque is. All that I understand is that a mosque is some sort of church. I wonder what it will look like on the inside, but I'm sure that with such a splendid exterior it must be choc-a-bloc with treasures, like a cathedral maybe.

As we make our way up the steep spreading stone staircase to the entrance of the mosque I am apprised of the fact we must now all take off our shoes.

'Everyone has to take them off, else they can't go inside. That's the custom,' informs Anthony. I see that all the others are removing their shoes so, somewhat hesitantly, I take off mine too and cast them onto the pile of rubber and leather at the entrance of the mosque.

Though, momentarily, the beauty of the ornamentation on the walls of this staggeringly huge building sidetracks me, I can't help but worry about the safety of my shoes.

Soon after we enter the main building I am struck by the utter emptiness of the place, for there is no furniture at all, in fact there's nothing here other than the vast sea of richly coloured carpets, and but for the few other tourists, the place seems totally deserted, just a huge and empty void.

I stand wondering what the point is of such a large empty space, asking myself how this is useful in getting to plumb one's own inner feelings, or getting in contact with God?

'I'm going outside. I want my shoes back,' I explain to the others.

It's a relief to be outside again! Seems I'm not cut out for sightseeing, but, that said, I would like to go back to the bazaar to look for a passport pouch; it would be such a very useful addition to our kit. I am transfixed by the idea of getting the pouch.

I have to wait a long time before the others emerge from the mosque.

'Do you want to see Top Kapi and Saint Sophia,' Anthony asks.

Right now I'm in no mood to traipse around more old buildings, and what's more I'm hungry.

'What are they selling?' I ask, pointing to a row of street vendors.

'Roast corncobs. Shall we get some?'

The fresh ripe corncobs are immediately stripped of their green covering and roasted on an open fire. To my surprise I find the charred toasted corn tastes so much better than it does when boiled, it has a lovely nutty taste similar to that of chestnuts.

Today the whole gang sticks together, mooching about the old quarter, wandering quite aimlessly, stopping first to look at one shop and then at another, before going somewhere for a snack. In fact we have evolved a daily ritual, which revolves around staying at the *'otel*, going to the local cafes, plus repeated trips to the bazaar and the area immediately around the bazaar, where the lanes and alleyways seem to abound with well stocked shops, often full with people milling about.

As all too many of the footways are extremely steep and narrow, therefore moving heavy goods must present a great challenge here.

'Did you see that?' Yolanda gasps.

Apparently, she'd felt a tap on her back but did not respond, thinking that perhaps it was unintended. Then to her surprise she felt a searing pain, as if her bottom were being pinched very strongly - I'm aware that whilst in Istanbul the girls have had to get used to this, having their bottoms pinched by passing men - so on this occasion she turned around thinking to confront the perpetrator, only to find herself staring at the long tired face of a horse, waiting to overtake her.

On another occasion we see an old man struggling up a hill carrying an upright piano on his back, his load secured with a rope across his forehead. Heavy, Man!

Interestingly, these crowded cobbled streets also attract street entertainers, and it's in one such street that we witness a most bizarre spectacle, a dancing bear. I feel extremely sorry for the animal and wonder that there must be a very dark side of human nature that subscribes to such displays.

We revisit the main bazaar and surprisingly it's at one of the many touristy shops that I obtain my prize - a two-tone leather passport pouch at the modest price of TL 5, and I'm soon transferring our passports and papers into it. I buy another (a spare) in brown suede, for after all, we haven't exactly splashed out on luxuries since we've been on our travels - the *djellaba* in Morocco, the nail clippers in Libya, a dress for Yolanda, and now a zippered pass-a-port case!

On the subject of souvenirs; whilst in London, when Yolanda worked for the gift shop in Trafalgar Square, *Admiral's Eye*, she had gotten me several rings from there. I wear these rings along with the one she gave me earlier in our relationship, the silver one embossed with small circles of gold hammered into it, giving the appearance of something mediaeval and romantic. Apparently it had been made for her, and given to her by a former boyfriend, a guy called Richard, in Amsterdam.

The other rings are not precious, though one in particular has fascinated me from the day I got it, it's a Turkish Puzzle ring, wrought of silver and consisting of four differently shaped segments which fit together into a pleasing pattern, rather like a knot, I had fun deciphering the puzzle, working out how to fit it back together. Back onboard the SS Kades I discovered that Anthony also has such a ring but a totally different method for solving the puzzle. Ironically, these Turkish puzzle rings seem surprisingly hard to find in Istanbul, so perhaps they're made for export only?

But they have antique signet rings here, which I figure are also aimed at tourists; they are attractive and each one contains a panel of brass with Arabic script inscribed upon it. But I doubt they're authentic, as most likely they've been aged by pressing dirt into the crevices. The shops and stalls selling these rings price them high, as though they're the real McCoy. But as I've set my heart on owning one in particular, impulsively I palm it and walk off, quashing the sense of shame I feel.

Serves 'em right I think to myself, *if they were more honest, I would have paid them the price.*

All of us seem to like rummaging around market stalls, so Anthony suggests it might be fun for us to visit the Sunday Flea Market. I've never heard of a Flea Market before but I'm mildly intrigued to find out what it's all about.

We discover that, unlike the regular indoor bazaar, the outdoor Sunday Flea Market doesn't seem to have any new items for sale, nor proper antiques either; the place is just stuffed full of rubbish, that is to say garbage, trash! Nevertheless, in spite of the complete lack of quality goods, the place attracts crowds of people who gather to turn over the mounds of assorted junk - the rusting nails, broken tools, buttons, soiled clothes, and rolls of sticky tape so weathered that they have fused together in a useless mass. How can anyone hold out any real hope of finding something useful, let alone a bargain here? What on earth induces people to come here?

Our Germans friends are really put out by the place, they don't like it one bit.

But Anthony appears to be quite home here, or maybe he just wishes to project that appearance. I ask him if such places exist anywhere else, other than in Istanbul? According to him one can find a Flea Market in Amsterdam too.

Now a great mystery that puzzles me even more, is why we cannot drink the tap water here in Istanbul. When I first heard about it, I thought it was a joke, but apparently the water is so bad that people actually prefer to buy purified water, sold in small bottles with aluminium caps at 20 *kurus* a throw. Imagine having to do that, to actually buy water? Had we been staying longer I'm sure I would have got around to trying the tap water. Surely it can't be that bad?

'Fancy a Fruko?' Anthony asks.

'Huh?' I puzzle.

'It's a fizzy fruit drink. But actually, the people here call the army the Fruko too.'

I don't know much about the role of the army here, but we do see quite a few uniformed soldiers on the streets. I do know what the president looks like though, his face is on all the coins and on the banknotes, and at every turn of the road and inside any old shop you'll see a picture of Atatürk, the man in charge of Turkey, Kemal Atatürk; his face is everywhere. Apparently it is he who established the modern Europeanised Turkey, and in order to modernise they phased out the public use of the Arabic script and replaced it with the more familiar Roman alphabet. The changes haven't stopped at that, of course, the commitment to western ideology shows itself in so many ways. Certainly, no one is wearing anything remotely resembling traditional costume. The gauzy veils of a land of Eastern Promise summoned up by the *Fry's Turkish Delight* ads seem to belong firmly in the past. But on the subject of this delicacy, when I have the chance to sample the real thing I am shocked to find I prefer the *Fry's* version. Though the delight here is tasty it lacks the smooth milk chocolate covering, not to mention the beautiful purple paper wrapper around it. In fact even the centre is no match for *Fry's*. Perhaps one day they'll be importing a variety of the British chocolate *Turkish Delight*.

Ever since reading Lewis Carrol's *'Alice in Wonderland'* and seeing the illustration of the *hookah*-smoking caterpillar, I've been curious as to know what it's like to smoke a *hookah* (a hubble-bubble pipe). In a cafe here I spot an ornate pipe and I'm curious to find out how much it costs to have a smoke, the staff assume I want to have a smoke so they fill the apparatus with fresh water and bring me something to smoke. I'm sure these pipes are only used for the smoking of cannabis, so I finger the substance, and to my surprise find it's not hashish at all but a dry dark strong tobacco. Filling the bowl with the tobacco I take a match and draw heavily on the mouthpiece. Whoo-oo-ah, it's pretty strong stuff in spite of the smoke being filtered and cooled by the fresh water. As the body of the pipe is made of clear glass I watch the smoke as it passes on its course through the Hookah. At just 1 Turkish *lira* it's a cheap thrill but not one I wish to repeat.

The Turks sure seem to like their tobacco strong, even the cigarettes tend to be harsh. Of the brands here the attractively named *'Yeni Harman'* brand has the most alluring packaging but on opening the ochre packet I find the cigarettes have all but emptied their contents. I guess the problem lies in the lack of plastic wrapping, so in the hot weather they can't stay fresh long. Curiously, some brands of cigarettes sold here are rolled into an oval shape, so to the unwary eye they look squashed, a little like they've been sat upon.

Sometimes Yolanda and I go out alone, and sometimes Anthony comes along with us, and on other occasions we join up with some or all of the Germans, and today we agree to all join forces and visit a genuine Turkish bath. The one we find is housed in an ancient looking building, which from the outside looks very similar to a mosque. However, we belatedly discover that this building is used exclusively by men, so Yolanda and the German girls must seek out the separate ladies facilities.

Inside I tread the most amazingly beautiful marble and alabaster floors, and make my way to the washing area where I find sinks and sunken hot water pools. Casting off my clothes and immersing myself in the water, I then sit naked in the humid hothouse by the side of the pool, soaping and washing my body, rubbing and scrubbing until every vestige of dirt and loose skin is washed away.

As I languish in the sunken pool I stare up into the vast vaulted domed roof, an impressive sight for lovers of ancient architecture. High up there, thriving in the intense heat and moisture, and providing a splendid sideshow far out of reach of the custodians of these baths, grow ferns and other plants which have rooted themselves in the crevices and cracks.

I wash myself repeatedly, over and over again; possibly a dozen times I lather myself, before the novelty of the experience of being in this hot steaming temple of naked manhood wears off. Of course, some might wish to languish longer, lolling about in the warm pools of water, savouring the cleansing experience longer, and possibly coming to some deeply rested state. A very conducive environment, very intimate too, possibly somewhere to hang out with a close friend or two. But I've had enough of Turkish baths for now, and as I figure I must be clean enough by now, I just want to get out.

The next step in passing through the baths is to have a dip in cold water, and the contrast is quite a shock to my nervous system. Almost immediately I feel frozen through, and I notice my bits and bobs shrivel up, so I wrap myself in the two large soft Turkish towels that have been brought for me, and I go and sit down in a small adjoining room where an attendant brings me a small glass of hot brown tea, proper *küçük çay (kuchuk chai)*. And after drying myself thoroughly, and finishing my tea, I get my clothes back on and make my exit.

Yolanda is outside, waiting. Apparently she's not enamoured with the experience, but listens as I tell her how much I enjoyed myself. However, as I sneeze repeatedly I reckon I might have overdone it. I wonder if perhaps I am now **too** clean?

I start to wonder if Anthony has got his facts right about 'following the sun' all the way to Australia, after all, we have moved from the intense heat of North Africa to cooler weather in Istanbul. In fact the nights here are decidedly cold. Perhaps that's the reason I'm suffering a minor head cold, or maybe it's the Turkish bath with its extremes of temperatures?

The Iranian consulate issues me my visa so we no longer need to stay in Stamboul.

The question though, is how are we going to travel across Turkey? The most obvious route for us is to go directly by road, via Ankara. But Anthony is full of enthusiasm for us joining up with him and travelling together by train. The idea is attractive, but it would place a heavy drain on our meagre funds. Another method is suggested by the small ads that are posted on the notice boards at the Pudding Shop and other cafes around and about the Blue Mosque. The idea is that extra passengers share the cost of petrol, but as luck has it there are no ads related to travelling East just now. Secretly, I entertain another plan. On leaving the SS Kades the captain showed me a sticker in our passports, resembling a postage stamp, which, according to him, enables us to travel at half the normal rate on another ship.

Trotting off to the shipping offices, I check out the situation with regards the cost of a trip across the Black Sea, along the north coast of Turkey. But I'm disappointed as apparently the half-price discount rate only applies to international voyages. However, when I quiz them further, as to what concession they offer on trips in Turkish waters, we strike gold, finding that we're still eligible to a decent discount and that there's a boat sailing almost immediately, which would take us where we want to go, a distance in the Black Sea, well on the way to the border of Turkey and Iran.

I fall to wondering why the Black Sea is so called. Is the water really black?

* * *

Anthony, the German couples and ourselves have fallen into a friendly familiarity during the time we've spent together, especially during our visits to our favourite cafe, in fact we've all grown quite fond of one another. In fact Christian and myself decided our cafe needed a menu that's more intelligible so that the owner could gain more business, therefore we spent a fair amount of time together discussing the project, but when Yolanda and I announce our decision to sail on the steamer, in a couple of days, it seems to significantly alter the *status quo* of our merry band. For starters I notice Christian makes no further mention of the topic of menus, and all the Germans start to look quite subdued, but maybe it's because they'll soon be returning to their homeland to resume their studies at university.

Regardless what the future holds for us all, it feels like it would be nice to finish our stay together on a high note, and someone gets the bright idea for us to go to the movies. Not a frequent cinemagoer myself, I am nonetheless curious to see what the homegrown Turkish product looks like.

As it happens the venue is sufficient in itself to throw us all into hysterics. This so-called cinema has been erected outside with sheets hung on ropes to form the walls and screen, with seating (such as it is) being on wooden benches, so upon one such bench the seven of us sit, tightly squeezed between extremely loud Turks. The heat is really up this evening; thank goodness it's an open-air performance.

The first short film is the most hysterical, ridiculous and melodramatic nonsense I've ever seen! And the one that follows is no better. Admittedly, we know almost no Turkish, but none of the films we see seem to require any great understanding, for they all have the simple basis *viz.* Goodies versus Baddies. The Goodies are instantly recognisable, as they are ones with a heroic and suave image, and if you are in any doubt about who is who, the Goodies are the ones that draw the cheers from the audience. The Baddies, and there are many, invariably have the most evil expressions and sport the longest drooping moustaches. It seems that the Goody usually prevails, but not always. And if by some mishap a Goody gets killed he is promptly replaced by another dapper chappy whom the audience cheers with great gusto. Film after film rolls by on the white sheet screens before we're done. The sheer disjointed banality of it all leaves us heaving with mirth. The outdoor cinema experience puts us all in lively spirits.

Night time is the best time to see Istanbul, for the lights from the boats, the cars, the stars and the moon, all contrive to turn the already impressive view into something really quite heady and magical.

As this is our last night together, I ask Anthony what he has planned travelwise.

'So, you're still going by train?' I ask him.

'Yes, via Ankara, you've heard of it no doubt, where Angora wool comes from? It would have been nice to go with you by boat, but there you go.'

'We might meet up again though, keep your eyes open for us!' I tell him.

Chapter 12

— ★ —

UP IN THE CLOUDS

Since ours is only a domestic voyage we very much doubt that accommodation will be provided for us deck class ticket holders. So, we arrive early to board the vessel in Istanbul harbour, in the belief that by getting to the boat earlier than other passengers we might find a comfortable niche for ourselves. But the ship is already very busy and we find ourselves at the end of a long line of Turkish passengers queuing for information about their sleeping quarters.

IÇ HATLAR = Domestic Lines,   YOLCU= Passenger,   YÜK= Freight,   BİLETİ = Ticket,
DENİZYOLLARI = Maritime

When it comes to our turn, our tickets are inspected and I'm dispatched below deck to look at the men's quarters, where the steward there shows me a cramped dormitory. I find it very hot and extremely claustrophobic, made all the worse by the smell of laundry, an odour that permeates the entire area below deck, and after inspecting the berth that's been allocated to me I return to where Yolanda is waiting.

'You have a look, see what you think,' I suggest to her.

Yolanda disappears down the other staircase, to the women's quarters but it isn't long before she reappears, a look of disapproval writ across her face.

'It stinks of damp clothes, I don't like it,' she moans.

We exchange uneasy glances.

'Well let's look around the rest of the ship,' I suggest.

And as we wander about on deck, I get an idea;

'What about the lifeboats?' I ask, *'Maybe we could hide in one of those?'*

'It's worth a try,' Yolanda readily agrees.

Checking first to see that we're not being observed, we climb into a nearby lifeboat, and find that there's easily space enough for the two of us to make a comfortable camp here, but I'm concerned that we might be discovered and get thrown out, so we crouch down low in the hope of avoiding detection. It's pleasant enough here, just staring up at the sky, but I'm interrupted..

'Oh sorry, I was just looking around,' says the man - he's a European. *'You've got a good idea staying up here.'*

'It will be nice to sleep under the open sky,' I answer him.

'I think I'll find my bag and get in one of the other boats. See you...'

A few minutes later, someone else discovers our quarters.

'No, you find your own place. We got here first.' I tell the intruder, but he climbs in anyway, deaf to all objections from Yolanda and myself. After hauling a load of luggage into the life craft, he stands facing us, resolute, determined and belligerent. Never in my life have I come across someone more thick-skinned. I get really furious with him, but he appears unmoved. Undeterred by our attitude towards him he sits himself in the boat.

'My name his Fritz. Vhat is yours?' he asks in a strong German accent and offers his cigarettes around. His efforts are met with measured politeness from us, and eventually he gives up and goes to look for his own boat.

'Good riddance,' I mutter, right after he's gone.

'Rude sod. Arrogant swine,' remarks Yolanda.

Before long we get more visits, all from other western passengers, most of whom become keen to move into one or other of the lifeboats. The ship is now on the move, and we're now a little less shy about being seen in the lifeboat.

I peer out at the water, the huge inland reservoir of water called the Black Sea, which to me resembles a vast unending lake, indeed it appears very dark to the eye but I don't think this is the actual colour of the water. More likely it's the rock below the surface that gives it its black appearance.

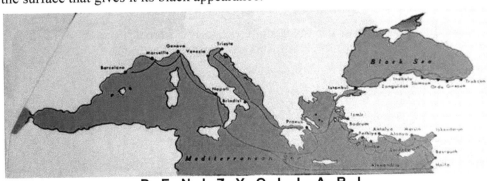

D E N I Z Y O L L A R I
TURKISH MARITIME LINES
means
Elegance, ... Fun, ... Relaxation, ... Security
Always at your disposal

The coastline stays in view at all times and the vessel maintains a fairly steady speed. Although the views are of no great interest, they hold my attention, and I convince myself the journey will be restful and undemanding. Certainly, we have prepared ourselves with some basic provisions, which with care we are determined to eke out for the duration of the trip.

We become quite friendly with the few other Europeans on board, even with Fritz. We discover that our fellow travellers are, without exception, joy riding, for after leaving Turkey they are all going back home to their respective countries.

Back in Istanbul we'd met another English couple also intent on getting to India.

'Where are you from in London?' I had asked.

'Richmond, Man,' he answered

'What a small world. Of the two other people I've met going to India, they're both from London, and from places I know well.' I tell them.

'That's the way it goes..' he replies knowingly.

But since there was nothing to tie us together other than this thin thread of coincidence, we soon parted. I'm beginning to realise that the peculiar thing about meeting folks from England is that it's very much a love-hate thing. On the one hand it's a relief to able speak to someone in proper English, but on the other hand it can really put my back up to be reminded how reserved and stuffy the British can be, Anthony being a notable exception.

The first stop on our journey is the port of Sinop, and when we dock there I'm eager to explore the place. Yolanda, myself and a motley handful of others go ashore, but being a port there's precious little of interest to see, just the usual industrial stuff, the cranes, loading bays and what have you. Our main purpose for visiting here lies in replenishing our food supplies and soaking up the local atmosphere, so we forge on and are repaid for our efforts in that we find some useful shops. The walk has done us good and we return to the ship refreshed and sharpened by the exercise.

So it is with the next port, Samsun, a name that for me conjures up the longhaired lover Samson who lost his mane. Samsun has another association for me; it's the name of a popular brand of Turkish cigarettes.

As the trip draws to an end I find myself clutching at straws to find entertainment; the trip is getting decidedly dowdy. But as we still have night more on board before we're due to arrive at our destination, I really hope things pick up before then.

* * *

With only minutes to go before disembarkation at the port of Trabzon we make the rash decision to order breakfast in the onboard cafe. I'm yearning for a breakfast of cornflakes; toast and marmalade, so when our food arrives I stare at it in disbelief, for in front of us are two glasses of *küçük çay*, a plate of large black shiny olives, some dry white cheese and a hunk of bread. It seems I must be destined for disappointments.

I take a bite out of the bread but there's something unfamiliar about it

'Is there something wrong with this bread?' I ask Yolanda.

'There's no salt in it. Strange isn't it?'

'It's disgusting, it all is,' I snort, *'what a waste of money!'*

Strangely enough though, the more I eat of the breakfast the more I enjoy it.

I become aware the ship is no longer moving and now that we have docked passengers are rushing to get clear the ship. Unhurriedly we finish our meal, get up and join the tail end of the mass exodus.

After we disembark we walk slowly through the port and sit ourselves by the roadside, thinking it a likely looking spot to hitch a ride.

'Do you realise we haven't hitched since Africa?' I point out to Yolanda.

'Yes, you're right, it's simply ages.' Yolanda replies, sounding genuinely surprised.

'Our last lift was the truck from Tunisia to Tripoli. That was a near thing at the washhouse wasn't it? I think they were out to lynch us you know? We got out in the gee nick of time. That driver was brilliant.'

'But what did we do wrong though?'

'Perhaps it was our singing,' I suggest.

'The weather's getting colder isn't it?' Yolanda points out.

'It's not so bad, but I see what you mean.'

There's clearly not much traffic going out of Trabzon today, so it looks as though we're in for a very long wait. But we have time, we just have to get used to waiting for lifts again. We've been used to having to wait for lifts but I'm never quite sure when an occasion will arise when we don't actually get one, when we'll have to find an alternate mode of transport, and if there are no alternatives, what do we do then?

Suddenly a car screeches to a halt beside us, and the occupant stares directly at us, rather dramatically, waiting for a reaction. It's almost as if he expected us to be here! He resembles one of the villain types we'd seen in the movies in Istanbul, although he seems friendly enough.

To be back on the road feels exquisite, and as far as I'm concerned you can keep all your mod cons, tickets, reservations, queues, and all that jazz. There's something special about hitching a ride, after all, no one has to give you a lift and by the same token no one has to accept one. Ergo, it's by choice, mutual choice.

As we motor further away from Trabzon the scenery becomes more and more pleasing, so much so that I find myself making positive comparisons to the countryside back home, specifically to the wonderful landscapes in Cornwall.

Our car climbs a fairly steep incline and at last comes to the top of the hill. The view fairly blows me away, for nestled here in this valley are beautifully rustic dwellings, rolling countryside, fields of waving crops and to the sides of the lane, kerbside flowers.

'My mum would love it here,' I enthuse.

'It's beautiful,' gasps Yolanda breathlessly as she takes in the stunning view.

Just now our driver distracts me, fumbling about in the pockets of his jacket. By and by he produces the fruit of his search, a shiny handgun! As he brandishes the revolver in the air I struggle to keep my composure. With one hand he waves the gun whilst with the other he holds tight the steering wheel, and fixing me with a defiant, unwholesome grin, he nods gently.

I gaze back at him as nonchalantly as I can; but it's sheer bravado, as I'm completely powerless to deal with the situation.

He leans over and jabs his finger on the chrome button of the glove compartment, then throws the weapon inside, but as he does so, he's less than attentive over his steering, and nearly causes the car to run off the road. Arighting the steering wheel he then snaps shut the glove compartment.

Whether our moustachioed driver is a villain or not is a matter of conjecture, but though we travel many miles with him, I never see the gun again.

As ever, all good lifts come to an end, and rather than sit around and wait, we find ourselves rediscovering our legs again as we take to walking along the country roads. Rambling our way through the beautiful countryside, we pass through the occasional simple hamlet, and as we do I notice that we sometimes attract the attention of the local children.

At the next village we stop to enjoy a glass of tea, and to also purchase some bread and tomatoes, before proceeding onward along the road, eating the food as we go.

I notice we are being followed by a group of children, so I smile at them for a moment as we continue on our way.

An object strikes the ground in front of us. I look down and see that it's a stone. Almost immediately there's another stone, and others follow after them. There can be no other interpretation; they are aimed at us! Paying no heed to our shouts of disapproval, the children continue to pelt us with stones,

It's an uneasy situation, for though we try to ignore them, in the hope they will stop, they do not. As I become increasingly concerned for our safety I lean down and start picking up stones myself with the idea of defending ourselves, but when Yolanda sees me doing this she tugs at my arm and tries to stop me.

'Don't do it Paul,' she shrieks, *'You'll get their families killing you. That's what they'll do. Paul, don't!'*

I heed her words, and we hasten our pace until we are all but running, and the air is thick with ever-larger stones being hurled at us, and many hit their target. But I feel that Yolanda is right, so I resist the burning temptation to retaliate, though I resent having to let the kids have their way.

As luck has it, they tire of their sport, and we get away with no more than some minor bruising.

So, why did they pick on us?

Yolanda is convinced she has the answer to this question, and explains that it's on account of their having seen she has hair under her armpits!

I wonder. But personally I think it's simply that to them we're strangers, and they need no other excuse.

Anyway, we continue walking, and eventually make it to a fairly big town, Ezerum, by which time it's getting dark, so we seek out a cheap hotel, for the temperature is now getting exceedingly cold and we see no point in sleeping rough tonight. The room that's provided is ill lit and run-down but it has plenty of blankets, so at least we are safe for the night, and though cold, not quite freezing.

* * *

A bright new morning dawns, and after freshening up we set off again for fresh adventures. Studying our map, it appears that Persia is but a day or two's travel away from here.

Before we find a place to hitch a ride from, we take a quick *shufti* around the town. There are the usual facilities available here, a bank, a Post Office and handful of shops. And though I'm not exactly sure what a citadel is, I'm convinced that the unusual looking tower on the skyline must be one, for it looks like a place of worship and it's like no other church or mosque that I've seen. I recall seeing such a building on the cover of a Rolling Stones LP, on which there was a song called *'Citadel'*.

But I wonder if these people around here are particularly religious? If they were, why would they let their children throw rocks at strangers?

Today we are involved in another such incident of stone throwing, which is altogether as intense and dangerous as the one yesterday. Just one of these rocks could kill, so again we take flight, this time only narrowly escaping severe injury. I'm really starting to wonder if we're not being warned off from travelling any further?

Bob Dylan sang that *'Everybody must get stoned'*. But had he ever been to Turkey?

Truth is, we could really use a lift to get us out of this district; as it's about time we got a move on.

And it's not too-o-o-o long before I notice far, faraway, a van winding its way down the road towards where we're standing, and even at a distance I can see it's a *Dormobile* camper van, driven by a young western woman.

166

The flash of a thumb brings an immediate response, the vehicle stops. Brilliant!!!!!!

The van belongs to an English couple who without hesitation offer us a lift.

Once we are settled in, and on the move, we tell them of our most recent escapades.

They respond coolly. *'Yes, common practice in these parts. Haven't you heard the Biblical story of Stephen the Martyr? He was stoned to death?'*

'Here? Really? So, they've been at it as long as all that, have they?' I muse. This means the locals have been at this stone throwing business for at least two thousand years!

'Where are you going?' asks the English guy, who has a somewhat aloof air about him.

'To the border,' I answer simply.

'And after that? Are you going to India?'

'If we survive that long! Yes, we hope so. Hey, isn't that Tyrannosaurus Rex you're playing? But it can't be the radio, where on earth is the music coming from?' I ask, my flabber well and truly ghasted.

'Cassette tape machine,' he replies nonchalantly.

'Well I'll be jiggered!' I ejaculate, genuinely amazed.

'The machine has these tiny tapes, quite unlike conventional reel-to-reel,' he explains.

The couple have a stack of tapes, which include some of their favourite sounds. Very impressed I am. Mind you, of choice, although they're more compact, I think I'd still much prefer to have the records. Something you can see, locate the track and 'Bob's your uncle'. And what about the record covers? I've been known to buy records simply for the covers - crazy but true! No, I can't see people enjoying tapes in the same way but I have to admit, they seem ideal for travelling.

Eagerly I drank in the music. It's nice to hear Marc Bolan again. I'd met Steve Took, his percussionist, just after the duo split. Nice guy, very nice guy. And now Bolan has 'gone electric', but I love this new stuff, lots of energy and of course, still lots of quaint poetry.

This is the life, motoring along, catching up on the new record releases.

This couple has it all sewn up, they've kitted the van out with all the necessaries (and have even taken the precaution of bringing along a vast supply of toilet tissue). In fact they seem remarkably well-informed about all sorts of odd things, such as how it makes good sense to take chewing gum to India, where apparently a thriving black market exists.

'I'll chew that over,' I assure him, but it raises not the faintest smile.

As the journey gets further underway, conversation drops, and we just listen to the tapes. The young woman throws back the odd comment to us while her chap sits reading a book on India, which is packed with lots of pictures, facts and information, all of which will likely go to make his journey all the more worthwhile.

When we arrive at the town of Agri we break company with our new friends in the camper van, and sort ourselves out a cheap hotel. The room is really grim and as it's too cold to sit about yapping, we wrap ourselves up in eiderdowns and blankets, and lay ourselves down for the night.

* * *

This morning, hoping to glimpse the couple that own the camper van (who I figure are still in Agri buying further provisions for their journey), we look around for them a bit before finding a spot to stand and hitch.

As luck has it we get no chance of a lift for several hours, but we decide not to wander off blindly down the road, as we don't fancy getting stoned and becoming headlines on today's tourist casualty news report.

Our waiting pays off and eventually we are offered a lift in a large modern truck, driven by a very friendly man, accompanied by one of his fellow countrymen.

They tell us they are both from Armenia.

'Never heard of the place,' I say truthfully.

'My blouse comes from Rumania,' Yolanda chirps *'perhaps that's near there?'*

The men are in cheerful mood and I come to suspect the secret of their cheerfulness lies in the bottle of *raakhi* they pass back and forth. To say they are drunk would not be far short of the truth, but they handle it well.

The truck takes a very steep climb, and the winding road ahead is narrow and largely unfenced, and as we are now ascending into a mountain range the way ahead looks perilous. From time to time, one or other of the Armenians takes a look out of the side window, down the steep drop to the side of the road, apparently in search of something. It transpires that he's looking to see whether he can spot any lorries or buses that have crashed lately. Phew, this is a dangerous area all right!

Things get worse; for I notice the road immediately ahead of us is shrouded in thick cloud, white and fluffy and dense, but the lorry doesn't even slow down! Forging ahead, with almost nil visibility, in what seems somewhat a desperate bid, with no regard for safety, I fear for our lives. It's a nerve-wracking experience!

A few minutes later and we are still in the clouds, though eventually we emerge, and with no more to remind us of the dangerous episode than a thick layer of moisture on the windscreen.

To the left of the road is a vast solid wall of rock, vast and imposing. Then, when we get some perspective, a great mountain rears before us, and whilst the higher reaches are covered with snow, the peak is totally obscured by clouds.

The driver tries to get our attention, and as he points at the mountain he grins maniacally,

'Ararat. Ararat,' he shouts.

'Really!' I gasp in surprise.

'I don't believe it!' Yolanda enthuses.

The name Ararat has long been etched on our minds, as it's the mountain where Noah is said to have landed after the 'Great Flood', and the driver seems to have heard this too, for he explains (with the help of gestures) that recently some wood has been found there on the mountainside, some timbers from a ship.

'Wow!' I exclaim.

The Armenians nod and smile at us.

Having lost the opportunity of going Israel I had assumed that we'd missed out on contact with anything to do with *The Bible* lands, but not so, for here is the site of one of the most important stories of the *Old Testament*!

'The water receded steadily from the earth. At the end of the hundred and fifty days the water had gone down,' (v3) *'and on the seventeenth day of the seventh month the ark came to rest on the mountains of Ararat.'* (v4) *'The waters continued to recede until the tenth month, and on the first day of the tenth month the tops of the mountains became visible.'* (v5) - Genesis 8:3-5*

But actually, with regards Israel, Anthony had told us that it was a good thing that we hadn't gone there. *'You wouldn't have been able to get any further. Can't go to any Arab country after going to Israel. Only way is to have two passports, that's how journalists cope.'*

The lift with the Armenians has taken us a long, long way, and despite their inebriation we have travelled safely; and now they drop us off.

We have some way to go to get to the border and we are fortunate in not having to wait too long before being picked up by a party of Britishers, speeding the last few miles on their way towards the customs post.

But when we arrive at the border the door of the customs office is locked shut, so it looks at first as though we'll have to wait outside until morning, but we're not so easily deterred, and we hammer on the doors, hoping someone will open up.

It works, the door is opened and we are all let in, but from their manner the border guards appear to be very annoyed and huffy with us, but they do get on and process our small party through, with the formalities of form filling, passport checking and baggage control being dealt with very quickly.

As I study my passport I realise it has been stamped 18-IX-70, which is a mistake, as today is the nineteenth of September. Oh, how the days and weeks are rolling by!

The English guy who drove us to the border nudges me on the arm, *'Wrong date on the passports!'* he says.

'Yes, I know.' I answer. *'But we're through and that's the main thing isn't it?'*

I wonder that he's going to make something of it with the customs people, but I decide to leave the matter there, and get on.

So Yolanda and I walk onwards across the divide, towards the Iranian customs point, and I realise, with barely repressed excitement, that we'll soon be entering that fabled land of magic and beauty, the fairy tale land of Persia.

Unfortunately though, we find our way barred by locked gates.

Turning to check out where the party of Britishers have got to, we find ourselves alone.

As the nearby restaurant-cafe is closed, we have little choice than to settle ourselves down, next to the road, and wait.

As the night passes, slowly, very slowly, I gain some solace in the certain knowledge that the long night will eventually give way to a brand new day.

There's no sleep for me here, for as ever I'm awake to the dangers that lurk, particularly in the form of strangers who get over interested in my girlfriend.

I notice a man, who seems to be serving in the military, who's staring and smiling across at us, in a way I find rather unfamiliar and strange, and I draw Yolanda's attention to him.

'I think he's got his eye on you,' I whisper to her.

*'Actually, I think he's smiling at **you**,'* she says, smirking, *'I've heard they prefer men in these places.'*

The soldier stands by the door of the men's toilets and looks over at me, and it does appear he's beckoning me, gesturing me to join him, and though I'm in need of the toilet I stay put, chatting to Yolanda, with half an eye on the soldier, to see what his next move will be, and when I remember to look again, he has gone.

It turns out to be a long cold night, a **very** long cold night.

Chapter 13

OUT OF THE STERLING BELT

Long after the first flash of the rising sun on the new day, there are still no signs of life at the border.

Parched and rattling, we are desperate to break our fast.

When at last someone comes to open up the cafe, I have had plenty of time to fully digest the menu before our order is taken. The interior of the cafe seems oddly familiar, the net curtains, plastic tablecloths, even the surface of the counter covered in that sticky-backed plastic stuff - *Fablon* - that after enough use eventually chips at the corners. The atmosphere, the fittings and the fabrics, and not least, the entire menu, all of them would fit in well, back in London.

In time, our breakfast is served and we wolf it down, our double fried eggs and beans on toast washed down with cups of coffee. We are nicely set up for the day.

I pay for our meal with Turkish money, and the owner thoughtfully gives us the change in Iranian *rials*, thin silver coins on which is cast the beautiful image of a lion stood against a sunset, a similar image to that which is printed on the postage stamps stuck to the visa.

Before leaving I deftly pocket a chipped glass saltshaker, figuring that we're going to need it, as fresh tomatoes taste all the better with a little salt sprinkled on them.

The border post receives its first travellers of the day, who draw up in a van, all exuding an air of confidence and affluent self-importance. It transpires they are Indians who have taken the overland route out of their country and are travelling to Europe. The meeting is a good one, and I for one feel that it can't be that long now before we'll get to India.

From the other direction comes a long articulated container truck, and the driver parks up nearby, leaps out of his cab, and strolls purposefully towards the cafe.

'Any chance of a lift?' I ask him.

'After, after! First I go eat,' he snaps back breezily.

I suppress my excitement, but it rather looks as if we might have a good lift lined up.

Eventually, some half an hour or so later, he returns back from the cafe and fixes me with his dark eyes.

'You come England?' he asks.

171

'Yes, from London.'

'Me, I also come. I coming London,' he tells us with evident pride.

Then he signals for us to climb up and into the spacious cab beside him, once we are all in and sat comfortably, he shifts the gears, and drives the truck slowly back towards the customs post.

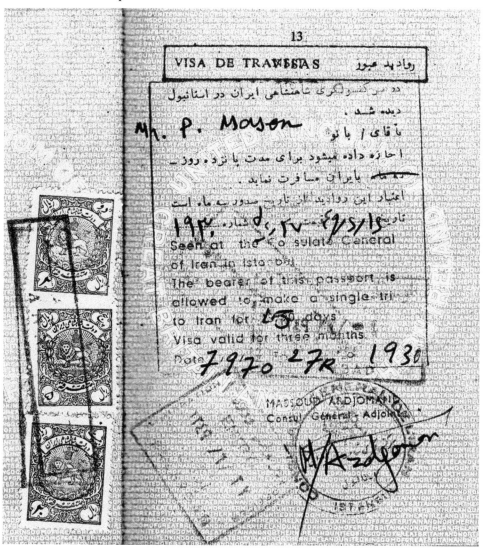

Passport control deals with Yolanda and myself in no time at all, and I get another stamp in my passport, on my visa, to add to my growing collection. Then the driver shows his papers.

Our lorry soon gets the all clear to go, as it's a sealed consignment and needs no inspection. I don't really understand the ins and outs of this, but presumably there's some sort of international agreement on such things.

Our driver seems quite an energetic man, tall and dapper, and dressed in a red checked shirt, with sharply creased casual trousers.

Once we're clear of the border, he lets us know he's headed for Teheran.

What brilliant luck! This lift promises to be a really long journey, perhaps our longest lift yet and our driver's good fun, and spends his time gaily chatting with us in broken English.

Apparently he's doing a removal job and he tells us with a grin that he's picked up other hikers (female) along the way. *He's a saucy one,* I think to myself, *but he seems safe enough.*

The cab is much higher than on most vehicles and what with the smoothness of the tarmac road, travelling is a real pleasure now. But as we slide along through the endless dry arid plain, the temperature seems to soar and get hotter by the moment.

To our right a chain of low dark mountains loom, which provide focus for my attention, and I notice in the far distance a bird, perched on the peak of one of the low hills, a magnificent bird.

'An eagle, an eagle, I just saw an eagle back there,' I rant, logging the sighting in my mental *I-Spy* book.

The stillness of this part of the world feels divine and fortunately, as our driver seems very relaxed, we don't become uncomfortable when the conversation lapses, as it does from time to time.

'You like picnic?' our driver suddenly asks.

After the long morning's travelling, the mention of a meal seems like a godsend. But I wonder where the picnic will be, as most of the land we are passing through is arid and pretty much only desert land.

We chug along for a while more before the vehicle pulls up, and parks on the side of the road. Our driver clambers up on top of the cab, where he opens a compartment and extracts all the necessary bits and bobs from a cold box there, including fresh eggs and butter.

We walk a little way and come to a grassy bank by a pretty narrow river, a good spot to picnic. It's great to be out in the nature. Our driver gets his *Primus* stove alight and fired up, and soon there's hot tea brewing and omelettes cooking.

Everything this guy says and does reinforces the confidant image he projects, one of unwavering pride and self-respect. Well, better that than having an inferiority complex I guess.

After a good meal we all light up cigarettes, and I think to show him the Turkish signet ring that I came by in Istanbul.

'This Farsee name, Saphiee,' he exclaims, pronouncing the name with passion. The name is inscribed back to front on the ring, presumably so that if it were pressed onto hot wax it would form a seal on an envelope, and the name would then be able to be read properly, the right way around. Though I don't believe the ring is authentic - it looks almost like new when the grime is brushed off - it has a curiosity value, with its inscription in what look like Arab script, but it's actually engraved in Persian, or more correctly 'Pharsee' lettering, according to our driver.

'If we ever have a girl I would call her Saphiee, it's a lovely name. Don't you think so?' Yolanda enquires of me.

'It's got charm; I suppose it's a variation of Sophie. I once knew someone called Sappho, Sappho Korner, daughter of Alexis Korner.'

I feel inspired to sing aloud the lyrics of *'Rosie'*; one of Alexis's songs:- *'Whooah Rosie, Whooah gal, Whooh Ahh Rosie, Whooh Ahh Gal, When she moves you know she really rocks, when she moves you know she really grooves...'*

As I sing I look over at the trees that grow there, close by the river, this is such an enchanting place; I've never seen anywhere else quite like it before. A fish splashes in the waters and I hear some birds chirruping. The sounds are quite delightful, we've all been well fed, and all seems well with the world.

* * *

Back in the truck we resume our journey, fortified and refreshed.

The passing hours are marked by nothing other than the movement of the sun, for in this wilderness, out of sight of mankind, any signs of human habitation are few and far between, being something of a surprise when they are seen.

Although it's far away, no more than a dot on the landscape really, I think I can see a town looming a great distance ahead of us. As we get much closer my eyes gradually light on a structure of immense beauty amongst several other lesser buildings. It's studded with stones of many shades of blue, predominantly that rare and serene colour, turquoise, intricate patterns of different hues of turquoise are spread over the curved surfaces of this holy structure, a mosque, no doubt; it's a most wondrous building to behold! And I get to thinking about the word 'turquoise', that it likely means 'Turkish' in some foreign language or other.

As our truck forges on and through the town, I puzzle at the many people here who appear to be carrying mackintoshes over their arms. On a day so incredibly hot, the sight is just too bizarre, in fact it defies understanding, and I can only guess that, uncannily, they must have some foreknowledge of rainfall.

As we get closer I stare very intently at these people, and am startled to discover that the items draped so elegantly over their arms are, in fact, incredibly long, wide, flat, breads!

Surely I can be forgiven for misunderstanding the situation since I've never seen nor imagined such large breads before. I mention my error to our driver who laughs so uncontrollably that I worry for him.

Night comes on but gradually, but when darkness arrives it feels intense, and though tiny stars twinkle and sparkle poetically they offer us no light, so henceforth on our journey it becomes more hazardous, as we have only the headlights to guide our way.

We ascend into a hilly area and our driver explains that we will be travelling on for only a few minutes more.

'Soon, soon we are stop,' he assures.

But we drive on and on, not for a few minutes, but for more than an hour!

Finally we arrive at our destination, an out of the way restaurant that lies snuggled in a fold of the hill. The building is a wooden structure with numerous windows, which puts me in mind of photographs I have seen of Alpine chalets and restaurants. If the Greasy Spoon style border cafe was a little incongruous in its appearance then this Swiss styled *l'auberge* is definitely a very close relative. Although this establishment appears closed for business, the owner soon emerges and greets us quite cordially.

Thus we all sit down to a light supper and a drink before our driver sets about establishing our sleeping arrangements. For reasons better known to himself, he seems to assume that we'll all be sleeping next to one another. Shades of Algeria! And I'm surprised to see the driver arranging his bedding underneath his lorry, but perhaps this is to ensure that if the vehicle were to be stolen that he'd be the first to know about it?!

Yolanda and I look elsewhere for somewhere to lie down, and in the event we decide to spread our sleeping bags across the veranda of the restaurant. I figure that even though it appears comfortable enough there, a very cold night lies ahead of us. I'm just so thankful that I don't feel I have to perform an all-night vigil to watch over the body of my girlfriend, as I've done on several occasions already during this trip. Gratefully, I settle down to getting some sleep, under the starry Persian sky.

* * *

Mercifully, our sleep is uninterrupted, and in the morning, after it gets light we arise to do our ablutions, and roll up our sleeping bags. Our driver generously treats us to a continental breakfast (coffee and a pastry), after which he gives us a signal that it's time to leave.

The morning sees us moving ever onward, through many, many more miles of semi-lunar landscape, interrupted only occasionally by a brief flurry of vegetation.

But the road is not quite so devoid of traffic today, for now there are lots more cars about, lorries and oil tankers too. I notice that the vehicle number plates in Iran are displayed in both normal text and Pharsee script, which gives me an unexpected opportunity to occupy myself in memorising the Pharsee numerals.

The closer to Teheran we get, the faster the truck moves; well, actually our driver is now driving as one possessed and so seems less inclined to talk.

Eventually though, something causes him to slow down and haul on the brakes. Opening his door and whipping out of the cab, he darts off towards a makeshift tent at the side of the road and disappears inside. Meanwhile we're left to sit and ponder, to imagine what lies behind his curious behaviour.

I keep a close watch on the tent, hoping to understand what's going on with our driver. He spends a long time there before re-appearing and beckoning for us to join him. There we are introduced to the locals, who seem a jolly enough crowd; and it looks as though our driver sees us as a good talking point.

It turns out that the tent is the business end of a fruit farm selling fresh produce - melons and grapes. We all set to gorging ourselves on the green pearl grapes, which prove compulsive eating, and we are soon gnawing our way through a few pounds of the juicy fruits, leaving only one or two brown ones, shrunken and wrinkled. I gaze at them a moment and give a start as I notice, for the first time, that a dried grape resembles a raisin, and I recall that the French for grape is *'raisin'*. I suppose everybody knows this, but I'd never spotted the connection before. I hadn't realised this simple truth in 18 years, so what else have I missed!

Our driver purchases a couple of crates of grapes, then we all return to the lorry.

On the road again and we're simply belting along.

My eyes turn to the rugged mountain range to our left.

'Elburz mountains,' the driver informs me.

'Beyond? Beyond the mountains?' I ask.

'R-o-o-s-sia,' he answers, his teeth clenched.

Though this is undoubtedly a good lift, I really would prefer to be going at a more moderate pace, but it's clear that the driver has something on his mind and it's beginning to affect the atmosphere between the three of us. Things are getting a bit uneasy.

He stops the vehicle once more, and this time he swings one of the wing mirrors around, and stoops down to study his face. Then, after taking out a little pair of scissors from a bag, he trims his moustache, after which he gets out a razor and soap, and proceeds to shave himself.

After all this he dons a fresh set of clothes then resumes his place in the cab. He appears in an exuberant mood now, thankfully.

'I see my wife,' he grins.

With gestures none-too-subtle he indicates why he's so eager to see his wife again. Sex!!! And he now engages us in talk about pubic hair and his dislike of it. I notice how uneasy Yolanda looks as he continues to talk on the topic, as he further states that it's his belief that women should remove all such hair from their bodies, particularly from between their legs. I can't be sure whether he really believes what he's saying or if he just wants an excuse to talk about women's private parts.

We're now coming to the climax of our lift, as we're shortly to arrive at the city of Teheran, the capital of Persia; it's so exciting, I just can't wait!!!!!

We breeze along, overtaking and overtaking some more, and I figure it can't be that much further before we'll have our first sight of the city, but as we near the outskirts of Teheran, at the start of dual-carriageway, our driver brings the lorry to a sudden halt.

Though I'm surprised he's given us no warning of his intentions, we shift ourselves, clamber down the few metal steps and jump to the ground, all the while giving thanks to him for the lift. Waving us a cheery goodbye, he revs up the engine and pulls away at speed.

After travelling so long on the open road, with only occasionally there being any other vehicles, it's a shock to all-of-a-sudden see so many cars speeding about. It's surprising how glum the expressions on the faces of the people inside the cars are, and though they are seemingly affluent and well-to-do, they appear unsmiling and tight-lipped and drive right by us.

We stand and watch as streams of cars come and go en route to Teheran, and I feel frustrated that having come so far, we've been abandoned just as we were about to enter the capital.

But patience is our paymaster and we resign ourselves to standing idle, waiting on the whim of fate for as long as it takes.

As ever, a car eventually stops and we are offered a lift.

The drive to Teheran is much longer than I expect, but when the city does eventually loom, I am staggered at the concentration of modern structures there amongst and contrasting to the countless older more modest buildings.

We are pulling into the centre of Teheran, and I figure we should make up our minds about where we want to be dropped.

'Post Office. Could you take us to Main Post Office please?' I ask hopefully.

We strike lucky; our driver understands and seems happy enough to drop us off there. The Post Office is on Avenue Sepah, and is a modern well-built affair; surrounded by rolling lawns, flower beds, with flags waving on high, atop tall poles standing along the perimeter of the grounds.

When we enter, I am struck by the feel of the place, which is more like a large church, or cathedral than a government building, it's cool and air-conditioned with an atmosphere of peace and serenity. Round about us Post Office workers move about their work, slowly, and with evident self-importance.

I seek out the appropriate counter and find myself facing a clerk, a middle-aged lady, looking through a window at me; she is well turned out, her makeup very carefully applied, and she's wearing a stylish European looking dress with a broad scarf of thin material draped around her neck and shoulders.

'Post restante? Mason?' I enquire, simply and earnestly.

The stylish lady slips away, and when she returns she carries a letter in her hand.

Only after I show her my passport does she pass me the letter.

A letter…! A letter for **me**…! I instantly recognise the handwriting; it's from my mum! But I don't open the missive immediately; I wait to open it until after we are comfortably seated outside out on the lawn. With a pen, I slit open the envelope, very slowly and carefully, then take out the letter and open it.

Apparently mum is fine and she writes that she's glad to have heard from us. I read her messages slowly, savouring her every word, and then re-read the letter again, several times.

Yolanda sits at a slight distance away, and when I'm finished I look over at her, whereupon she asks if she can read the letter too.

I'm really glad that we've heard from my mother, and her letter is so reassuring and homely.

Now we're set to explore Tehran and find somewhere to stay. I recall Anthony recommended we find a place called the Amir Kabir, which I discover is not too far away from where we are, and then, by chance, we meet another European also in search of the same place.

We walk together, and as we walk we talk. Apparently he is also British and is set on getting to Australia, where he intends to settle down and build his own house. I am impressed that he's self-organised, and that he has a goal too.

Right now I'm confused as to where Anthony was recommending us to stay, for Amir Kabir turns out to be both the name of a street and a popular hotel.

As we make our way along the Amir Kabir Road I am totally amazed to see someone here that I recognise, who we last saw back in Istanbul, since when we've travelled across sea and by road some 1500 miles (about 2500km).

'It's Anthony! Hi Man! What a small world…. How you doing?'

As we walk along, the three of us, together again, we exchange our news, and as we approach the Hotel Amir Kabir, Anthony sets himself to persuade us to stay there, but he helpfully points out that since it's still quite early in the day and we have several hours to make up our minds about choosing where to stay.

So, leaving Anthony at his hotel, Yolanda and I continue traipsing further along the broken sidewalk that runs alongside the busy street, through an area which seems to be a haven for motor spares' businesses, with tyres and hubcaps littering the pavement, and spare parts spilling almost onto the street itself. Although it's hot, we are shaded for much of the time by the many trees that line the route.

We check out another place, the Mehr Hotel, where we are shown a basement room, inside of which are potted plants and rush matting, and vegetation just outside the window; the room has a faintly exotic feel about it, and has a natural, interesting air.

Whilst it's true that we enjoyed Anthony's company back in Turkey, but we nevertheless feel wary of shacking up with him at the Amir Kabir Hotel, as the place is clearly a magnet for many western travellers. So we take the room here, and at 35 *rials* it's a good 10 *rials* cheaper than the competition. Then, after locking our bags inside our room, we set off out to see the city.

The first thing we want to do now is to find somewhere to eat, so we begin exploring the honeycomb of backstreets near to the hotel, and there we find a suitable place, which is both cheap and cheerful, selling bowls of hot steaming vegetables; chickpeas, tomatoes and potatoes at 4 *rials* per portion, and for 5 *rials* we get a large flat bread too. The eating-house uses what little space it has to the maximum advantage, and though the ceiling it not very high, there's a narrow iron staircase enabling customers to eat 'upstairs', however, I suspect that if I were to suddenly stand to my full height I would likely suffer concussion!

The food, which appears really wholesome and nutritious, if a little unseasoned, is delicious and filling, and whilst we eat we refresh ourselves with copious quantities of water from a jug.

What with being sat in a truck for two whole days, and having to endure the ever-present noise of the engine and the glare of the sun too, life's been pretty wearing and has left us much in need of some rest. Now we reckon it's time to give ourselves a break from all that and to unwind and relax for a couple of days.

When we return to the hotel we set ourselves to wash off the dust and dirt. Actually, after my shower, I feel almost uncomfortably clean and extremely tired, as does Yolanda. So, even though it's still some hours before nightfall we decide to turn in for the night. Slipping into our sleeping bags, we murmur some good night pleasantries to one another before turning over and closing our eyes.

* * *

On awakening, I open my eyes slowly and try to figure out where I am. I look about the room, and out at the foliage behind the low windows lit by the sun peeking in through behind the plants in their earthenware pots. The room feels cool and fresh; it's great that we decided to stay here, as there's an atmosphere of peace and harmony here, almost sacred, unlike anywhere we've stayed so far on our travels.

Today we'll need to change some British currency, for so far in Iran we've been relying on the money we got from changing our remaining Turkish cash at the border cafe. So, after a brief freshen-up, we set off to see some more of the city.

We walk back towards the Hotel Amir Kabir and decide to pop in and see Anthony and the others, which entails crossing over the main road. We've already noticed that the drivers here seem to ignore all known rules regarding sensible behaviour whilst driving, and instead steer haphazard courses at maniacal speeds; in fact the Amir Kabir resembles a glorified bumper car arena. The drivers' total disregard for one another, or for pedestrians, is most disconcerting, and since all commonly adhered to standards of safety are lacking, I can only assume that driving licenses are issued here without any reference to the driver's ability.

It is no exaggeration to describe our situation here, crossing the road, as potentially fatal.

Now, the prospect of darting blindly across the traffic flow has no appeal at all, but after repeated unsuccessful attempts to cross the road, we take a leap of faith and rush across to the other side, arriving breathless and flustered.

*'They're **crazies**,'* Yolanda pants.

In a state of nervous exhaustion we make our way our way to the hotel, where, to our surprise, the main door bursts open and out come our British friends.

'What can I do?' asks the Englishman, the one we met with yesterday after our visit to the Post Office, *'I can't get any money here in Teheran. Cheques from a British bank are useless here. We are out of the Sterling Belt.'*

'What do you mean?' I puzzle.

'They don't deal with British banks. Only hard cash.'

'American dollars are best,' Anthony eagerly suggests.

Though this guy with Anthony clearly has no lack of funds - if he has enough to set himself up in Australia and to build a house there - but it seems he cannot arrange to receive a penny of it here in Iran. It appears ironic that we, who have so little money, are actually better off, in this instance, than he is, at least until he gets things sorted out.

'If you get really stuck we could let you borrow a few rials,' I offer vaguely. *'See you around.'*

When we are safely out of sight I allow myself a grin and a chuckle at his expense, after all it was only yesterday he was so very cocksure of himself.

We now make our way to the main street, Avenue Ferodowsi, where I notice signs advertising the many *'saraf'* or moneychangers; the rates are displayed, listed and set so we know we won't get burned. Seems we can hope to get about 200 *rials* to the pound, so I feel comfortable we can afford a few days stay in Teheran.

We're now in search of breakfast, but this does not stop us pausing to look in the numerous clothing shops that offer an array of western style shirts, blouses, jackets and trousers.

On our search for the elusive cafe we pass a grand looking building, the National Bank Melli Iran, and then we go across the Avenue Naderi.

Reposing at the end of a tree-lined avenue, safe behind the vast gilded black wrought iron railings and guarded by a sentry, is the British Embassy. To my eyes the whole place looks extremely ostentatious.

We continue on our way and move further up Feredowsi and come to a particularly posh area, which reminds me very much of Bloomsbury in London, with grand arcades, hairdressing salons, continental cafeterias and up-market clothes shops, all set amongst the most elegant and graceful architecture.

Swiftly we leave this quarter in the hope of having better luck finding breakfast back on Feredowsi.

At a restaurant adorned with the ubiquitous red and white sign, we stop and study the menu, and discover they offer a reassuringly wide array of European fare.

'A bit expensive! They do breakfast though... Let's treat ourselves. You only live once eh?'

'Why shouldn't we?' Yolanda asks, then adds, *'There's a lot of richies around aren't there?'*

'Yes, they all seem frightfully well off.'

After a hearty breakfast, we continue our walk along Feredowsi, whereupon a young guy introduces himself and asks us if we would like to see the city in his company. Since he seems pleasant enough we accept his offer, and he takes us on a tour of the city in his car.

'You have heard about Jimi Hendrix?' he remarks casually.

Back on the SS Kades, Anthony had told me that apparently Jimi had been seen in Morocco. So, maybe now he's here in Persia?

'What about him?' I ask.

'He's dead,' the man answers.

'What? Surely you've got it wrong, someone else perhaps. Who did you say?' I ask.

'Jimi Hendrix, the guitarist, suicide I think.'

'I don't believe it,' Yolanda moans loudly.

I notice we're near to the Post Office, and I ask our Iranian friend to stop the car, telling him we have some things to sort out.

When we are alone together, Yolanda and I stand facing each other in silence. Could it be true, a man who veritably crackled with positive energy is really dead? It's Yolanda who breaks the silence.

'Do you believe him, that Jimi is dead?'

'Yes and no,' I answer glumly.

'Maybe it's another guitarist. Perhaps he's got it wrong.'

'On the other hand ...?' I mumble vaguely, lost in thought.

We revisit the Post Office but find no post for Yolanda or myself, so we wander slowly back to our hotel.

I'm still thinking about Jimi, my hero, the guitarist and dreamer *extraordinaire*.

'Foxy lady, I'm coming to get ya..!' I sing quite loudly.

By the time we get back to our room the words and music to many of Jimi's songs are gushing forth through me.

Strutting up and down the floor of our bedroom, I wrench the chords and solos off a load of his songs, strumming and tugging the strings of my imagination. I set myself to perform each and every song I can remember. For *'Burning of the Midnight Lamp'* I even treadle at a make-believe wah-wah pedal simulating the sounds, making different shapes with my mouth, with nasal sounds escaping my nostrils.

'Oh don't. Stop it. Stop. He's dead, he's dead.'

'His music isn't! Never will be and that's for sure.'

High as a kite, that's how high I feel right now.

'Well mountain lions found me there, waiting, and they set me on an eagles wing,' I drawl. *'Yeah, eagle's wing baby.'*

'How could you? You just keep reminding me he's dead,' Yolanda pleads.

'Well maybe he's not,' I answer thoughtfully.

Towards the end of the day we go out and scout around the local shops for fruit and vegetables. We are successful and scurry back to organise our supper, which consists of fresh baked flat bread, onions, tomatoes and grapes.

'I've had ample sufficiency, as my grandfather used to say,' I sigh.

Yolanda smiles.

'I feel like a cup of tea and after that maybe we'll go to bed?' I suggest.

'I can't sleep if I have tea or coffee before I go to bed.'

'You must be losing... uh .. your sweet little mind,' I sing, mimicking Jimi's style some more.

* * *

Though we would dearly like to explore some more, Yolanda and I agree that we should avoid the temptation of staying in Teheran too long. So, thinking we should press on, we decide that this will have to be our last day here. But before we go we want to make the most of the facilities at the hotel, so we set about washing our hair and our clothes. And in searching out a bucket to soak the clothes we begin to discover the rest of the hotel. In the midst of it all we find an attractively paved courtyard, and here, amongst the balustrades, fig trees and potted plants, we locate a bucket next to the communal tap, as well as a fellow guest, a Yugoslavian lad, sitting there resting.

'Have you heard about Jimi, Jimi Hendrix?' I ask him.

'What?' he answers me cautiously.

'Someone told me he's dead.'

'Oh, really?' he replies; though he appears unmoved by the news. I can't be sure that he has understood properly. But perhaps he is just being 'cool', yes that's it, for I discover that whatever topic is being spoken about, that I find him inexplicably distant.

We leave the washing hanging in the courtyard, where even the sunshine has difficulty finding it's way in; but the air is so warm it should all soon be dry.

* * *

The next day, when we make ready to leave, Yolanda discovers that our clothes are still damp, so we are forced to pack them away anyway just as they are.

Hereabouts not many speak any English and of those that do, few are very proficient, so we find it difficult to glean any useful information. We are unsure which route to take, for we have no plan of the city, so we have to rely on our intuition as to which direction we should take to find a good spot to hitch from. But as we are in no particular hurry, we dilly dally about on the way, nosing around the back streets behind the main road, where we discover a marketplace of traders eager to ply their trades.

Yolanda wants to sample some of the edibles on display.

'Ooh look...! Pistachio nuts... I love them! Oh, and look they've got pine nuts too, I haven't had those since I was at college,' she exclaims. By college she means the convent school she attended outside her hometown of Siena, Italy.

'Yoghurt?' she asks a trader uncertainly.

'Yaourt,' he replies rolling his head to and fro.

Yoghurt has only recently been introduced into London shops in the form of slimmer's desserts, and up 'til now I've not been tempted to try any myself, but Yolanda is keen to sample some here, so the shop owner serves it to her in a shallow bowl - but with a thick skin on top of it it looks altogether unappetising.

'Yuck!! It's off, it's sour, really horrible, ugh!' Yolanda hollers disdainfully, and she begins to rage at the shopkeeper. Then she storms off without paying and tries

sampling the yoghurt on several other stalls, before finally realising that they can't all be 'off', and then, shamefacedly, she admits that she must have been wrong. She now asks for a little sugar, to add to the yoghurt, and apparently this makes it taste more palatable, and she eats it up hungrily. When she's finished we get on with our walk across town.

Trekking through the avenues of uptown Teheran I glance up at the names of the streets. This one, the Avenue Shah Reza, seems interminable, frustratingly so, and as I fight to control my impatience to find a place to hitchhike, my attention lights on two guys walking some way ahead of us. I wonder that one of them looks slightly familiar?

'Isn't that the Yugoslav cat?' I ask Yolanda.

'Where? Oh maybe.'

We quicken our pace and soon catch up with them.

'Where are you off to?' I ask them breezily.

'Same as you, probably,' one of them answers, smiling.

There's something about him; he's quite different from any of the other travellers we've met.

'We're hitching to Afghanistan,' I tell him. *'What about you?'*

He just nods and smiles a big, big grin. It transpires that he, Yani, and his friend, Jorg, are both from Yugoslavia and are both of them hitching to India together. We walk, the four of us, Yani and Jorg, Yolanda and myself, until eventually we find a convenient place to hitchhike from.

Having dropped our baggage down on the pavement beside us, we stand around, a little ill-at-ease with one another. I break the silence;

'Jorg. I think maybe your name in English would be George?' I suggest. He stares back at me, possibly without comprehension. I'm not sure he speaks any English.

'Since we're all going the same way, shall we share a lift?' Yani suggests.

Now it's my turn to be cool, and I turn to Yolanda for her response, only to find she is transmitting her 'no comment' expression.

'All four of us?' I ask, surprised, *'well I guess we could give it a try.'*

'You have cigarette?' enquires Yani.

I nod and pass him one.

'And one for Jorg, yeah?' he adds.

I get the distinct impression that they are both financially worse off than us, and if we are to travel together this could potentially put a drain on our resources if we are not careful.

But no one stops to offer us a lift; perhaps it's too much to expect for anyone to pick up four bedraggled foreigners. It would seem like a better idea that we should split up and stand separately; like that we might stand some sort of a chance.

As I toy with what to do about our situation, a big black *Rover* car lumbers down the road towards us, all shiny black paint and gleaming chrome, an old style vehicle with a humped high roof. The car stops just a little way ahead of us. Frankly I am surprised.

'All of us?' I ask nervously.

The driver and his friend get out and move some items from the back seat to the boot, then gesture for us all to get in the vehicle. We squeeze ourselves into the car and it starts to move off, very slowly; the pace is sluggish, almost unnatural, but who am I to complain?

Yani assumes the role of self-elected leader and spokesman, which comes as a relief to me, as I don't want the responsibility of speaking on behalf of the four of us. So leaving him to talk with the driver and his friend, I take to staring out of the window, noticing that we are now leaving the built up capital and going north.

Yani turns his head to announce that he has agreed that we'll all join the Iranians on a picnic. Inwardly I groan, as personally I really don't want to delay our journey picnicking with these middle-classed middle-aged men.

The car maintains its ludicrously slow speed as it negotiates the winding, climbing road, but in less than half an hour we arrive at a local beauty spot. I am heartened to discover that the boot of the car contains lots of food and drink, though I can't help but wonder why it is that they packed enough for six people.

What a queer assortment of companions we are, sitting around doing rough justice to the spread. But it's a nice leafy spot, and the food is good; so life could be a lot worse, for sure.

'Paul, you are Music Man. Sing a song!' comes a request from one of the Iranians.

'Really, I don't feel in the mood, not just now, maybe later, huh,' I mumble.

The other Iranian guy shouts his encouragement and claps his hands, and I notice that Yani is staring at me, challenging me. But I ignore him and carry on eating.

'Come on Paul, sing us a song,' the driver calls to me.

I look again at Yani and know that I'm beaten, so I capitulate and falteringly give a rendition of Donovan's hit, *'Mellow Yellow'*.

'I'm just mad about fourteen year old girls, they're mad about me. They call me "Mellow Yellow"' I sing, then I then explain to them, *'I'm not a singer, I play guitar,'*

'Good. You good. Thank you,' says the Iranian courteously.

No one seems to have much to say, so this is really not my idea of a picnic, and I suspect Yolanda isn't enjoying herself either.

'I hope we go soon,' she whispers to me.

But in spite of a lot more wishing, hoping and waiting, it's a long, long time before anyone makes a move.

I'm surprised that Yani should find these guys' company any more enjoyable than we do. He's being so polite to them, so I wonder what he likes about their company. But by Yani's expression I guess he's up to something, but I can't think what it is, I just know there's something on his mind. Then, whilst he's chatting to the driver he suddenly stops speaking, takes a deep breath, and after a dramatic pause he asks: -

'Opium? You have opium?'

'Opim, opim, Yes, you like? You come to our house. Plenty opim,' the Iranian answers excitedly.

My heart sinks. This journey with these Yugoslav guys has been strain enough already, and I have no desire to prolong it by going back to these Iranian guys' house. But Yani appears delighted with the news of the opium, and takes it upon himself to accept an invitation for us all to stay the night at these mens' house.

Thanks a lot, I think to myself.

We arrive at the house, a European style affair, shortly before nightfall, and the Iranians produce a quantity of the sticky black drug, and together with Yani and Jorg they set about smoking it, and as it has to be mixed with tobacco, muggins here is asked to provide some cigarettes.

Whilst the opium smokers are indoors smoking, Yolanda and I go outside where the air is fresh, and we sit down on a bench in the garden at the back of the house, chatting and sipping some refreshments we've been given.

After some minutes one of the Iranians emerges, and wanders rather unsteadily over to join us, and I note, from the way he walks and the expression in his eyes, he appears **incredibly** stoned.

As it happens Yolanda needs to use the toilet and therefore asks our host where the toilet is. He responds by pointing vaguely to the back of the garden.

'Here, you can go here,' he tells her, gesturing to the garden space.

It's obvious to me that she's puzzled, that she can't tell whether he's joking or not, so at first she doesn't move, but eventually, seemingly out of desperation, she goes off and finds a secluded spot to relieve herself. But, as she tells me later, when she went to pull up her underwear she noticed the Iranian was but a few feet away from her, with his eyes fairly popping out of his head.

Clearly our host has 'ideas', and from now on, wherever she goes, he follows her, and I can see she's getting very anxious, and coming close to me she confides in hushed whispers how she fears for what the night might bring.

I've smoked 'O' myself, some years back, so I'm aware of its cycle of effects. First there's the initial nausea, then the extreme hunger, followed by an inability to move, and when this is over the charm of the drug then becomes evident, in the dreamy easiness and heightened sensory perception it bestows. It had a very soporific effect on me, made me feel very mellow. But these Iranian guys are probably old hands at this game, so who knows at what stage they are at, or what affect it has on them, or even what quantity they've had. What I do know is that on an opium high, life can appear very dreamy, as though one were watching oneself in a movie.

With Yolanda sticking close to me, uncomfortably close, I go in search of the Yugoslav cats, and find Yani and Jorg totally smashed and completely 'out of it', slouched against a wall, their speech slurred and only barely intelligible. Then our Iranian hosts enter the room, and they appear agitated, angry even, at finding us all sitting together. Now, it's one thing to be a little stoned and disorientated, but quite another to get oppressive and heavy. This is not like any 'turning on' scene I've ever been in, not at all. Judging by their faces, I note that not only do they look crazed, but also they seem disturbed, aggressive even. Actually, to my absolute horror, they appear chillingly murderous - I've never seen such looks before! Not ever. Not even when I've been with people who I've known to be really, really stoned.

Things have really been moving on at an alarming rate and I feel very uneasy about the situation with these guys. I can't begin to imagine why they're in this state, as it's not as if anyone has insulted them. So, most likely, it's a lust thing, that they find Yolanda attractive and they can't control their desires. I do know that drugs can affect people in different ways, sometimes quite strongly, but I never saw anyone look so demented as this before.

As I'm the only guy here who's still straight, I feel I have a duty to the others to look after them, and the responsibility hangs heavy on me; but it's obvious that somehow I have to get Yolanda out of here to safety, and the others too if they'll come.

I bide my time and wait and wait, until the Iranians get up and leave the room for some reason, and then I try to whisper my plan to Yani, but he just sits there staring, his eyes unfocused, a slight smile on his lips. So I try again;

'These guys are dangerous. We are getting out. How about you?'

'Are you sure, Man?' Yani asks, looking me squarely in the eyes.

'We go!' I state emphatically.

I can see it takes him an immense effort, but Yani pulls himself together and gets to his feet. Then, with each of us clutching his and her own baggage, the four of us slip out through the front door and out onto the road.

Fate has been kind to us so far, as it appears our escape has gone un-noticed, but now we need to help ourselves.

'Run for it!' I urge the others, and with that we all race off blindly into the darkness, just as fast as we can go.

Chapter 14

UNLIKELY PROPOSITIONS

D own the darkened lane we run in order to get Yolanda away from the house of the two stoned foreigners who seem to have gotten way-y-y too interested in her, and most worryingly of all seem to harbour homicidal tendencies too.

'Just keep going!' I shout, trying to give encouragement to the others; but I realise we all lack the stamina to keep on running for very much longer.

'What are we to do? We can't keep going like this,' comes Yolanda's anguished voice from the gloom.

'We need to get the hell out of here. We've got to get away!' I insist.

I worry that as we don't know the area, we're running blind, and we might easily come to a dead end.

I hear the sound of a vehicle approaching, and due to lack of visibility I can barely make out whether it's a car or a truck.

'Let's try and get a lift,' I shout to the others.

So the four of us stop still and stand in the middle of the road.

To my relief the lorry brakes and the driver gestures for us all to get into the back of the vehicle, so we hurriedly clamber on. As we pull away I hold on as best I can, in fact we all cling on to the back of the cabin for dear life as the lorry lurches and bounces, negotiating the uneven track. The dirt thrown up by the spinning tyres creates billowing clouds of dust that fairly fills the air. Coughing and spluttering we cover up our faces with our sleeves.

The lorry moves on at quite a pace along the long rough track and then it turns a corner and gets onto a proper road. Here the driver brings the vehicle to a sudden halt and calls to us.

Bruised, choking and dazed we stumble back and lower ourselves onto the road before then going to speak with the driver.

By the light of the headlights I see my companions, who look truly comical, like extras from a Buster Keaton comedy, plastered as they are from head-to-toe with fine white dust.

The lorry driver cannot take us any further - I'm not sure why - so we stand stranded, nursing our eyes and coughing incessantly.

Here we are - God knows where - sore, tired and desolate, in almost pitch-black darkness.

'What next?' I ask, hoping that maybe Yani can think of a way out of this dilemma.

'Go to the police?' he suggests.

'We can't go anywhere. In this darkness I can't see a thing, let's just wait for another lift.' I answer Yani.

As we stand about, waiting in the darkness, occasionally I strike a match, and by the flashes of light we are at least able to get glimpses of one another's faces from time-to-time.

'You know, we take our eyes for granted,' Yolanda observes quite suddenly, *'we've got a lot to be thankful for. Think what it would be like to be blind!'*

How long we are waiting here, I don't know, but the darkness makes it feel like a long time, though it's likely only a matter of twenty minutes or so before the lights of an approaching car brings forth a loud cheer from us all. And as luck has it the car stops, and the man who's driving it gestures for us to open the door and get in.

It's a tight squeeze for the driver has his wife and child with him.

As we get on our way the family show themselves to be exceptionally hospitable, passing us soft drinks and nuts, and chatting away excitedly, and I notice Yani in particular looks as though he thrives on the attention from them.

We are fortunate as this lift with the family is a long one, but as I'm tired I would much prefer to be able to go to sleep somewhere. As it happens I'm not at all sure of our whereabouts, but that said, I'm way past caring.

We journey onward through much of the night until eventually the car comes a halt, and it's apparent we've now arrived at the town these people hail from, and Yani, Jorg, Yolanda and myself get out and sit by the roadside, thinking that even if we have to stay here for the rest of the night, that it's no big problem, at least we're out of danger now.

* * *

As the town awakens early in the day, we all file into a local *chaay* shop where the silver-tongued Yani quickly ingratiates himself with the owner.

To the applause of all the other customers there, Yani makes a great show of drinking his tea out of a saucer; so I gather it's a local custom. It's something I used to see my grandfather do, he would sometimes drink his tea like this, out of a saucer, in order to cool his over-hot drink.

The teahouse also sells fresh *halwa;* a sweet preparation made from honey and crushed sesame seeds. Yani is full, so full of praise for this and so we all tuck into a piece. I find it pleasant enough, though dry and hard to swallow.

'Cigarette?' comes a request from Yani.

189

It seems he has no money whatever. So I purchase a packet of Iranian cigarettes - a brand called *Homa*, which are smaller than normal sized cigarettes, being closer in size to matches, short and thin - and opening the packet I hand them around.

Yani focuses his attention on the other customers of the cafe.

'*Pool naderi*,' he announces.

Whisperingly he explains to me that this short phrase simply means '*I have no money*'. He's lucky in getting the locals to part with a little cash, and then he shows his willingness to pay for his tea, but though the owner waves him away, he doesn't hesitate in accepting payment from Yolanda and myself. I still have strong reservations about travelling with Yani, his patter is just too well oiled, but for the time being I decide to stay silent about my concerns.

Outside, on the roadside, we all stand about waiting again, hoping for a lift, and the day takes an upturn when a lone driver picks us all up, and seems genuinely pleased to have our company. But before long the driver stops and explains he has some business to sort out before we can go any further.

As it happens he is not gone very long, and on his return he invites us to pick some walnuts from a nearby tree. Now why is it that things taste so much better when they are freshly picked? Back at home we generally only had nuts at Christmas and those always tended to be a bit dry and brittle, but when I crack open my first fresh walnut I discover the contents are surprisingly warm and oily.

'*Delicious, fantastic. I don't usually like nuts,*' I remark. But Yolanda doesn't reply, her mouth is already full.

I get chatting with our driver.

'*Where are we?*' I ask.

'*Near Caspian Sea. Next we go Amol, then Babol.*'

Amol and Babol! They sound to me like Biblical names. And Caspian? Well, there was a '*Prince Caspian*', which was the name of one of C.S. Lewis's inspiring and imaginative *Narnia* books. I check my map and establish our location. To my surprise I find we're still not so very far from Teheran. Yet after all the travelling we've been doing I would have thought we'd be further away, so we must have been going around in a circle or something!

As the day wears on, the effects of our sleepless night really start to take their toll, and when our lift finally comes to an end we're all desperate to get our heads down, at which point Yani confidently claims that he's sure he'll be able to get us all a free night's lodging in a hotel.

I do not openly doubt him, preferring instead to see what tactic he intends to use to get us a place.

At Yani's insistence, we all go in search of the police station, the four of us, with Yani leading the way, then Yani apprises the police of our situation, and we are soon being escorted to a hotel close by, where two rooms are given over to us for our use. Just like that!

In truth, I would sooner have paid for our room, but clearly, for the sake of the group, it's better to work on the basis of 'all for one and one for all'. My feeling is that the hotelier is not too greatly enamoured with our presence, but he refrains from giving voice to his feelings.

After sprucing ourselves up a little we make ourselves a meal of bread, tomatoes and grapes, before turning in for the night.

* * *

The wicker blinds in the hotel are insufficient to keep the bright sunshine out, so, come morning, none of us lie in bed for long.

When the four of us regroup I'm glad to discover that the night's rest has worked wonders on us. The tension that was beginning to mar our relationship has abated somewhat.

'Do you reckon we'll make it to Mashad today?' I ask Yani.

'Sure, and we must get to the Afghan Embassy, but we might have a problem there though.'

'How's that?'

Yani explains to me that from what he's heard, we'll need visas to visit Afghanistan, which we can pick up whilst we are in Mashad, which is not a problem. But the rumour is that the Afghans only allow entry to people who have lots of money to spend, so accordingly they require that everybody show them the equivalent of $100 when they go for their visas, which is a problem, and something to reflect on ahead of time.

That isn't the only bad news; nobody seems to want to give us a lift, so we talk about splitting up and standing as two pairs by the roadside in the hope this will give us a better chance. But still nobody stops to give us a lift, so, seeing a bus speeding towards us, Yani waves it down.

When the bus slows to a halt and stops, Yani uses his standard lament,

'Pool naderi, pool naderi,' he pleads.

The driver smiles and gestures us all aboard where we sit down alongside the other passengers. Immediately we become objects of attention, and then of amusement, as one man in particular seems intent on making his presence felt.

'Pool naderi?' he asks, pointing a finger at us.

We all affirm, for what else can we do after Yani has told the driver we have no money?

'Pool ma dharam, pool ma dharam,' he states repeatedly, telling us he has pots of

money, and he continues to gesture with his hands so we get the full import of his words, which is that he has a lot, a lot of money and that we don't. And this news seems to amuse him hugely.

By the time the bus finally arrives in Mashad, it's well after nightfall, and after debating the subject of what to do for the night; we all agree that we'll camp out on a patch of lawn we've chanced upon. After only a short time though we begin to re-think our position and Yani again suggests we deliver ourselves up to the police.

But tonight things are very different here, as there's no hotel on offer to us; all that's available is to stay in the police station cells.

Yani and Jorg disappear into the first cell, and though we're initially reluctant at accepting the offer, Yolanda and I lie down in another cell. Of course we leave the door of our cell unlocked, and I'm put out when I notice a police officer comes into the cell to lie down too, but he soon falls asleep, clasping a machine gun tightly to his chest.

I wish, hope and pray - and pray some more - that he has correctly secured the safety catch!

Though I don't exactly sleep (as I keep peeking to re-assure myself the gun is not pointing at us), I do rest and feel quite safe, it's better by far being here than lying out near the street all night, under the gaze of passers by.

* * *

When I awake I'm relieved to find that I'm unscathed and that I've slept right through the night. The truth is that I'd been really concerned about the machine gun pointing at us, and had only got to sleep by blotting out the worry from my mind.

We don't linger at the police station and are soon up and outside; but what with hunger, weariness and an overall disinclination to walk, we are all a little difficult and prickly with one another.

We're all plodding along the pavement, with no particular destination in mind, until, quite suddenly, Yolanda sits herself down on the pavement with a bump, and looks up at us all with a belligerent expression upon her face.

In response we say nothing (well what is there to say?) so she bounces back up again, and walks on as though nothing has happened. Like the rest of us, she has clearly had enough, and this is her way of showing it. This is the only sign she gives of her feelings. The episode takes only seconds, but it speaks volumes about what we all feel. She's been a brick and has so far endured everything with resignation, with utmost patience.

After the pavement incident Yolanda is embarrassed and tries to hide her face from us.

'Let's find a chaay shop,' I suggest.

'Where else?' Yani responds affably.

192

Here we are in another town, sitting in another *chaay* shop, and here we have another chance to contemplate a portrait of the Shah of Iran. I really cannot fathom why every shop here seems to have a portrait of the king on display.

I study the photograph, the Shah has his hair swept back (in the style so often associated with actor Tony Curtis), and he's pictured in uniform with a broad light blue sash across his dark high collared jacket, which is simply dripping with gold braid and medals, the Shah is flanked by his attractive wife and young son.

'He divorced Soraya, his other wife, as she couldn't give him a son, only a daughter,' explains Yolanda. *'That's the Empress Farah and the boy's name is Reza.'*

Reza's mother looks faintly Italian; which might go some way to explain why Yolanda knows so much about the royal family here and it might also explain why she, as an Italian, is not required to obtain a visa for Iran.

'We need to get cleaned up before we go to the Afghan embassy,' I point out.

'Definitely! My face feels unreal. I'm filthy,' Yolanda admits.

'Yes, we should do that,' agrees Yani. *'I must get some money sorted out too.'*

Well this sounds interesting; I wonder how he's suddenly going to get some money?

Our own task is to set out and track down some washing facilities, and we're surprised at how modern the facilities are, but then I discover we are expected to pay.

'A sauna bath! That's a bit unexpected; I never had one of those before. I thought they only had them in Sweden,' I puzzle.

'Meet you guys back here in an hour,' Yani calls, before disappearing.

Clearly Yani is going to look for somewhere to wash for free. I'm thankful that he didn't expect me to pay for him (or maybe he did?).

Anyway, after purchasing some soap and shampoo, the manager of the sauna issues us with towels and wooden sandals. Putting on the sandals we step into the sauna room, which has both hot and cold water on tap and a raised surface to recline on. I slip off the sandals only to discover the floor is heated from below, and is very, very hot. And soon the temperature in the room becomes almost unbearable, which encourages us to get on with the business at hand.

We get though half a bottle of shampoo and a cake of soap before we're satisfied that we've cleansed ourselves of all the foreign matter we've accumulated whilst on the road, and when we emerge from the sauna we are both of us squeaky clean.

We find Yani and Jorg waiting outside, so I share my enthusiasm for this new experience.

'Brilliant. You should try it. I feel really so-o-o clean. Fantastic Man.'

'Oh yeah? We cleaned up too. So, are you ready to go to the embassy?' Yani asks.

He has already sussed out where we have to go. We find the consulate, obtain the necessary papers to apply for our visas, and are soon sat in the local cafe again, filling out our forms.

The consulate requires passport-sized photographs too, and fortunately I still have the remainder of the strip of photos I obtained when organising my passport.

It becomes obvious to me that Yani is still worried that he will have to front up a lot of hard cash.

'Some guy says he'll lend it to us if we need it,' he tells me.

Well, I'm impressed that at least he's got on and found a possible solution to the problem for himself.

Anyway, we're all in agreement that Yani and Jorg, and Yolanda and myself, will visit the consulate separately.

'Let's go, Yolanda,' I suggest, *'the earlier we get the forms back to them, the sooner we'll get the visas.'*

Everything goes well for us with the Afghans, very smoothly, without so much as a hint of a problem. Mind you, had they seen us a few hours ago things might have been different!

On our return to the cafe I am able to reassure Yani, that we haven't been asked to front any money, let alone $100 each. Now he and Jorg scuttle off to hand in their forms. They're not gone long before they return, looking very satisfied.

We've been told the visas won't be ready until late afternoon, so we have some time on our hands, as it isn't even midday yet.

We stand about in the street while Yani sets off out to do some hustling, and he returns pretty sharply with a satisfied smirk on his face, so by the looks of things he has got himself some money.

We sit ourselves down in a *chaay* shop and attempt to order some food, but to my surprise, instead of showing us a menu, we are pointed to the adjoining shops, where we are able to buy some bread, vegetables and fruit.

I wonder just how irate the owner is going get with us, for taking our food into his cafe to eat with our *chaay*. However, not only does the owner agree to us eating our food in his shop, he even offers us some salt, and the use of a knife.

Imagine being able to do this back in England! It would like be begging for trouble.

After our improvised meal there's another surprise in store for us, Yani pulls out a pack of cigarettes and offers them around! It's such a relief to see that Yani's dealing with his financial problems and apparently sorting them out. I really don't like to think that I ever buy friendship, so I'd much prefer not to be leant on, and to see these Yugoslav cats independent of us. Hey, with his newfound wealth Yani is even offering to pay for a couple things for us - I guess it's his way of balancing things out. We continue to hang around the *chaay* shop, using the place as our base until it's time to go back to the consulate, though we sometimes slip out for a few minutes just to get some exercise. It would be nice to go and explore Mashad and take a closer look at the vast and fabulously huge mosques we passed, the one with an amazing turquoise dome and the other with a gold one. When it's time for us to set off for the consulate again we're still apprehensive as to whether or not we'll get our visas, so we keep our fingers well and truly crossed. But we needn't have worried; our passports are there, ready for collection, though when I check the validity of my transit visa, I find it's limited to just one week from entry 'Via Islam Qala', leaving us precious little time to get across Afghanistan!

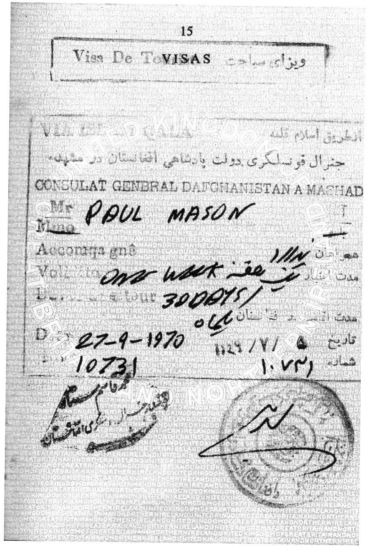

'How are you getting to the border?' Yani asks me.

'Hitch I suppose. Why?' I query.

'We're catching the bus, you should come!'

Yani amazes me.

'But how can you afford it?' I ask him.

Yani merely raises his eyebrows.

Actually, Yani is spot on about the bus, it's a great idea not having to having to depend on a lift tonight, pure luxury, and we all settle down to enjoy the ride, one that's likely to be quite a long one.

As we race towards the border, the last light of the day faintly illuminates the barren wastes about us.

All night long we travel, hour after hour, through the remote towns of Torbat-e-Jam and Tayebad, and onward until we stop and are processed at the Iranian customs post.

Then we continue, hurtling on through the desert until at last we come in sight of the Afghan border post.

By the time we arrive at the border, dawn is just breaking, yet already the place is crawling with porters hauling freight about. It's exciting to be entering another country, especially one so close to India. But first we have the monotonous chore of filling out all of the necessary entry forms, for which we have to queue, and then fill the things out, only to queue again when they're completed!

When we present our forms the customs official looks at us attentively. His face is wizened and his beard long, he wears a white turban tied loosely round his head; ill-fitting khaki clothes hang loosely on his slight frame.

He attempts to speak with us in his own language and appears amused that we don't understand what he's saying.

He tries again, this time in broken English, very courteously wishing us a good visit.

Clutching his pen, he makes his own inimitable oval shaped mark on our passports, his hand tracing a spiral pattern.

'Salamun alaikum,' he says to me, his dark eyes smiling intently, looking deeply into my own.

I smile mutely

'Okay?' he asks.

I nod.

He now turns his attention to the next person in the queue; so from this I get the impression we are now done.

There's a money-changing facility nearby where we think to obtain some Afghan money, after which we walk a distance further, and coming to a barrier we hesitate until the barrier is raised, then, under the scrutiny of a group of officials we walk on through.

'Wow, we're in Afghanistan,' I exclaim, before showing Yolanda our Afghani money, noting that Afghanistan is a Kingdom; *'Look at their coins, they all have ears of wheat on them.'*

We look back but seeing no sign of Yani and Jorg, we continue a few yards, before stopping awhile, but when there's still no sign of them we start to walk on slowly without them.

As we walk we look about us, vaguely in search of a lift, but there are no vehicles here. Perhaps it's a bit early yet?

We haven't gone very far when we come across a group of camels tethered to some trees, surrounded by a colourful troupe of Afghans. We settle down nearby them, ostensibly to put our passports away, but in truth to give us a chance to get a closer look at these desert animals and their owners.

The camels have on their backs enormous mounds of baggage, and their grumpy facial expressions seem to speak something of their dislike for their burdens. When they spot us looking at them they respond aggressively and bellow loudly at our approach. I notice swarms of flies are buzzing about them, some of which settle on their coarse matted unkempt coats, and nearby, seated neatly in a row, are a group of people, adults, and children with dishevelled hair, their clothes in tatters, who are scarcely in better shape than the beasts, and who all stare intently at us.

In response I smile, first at them and then at the camels. However, the people remain silent and unresponsive, all maintaining the same steady expressionless stare.

'Let's go now,' I suggest to Yolanda.

But as we get up to leave, suddenly a crowd of eager faces spring up and surround us, and by their gestures we understand they are offering us to join them and travel with their caravan. They become really quite persistent.

Though it's a fascinating and novel idea, it doesn't seem a practicable answer to our travel needs, so we go to leave, but only with difficulty are we are able to peel ourselves away from the camel train (all the while wondering what we have turned down).

Onwards we walk, on and on and on.

We have had nothing to eat in quite a while so we are becoming quietly desperate to find somewhere to get some breakfast. We continue to wander quite aimlessly but are no closer to finding a cafe, when I see an Afghan on a bicycle and I stop him to ask directions.

He dismounts from his bike and gazes long and hard at us with apparent interest; so, using a mixture of basic English words and easy-to-comprehend gestures - as for instance pointing to my mouth and clutching at my stomach - I communicate our need for food and drink.

For his part he nods to indicate his understanding, and motions for us to wait for him, then he cycles off along a path at tangents to the road and disappears from sight.

We wait a very long time for him to return, during which time we seriously wonder if he ever intends to come back, but we are heartened when, at length, we see a figure some distance away come cycling in our direction, from the vicinity of a clump of low flat dwellings. When the cyclist gets closer I can see by his face the signs of his exertions - perhaps he has cycled a long way?

Coming abreast of us he stops and hands me a paper packet, which I open at once, and find it contains a piece of hardened dark brown flat bread.

With difficulty I bite off a piece - the bread is stale - so I chew it until it becomes moist.

Many minutes pass, and whilst we try to eat the bread the man watches us attentively.

'Well thank you,' I say, after managing a few mouthfuls, then I start to pick up my baggage with the intention of getting going again.

'Wait!' he says.

I look at him in surprise, wondering what he has to say after being so quiet for such a long time. He pulls something out from his shirt pocket and looks over at me. Slowly he gathers his words.

'For.... Five, yes, five minutes, with her,' he says pointing to Yolanda and gesturing at his wristwatch, *'and I, I give you this.'*

He hands me a huge block of jet-black hashish weighing well over a pound (about half a kilo).

'What?' I exclaim in surprise. I find it hard to believe his offer is for real.

I glance over at Yolanda, who looks back at me uncomprehendingly, maintaining a stiff silence.

Here we go again! This idea that having sex with a woman is just about offering a fair price! We are tired, hungry, and have nowhere to stay, and yet here we are being met by a guy who just sees in us the opportunity to buy sex.

'No,' I tell him, *'No! No! No!'* I say repeatedly, shaking my head.

Undeterred he remains standing there, apparently thinking, and then, after a short while, he signals he has something else to say.

'And the bike!' he adds, pushing the heavy framed machine towards me.

What a bizarre situation this is turning out to be. And to think, initially, I hadn't even realised he could speak English.

But it's his coolness that unnerves me. Does he actually think I'll accept?

I shake my head vigorously, but then remember that both Anthony and Yani have warned me that in these countries the meaning associated with nodding and the shaking of one's head is reversed. So by nodding one is saying *'No'*? And by shaking the head one is saying *'Yes'*? I just hope my gestures won't be misread.

We gather up our things, and fortunately he makes no attempt to stop us as we resume our journey.

'What a bloody cheek!' Yolanda fumes. *'Why did he ask you? Are women bought and sold here? Huh? Are they? Bloody cheek!'*

We continue walking on in silence for quite some time, with no opportunity of a lift presenting itself.

I wonder should we get another bus? It could turn into a costly habit.

'We could have cycled to India though, at least it would have been quicker than the camel train,' I quip.

Yolanda laughs. I'm relieved that she's not too upset by the episode.

Well, the thing is, it was all so matter-of-fact, with neither of us feeling threatened or sensing any kind of danger.

Though we have to walk for quite some time more before a vehicle stops for us, eventually we get offered a ride, in a jeep, and lose no time in clambering aboard, where we join a fellow passenger, an Afghan, who appears to be a member of the military, for he wears a *khaki* jacket.

As the vehicle pulls away and we get some distance, I observe some low mountains flanking us to our left, and as the jeep storms along through a cloud of dust we drive across a ford, now all but dried up, a cracked mud riverbed.

Travelling in an open jeep silences us, for it's not possible to hold any proper conversation with the rush of air current, or even light a cigarette.

In time we approach a major town or city, Herat, the sight of which immediately lifts my spirits. The skyline here is packed with domes and minarets and is pretty staggering by any standards. The minarets stretch high into the sky and appear like enormous columns or chimneys; in fact to me they seem to belong to an older world, broken relics of some forgotten former dynasty.

We have no desire at all to sleep rough here, so the order of the day seems to be for us to find a cheap hotel where we can leave our bags and then go in search of food. As we don't feel like scouring all over town to check every last hotel, for us the choice of hotels falls between Nawasi Behzad, Grand Behzad and the Super Behzad, and after discovering one where for just a few coins we can rent a comfortable room, we book in.

After locking our room we leave the hotel with the intention of exploring Herat, but no sooner are we out of the main door than we bump into some people we know; none other than the very lads we left back at the border, Yani and Jorg, but I notice that their eyes have become unusually fixed and staring.

'We just got a room here, really nice, and you?' I say.

Yani smirks, looking very pleased with himself.

'The manager he gives us his own room for free. You wouldn't believe what I found under the carpet?'

I gaze at him inquisitively.

'Hashish, Man, wall-to-wall hashish! Wow!'

'Looks like you've smoked your way across the room,' I quip, half seriously.

Their grinning stoned expressions confirm to me they must have made a start. Well, good for them, probably just what they wanted, an unlimited supply of hash. But for myself, right now, I just want some food.

'Hey, look, Yolanda and myself are starving, we've really got to get something to eat, so, see you later huh?'

Daylight is fading fast and as we make our way through the local alleyways I notice the occasional paraffin lamp has been lit. In fact, there's a delightfully mysterious atmosphere to this place, an aura of enchantment, but what with not knowing what might be lurking in the shadows, the feeling of wonder is somewhat tainted by a faint tinge of menace.

In search of somewhere to eat we peer into all the shops we pass.

Full of curiosity we check out the clothes shops, in which are hung countless woolly skin jackets (some appear to have just been ripped off the sheep!), embroidered waistcoats, shirts and skullcaps. There's also a variety of silver jewellery on sale, chunky pieces, some set with turquoise, others with orange stones.

Everywhere we go we breathe in the smoke of wood burning fires, which permeates the air.

At last we find a place to eat, one that looks reasonably clean and tidy, a barn-like eatery with a pitched roof resting on great solid wooden beam supports. We sit ourselves down.

A man dressed in a long loose baggy shirt comes over to our table and looks at me enquiringly.

'Rice? Kabuli rice?' he suggests.

We order some rice, some bread and some yoghurt.

As we sit waiting, we look about us at the other customers, at all the ancient looking bearded Afghans, some wearing turbans, others skullcaps, all attired in baggy shirts (many of which seem to be army surplus).

First to arrive is the rice, which we find contains carrot and raisins.

'This tastes brilliant,' I enthuse.

Yolanda nods appreciatively, her mouth full of rice. We demolish the heaps of this mouth-wateringly delicious food between mouthfuls of fresh warm unleavened bread and gulps of water, and when we've finished the main dish we turn our attention to the yoghurt, crushing crystallised pieces of sugar into it. Oh, the yoghurt is just so-o-o creamy and tasty.

To round the meal off we have a pot of tea without milk, actually we've not been offered milk tea in ages, not since being in North Africa! The food and the drink restores me to some sort of norm, and feeling fairly well satiated we make our way back to our hotel room for some long overdue sleep.

* * *

The new morning sees us ripe and ready for the new day's travels and adventures. Today our destination is the next major town, which according to the map is a city called Kandahar.

We soon locate the road leading out of Herat, and though there's precious little traffic to be seen, the day is yet young, so we're not about to get disheartened.

We prepare ourselves for a long wait and are pleasantly surprised when a car draws up. I'm particularly surprised to note how small the car is, compared to those we've travelled in so far, for it's a *Mini Cooper*, a particularly small town car. I'm surprised too that the driver speaks passably good English, and for some reason I get the impression he's still doing his studies.

We haven't gone very far out of Herat when the car takes a sudden turn to the right, whereupon I soon ask the driver where we are going and he explains that he's taking a short cut. But I remain concerned, as from my dim understanding of the local geography; I am convinced that if a short cut were to exist, it would lie to the left of the main road rather than the right.

As we tumble on down the pitted, rutted minor lane, I nurture misgivings about having accepted the lift, and start to get concerned about what the driver's intentions towards us are. I cannot work him out at all, he seems affable enough, and he smilingly mentions that he intends to pick up some of his friends along the route. Indeed, we end up stopping several times for other travellers, but my concern only deepens when I see the car has become overcrowd and possibly overloaded.

However, as I'm in no position to give the driver advice, I keep my thoughts to myself. But the inevitable happens anyway.

When the car breaks down we all get out and stand around and stare. The Afghan guys are looking under the bonnet, looking under the chassis, and then they stand around talking.

Whilst they're all busy, Yolanda and I start to walk away, and call out to them to tell them that we've decided to walk back to the main road.

'That was a close shave,' I confide to Yolanda with a sigh. *'Where on earth was he taking us, I wonder?'*

'I didn't trust him,' Yolanda mutters suspiciously, *'What did he want to pick up all those people for?'*

'I think we should stick to main roads in future.' I offer.

We put our best foot forward and start to retrace our way back to main road, when after a few minutes we hear the noise of a car behind us, so I turn around, only to see the Mini drawing up. The driver stops the car and jumps out, and calls for us to get back in the car.

'Car fine, no problem.'

'No thanks,' I answer decisively.

'You get in my car!' he demands.

'No. No thanks!'

I see his expression, that same expression I'd witnessed on the faces of the opium smokers back in Iran.

Yolanda lets out a scream.

'Look out Paul, he's got a knife.'

'You're too crowded,' I point out, *'your car broke down. We'll take our chances on the main road, thank you.'*

The young Afghan lunges at me with the knife pointed directly at me, and I notice to my horror that it's held in his hand by a set of rings, it's a 'knuckle-duster' knife.

He lunges at me, again and again, and the knife flashes before me, and each time getting closer, dangerously closer to stabbing me.

'Stop it! Stop it! Stop it....!' Yolanda shrieks.

Instinctively, faced with my assailant getting ever closer, I flail out with my feet, aiming at his outstretched hands, which at least serves to keep the blade away from my flesh; and by swinging my leg high I keep him at a distance, and this seems to make him back off a bit, until, now he realises I'm going to defend myself, he stops trying to fight with me and instead staggers back towards his vehicle.

We don't hang about any longer than it takes to pick up our bags again, and we are off again attempting to put some distance between the driver and ourselves. But we haven't walked very far up the lane before I hear a wild revving of an engine, and the car speeding towards us, bearing down on us - and as it comes close to us I turn just in time to see an arm leaning out of one of the windows.

One of the passengers snatches Yolanda's black fur coat from its place on top of the sleeping bags she carries, and a roar of laughter issues forth from inside the car.

'Idiots, give it back right now, give it back!' Yolanda shouts, but to no avail, the car is soon out of sight.

If she's no longer got her coat I think it only reasonable to jettison mine, as I don't like there to be any inequality between us. So I offer to dump my coat in an adjacent field.

Yolanda won't hear of it and we argue the pros and the cons as we walk along, and before we've resolved the issue, we turn a bend in the road and I again catch sight of the car, for it has broken down once more.

As we approach we glare at the embarrassed looking occupants, and one of them throws the coat out across to us, and we continue on our way.

We continue up the lane and arrive back at the crossroads, hot, bothered, furious and fuming over the happenings of the last hour, so we seek refuge in an ancient looking *chaay* house here, where we enjoy a pot of tea and some cake, as we sit bemoaning our fate.

Because of the incident with the knife, I now view all those about us with a high level of suspicion, I feel that these people, just because they're in the same vicinity, are in some way to blame for the skirmish. So, after we've finished our tea we get up, walk out through the smoke-filled room and leave without paying!

As we wait for another lift we keep a watchful eye on the *chaay* shop wondering if anyone will come and ask us to pay our bill, but before that happens we get a proper lift again, this time from a large colourfully decorated Afghan truck.

The lorries we see here in Afghanistan are British-built. It seems the Afghans import *Bedford* chassis's and local labour adds the rest, building up high slatted wooden sides and back. The individual panels, as on this truck, are painted with compelling images of landscapes, people, flowers and machines.

The inside of the cab is surprisingly roomy and spectacularly colourful, with mirrors adorning the decorated walls. The sway of the truck, as it speeds off on its way, causes the worry beads hung on the rear view mirror to dance about merrily as we zoom along the well-constructed highway.

Up until now I have hardly been aware of the rings on my fingers, but they don't escape our driver's keen gaze. In all our travels I've never before been propositioned by a driver to sell anything. But this is Afghanistan and as we've already found, things are rather different here.

He now hassles to buy my rings, by writing numbers in the dust on the dashboard. It's a reasonable way to idle away the time, but after protracted haggling we fail to come to an understanding, and I resolve to take my rings off at the earliest opportunity after the lift is over, to avoid any repetition of this sort of interaction.

Looking outside, I notice we're now passing through a village or small town, with concentrations of dwellings spread across several hillocks, with houses and shops lining the road. But there's something wrong here, for not a soul stirs as we drive by, the place is totally deserted. Where has everyone gone? It looks as though the entire community has abandoned their homes, very suddenly.

'Ghengis Khan again?' Yolanda suggests.

'Huh?' I puzzle.

At length we draw into a pull-in cafe where our driver gives his order and beckons us to join him. Our driver is a man of few words, and after he discovered we can't understand him very well, he virtually gave up trying to speak with us. So without conversation we sit there and help ourselves to the water jug on the table, and when the cooked food and bread is brought to our table, we tuck in. And after we're all finished the driver gets up, which we take to be a sign that we're back on the road again.

At our next stop Yolanda makes it known she needs to use a toilet, and though she follows the directions given her, she returns looking bewildered and flustered. The instructions are repeated but this time it's made clear that *anywhere* at the back will do. In other words, there is no toilet!

As evening fast approaches, I wonder whether we should strike out and find ourselves a hotel. But as it turns out, our driver is all set to drive on through the night, so we stay on with him.

As it happens, during the drive, the lorry stops but occasionally, and only infrequently do we see any other trucks amidst the gloom. And on this long, long drive, our driver never once tries to introduce us to any words of his language, surprising, since up until now, in other countries, it's been routine for our drivers to try and educate us.

We travel on throughout the night, but when, at the first light of day, we pull into a yard where many other trucks are already parked, our driver signals to us that he's going no further.

From the truck-park we amble wearily back out along the lonely road, drinking in the fresh cold morning air, when all of a sudden there's the puffing sound of a locomotive engine, which is curious as I'm sure there's no railway anywhere hereabouts or anywhere else in Afghanistan, though I've heard that long, long ago, the British wanted to build a railway through the country, but their scheme had been thwarted by the King of Afghanistan, who objected, and banned the building of railways, allegedly saying that 'if a railway was built then people would use it'!

To my surprise, coming towards us, chugging around the corner is a steaming smoking vintage traction engine.

Stunned, I gawp at the approaching vehicle with disbelief. On the front of the engine is tied a bucket, which swings back and forth, keeping time to the machine's lurching rhythms, and on the side, amidst a mass of brightly polished brass pipes, is a painted sign, boldly and clearly advertising *'Lipton's Tea'*.

A pair of grimy faced westerners in serge boiler suits and shiny black engine driver hats stand on the footplate, driving the engine.

'Hello there!' I shout to them.

'Morning!' they answer, somewhat glumly in their heavily North of England accents.

And the wonderful old machine continues chuffing, chugging and clanking off on its way around the next bend, lost to our sight.

Chapter 15

WHAT DID I SAY?

Carpets on the ceiling, carpets on the walls and, less surprisingly, a carpet on the floor.

From amongst the array of patterned teapots, the tea vendor chooses one, then places a handful of green leaf tea inside it and from his urn fills the pot with boiling water. The pot is then placed alongside two china bowls on a wooden tray and brought to us.

I wait a few minutes for the tea to brew, and as I do, I study the pot, noticing signs that it's been broken many times, but that it's been successfully repaired by the use of tiny metal rivets. No sugar bowl is provided, as in each tea bowl is placed a large lump of crystal sugar which gradually dissolves over the course of several top ups of tea.

Having been travelling the whole night, what we really need is a slap-up breakfast and then to lay ourselves down between fresh clean cotton sheets. Standing outside the *chaay* shop, we look about up and down the road, hoping to catch sight of somewhere we might obtain these delights.

From the squat hotel across the road come signs of life; it's a bunch of fellow foreigners who are taking the morning air.

We make ourselves known to them and cross over to chat.

Helpfully, they show us inside their hotel, which proves to be clean, neat and very inviting.

From talking to these guys, the purpose of their staying in Kandahar becomes clear to us, which is quite simply to smoke lots of hashish and have an easy life.

'Don't get cash sent to you in Afghanistan,' comes their friendly advice, *'it'll never get through! If you're sending letters, make sure the postage stamps are franked while you're there, else as soon as your back's turned the stamps are off again!'*

But though it's tempting to book in here, there's something about the sleepy atmosphere of this hotel we don't feel comfortable with, which decides us against staying here. So instead we again try our luck at hitching and soon strike lucky, as a truck pointed in the general direction of Kabul stops to give us a lift.

'Why do you think they have concrete roads here?' I ask Yolanda, confused as to how such a poor country can afford to install such an expensive road system.

'Search me,' she responds vacantly.

Apart from the ritual halts at *chaay* shops *en route*, there's little of interest for us to see this morning. I notice that at all the simple truck stop places we stop, there always seems to be a carpeted area set apart from the *chaay* shop, for the faithful to bow, prostrate and mutter their prayers.

The lift takes us on to Ghazni, some 70 kilometres short of Kabul, and, as it's but early afternoon, we keep trying to hitch but get no lift before a beaten up old double-decker bus stops for us, though I hesitate before climbing aboard.

'Pool naderi,' I call to the driver. But he beckons us to get on anyway.

It's a local bus for Afghans who sit about with their luggage at their feet.

Climbing upstairs we sit at the back from where we get a good view of the surrounding area, which just appears to be countless miles of barren, dusty, rocky terrain, dotted with the occasional village.

As we speed towards the capital of Kabul, it occurs to me that having declared ourselves penniless, we've trapped ourselves, that we can't buy anything at wayside shops, that is, until we break company with our driver, and only then can we pay for anything ourselves. So, when we there's the occasional stop we are unable to buy any fruit or cigarettes, thus we eagerly await our arrival in Kabul.

But when the bus does eventually pull to a halt somewhere on the outskirts of Kabul, it proves difficult to separate ourselves from the driver, as it looks as though he wants to look after us!

Despite the man's protests, Yolanda and I set off on our own, along a road we hope will take us to the centre of the city. Soon we find ourselves wandering through a modern housing estate with neat detached dwellings for its wealthy occupants, and as we go to cross the road, all of a sudden I find my leg sinking knee-deep into some filthy odious sludge; I hadn't noticed but between the kerb and the pavement there lies a deep drainage ditch filled with God knows what.

'Shit, how revolting!' I exclaim in disgust.

Impulsively, in order to get myself cleaned up, I go and beat on the door of a nearby house, and fortunately a man comes to the front door, so I point to my leg and indicate to him that I need water. He seems to understand, and shows me to an outside tap where he assists me in cleaning the mess off.

My efforts to douse the filth off, leaves the leg of my jeans and one of my socks sodden, but at least the muck is cleaned off, well kinda sort of, so despite my wet trouser leg and wet foot, we resume our walk, trudging onward, intent on locating the heart of the city.

Finding a run-down but suitably cheap hotel, and convincing ourselves we've walked far enough, we book in, dump our luggage in our room and set out again, determined to find somewhere to eat.

It feels like we're in the centre of town, so it's not hard to find a cheap cafe where we can tuck into some fried eggs, some rice and some fruit.

Re-energised, we decide to check out the general area, and in particular the local shops.

Bootlaces, hair clips and reels of cotton are on sale from the street vendors - I buy some Kirby grips to clean my ears. Yolanda wants some shampoo and I'm surprised to find she has the pick of many western brands. We want some cigarettes too, and soon discover an unusually wide choice of packs available on stalls that display wooden racks of king-size packs, from Russia, from China, from the USA and even Great Britain, cigarettes at half the price they would sell for in London.

The gathering gloom of the approaching night forces us back to the security of our hotel, for the ill-lit streets seem to threaten danger, and we really don't need any more excitement for a while, not after so recently having warded off a maniac brandishing his lethal looking knife; we just need to sleep.

* * *

We find the new day extraordinarily sunny and hot again, and are soon out of our room and off to explore the city, in search of a bank to change some money. However, we discover that unexpectedly today has been turned into a national holiday, to mark the death of Egypt's President Nasser. So, it appears we must stay another day in Kabul.

Just as I'm weighing up our situation, I see a familiar face.

'Anthony! You again? How are you doing, Man?'

'Hi Paul. Hi Yolanda. You've done pretty well getting this far. I've only just arrived myself.'

But it looks to me as if Anthony isn't well, though I think better than to mention it to him.

'We had wanted to move on today but they've closed up the banks, so we're going to have to stay in Kabul until they open.'

'Nasser! Yes, I heard the news. But look, you can always change your money on the black market,' he suggests.

I hearten at the news that we might still get to leave Kabul today.

'Have you got your rupees yet?' Anthony asks. He then goes on to explain that here in Kabul one can buy Indian and Pakistani currency at a very good rate. *'Be careful though, old Pakistani notes are worth less than the new ones, about seven eighths of the value.'*

'How should I know the difference?' I ask.

'The old notes are bigger, oh you'll manage it,' he replies nonchalantly.

By following Anthony's directions we soon arrive at a market area where we discover several apparently empty shops, but on closer inspection I see that each is attended by a man of massive size sitting in front of a large iron safe.

By checking from shop to shop we quickly discover the going rates of exchange, and I'm able to change some of our British paper money into a fist full of Indian and Pakistani currency notes. None of the *rupee* banknotes look very old, or any larger than what I'd assume is normal, so I assure myself that things have gone well for us. But before leaving I count all the notes, to check that I've been given the correct amount of foreign currency, there being 25 Pakistani *rupees* to the pound or 30 Indian *rupees*.

Whilst we're here we also take the opportunity to pick up some more Afghan money, and then look around the other shops and booths, some of them sell clothes, with some of which appearing to be antiques, such as old waistcoats and hand-me-down dresses, hung amongst brand new garments.

Here too are old muskets and beautiful old musical instruments - small multi-stringed affairs with dried cracking animal skin on them. I give one a twang but am unable to coax anything like music from it.

Walking down a narrow alley I spy what appears to be a one person tent proceeding towards us; I stop and look more closely and see a pair of eyes twinkling from behind the cloth grill.

'I wouldn't want to be a woman here,' Yolanda exclaims in shock.

Then we catch sight of what seems to be a river winding its way through Kabul, but it's all but dried up and is just a meagre trickle of water amongst some shallow putrid puddles contained in a concrete riverbed.

On our way back to our hotel we find an Afghan standing in our way!

'Hashish, opium, heroin, cocaine?' he offers.

Uneasily, I look about us and see that just a few feet away is a traffic policeman.

The dealer questions us again as to what sort of drugs we want, and as I reckon his voice must be audible for quite some distance, I attempt to gauge the reaction of the policeman, who appears unmoved.

'Very cheap,' the voice continued.

'No, no thanks,' I tell him, as we move away.

We meet with other foreigners here in Kabul, and they all seem to like Afghanistan a lot; some of them tell us they're planning to travel northwards to visit the towns of Bamian and Mazar Sharif. Indeed, there are pictures here of the colossal rock-cut Buddha situated at Bamian, which are the only images available as postcards here.

'You should stay man,' a fellow traveller tells us, *'what do you want to go to India for?'*

'We're only on transit visas. We have to be out in a couple of days more,' I explain.

But, honestly, I have no great desire to get off the main route or to stay in Afghanistan any longer than necessary. Our experience with the guy wanting to rent Yolanda, and my almost getting myself knifed, have done nothing to make me want to stay here any longer than need be.

* * *

So we are up fairly early and making our way out of the city in the hope of getting a lift onward, in the hope we might possibly make it to Pakistan today.

As we walk the road that leads out of Kabul, we see further lengths of the dried up stagnant riverbed before eventually arriving at the city limits. Here we are met with a very grim sight indeed, of an incredibly sprawling concentration of people dwelling in makeshift tents. The spectacle shocks and horrifies me; I suppose this is what is called a shantytown, a ghetto or a tent colony. It's a disgrace that people are reduced to having to live like this, and I can't begin to comprehend how these people can survive in such a situation. I'm in no doubt that these must be some of the poorest people in the world, certainly the poorest I have ever laid eyes on in my life.

There are barely any cars or lorries on the road today, so we walk for a very long time without ever coming close to getting a lift. But as the saying goes, 'All comes to he who waits', and in the fullness of time a vehicle does eventually pull up.

It's a Japanese version of a *Land Rover*, almost brand new by the looks of it. The driver speaks immaculate English, and he makes light conversation with us as we travel on past the town of Sorabai, from where we head for a town called Jalalabad. On reaching there the driver proposes we might like to visit his home, and perhaps to stay over for the night. It seems a nice invitation and we accept.

His house is luxurious, even by western standards, and has an immense garden at the back where many exotic species of flowers, plants and trees grow. The whole place has an air of tranquillity, and as we sit on the balcony chatting, the only other sound I hear is birdsong emanating from the garden, which is quite enchanting, and the prospect of staying here further is tantalising.

A servant brings us tea and cake, and all seems well in the world.

A sharp ring at the doorbell interrupts the peace, and after opening the front door, our host returns and introduces us to the visitor, a Russian. Then on some pretext, our Afghan host excuses himself, and we are left together with the visitor.

'Have drink?' the Russian asks.

'No thank you,' I answer.

'Have drink with me?' he growls, but we decline his offer as politely as we can.

'Whisky, vodka, what you drink?' he persists.

Our host returns and he and the Russian exchange words.

'Drink, drink! What drink you want?' the Russian again asks.

'No, nothing, nothing to drink,' I answer firmly.

Our refusals seem to anger him.

'You have sweet maybe? You want hashish sweet?'

The Russian's demeanour is dark and moody as he repeatedly asks us why we refuse his hospitality, so we answer as best we can, but it seems he cannot be pacified, in fact he becomes downright offensive.

Clearly we cannot stay and I anxiously await an opportunity to get out of the house.

When he leaves us on our own for a few moments, I'm on my toes and off in search of the driver of the jeep.

'Can you take us away from here, to a local hotel,' I ask our Afghan host.

He agrees to my request and in silence we leave together. He drives us into town where he stops outside a very posh looking establishment, the Hotel Jalal Abad. We step out of the jeep and the Afghan brings us our luggage and offers his apologies for the conduct of his friend. But it's not enough, I feel really angry.

I stand facing him and glare at him.

'You have let us down. You offered us to stay with you and then you put us through all that. I think you should pay the hotel.'

The Afghan looks ashamed.

I notice a crowd gathering about us.

The Afghan looks nervously about him then presses a handful of change into my hand, but without taking my eyes from his for a second, I throw the coins across the road in contempt. He doesn't wait around for me to say another word, but gets back into his jeep and is gone in an instant.

We leave the money in the road, and go in search of an affordable hotel, and are lucky in finding one for only 10 *Afghanis* for the night; never have we found a cheaper room (the price would barely pay for a bar of chocolate back in England). On the downside the room offers little privacy as there are no curtains at any of the windows and the door has no lock. But we improvise by hanging up bed sheets and joining them together with safety pins acquired from the manager. The manager seems a gentle fellow who only wants to please; why he even brings us a gift of some nuts and raisins, which will have to serve as our evening meal.

Since we have made enemies with the well-to-do Afghan and his Russian cohort, we decide not to go out in the town tonight; and after securing the door, by moving our bed in front of it, we get our heads down for the night.

* * *

Leaving Jalalabad early we don't wait about for a lift but instead carry on by foot.

After a while we both find ourselves in need of a toilet, so, being close to a house, we ask the owner if we might use the toilet there. We're in luck as the owner speaks a little English, and seems only too happy to oblige.

First Yolanda, and then I climb upstairs and use the bathroom, after which we shout our thanks to the owner and leave. Once we are out of earshot Yolanda turns to me.

'Incredible!' she gasps, *'It was just a hole in the floor! Did you see what happens to the shit? Did you? You know there is a pig wandering around underneath? I saw it!'*

I agree, it was quite a shock.

'Mind you,' I point out, *'there was a roll of toilet tissue, wasn't there?'*

'A pig, there was a pig down there! I can't believe it!' continues Yolanda.

Yolanda's right, of course, I have never ever seen the like of this ever before.

As we resume our walk along the main highway, fortune smiles on us in the form of an oil tanker, which pulls up alongside us to offer a lift.

Like most commercial vehicles here in Afghanistan, it's gloriously decorated with a rich variety of colourful designs and motifs.

The journey goes well, that is until we are diverted, then the tanker has to bump along a rough track cut through a strip of jungle. Along the way a figure emerges out of a hut and stands in front of us, blocking our way, brandishing a long syringe. He looks incredibly stoned and seems so disappointed that we refuse his offer of a jab. He remains over eager to stick the needle in us and it's hard work convincing him we don't need another jab. We tell him we've had our injections though I'm not sure he understands. But God knows if the needle is sterilised or not, I hate to think what we might catch should we give in to his demands.

Though our lift in the tanker takes us a little further, unfortunately it's all too soon over, and afterwards we have little joy in obtaining another ride. So, when we see a smart *Mercedes-Benz* bus approaching we make a quick decision to hail it, and we're happy enough to pay the few '*Afs*' charged for a ticket to the border. We settle down alongside our fellow passengers, and watch as a chicken struts about; the atmosphere on the bus is jovial and lively.

I notice with some amusement, that when the other passengers, most of whom are women, see a truck coming towards us, they start cowering and praying loudly; so the driver slows the bus right down, and by the time we're actually approaching the oncoming vehicle we are hardly moving! After we pass the other vehicle everyone breaks out in screams of jubilation. I look on, bewildered, and wonder how they would cope with the busy traffic conditions we have back in England.

This bus is a local one and stops frequently to let off and take on new passengers, and at one stop I notice a young western couple with their infant son get on. They explain to us that they've travelled all the way from England with their 3-year-old, taking buses all the way, and reassure me that the young lad is faring well.

'Just so long as you eat and drink local, everything's alright,' the guy tells us. Well, though I'm doubtful about the sense in exposing a young child to such dangers, I'll just have to take his word for it.

'Don't overstay your visa or they fine you. The longer you stay over, the more they fine you, if you can't pay ... it's prison!'

I ask him about the concrete roads: -

'Russians made the roads. Americans built the laundry in Kabul. The Russians and the Yanks are in hot competition to outstrip each other.'

I tell him about the Russian hospitality we were offered in Jalalabad.

'They can be pushy, sure! But did you not know that the British all had their throats cut at Jalalabad years ago? Only one guy escaped out of thousands. By the way, you know of course that Pakistan was part of India until recently? Then the partition.'

We arrive at the Torkham border post, and offering up our passports we are soon cleared; then we walk on over to the Pakistani border post.

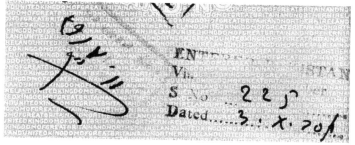

I am euphoric that we're actually entering into what was, until recently, a part of India. So as I stride over to the customs officer I shake him by the hand.

'Pleased to meet you,' my words sing out.

The customs guy responds in like, by offering us tea and cake, which we sit down and enjoy in the shade by the customs hut. Once we've had our tea we get on with filling the inevitable forms, questions which I can answer now from memory and soon we're through.

This is really something; here we are standing overlooking the world-famous Khyber Pass! Wow! I stop and stare around, taking in the view over the trees, and at the road winding down through the pass. I notice the traffic here uses the left-hand side of the road, just as it does back in England, and we don't walk far before a car stops for us; a modern American affair; a cream coloured *Cadillac*.

Down the pass we glide, with hills appearing and disappearing on all sides, and I see railway tracks, snaking there way through the hills, disappearing into dark tunnels in the mountainside.

As on so many previous occasions of our journey, I seem to be able to sense when something's not right. The driver seems distracted; he keeps looking in his rear view mirror at the car behind, which seems to be tailing us. Perhaps I'm getting paranoid but I could swear that our driver is right now making signals to the other car driver. Thinking about it, I am worried that he intends to drive us off the pass, so I ask him to stop, but he ignores me. I ask him again but he refuses to stop, so I wrench his foot off the accelerator and we gradually slow to a halt.

Hurriedly, we haul ourselves out of the car, and make our own way down the Khyber on foot, concluding that we have again torn ourselves from the clutches of danger.

Yolanda lets out a long moan.

'Oh my hat! My straw hat, I must have left it in that car.'

After walking quite a distance through the Pass we turn a bend in the road and pause for a few moments to rest. I look up at the stone walls of the pass and study the insignias of the regimental coats of arms of the many forces that have served here. I ponder awhile whilst reading them, the 'Gordon Highlanders 1932', the '22nd Cheshire Regt. 1933', the 'Punjab Regiment', and there are so many others.

Then I catch sight of a bus hurtling down the Pass and as I'm fearful the driver won't notice us, I begin shouting and waving for it to stop, and it does

'What were you doing man? It's dangerous here,' a voice calls from the bus.

Once onboard the bus we are reunited with the English couple, who explain that the Pass is bandit country, that the Baluchi tribes that live here are quite beyond the range of national police, and that they continue blood feuds for generations.

According to the English couple, everyone coming through the border at Torkham, from Afghanistan, is issued with bus tickets on the Pakistan side. Fumbling around in my pocket, I pull out some crumpled paper.

'I wish we'd known about the tickets before,' I confide to Yolanda. *'It could have been curtains for us back there.'*

Once we're clear of the Pass, the Landi-Kotal area, the bus motors onwards to the city of Peshawar, where most of the passengers get off. We watch them alight and see them being met and picked up, by any one of the many gaily-decorated motorcycle rickshaws that ply for trade nearby. Though it's interesting here, we decide to ride on to the next town, in the hope it will be less busy.

The next town is Nowshera, and we find it easy enough to find a suitable hotel, and once we've set our baggage down and locked our room, we go off in search food.

Everywhere and anywhere we walk here we are stared at and followed about; it's as though the people here have never seen a tourist before.

So many times we are offered directions, or offered to go back to people's houses for meals. Finally, after finding a suitable eating-house, we take refuge there, ordering up a plate of curry and rice.

After paying for our meal, we launch ourselves back out into the street and try to retrace our steps back to the hotel, only to find we're continually pestered by local men, even more so than before.

Though the situation is challenging we eventually make it back to our room, which, with its old-fashioned dark heavy furniture, feels very gloomy. Maybe it's because the hotel was built long ago, in a different age, but the place feels decidedly spooky. Our room has many windows and we find that it's not possible for us to block the higher ones, but over the lower windows we do manage to draw the accessible curtains tightly together before lying down on the double bed to get some sleep.

A few minutes elapse, I relax and feel myself starting to drift off.

'Aaaa-a-a-a-aggghhhhh! Paul, Paul, look....!'

Quickly turning the light, I find Yolanda on the verge of hysteria as she points up to the higher windows, where I can see a cluster of men's faces are peering in at us. I also see a man withdrawing back through the fanlight over the door.

Jumping out of bed I stand and shout at them and they all immediately disappear from sight. After turning on the light I draw up a chair and climb up to secure all the windows and doors as firmly as I can. I try to reassure Yolanda and I'm successful in that she calms down a little. We decide to try to go back to sleep, so I turn the light off again.

I'm not sure how long I'm lying here, trying to sleep, but again I hear Yolanda scream out, and turning on the light confirms that indeed the faces are back. This time I race off to call the manager, but I doubt he knows what I'm talking about or that he even cares, I hope he gets the message anyway, that he should make sure no one else disturbs us in the night.

Before I lie down again, I get out my penknife and open it, just in case I need it to defend us.

* * *

When I awake I lie for a few moments wondering where I am, and then notice the open penknife tightly grasped in my hand. The events of the night now seem distant and unreal. It's time to move on.

Today we get lift in a car going to 'Pindi' (the local abbreviation for Rawalpindi), from a friendly Pakistani guy wearing an Oxford blue anorak, which appears to have been imported from Britain.

I wonder that he wears such a jacket on a hot summer's day.

'You are coming from Englandstan, yes?' he asks. *'You are very welcome here in my country, you and your girlfriend, yes. But, I ask you this. Why are we not welcome*

to visit U.K.?'

'I'm sorry to hear that,' I answer him sincerely.

But I cannot begin to answer his question, as I've absolutely no idea what Britain's policy is for dealing with foreign visitors. But I take his point; it does seem unfair that I can go where I want yet he cannot.

The cantonment area of Rawalpindi, where the military headquarters appear to be situated, proves an eye opener; as in the market place we can't help noticing the beggars and cripples who cry out for attention.

'Baksheesh!' they implore.

There's a man here without any legs, who sits on a small trolley and has but one arm with which he pushes himself along.

As the sights and sounds of this busy marketplace threaten to overwhelm, we extricate ourselves from its clutches and look about for a place to stay, and we soon find an old-fashioned looking hotel; one with beautifully constructed wooden landings and terraces. Even the vendors downstairs seem to belong to the past, with their wide assortment of old-fashioned boiled sweets; even the designs on the cigarette packets speak of the past. There are other sweets on sale too, beautifully displayed coloured fudgelike sweetmeats. Also on sale are green leaves into which preparations spices and nuts are added.

'Paan,' the cross-legged old vendor informs me.

Customers chew the *paan* and then spit it out, leaving their mouths stained bright red. The bespattered pavement all about bears witness to the popularity of this pastime. The streets all around throng with crowds of people and the air carries the sound of busy traffic, with horns tooting a variety of notes and tones, creating some sort of crazy but faintly melodious street orchestra. As we pick our way through the old town of Rawalpindi we have to be careful to step over a stream of dark liquid in the gutter, and try to make sure we don't slip on any discarded fruit and vegetable matter strewn about. Horse carriages and motor scooter taxis race dangerously around the narrow roads. Ironically, despite all the filth, the grime and the noise, I feel very happy to be here and to be able to enjoy the collage of busy colour about me, and the friendly attitude of the people, all of which enlivens my spirit.

* * *

After a good night's sleep, we decide to check on whether or not the rumour we have heard is true, that we will need visas to enter India.

In order to go to the Indian Embassy, we must first find the correct bus stop, on the Muree Road, and then take the grey bus to the 'new town' of Islamabad. This developing area is intended to be the new capital of Pakistan and apparently this is where the diplomatic enclave is already situated.

Happily we find the Indian Embassy easily, and I'm assured I need no visa, but it seems that Yolanda, being an Italian citizen, does need to apply for one. So she settles down to the task of filling out the forms, and lodges them with the embassy staff before we go off in search of lunch.

At a local restaurant we discover a dish called *Peshwari Biryani*, a rice dish topped with sliced egg and served with *naan,* an oven-baked bread. The meal is delicious.

Our mission accomplished, we return to Pindi and spend the rest of the day idling, and wandering about the market place. As my throat feels unbearably sore I locate a chemist, and buy myself a bottle of cough linctus. Downing a slug of cough mixture it makes me feel better but I start to feel a little drowsy, making me wonder what it contains. I suspect they must put opium in it

'It's reall-l-l-ly strong stuff,' I tell Yolanda, *'I feel re-a-l-l-l-y stoned....!'*

* * *

We're up early in the morning, as again we've to get the bus to Islamabad. Arriving at the Indian embassy we're dismayed to discover that Yolanda's visa hasn't been issued yet, so we ask to see an official. When someone at last appears he states that a visa will not be ready for several days and that its validity will be for six weeks only.

'That's ridiculous, she needs a six month visa at least,' I point out. But though I try to reason with him his mind's made up, so I remonstrate with him further, saying, *'If the British were still in charge she wouldn't even need a visa.'*

'McPherson!' he shouts commandingly.

Immediately an unbelievably tall, muscular Indian appears on the scene and orders me to leave. Naturally I refuse but he's not so easily put off, and grabs me bodily, lifts me off the ground and then attempts to eject me from the building. After a brief struggle he carries me out of the front door and he dumps me on the pavement.

I sit there for a few moments, temporarily in a state of disarray.

'Are you alright?' Yolanda inquires.

'Mmmmmm-m-m-m-m.'

'What's happened to your watch?' Yolanda asks, sounding concerned.

I look down; my watch has been wrenched from its strap.

'Idiots,' I moan, *'Stu-u-u-upid idiots. What did I say?'*

We don't discuss the incident but instead walk along in silence for a while. We move away from the embassy and start walking towards the shopping area, and once we arrive at the shopping precinct I locate a watch repairer and pay him 50 *paise* (half a *rupee*) to fit a new spring clip on my watch. Relieved to have my watch back, we make our way out of the shopping mall, when we bump into a couple of fellow travellers, Jonathan, an English lad, and Donna, a Brazilian girl, who encourage us to join them at the local campsite. We tell them of our difficulties in getting a visa that will enable Yolanda to stay in India for a reasonable length of time.

'Go to Karachi. There's a High Commission there,' they advise.

Chatting with Jonathan and Donna makes me feel just a touch better about the situation we're in. But I can't help feeling that the official was being mean with Yolanda. If only they had offered her a decent visa, if only they had listened to us. Although I don't suppose I made matters any better by reminding him of the days of British rule. I just couldn't help myself.

'You've still got a bad cough, you should take something for it,' Yolanda points out.

Back in Pindi I replenish my supply of cough linctus, but unlike the reaction I had before, of feeling pleasantly stoned, over the next few hours my state of mind takes quite a nosedive, and I begin to become obsessed with the idea of getting married to Yolanda here in Rawalpindi, and I spend ages endlessly talking about it.

We go out and explore Rawalpindi, and as we walk the sky suddenly darkens and issues forth a torrent of ice pellets that bounce as they hit the ground, each one the size of a large coin, such as a half-crown. The redbrick Post Office nearby positively glows in the strange light!

Minutes later, the hailstorm spent, all is as it was before, and the sun reappears.

* * *

Another night in Pindi and I'm still crazed from the doses of linctus, but I'm focussed enough to realise we should be moving on. However, in order to obtain Yolanda's visa we must first travel the huge distance down to the port of Karachi - about 800 miles (or 1,250 km) away - a massive detour taking us right across the other side of the country. So, initially we set off in the direction of the city of Lahore, which I understand is close to the border with India. This new leg of our trip starts when we are offered a lift with a rather old-fashioned looking middle-aged couple, to Jhelum, a city midway between Islamabad and Lahore. The man wears a flat cap, and with his swirling military moustache and continual praise for the British, he seems to be a fascinating leftover from the days of colonial rule.

'Why are you going to India?' he asks, *'All those so-called holy men with no homes, just drifting around on charity!'*

We listen attentively.

'Those Hindus pray to trees you know? Huh! We'll give them trouble, you see if we don't. We'll show them what we're made of! Praying to trees indeed, huh!' he complains.

Praying to trees? I can't wait to get to India. It sounds fascinating!

The car passes through a heavily wooded area.

'Wow, did you see that bird?' I rave. *'Pure turquoise colour, the most magnificent*

bird I ever saw.'

Soon our lift is at an end and as we alight from the spacious car I swing the door closed with some force.

'Ahhh, ah, ah, ohhhhh!' I gasp, as my thumb gets crushed in the car door.

Our driver offers me a linen handkerchief, which I wrap tightly around the throbbing soreness, which curiously seems to make it feel a little better.

Reassured I'm okay, the couple motor off, and we remain where we've been dropped, standing on a bridge overlooking the River Jhelum. I notice nearby is a signpost that warns photographs must not be taken. I wonder, *what's the problem?* Judging by the way the guy was talking just now; perhaps they're expecting an attack from India? I wonder?

Following our habit, we don't wait long before starting off down the road; we walk under the lush foliage of the overhanging trees, which protects us from the severe heat of the sun. The trees bustle with birds that fly about above our heads.

We haven't gone very far before we meet with a young man who tells us he's a student; he befriends us and offers for us to go back to his home for a cup of tea. We accept his invitation of hospitality and return to his quarters where we get to meet his friends. I notice that, despite the very hot weather, they all wear long thin scarves around their necks, and long shirts and leggings too. I guess it's the fashion.

We enjoy their cultured conversation and share some refreshments with them, but ultimately decide against staying on with them, as experience has made us somewhat wary of certain sorts of full-blooded males.

Leaving the student types, we start exploring the locality, and passing by the gates of the local park we continue our search, looking for somewhere suitable to stay. After walking a good distance out of town we eventually find something which halfway resembles a guesthouse.

Here we eat a meal of omelette and *paratha* (a flat round bread smeared with oil) and a drink of hot milk, before settling down to sleep in an upstairs room, on *charpoy*s, crude rope-strung beds.

As evening turns into night, more and more guests come up to lie down in the dormitory room. But since darkness has already set in with a vengeance, it's too late now to find anywhere else. So I spend an uneasy night trying to keep myself awake, once more watching over Yolanda's sleeping shape.

* * *

Yolanda surfaces and seems blissfully unaware of the comings and goings of the night. The sun is by now up and shining brightly, and all the other guests are gone.

We find it's a very long walk along a country road before we're able to rejoin the main highway, and accompanying us on our walk are groups of children, carrying bags of books and packed lunches, and there are also grown-ups, some on heavy looking 'sit up and beg' bicycles, carrying large packages and bags.

On the main road, the traffic mainly consists of *Massey Ferguson* tractors, ox carts and camels, all pulling heavy loads whilst energetically jostling for position in the stream of traffic. The carts are piled so high as to resemble mobile haystacks.

From a roadside stall I buy a packet of small tapered primitive cigarettes, called *bidees*, each having a small quantity of dried smoking material (tobacco) wrapped in a dry leaf tied and knotted neatly with red cotton thread. For the equivalent of an English penny I get a packet of 25 *bidees*.

Watching the over-laden vehicles trundling past us, we despair of ever getting a lift away from here. The smoke from a *bidee* tickles my throat and stirs my hacking cough; my tired eyes remind me of my lost night's sleep.

It seems that most of the traffic on this road is local farmers going about their business, but we still maintain a hope that someone might eventually stop for us.

It looks like being a long wait today, but before we become totally dejected, we spy two large white vans heading toward us, and - miracle of miracles - they both stop, and from one of the *VW* microbuses a lanky westerner jumps out.

'Hop in, Man,' the American invites us, as he walks over and introduces himself.

When we get into his vehicle I immediately realise Pete's van has no windscreen.

'A stone,' he explains, *'but it's okay, in fact with the gauze over it for protection, it's better than having the glass, it's way cooler anyway!'*

The American tells us that he and his two mates (both of whom are in the other van) have been exploring the other side of Pakistan, and they're now all set for Karachi where they plan to sell their *VWs* before returning to the States.

I try to light a *bidee,* but every time I strike a match it gets blown out by the steady stream of air passing through the windscreen gauze. Yet when Pete tries, he cups his hand around the match and lights up easily. I'm impressed, but make a mental note to buy some real cigarettes as soon as I get the chance.

Just now I'm puzzled about the sound coming from the *VW*, for there seems to be something amiss with it, and whatever the problem is, it seems to be getting worse as I notice the van lurches from time-to-time.

I mention the noise to Pete who confides that he's known about the problem all along, that it's the front brake, which has gone faulty and is now becoming permanently locked. We lurch fairly continuously now but he doesn't seem particularly bothered, so I try not to get alarmed.

The more time I spend with Pete the more I'm convinced he's ill. It's a relief of sorts when he explains to me that he's trying to purify his body by subjecting himself to a starvation diet!

After many hours of driving along the fractured road, Pete at last announces his decision to pull up and have a rest. It's going to be our first opportunity to meet with his friends in the other van.

'Taste this!' Pete challenges, handing me a bottle of drink, *'Guess what it is, Man?'*

'Umm, apricot, peach, or maybe orange,' I hazard, *'I don't know really. What is it? It's fa-a-anta-a-astic!'*

'Mango. Really wild isn't it?' he enthuses, *'Shezan or Benz, we drink them all the time.'*

'Have you all just come back from India?' I ask.

'No? We've just been cruisin' around Pakistan,' he beams, clearly surprised that I might assume they've been to India.

The other microbus couldn't be more different than the one we've been travelling in, for whilst Pete's is virtually empty, this one is choc-a-bloc with possessions.

One of Pete's friends shows me a hash pipe, by which he seems to be suggesting that I might like a smoke.

Proudly he points out that the pipe is made from a shark's tooth!

But my attention is already taken, for I've just spotted a guitar, a *Gibson* Jumbo.

'Bob Dylan had one of these on 'Nashville Skyline',' I point out.

'Yeah cool,' comes a voice enveloped in a cloud of smoke.

There's now a chat about when and where we'll stop for the night, and it's soon decided that we should call it a day and stay right here where we are.

Thoughtfully, Pete offers Yolanda and I to sleep in his van, whilst he joins his mates in van number two.

* * *

It's an early start in the morning, and when we're all up and awake the vans pull away, but we make only slow progress, as the road is surprisingly rough and broken, and we encounter numerous roadworks where we are diverted onto ever rougher and more treacherous dirt tracks.

The air is thick with dust, thrown up by the wheels, along with the stones and rocks that repeatedly impact on the wire gauze windscreen.

Pete is still on his starvation diet, so he doesn't tune in to our need to stop for snacks, and consequently, we get even less to eat today than usual.

Eventually both vans stop again and we all hang out for a while together outside a western style cafe, where I drink a *7UP*.

Perhaps because of hunger or maybe because I'm still glugging the cough mixture, I feel very 'out of it'; my brain whirrs, and I can't stop talking. From out of the shadows come pastel puffs of colour whilst the lights about me buzz and shimmer.

* * *

It's our third day of travelling with the Americans and I sense we must by now be getting quite close to Karachi, but first we get to the city of Hyderabad, a seemingly sleepy place lying on the banks of the Indus River.

Here our new friends introduce us to the delights of the local milkshakes - utterly delicious - and whilst we're in Hyderabad we take the opportunity to walk about a bit and to go and buy some fresh fruit.

It appears that our companions are really in earnest about getting to Karachi, they tell us how much they're looking forward to booking into a luxury hotel.

Once we're back in the vehicles, there's no further delay, we're off in moments.

On our way out of the city I spot a vast lake, whereupon I cry out. *'Look, look! There's a house under the water. Look, you can see the roof sticking out! Look over there, there's another and another.'*

'River's flooded,' Pete informs me matter-of-factly, as though such incredible flooding were an every day occurrence.

The problem with the front brake has been getting worse, and it's clear that Pete is becoming more concerned about it, in fact he's getting quite obsessed, and at the next garage we pull in, Pete hoping to get a mechanic to check over the brakes.

A young guy, covered from head-to-toe in grease, comes out to see what's up, and after hearing what the problem is gets underneath the vehicle.

Yolanda and I get out to leave them to it.

About an hour or so later, we are still sat sitting waiting for Pete, when he drives up beside us. He appears jubilant.

'I've paid him with a long sleeved sweatshirt. He was really happy!'

'The brake, did he fix it?' I ask.

'We'll have no more trouble with that!'

'He put a new one on?' I puzzle.

Pete laughs nervously as we get back into the van.

'I told him to rip the brake out!' Pete admits, after we're seated and back on the road.

I'm concerned, I wonder whether having only the one brake will be enough, but Pete seems confidant, and there appears nothing more to do other than trust that nothing will occur during these last few miles of the journey.

It's not too long before we have our first sight of the huge and sprawling port of Karachi, and soon the two vans are parked up in a side street of the city, and we're all crowded into another milkshake bar.

The Americans sit exercising their imaginations as to what to order, and soon they are downing honeyed shakes with various combinations of different fruits.

'What are you going to do now?' I ask them.

'Find the best hotel in town, have a shower and then crash out. I'm wasted!' Pete sighs.

So it's time now to go our separate ways, and before setting off in search of accommodation we thank them for giving us the lift, and wish them all the best.

But we discover, after trudging the grimy streets of Karachi, that though it's still early in the day, no rooms are available here, other than at one hotel that we think is rather too expensive for us. So, as everywhere else seems to be full up, we turn in desperation to the Salvation Army.

'No, not together, definitely not,' the official there states emphatically, *'Maybe, if you come back later we might find you separate lodgings, but I'm not promising anything.'*

As he admits that there are vacant rooms here, it's obvious that he's just being awkward and extremely un-Christian. However, I have no wish to make myself beholden to him I make ready to leave, but before doing so I offer him my riposte: -

'They refused Jesus too, you know? And you call yourself a Christian! .. Shame on you!'

There's no denying it, we're in a tight spot, and we brood over our situation awhile before deciding to go back to the hotel we'd turned down on account of the cost. Now the man behind the counter tells us that they have no rooms left.

'Show us the room!' I growl, *'Now!'*

Moments later and we have the key to a room and are soon enjoying having somewhere to lie down, but before long the increasing humidity causes us both to get terribly thirsty, so we go in search of a tap, and though the water is warm, we drink pints and pints of it.

The heat is becoming so, so-o-o-o oppressive; it feels like it's almost too much of an effort to breathe.

In the evening I go downstairs and investigate the cafe, and looking about as I wait to be served, I see a huge fly hovering around the light, and other different species of monstrously large insects too, all attracted by the lights, flying around the airless room, the SIZE of them is ... is just ENORMOUS.

Grasping the bottle of fizzy orange I've bought, I stagger back upstairs to the hotel room and call out to Yolanda; *'Wow, it's been like being on a bad trip or something. There are dragonflies down there as big as your hand! And that's not all... there are people wandering around down there who seem a bit odd, without any clothes on either. Weird! Really weird! Just too weird!'*

Chapter 16

— ★ —

PROPER - IN PYJAMAS

For the first time since we left London, Yolanda digs out her make-up and titivates herself, in an attempt to cultivate a respectable secretarial image, for today we're on a mission to locate the Indian High Commission and obtain the precious visa for her.

We don't discuss what might happen if we fail to get the visa, the idea is just unthinkable!

Outside the High Commission stands an armed soldier wearing a bright red starched turban. Yolanda approaches the building alone and readily gains admission.

Eventually, she re-emerges and rejoins me where I'm waiting, some way up the road. Apparently, she has completed her application and is confidant that the visit has been a success; we'll just have to wait and see.

Whilst we're here in Karachi, I think to try and contact the family of an old friend of mine, Heck (Heckmath or Hikmat) Khaleeli; so, in a mood of optimism I scan the pages of the local telephone book. But after searching his family name by a variety of spellings, I am left disappointed, and conclude they must be ex-directory.

Walking the streets of the city we swelter in the mounting humidity.

Hand-painted hoardings make for interesting reading, advertising as they do a spectrum of services from palmistry to sexology to medical treatment for specific ailments such as urinary problems.

As we wander, the sight of a naked couple walking down the middle of the street leaves me momentarily baffled and confused, for surely it's not usual for people to walk around naked?

Curiously, as we continue to explore Karachi we find no evidence of any business convention, so we're left to wonder as to why there's a shortage of hotel rooms.

Since arriving in the city we're persistently being offered to change money, and since we need some extra cash, and as we've discovered the government rate is a mere 12 *rupees* to the pound compared to the 25 *rupees* back in Kabul market, we become interested in the repeated offers of black market exchange. The best rate seems to be 20 *rupees* to the pound, and after making an exchange we are left feeling temporarily flush, enough for us to buy a good meal from what we see as our profits.

Back at the hotel I get talking to an English chap who's staying in the room next to ours, who has bought himself an unusual musical instrument, which he's in the process of packing up and sending home. He confides to me something about the nature of the 'extra' contents he's included in the parcel, but urges me not to tell the American girl who's also staying in our hotel.

'She's with the Peace Corps, Man. She's a spy! If she found out I'd get bust for sure.'

It's odd that he trusts me then, as I'm a complete stranger, but I have bigger things to worry about than someone sending a block of Pakistani black hashish home.

In the back of my mind there lurks a big worry about a certain someone's visa.

* * *

Yolanda is due to return to the High Commission today, so again she tidies her hair and adorns her face with a little makeup.

As I wait for her I focus only on a positive outcome to her visit.

When at length she returns, she waves her passport triumphantly.

'They've given me a 3 month visa!' Yolanda beams.

'Now that's more like it! Well done!'

'And they gave me these brochures too, and a map of India. They were really nice to me, extremely polite,' Yolanda says, surprised.

'So should I go back and try and get you a 6 month visa?' I joke.

'You wouldn't?' Yolanda asks, for a moment becoming very serious.

There has been so much unspoken worry over the visa since the incident in Islamabad.

'Let's get two bottles of Benz and some biscuits,' I urge. *'It's time to celebrate.'*

* * *

We're up early in the morning and back on the road.

As we wait for a lift in the direction of Lahore, we both have but one thing on our minds: -

'Another bottle of Shezan. Another bottle of Benz. Yes let's!'

Again and again we buy another bottle or two from a nearby stall that is storing these precious bottles of nectar on blocks of ice to refrigerate them.

'I could get addicted to mango juice,' Yolanda confides.

'I already am!' I admit.

We have a long way to go to get to Lahore, and once we get going on the journey it proves to be one of the most rigorous and grinding yet. The highway is in such a state of disrepair, and as we travel towards Lahore in Japanese replicas of European cars the road seems even worse than I remember it from our journey with Pete.

We consume little food on the way, stopping only to eat at wayside cafes where the choice is usually limited to preparations served from a row of billycans.

On this occasion the main dish is some overcooked, over-spiced, vegetable matter, and as we put our spoons in, we find pieces of bone in it! The other cans contain a variety of dubious looking preparations, but we eat what is available, and submit to the inevitable long-running difficulties in the toilet department.

Our trip is really turning into a nightmare, as night and day we suffer severe discomfort and tiredness. It's really ghastly, and this particular leg of the journey is definitely a very low point in our trip so far, and two days and nights of sleepless travelling leaves us totally exhausted, but thankfully, reasonably close to our destination.

We find ourselves stuck behind an oil tanker, but the landscape painting on the back of it alleviates at least some of our impatience. One of the good things about Pakistan is that wherever we go we get to see attractively painted goods vehicles.

We are dropped off on the outskirts of Lahore and it's not too long before a large *Bedford* truck pulls up. The vehicle is hand-built, in the Afghan style, and similarly decorated. We climb up high to a wooden turret that's been constructed above the cab and we stand alongside a band of turbaned workers with their shovels.

Lahore is a big, big shock for us; it's way too busy, crazily busy and so noisy. But we're fortunate in that we're dropped in an area where we find somewhere to stay the night; though I don't feel entirely comfortable here, there's a slightly sinister feel about it.

We are pleased and relieved to get the chance to meet with a fellow European who proves helpful in telling us how we'll need to get a permit to travel the road to the Indian border, and importantly, he tells us where to obtain it. Where would we be without the continual flow of advice from others, concerning visas and the like?

At each and every place we stay we seem to have to fill out forms, and we get hold of a fountain pen and try writing with it:

Pakistan (Lahore) - I write, but the black ink seems to be a bit thin.

I love you - writes Yolanda, but now the ink is getting very weak, almost unreadable.

I love yooooooo - I write, and the ink gets progressively darker the more I write.

When we go to pick up some cigarettes, Yolanda points excitedly over at the stall.

'*Kappa dooay, Kappa dooay,*' she chants, '*See over there, the picture on the box, it's a very famous mountain.*'

'*Never heard of it,*' I confess, turning the box over in my hands and studying the image, printed in turquoise blue, of the K2 Mountain, a timely reminder that we are near some very high mountains, it feels good to know.

We return to our windowless room, padlock ourselves in for the night, and try to get some much-needed shut-eye.

* * *

In the morning we find that locating the Ministry of the Interior is straightforward enough, and are supplied the necessary chits giving us permission to travel along the restricted road to the border, so we then head off out to pick up the bus. At 2 *rupees* apiece the tickets are very cheap, and soon we are headed off down a dusty track out of Lahore on our way to the border crossing, but the trip takes far longer than I expect, and it's mid-afternoon before we arrive at the Pakistani customs, 'Via Ganda Singh Wala'.

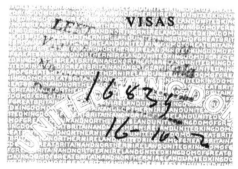

I had heard - I think it was from Anthony - that at the Pakistan border, car owners are expected to pay a significant amount of money in order to be allowed to take their cars into India, but nothing prepares me for the sight of field after field full of hundreds of abandoned vehicles. Apparently, before driving into India, car owners are required to first deposit the full value of their car with the authorities, with the result that many leave their vehicles on the Pakistan side, presumably with the intention of reclaiming them when they leave India.

Clearly, we don't have a car to be concerned about, but I do have a worry of my own, for someone has told me that we're not allowed to import any *rupees* into India, or that if we do we could find ourselves in deep trouble. Rather than ask at the border whether the rumour is true or not, I make a quick decision to hide the *rupees* in my underpants, and hope for the best they'll remain undiscovered.

At the customs post on the Indian side of the border, is a young woman who reminds me a lot of my elder sister, Margaret.

She appears to me to be worryingly intelligent, as first she eyes me very slowly and deliberately, and then exchanges a few words with me. I answer her questions carefully, and do my best to conceal my anxiety about the hidden roll of banknotes. To my relief she soon turns to the next person in line behind me, without acquainting herself with the contents of my underpants.

I take a look at the fresh stamp my passport that states simply;
'ENTRY 16-10-70 Hussainiwala Distt, Ferozepore'

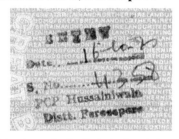

We've made it to India! We're here in India! At last! Amazing, amazing, amazing!

We keep with the flow of other new arrivals, walking along a path beside a wide still river, the Sutlej. I notice too also disused railway track here, which presumably was at one time used to connect the two countries.

'We're here! Do you know it's taken us almost 12 weeks by my reckoning?'

'I've lost all track of the time,' Yolanda murmurs contentedly.

I find it difficult to come to terms with the reality that we have finally actually arrived in India, but we have!

As we walk the path alongside the waters of the Sutlej River we see no one praying to trees here, but I do notice, on the riverbank opposite, a group of colourfully clad women wandering to and fro amongst the trees, and some of them are crouching near the water's edge, cleaning shiny cooking pots made of brass.

I stay watching them awhile, noticing that a soft light emanates from the area where they are gathered. As I stare at the spectacle, the figures gradually fade, so I watch with ever greater attention, but their forms seem eventually to evaporate and do not re-appear!

I'm confused, how could these women just disappear into thin air and leave no trace? How could they be there one minute but not the next?

We continue along the pathway until we come to a large throng of travellers gathered outside a large building, which I discover is the railway terminus for the Indian Northern Railway.

Amongst the crowd I spot a couple of Europeans.

'Are you going to Amritsar?' one of them enquires of us. *'You can stay in the Golden Temple for free. Just watch out for the bed bugs and don't smoke,'* he cautions us.

'Where are you off to?' I ask, *'Are you going to Amritsar now?'*

'We're catching the train to Delhi.... It will leave in a few minutes,' he informs me, before padding off to the ticket office.

'What do you reckon?' I ask Yolanda, my eyes fixed on the pair of hissing coal black steam locomotives that stand ready to pull the waiting train away.

'Yes, let's,' she declares.

Of course, everyone's heard about Indian trains, that ofttimes passengers cling onto the sides of the coaches whilst others sit up on the carriage roofs. Fortunately, this train is not like that, but it's still very crowded, with no seats available, but thankfully the corridor is empty, so we have space more than enough to settle down.

The unmistakable smell of coal smoke and the sound of blasts of compressed steam, fill my senses, then a shrill high-pitched whistle blows..... and we're off!

I wonder how long the train trip will be? I reckon it's likely to be about half an hour, or so, perhaps a bit longer, but I pay careful attention to the names of each station we pass, hoping that we'll soon be arriving at Amritsar.

As time rolls by, more and more passengers cram themselves into the already crowded train, and I ask one of them when we are due into Amritsar. I catch but a little of what he says:- *'Amritsar nahin. Is train Delhi ko.....'* he explains.

Oh dear, I get his drift, the train isn't going to Amritsar after all, it's bound instead for Delhi.

As the night has well and truly set in, it seems crazy for us to get off the train now, so we settle down and accept the inevitability of another long journey ahead of us. Unfortunately, our spot in the corridor turns out increasingly to be a magnet for the dozens of passengers who come from neighbouring coaches to use the toilet. Situated as it is, only a couple of feet from where we sit, I can't help but notice a rank odour wafting our way from time to time, and I find myself holding my breath and blocking my nose for long periods on end, and what's more is the smell only worsens as more and more passengers keep piling in.

At the frequent station stops, more and more people climb aboard the train, many of them clutching brief cases.

'Where are you from? Englandstan?' we are asked again and again.

'Yes, from England. From London actually.'

'London? Proper London?'

'Yes. Proper London,' I tell them, somewhat puzzled as to where improper London might be.

Some passengers rummage about amongst their luggage and produce food and drink, which they kindly offer to share with us. Moreover, we are offered advice on the best places to visit in India; we are told to see the Taj Mahal in Agra, and also encouraged to visit Bombay, Calcutta and Madras too.

Time moves slowly as the train sways and clatters along on its long, long journey through the darkness, and I guess we still have a very long time to go before arriving at Delhi.

I become increasingly more uncomfortable and I yearn to get off the train and breathe some fresh air again. My skin has become extremely itchy, and as I rub and scratch my arms, legs, face and head, my whole body becomes ever more sore.

Yolanda and I have by now come to dread anyone coming and opening the toilet door, and when they do come, we cover our faces and almost throw up at the stench; things are getting really grim!

As we sit hunched uncomfortably over our belongings a new day gradually dawns, but this is hardly the best way to enjoy the start of our first proper day in India.

When the train eventually stops, hordes of people all try to get off at the same time, and the ensuing panic is truly alarming. We are engulfed in a surging sea of hurrying Indians and are simply being swept along.

'We've lost our tickets,' I blurt out in desperation at the ticket barrier.

The ticket collector just smiles, and moments later we find ourselves on the station concourse, and making for the exit, where the brightness of the morning sun causes us to squint as we take in our first sight of Delhi.

'Hotel sahib. I take you good hotel,' comes a voice.

'Cheap hotel, come I take you,' another voice tells us.

'You come with me, do not listen to these fellows,' says someone else, gripping me firmly by my sleeve.

I am in no mood to argue and with this guy's help I see an opportunity to escape the crazy din of the railway station. So, in the company of our guide and the few other travellers he leads along, we find ourselves shepherded through bustling streets near the station, to a quieter, calmer neighbourhood, where we enter a complex of low attractive redbrick dwellings, and here our guide persuades us to take some tea with him and await the proprietor of the establishment.

In the shaded courtyard we sip our cups of scalding hot over-sweet milky tea. Then a middle-aged lady joins us, clad in white cloth wound around her, wearing a red mark on her high forehead, she offers to show us a room.

Yolanda seemed hesitant; she gives me a pleading look.

'It's early yet,' I announce, *'We would like to see more of Delhi before getting a room.'*

Quickly we find our way back on to the street, and instantly notice the mouth-watering smell of food cooking, coming from a snack stall.

'Let's have one of those,' Yolanda encourages.

'Potato cakes are my favourite,' I admit.

The fried potato cakes are simply scrumptious; they don't just contain potato but are stuffed full of herbs and spices, and served with a portion of chutney too.

About us birds twitter and squawk, seemingly responding to the blare of horns coming from the plague of cars and motor-rickshaws.

I notice a corpulent businessman reclining on the back seat of a cycle-rickshaw; his dark waistcoat announces his status, for otherwise he is dressed much like everyone else in the area, with long white shirt over a white skirt-like arrangement, and wearing open sandals on the feet.

We explore further, and wherever we wander voices greet us, with some offering us hotels whilst others offer hashish, all are open and friendly in asking questions, especially the proper one:-

'You from where coming?'

'London, from England,' we tell them

'London proper? Proper London?'

We nod. Someone reaches out and thrusts a hand-rolled cigarette between my lips. I inhale and am not surprised at the sweet pleasant taste of hashish smoke; I exhale it through my nostrils. Yolanda tries some too before handing the cigarette back to its smiling owner, who then disappears into the crowds.

'Hotel, hotel, hippy hotel,' an eager voice cries out, *'Come this way.'*

I look to where he's pointing and notice some bedraggled, emaciated Europeans gathered about there. They speak to us:-

'Comment ca va?' they ask.

'Hi. Do you speak English?' I ask hopefully.

Perplexed, they turn to one another, and then they call someone else over, who says; *'Deutsh, sprocken zee Deutsh?'*

'Nien Deutsh sprocken zee, I'm afraid,' I try.

'Hey I'm English, Man,' says a rather pop-eyed passer-by. *'Are you staying at The Green?'*

231

He seems to have difficulty in speaking, and it's my belief is that he's mightily stoned, and that this Green Hotel is for stoners.

So we decide to look a bit further for a place to stay and someway down the road we come to a signboard for the 'Eagle Hotel'.

Stumbling up the steep staircase we enter a cool and extremely tidy room, where we find a group of men sitting about on polished wooden high-backed chairs. One of them speaks:-

'You are looking for manager?' comes a familiar Goon-like voice.

I look hard at him, for not only does he sound like popular comedian 'Goon' Spike Milligan; he also looks a lot like him too. I laugh out loud and the men laugh too. This decides us; we have to stay here, I like the atmosphere.

We are taken to the top floor, to a row of rooms outside which are garments hanging out to dry. The manager opens a padlock and shows us into a small low whitewashed room containing two rope-strung *charpai* beds.

We decide to take the room, though before we can get comfortable we have first to go downstairs and deal with the monotonous duty of filling out the dread registration forms (this one is so detailed it even requires that I state my father's Christian names).

After filling out the forms we return to our room to unpack our toiletries and towels. I open the shutters revealing a barred aperture in the fragile wall.

As we settle down to rest for a few minutes, a little bird flies in and has a quick look around, then sits down itself outside the window and sings.

Downstairs there's a restaurant and we decide to lunch early, ordering ourselves a vegetable *pilao* (fried rice, peas and potatoes) each, and to quench our thirst we try the fresh limejuice. The vegetable *pilao* is a knockout - **so** tasty - and I make a mental note to buy this dish again, given the chance.

After our meal we go back upstairs and laze around, seating ourselves down on the terrace and gazing out at the local houses, shops and lanes of Old Delhi.

I need to sew up my jeans as they are coming adrift at the seams, but when I take them off to check them, I find, to my amusement, that they fairly well stand up on their own without support, so it's clearly time to wash them, and some of our other clothes. However, that will have to wait until tomorrow, for today I really need to buy some new shoes; the cracked sole has been pinching my foot since it came apart in Algeria; they just have to go!

On the balcony we meet some of our fellow guests; there are both Indians and westerners staying here, and we take the opportunity to fraternise awhile.

'Where are you going?' comes the repeated question.

'Hmm, we've only just arrived,' I protest.

What with all the travelling we've been doing - weeks and weeks of it - I've given very little thought to where we're going, only about getting to India reasonably quickly, within the timing of our visas, and whilst the money lasts. But now we're here in India, I realise that we'll soon have to work out where we want to visit.

Actually, I'd never really thought about whereabouts I wanted to go in India, I'd just entertained a vague image of Yolanda and myself drifting about, learning the language and perhaps finding some sort of solace amongst the religious people here. But, now we're here, that all seems a bit desperate and unnecessary, though I have no clearer idea about where we should be heading.

According to the people we've spoken to, Goa seems the most popular destination, and from what I gather Goa is a palm-beached paradise for drug-takers, down the coast somewhere. But we haven't come all this distance just to re-involve ourselves in the company of people who are stoned out of their minds. So I suppose I have to think of somewhere else I'd like to go, and I think for a few moments before realising that rather than go 'somewhere', it might be better to go and visit 'someone'.

I vaguely remember hearing that The Beatles visited India a couple of years ago. Now where did the group go? I recall they stayed with some old bearded Indian philosopher fellow, and of course there's also Ravi Shankar, who plays the sitar. Though I'd never bought any of his records, I really liked the twangy, buzzy drone sound of the instrument.

By button-holing a member of the hotel staff I embark on some research, and soon discover that Ravi Shankar lives in Bombay, and that the philosopher guy is called 'the Maharishi', and that he lives to the north of Delhi, at a place called Rishikesh.

'Which is closest?' I ask, pulling out the government produced Tourist Map of India Yolanda was given in Karachi.

I locate Bombay on the map, and then I find Rishikesh.

Bombay it seems is a long way away, several days journey perhaps, whilst Rishikesh is much, much closer, perhaps only a day's journey by my reckoning. Because of my passion for music I am drawn to find out more about Indian music from Ravi Shankar, but Rishikesh is nearer.

'I'd like to go and see the Maharishi,' Yolanda tells me, bubbling over with enthusiasm, *'I told you I was interested in him didn't I? My boss Mr. Lions went to see him, he told me so.'*

In truth I'm not much bothered where we go, just so long as we have a destination in mind. But for the time being, the idea of staying around Delhi for a while holds a certain appeal, I'm happy here.

This evening, as we stand out on the terrace watching the lamp-lit comings and goings in the street below. I strike up conversation with a fellow guest

'What do you think of the place?' I ask him, with some enthusiasm.

'What do you mean? Delhi? Just another city, yeah, just another city, Man.'

'What?' I gasp, *'Really?'*

But as he doesn't seem to have anything further to say on the subject, I bid him goodnight.

* * *

Waking up, I remember where we are, and am elated knowing that we have actually arrived here in India, that all we have to do now is breathe it in.

Before going out to explore the nearby shops this morning, we breakfast at the downstairs restaurant.

Set up for the day, we descend the concrete steps down to the street and immediately become engulfed in the hustle and bustle outside.

There's the sound of bicycle bells merrily ringing and there's a constant fanfare of car horns and motor scooter hooters resounding everywhere. As there are no pavements here we have to walk in the road, being careful to dodge the traffic. We walk up past the hippy hotel and head off for the market.

In the main market street of Chandi Chowk the stalls are piled high with a multitude of products, all attractively arrayed.

I have no desire to buy anything just now, only to look. We pass a shop selling brass objects and amongst the gleaming stock of vases and bowls I spot some perpetual calendars, amazingly clever devices, which give calendar days and dates for a period of many years, just by twisting two discs of engraved brass discs. I recognise them, on account of our family owning one, my parents having been given it as a present, I suppose.

'I really feel like spending now!' I announce gleefully, as we arrive at a row of shops selling clothes; we're spoilt for choice as to which shop to go to.

We walk into one and I ask to see some shirts, long loose white ones, and I also ask to see some light cotton trousers.

'Kurta, "kurta" is "shirt". You want kurta pyjama pants!' the salesman shouts.

He brings me a pair of white cotton lightweight baggy trousers - what one might call 'elephant pants' - and a large shirt with intricate embroidery around the collar. I imagine in this extreme heat the loose trousers will be a lot more comfortable than my denim jeans. Yolanda seems very keen on my purchase.

'For me too,' she insists.

But the shop owner only scowls at her and shows her instead some feminine looking clothes.

'For you lady, shalwar kamiz. Yes!'

'Kamiz that's similar to "chemiz" the French word for "shirt",' Yolanda explains to

234

me.

The shopkeeper finds some colourful tops and leggings to show her.

'Paul, I want the same shirt like you are getting, and the trousers too.'

We both pressure the shopkeeper to bring a set of whites for her, and at first he resists, but eventually, after a lot of cussing, he orders an assistant to go find a shirt and trousers in her size.

I detect Yolanda is very pleased with herself, in getting her way, as she now wears a smug look on her pretty face.

Our purchases are carefully wrapped in tissue paper and tied with string.

Clasping our neatly wrapped purchases, we move on to a nearby shoe shop where I look for a pair of sandals. In fact I scour several shops in search of a pair marked as Anthony described, stamped to certify the cow died a natural death, but without success. So instead I choose a pair I fancy, ones that have a thick ring of leather to hold the big toe, connected to a wide strap that holds the foot, all sewn with gold braiding. But I worry the heel and sole are stiff and unyielding to the touch, though Yolanda encourages me to buy them anyway, saying they will soon 'wear in'.

'Kalapuri chapal. Best. Excellent quality sandals,' the shopkeeper cajoles.

I buy them.

To round off our shopping trip we buy some bananas, clementines, various toiletries, a small package of *Surf* washing powder, a packet of incense (locally referred to as *agarbatthi*) and then our shopping spree is done.

Eager to try on our new clothes we get back to the hotel as soon as possible and extract the clothes from the limp brown paper and string that secures them.

'They'll need washing first, they're full of starch,' Yolanda counsels. *'I'll sew the buttons on too. I wonder why they don't come with them on. Whatever! It won't take me long to put them on.'*

So it is that we spend most of what remains of the day cleaning our new clothes, bathing, and washing our hair.

With my jeans and new pyjamas drying out on the roof, I don my Moroccan *djellaba*, which is ideal for mooching about in. I light one of the joss sticks, and its wonderfully soft fragrant smoke refreshes my sense of smell; I haven't lit any incense in several months.

It's great to sit around and relax for a change, and browse the tourist leaflets; well I give them a once over anyway. And from time to time I check to see whether the whites are dry yet as I'm impatient to wear mine.

Before my new white cottons are properly dried I've already got into them and am posing in front of the landing mirror. They look great! I try the sandals on too, they're still very stiff and awkward, but I'm consoled that at least they look brilliant.

235

All in all, we've had a good first day in Delhi, and we agree a plan, that tomorrow we'll set off northwards for Rishikesh, leaving the visit to Ravi Shankar for another time.

* * *

'It's Monday today. The traffic will probably be better than if we'd gone yesterday,' I comment, somewhat inanely.

'Probably,' Yolanda replies graciously.

My sandals rub against my toes and ankles, they also squeak, but this doesn't stop me from wearing them, and enjoying my new outfit too. I love it!

We have only a vague idea which direction we should walk in out of Delhi. First we head back towards the railway station where we arrived, and I notice it appears changed. Then it occurs to me that perhaps we are disorientated and that it's a different station. Yes, most probably that's what's happened.

As we walk on, a vast red sandstone fort looms ahead of us.

We stop to examine a poster on the wall, which proclaims a forthcoming attraction here: -

Son e Lumiere at the Red Fort

We walk on and as we do I notice a car stopping near us, a large black family car.

'Can I offer you a ride,' a suave voice asks.

Unhesitatingly, we accept the invitation and climb in.

We exchange names; discovering that this is Vijay, Vijay Mathur.

'I had a school friend called Deepak Mathur. Is he one of your family?' I ask.

'The name Mathur means we come from the city of Mathura, the holy city of Lord Krishna's birth,' he explains.

'Oh, I see, that makes it easy doesn't it?'

'Tell me, what is your father's profession?' he asks

'Physicist, Atomic Physicist amongst his jobs. Now he has passed on.'

'He was a clever man! Where are you going to? Have you seen the Red Fort?'

'Yes, we just passed it. Now we are going to Rishikesh.'

'That is good, it is a very holy place, you will be blessed. Unfortunately I cannot go with you, much as I would like to.'

We have gone but a short distance when Vijay stops the car and fumbles in his pocket.

'Here, take this for your bus fares. And this is my card; show it at the J.K. Ashram in Haridwar and the servant there will give you a room. My family is connected

with this place.'

'Are you sure it will be all right?'

'Yes, you are very welcome. When you return to Delhi give me a call. Keep well! You must know that they do not have proper facilities so far from the city.'

'That's really nice of you, thank you very much.'

'Don't mention it. The money should be enough for the bus fare, you catch it on this road; up there.' he directs.

We wave him goodbye.

We resume our walk and pass a patch of waste ground, where a man with a monkey is entertaining a small group of children. On seeing us coming, he feverishly rotates a small drum with little spherical clappers that beat the drum skins loudly, and the monkey dances about.

'Poor little thing,' Yolanda whispers.

'Let's walk on,' I suggest, not wanting to encourage the man.

The road leads us to a long iron bridge, which spans a broad lazy-running river, the River Yamuna.

The rucksack has been cutting into my shoulders so I unstrap it and let it down onto the ground, As I gaze down at the swirling flow below us it seems to me the waters cry out for my load. I pick up the rucksack, it's tempting, so very, very tempting.

'Would you mind if I chucked the bag in?' I ask Yolanda.

'What are you talking about? Of course I would,' she replies .

We have no reason to hang on to all this clutter, but then I reflect, maybe one day it might come in useful.

We continue crossing the bridge and on the far side we find a young chap selling bananas, huge clumps of them. For only *a rupee* he sells me twenty of the ripe fruits and we get stuck into a healthy breakfast.

I figure this as good a place as any to hitch a lift.

While we wait I get to pondering, about the nature of happiness.

It occurs to me, probably for the very first time, that it's impossible to experience happiness and unhappiness simultaneously. Furthermore, I see no merit in experiencing unhappiness, whereas happiness always feels right. Pursuing this idea further I wonder if, actually, we have a choice in the matter, as to whether or not we are happy or sad. So I decide to test this theory by actually choosing to be happy!

I am exhilarated at the implications of this idea of choosing to be happy, and log this as something I'll maybe be able to discuss with this Maharishi fellow when I get to meet him. I wonder also if there is anything else I might discuss with him, any other ideas I've come up with?

I do recall that I came up with a theory of sorts after following the 'No Entry' signs at Notting Hill Gate Underground station, in London, and I found it provided me a short cut to getting upstairs, it being a much shorter distance than going the prescribed route. I had then tried this at other underground stations and found it to work in other cases too. So I wondered, if I'd inadvertently discovered something, a secret of the universe maybe, that other signs of no entry might lead to other shortcuts, and perhaps more. So, I'd certainly discovered a philosophy of sorts.

There are few vehicles on this road, just the odd cyclist and the occasional truck, so when a grey government bus swings around the corner I have no hesitation in hailing it. Yolanda and I climb aboard and from the conductor we buy tickets to Hardwar, then we settle down to enjoy the ride. The first town we come to is a place called Meerut, which, according to a pamphlet I'd been reading back in Delhi, was the site of a 'mutiny' during the British rule. Through the bus window I spot a cemetery, an unfamiliar sight here, British perhaps, probably for Britishers who didn't make it back home?

As the bus navigates the twisting streets at the town centre, I spot a hand-painted sign for a 'Milk Bar', which sounds like a nice place for a stop. But the bus doesn't even slow, and soon we are out of town and back out on the open road.

Through the lush plains we race, glimpsing pleasant sights of rural India; we share the road with bicycles piled high with vegetation which swerve unsteadily as the bus overtakes them.

Speeding through villages and towns, we drink in all the sights, of the curious shops and *chaay* houses and the colourfully clad women carrying bundles on their heads. Everywhere we pass through we see the signs of religious worship, from small roadside shrines to impressive domed temples, freshly whitewashed and gleaming in the sun.

Not everyone on the bus is going as far as Hardwar, some are going only a few miles whilst others stay on a while longer. The comings and goings of the passengers keeps the ticket collector surprisingly busy.

There seems to be a traffic jam, and we are held up in a queue of cars, so I look out to see what the delay is. Just at this moment I see a massive gleaming locomotive steaming towards the road crossing, slowly hauling a long line of carriages; the air filled with pungent smoke smelling of bad eggs.

Once the train has passed and disappeared from view, the traffic begins to move again.

The landscape is gradually changing, and though it's still a flat plain to the right hand side of the road we see a range of pretty green hills coming into view. There's something very comforting about the sight.

'We must be getting near the Himalayas,' I remark excitedly.

'Sivaliks, they Sivalik Parvat are,' a fellow passenger informs us.

And it's not long before we see signs of a built up area coming into view.

'Haridwar! This Haridwar, sahib,' the conductor shouts to us.

Alighting from the bus, I ask for directions to the address we've been given. But nobody seems to have heard of J.K. Ashram, and after walking this way and that about town we begin to despair of ever finding the place, if indeed it exists.

Only after much more walking and worrying do we eventually locate its whereabouts, then, knocking at the door, we are met by a thin shabbily dressed man, who is clearly the servant Vijay told us about.

He looks at us suspiciously, so I think to show him the business card, and try to explain our situation. Unfortunately, he doesn't respond, he doesn't seem to understand English, but this does not prevent him from letting us in and showing us to a spacious room, which sports the most enormous double bed.

In the circumstances we think it safe to entrust our bags into his care before going back outside in order to discover the town of Hardwar (or Haridwar, as some call it).

We look about for somewhere to eat, hoping to find a place selling a vegetable *pilao* as good as the one we ate at Eagle Hotel in Delhi. We are fortunate in finding a place to eat, and get to enjoy a hearty meal. We also visit a chemist shop, in search of tampons for my girlfriend, then we return to our lodgings.

It's reassuring to see that our baggage is still intact and that it's been put in our room, and I notice too that the bed has been freshly made up with clean sheets.

For us the room is incredibly luxurious compared to any other place we've stayed in during our travels. I explore a little and notice that there's a door that opens out on to some slippery stone steps that lead down to a wide fast moving river.

'This is the Ganges,' Yolanda informs me, *'the Indians consider it holy, you know.'*

'Yeah, some time ago I saw a film about India, by some French guy. The way it looked in the film was that musicians played on every street corner. The only music we've heard so far has been from radio sets - apart from the records on the jukebox back at the Eagle. I really like the records here, the pop ones, they're so psychedelic, fantastic stuff! Actually, I like them even more than the Moroccan records we heard, and that's saying something.'

We go back inside to our room and lock the door to the river terrace so as to prevent anyone sneaking in.

I think about the water outside, it looks so very deep and dangerous. I've been apprehensive about going near deep water since I was a kid, having had some unpleasant experiences going out of my depth. But when I think about the river here I feel an unusually deep sense of peace and contentment within myself. Things seem to be really looking up for Yolanda and myself.

Chapter 17

AT THE ROOTS OF THE MOUNTAINS

A stray beam of sunlight glances across my face, gently waking me. The stillness of the room counters my urge to rouse my fellow traveller. At length though she stirs and smiles softly as she spies me gazing at her.

'What a lovely bed, pure luxury. I haven't slept so well in ages,' Yolanda announces, languishing contentedly.

When we've sorted ourselves out and are ready to leave, we go in search of the servant who we find downstairs resting on a mattress on the floor.

'We go now.' I announce.

The man stares up at us.

'Thank you. The card please, we need the card.' I tell him

He looks uncertain.

'The card please!' I demand, making the shape of the card with my hands.

Hesitantly he lifts up his pillow and passes me Vijay's business card, before taking to his feet and going to unfasten the front door.

He stands, bowing his head and courteously places the palms of his slender hands together, so I do likewise and then pick up our bags to leave.

From the road outside comes the sound of the tinkling of a bicycle bell. As we emerge from the doorway, we are in time to catch sight of a Western couple astride three-wheeler bikes, pedalling at an urgent pace, their loose clothes billowing out most comically.

'I wonder if they're staying with the Maharishi?' Yolanda suggests.

'It's possible I suppose. Let's get going shall we?'

A short walk finds us in the centre of Hardwar, from where we tread the wide walkways bringing us to the numerous ornate and attractively painted temples.

A notice on some railings informs us that we stand before 'The Footprint of Lord Vishnu'. Stopping here also affords a panoramic view of the distant hills. My heart rejoices realising that we will shortly be in sight of the Himalayas proper.

Onward we walk, stopping only briefly in order to gain directions.

Reaching the Rishikesh road it's soon evident that hitchhiking is not going to be easy, as there are no private cars, just the occasional bullock cart and someone riding past on a bicycle. Instead we just put our best foot forward, but have ventured no great distance before we find an excuse to stop.

Standing in the shadows, by a mossy grey rock wall beside the main road, an old man rests himself against a boulder beside a gurgling stream. There is something familiar about him, his bald head and his broken John Lennon type glasses perched on his wrinkled nose, tied on with string. His skin hangs in leathern folds; a white thread hangs diagonally across his chest. Bunched up cloth sheet clings round his bandy legs, his dusty feet poked into over-sized, scratched, shiny black lace-up shoes. He holds before him a tray of snacks that's strapped to him after the manner of cinema usherettes.

Curiosity concerning his unfamiliar wares forces me to go over and inspect the edibles he has on display, trying one, then another, and another, sampling each kind of snack. The snacks vary in price but all cost less than the equivalent of an English penny.

Soon I have tried his entire range of savouries, *samosa*, *pakora*, *bel puri* and many more, including a puffball containing water. For reasons better known to herself, Yolanda does not indulge, and is contented just to watch.

Quite suddenly, a single-decker coach grinds and swerves around the corner.

We jump up and gesture as we narrowly avoid being run down by it.

Luckily it stops and I find that Vijay our patron has got it just about right. What is left of the 50-rupee gift he gave us for the bus fares is now spent on tickets to Rishikesh, and with only *paise* to spare.

I ask Yolanda about the quaint old man back in Hardwar.

'He reminded me of someone,' I say absent-mindedly.

'Gandhi, he looked just like Mahatma Gandhi,' she opines.

'The very man!' I marvel.

The bus journey from Hardwar is pleasant enough, for the route is much softer than the one yesterday, with views of the verdant tree clad slopes of the soft rolling hills constantly causing me to lift up my eyes.

But the view vanishes, with houses and shops now lining the road, and it's clear we have arrived at a small market town.

Turning off the road, the bus pulls to a halt at a bus stand.

'Rishikesh,' the driver calls.

Alighting from the bus, we ask a bystander to point out the way to where Maharishi Yoga Mahashi, or whatever his name is, lives.

'English no speak,' the man explains. *'You Tourist Office go.'*

241

Helpfully he directs us where to go, further down the road, and on looking up, I see a wooden sign with 'Tourist Office' neatly painted on it, and then, after scaling the outside staircase, we enter a darkened room there.

The ascent of the very steep stairs leaves us puffed, wheezing and coughing, and we are also temporarily blinded by the almost total absence of light inside. From some distant corner of the office arises a voice, a cultured voice, only faintly audible.

'Yes please! What it is I can do for you? Please, come take seat. Yes you sir. Yes kind lady.'

As my eyes grow accustomed to the dim light, I notice a young man sidling over to us. Slowly, almost ceremoniously he shows us around the office, pointing out the piles of brochures, and the road and rail map stuck on the wall. He then shows us the visitor's book, after which he slumps back in his chair and peers over at us from behind his desk. And at his repeated request we too sit down and small talk with him awhile.

Of a sudden comes a flash of sunlight, and someone else enters through the doorway. It turns out to be another member of the staff, apparently the first man's boss, who greets us enthusiastically.

'Good morning, how are you? Where are you coming from, France, Germany?'

'England, actually,' I answer, not without pride. *'I say... could you leave the door open please?'*

'This is good! No problem! You want tea? You come from London?'

'Proper London,' I answer (somewhat tongue-in-cheek), and ask, *'Do you mind if we smoke?'*

'You like sigrat?' he asks, producing a pack of *Wills* (relatively expensive cigarettes) and offering them around. After smoking one of his cigarettes, and chatting with him for a time, I slowly get up from the chair and indicate our wish to leave.

'You need horse tanga. Maharishi Ashram is too much distance,' informs the official.

Turning to his colleague he says with an air of authority, *'Please find tanga for our friends.'*

Without a word the subordinate sets off on his errand, and soon returns, telling me that a horse and carriage taxi awaits us down below.

Bidding our farewells to the guys at the Rishikesh Tourist Office we climb back down to the street, to find a rather ragged unshaven man standing at the foot of the stairs.

The suspension of the carriage lurches and creaks uneasily as we climb up the swaying steps and sit ourselves down on the hard wooden bench. The roguish looking driver now joins us. Sitting down on the seat and tugging at the smooth

242

leather reins he cracks a whip across the hapless horse's mane. Notwithstanding my concern over the creature's welfare, as the driver drives him hard, a strange feeling of exhilaration floods my senses, for there is something very special in the atmosphere here, which feels very comfortable, a reassuring feeling of intense peace and tranquillity, which for me increases at every step of the horse's hooves.

The driver beats the horse, urging it to go faster.

'*Don't do that!*' I shout, trying to raise my voice above the sound of the galloping hooves.

Grinning and determined, the driver averts his bloodshot eyes and ignores me. Yolanda shouts at him too, but to no avail.

I survey the roadway for any sign of our destination, and ruminate as we speed along the tree-lined lane, about the Maharishi and his followers. *What's their belief system? Do they believe in self-sufficiency? I wonder if they grow their own food, do they tend vegetables and fruits here amongst these lush hills, which rise up on all sides?*

We pass a sign that points to somewhere called 'Yoga Niketan', which I assume must refer to the barely visible white building set far back up the forested left-hand side of the road. It sounds promising, and just might be the place we're looking for.

But the *tanga* doesn't slow, not even a little, and just continues at a brisk canter.

At a forked crossroads we swerve suddenly across to the right-hand turning, where our driver reins in the panting, frothing horse.

There are other horse *tangas* here, stood about forming a semi-circle, their masters seated atop or reclining on their respective carriages in a corner of the yard, talking and puffing on *bidees* held tightly in their clenched fists. Our driver signals for us to climb down. Then I go to pay him the fare.

'*Ek rupee chaar annas,*' he calls out gustily and helps himself to a *rupee* and a 25 *paise* piece from the coins in my outstretched hand.

Unsure where to go now, we move towards the cluster of buildings ahead, only to discover that everywhere is locked up here, with no sign of life anywhere.

Further down the pathway I catch sight of a well-to-do looking Indian gent shuffling about, and as we draw closer to him I ask him why everything is shut up.

'*They are closed, they are eating no doubt. This is Shivanand Ashram, the Divine Light Society. What do you want here?*' he asks softly.

Looking up I notice a sign, 'Shivanand Nagar'.

I answer the stranger; '*this is not the right place I think. We are looking for the Maharishi.*'

'*Ah, he is over the river. I too am crossing; I am waiting for ferryboat. You disappointed will be, I am thinking, Maharishi at present not there. Now in Europe is.'*

I let the conversation drop, and settle down to wait for the ferry.

After some minutes a khaki-clad figure comes sauntering along the riverside path, and producing a large bunch of keys he opens up the Post Office here, the smallest Post Office I've ever seen.

This spurs me to think of writing a letter to Vijay, to thank him for his help, so I set about purchasing an Inland Letter Card (which has a pre-paid postage stamp).

A timelessness fills the air, an easy restful feeling.

Through the tranquil silence I sense some activity behind me.

Turning I notice that a boat has moored at the foot of the wide steps, so I get up, pick up our rucksack and hasten down in order to climb aboard. The long ferryboat rocks gently as Yolanda and I climb aboard and sit ourselves down beside our lone fellow traveller, the man who we were chatting with near the Post Office.

The blistered paintwork reveals portions of smooth sun-bleached timber, my hand absent-mindedly picks at the flaking paint.

The old sunburnt ferryman yanks at the rope tied to the outboard motor, jerks the engine into coughing spluttering life, causing fumes to blast forth from the exhaust pipe. The ferryman's assistant unties the mooring line and we are off, puckering the nearly still mirror-like surface of the water with rushing waves.

Tracing an arc on the waters, the ferry throbs it's way towards the opposite bank, and the reflections of the buildings there dance on the river's silvery surface.

On reaching the riverbank, one of the boatmen athletically jumps off onto the steps, and makes fast the craft whilst we get up and step off, rather warily, as with any sudden movement of the boat, we could slip and fall into the waters. Once off we climb up the stone steps.

'You for some refreshment with me will come,' the Indian gentleman announces.

A quick glance at Yolanda tells me she would love to, so we agree to follow him along the concrete path, which is worn smooth and strewn with glinting silver sand.

'You like Indian clothes, I see,' he remarks to the pair of us. *'Very nice,'* he adds with an evident note of satisfaction.

We pass along a narrow walkway, bristling with businesses.

Behind the first stall hangs many brightly coloured printed calendars.

Our friend from the ferry crossing leads us to a spacious restaurant, the *Choti Wala* in front of which are displayed trays of appetising sweetmeats.

'You my friend meet,' says our companion, introducing us to another gentleman, who is eager to shake us both by the hand.

'Also you would like some food?' he offers.

'Thank you. No, just Fanta Orange, that will be fine. Thanks.'

So here we are, all seated at an extremely solid red table apparently inlaid with red alabaster, and we are cooled by the several electric fans that whirl above our heads.

An eager young man dressed in soiled whites, a towel draped over his shoulder, takes our order.

Waiting for his return we help ourselves to chilled water, which along with spotless gleaming stainless steel beakers is thoughtfully placed on our table.

Swargashram © Jonathan Miller

'In Swargashram you will stay?' our friend asks, *'I give you name of place. You will not have money to pay, it is for all pilgrims. You paper give me. For you I write.'*

On the back of one of the pamphlets given to us today, courtesy of the Rishikesh Tourist Bureau, the one on Buddhist Shrines, he writes for us the following information; *'Ved Nikaitan'*.

Ved NiKAITAN.

'I walking that way am. I will show you!'

Walking along the walkway on the riverbank, we make our way, and I see, for the first time since coming to India, cows, sacred cows, wandering loose, idly grazing on weeds and any edible rubbish.

Enjoying the calm restful atmosphere, I give only passing attention to the structures that line the pathway, white buildings trimmed with deepest pink, having numerous rooms and sporting grand entrance places, the signs advising the names of the institutions, Gita Bhavan and Parmath Niketan.

On the other side of the walkway is an eating-house and some little businesses selling wares such as cloth, vegetables and gifts.

Passing these shops and stalls we arrive at an attractive clock tower of reddish rusty pink stone, topped by an onion shaped dome. The hours on the clock face are marked using Indian numerals.

१   २   ३   ४   ५   ६   ७   ८   ९   १०   ११   १२

Coming to the end of the concrete walkway, there are no more buildings, and the River Ganges comes properly back into view again.

From here there is a vast foreshore with an abundance of smooth pebbles and boulders interspersed with large swathes of silver sand.

view of clock tower from foreshore © Jonathan Miller

Standing on the foreshore and looking across the river to the far side bank, at some goodly distance one can see the town of Rishikesh.

'I must here leave you,' announces our guide apologetically. *'Your ashram a little further is, on banks of Mother Ganga. May you benefit from your stay here, very holy place it is, much peace you will find. When to Maharishi's ashram you go, walk on, not far into the jungle it is.'*

Jungle, eh? I like the sound of that!

The feeling of well-being that I've sensed since my arrival in Rishikesh forges in me a determination to make the most of this opportunity of a respite from our endless travels. I make up my mind to stay here a while, maybe as long as a month. My only hope now is that we will find lodgings and are met with a warm reception.

I pause to take in the scene.

Ahead of us runs a rough path, and to the right is the foreshore of the river, silvery sands peppered with pebbles, some white, some dark grey, and dozens of large dark grey rocks too, with some few of the largest boulders partly submerged in the flow of the sparkling waters of the Ganges.

Some way off to our left, and some distance from the shore, are a couple of flat-roofed structures, which I take to be our destination - the *'ashram'* we've been guided to. And beyond these low buildings thickly wooded slopes are ranged, lush hills rising high up into the sky.

Deep drifts of sand slow our progress, and the sun-drenched picturesque views and pervasive sound of birdsong invite us to pause and enjoy.

As we approach the buildings, a lady garbed in faded orange cloth walks towards us. Of slight stature and short hair; and by her countenance and demeanour she appears self-assured and serene.

Following her is a small group of people, mainly young women, who seem, by their expressions, to be in awe of her. Their presence - they resemble a shadow - is surely not lost on the woman, who strolls forward purposefully, with an air of self-importance that, to be quite honest, I find slightly offensive.

Establishing eye contact with me she hesitates and stares for some moments, giving the impression she is reading my thoughts.

As I'm no great lover of game-play I immediately seek to break through the phoney baloney.

'There is room here?' I ask.

'English nahin,' she whines, spinning her petite hands together in a flurry.

A studious looking Indian gent appears by her side:

'What it is you are wanting?' he inquires of us.

I show him the scrawled name of the *ashram*, which is writ clearly on the leaflet I'm holding, just above a depiction of the crossed-legged Buddha.

'There is room here?' I repeat.

I'm confident the lady in orange understands my words, for she takes a grip of my arm and pulls me forwards, first past one row of doorways and then past another, until she stops, pushes open a slatted door, and ushers me inside a tiny room.

'Ek rupee,' she states loudly, clasping her hand upward to reveal one waving finger.

I look about inside, there's no bed and no furniture here, just an empty cell of a room.

I falter for a moment, recalling we'd been told the accommodation would be free.

'Bed?' I enquire. *'Something to sleep on? A lock, we also need a padlock.'*

'Nahin, Nahin ... Lock nahin. Lock Rishikesh men,' she says, her rather high-pitched voice soaring ever higher.

At this she shoots away, as agile as a young fawn, leaving the cluster of fans who have been watching the proceedings to disperse and disappear.

Yolanda and I wait in the room. We wait and wait.

Eventually the woman returns, carrying two thin rush mats, which she dramatically throws to the floor, as if anxious to be rid of their weight, before turning on her heel and is off again.

'She's a holy woman isn't she?' Yolanda asks in a hushed and bemused tone, after our landlady has quite disappeared from view.

'She didn't give us a padlock,' I respond.

Settling down to the task of laying down the mats, we unroll our sleeping bags and extract the towels and toiletries from the rucksack, after which I'm ready and eager to get back outside, as I want to see more of the area.

'Let's look the Maharishi up,' I suggest, *'I do hope he's in.'*

After closing the door, I go and look about in the nearby undergrowth, in search of a short sharp stick to jam into the iron hasp and staple latch, a symbol of our wish to lock the room.

We leave the *ashram* through a low wooden back gate and make our way out past a small but well-planted vegetable patch.

Our path takes us along an expanse of sand then straight into the jungle, where the sunshine seems to struggle to penetrate the dense foliage. Creepers wind themselves up and around the trunks of the many tall trees that line our way. The sounds of wild animals and birds, the variety of colours here, with so many variations and shades of yellows, browns and green, alongwith the sweet smell of the blossoms and the undergrowth; they come together to fairly intoxicate my senses.

Abruptly the path brings us into a clearing.

Only with difficulty can we venture forth, for all around us flutter butterflies, hundreds of exquisitely patterned delights, fluttering and flying about, engulfing us and fairly blocking our way. But after pressing on, we find the jungle from here on becomes ever less dense.

We halt at the remnants of an ancient building. Upon and around the smooth grey-stone foundations are strewn the remains of the crumbling walls on which cling splendid mossy growths. I stand amongst the ruins and try to imagine what the stonework once formed. There is something in the air; a presence that makes me wonder if it was a temple perhaps, for the spot feels special. It's possible to imagine it might even have some rudimentary sort of awareness of its own.

Close by is a corrugated-metal hut, near which stands some horned white cows grazing, lowing softly and glancing up at us as we pass.

With no path to guide us, we now hesitate. Maybe we should go back? But then again maybe we should walk on just a little bit further?

'Can you hear the monkeys?' Yolanda asks softly.

'I think so, but I haven't seen any yet,' I answer, listening intently.

Just at the point of deciding to postpone our visit, in the distance I catch sight of a low stone wall, and head on over to take a closer look. Affixed to an overhanging tree, a notice announces; '

SHANKARACHARYA NAGAR
Spiritual Regeneration Movement
under the guidance of Maharishi Mahesh Yogi

There's a steep path here, cut into the hillside, reinforced with staves of wood. The climb proves interminable and steep; we clutch at the low stonewalls on each side of the path to make the going that much easier.

Periodically we stop to regain our breath but after climbing upward for some time, we at last make it to the top. There's a white fence here inset with a gate, upon which is a notice;

JAI GURU DEVA - PLEASE NO SMOKING

As there are sounds of building work coming from the right, we take the left-hand path; past several simple but pleasing looking buildings, until we come across another hand painted sign with a wooden pointer nailed to a tree, '**OFFICE**' it reads.

A knock at the door pays off, for a European dressed in white shirt, casual trousers and open sandals opens the door.

He stands silently before us, eyeing us intently. After introducing ourselves I tell him the purpose of our visit;

'We've come to see the Maharishi,' I say simply.

'He is in Canada since some weeks,' he answers me, eyeing me quizzically all the while.

'That's amazing Yolanda. We come all across the world, and come to see him, and he goes off to Canada. Is he due back soon?' I ask the man.

'That I can't say. Whereabouts are you staying?'

'Ved Nika something, down by the Ganges.'

'Yes, I know it. Tell me, do you meditate?'

Meditation is a personal matter, essentially private really. I think for a moment, and ask myself what I've been doing all these weeks on the road, if I haven't been 'meditating'?

'Well.. , yes, I suppose so...' I answer vaguely.

Evidently my answer does not please him, for I see he's frowning darkly… then he asks if I have been 'taught' to meditate.

Though I don't know quite why he's asking me this, I have to admit that I haven't been taught to meditate. His expression rapidly clears; he begins to radiate a warmth not evident before, then he searches out something from inside the office.

'Perhaps you would like to talk with someone, you could come back tomorrow. In the meantime take this to read, you might find it of interest,' he suggests, handing me a small stapled pamphlet.

'The Beatles, they came here a couple of years ago?' I ask, hoping to find out more about why they were here.

'Beatles?' he asks, frowning for a moment. *'Yes, that's right, they were here,'* he adds distractedly.

Since the Maharishi himself is not here at present, so it looks as though we won't get to chat with him, and this man clearly doesn't want to talk about the Fab Four's visit, there seems no point in waiting around here.

I turn my attention to my fellow traveller:-

'Let's get back now, Yolanda, we haven't had a proper meal yet today.'

She agrees with me.

'Then come back tomorrow, say mid-afternoon, if you cannot find me, ask here at the office, Andreas, Andreas Müller,' he repeats.

'Thanks, we'll be back,' I assure him.

With no wish to lose ourselves in the surrounding jungle we carefully retrace our steps, keeping strictly to the way that brought us here. Finding ourselves back at the path, energetically in leaps and bounds we descend the steps, and soon find ourselves back in sight of the sandy bank of the river.

I pull off my sandals.

'The sand feels amazingly soft, doesn't it?' Yolanda observes.

I smile in agreement.

'Paul, your feet look really sore. Still, they'll soon heal up, new shoes always take a while to break in, mine really hurt at first.'

Nice to know she cares.

The Beatles seated around Maharishi Mahesh Yogi, in a clearing near the office at Shankaracharya Nagar, prior to a group photograph of course participants being taken. Rishikesh, India, February 1968

George Harrison, John Lennon & Paul McCartney of The Beatles, with Maharishi Mahesh Yogi, at a sing-along on the sandy foreshore of the Ganges. Rishikesh, India, February 1968

As we're both hungry, we decide not to go back to our room just yet, but instead to make for the restaurant, which we visited earlier, back in Swargashram village.

'I hope they've got vegetable pilao,' Yolanda exclaims excitedly. *'Oh look, look at that dog, isn't he sweet? He's just like my dog, Titi, back in Italy,'* she exclaims.

She stoops over the tail-wagging mongrel, which is all too grateful of her attention.

The sound of cloven hoofs diverts my attention.

'But look at the cows, it's so nice to see them walking free, see how noble they are, they look healthy too, don't they?' I observe.

Ambling along, soaking up the peace and tranquillity of this place, certainly beats being on the road, and the local people here seem so friendly, smiling at us warmly, sometimes even bowing their heads. Of the people we pass, a good half of them wear cotton robes. Occasionally the robes are white but more often they're of a variety of shades of orange or ochre.

We arrive back at the ferry crossing, after which we turn off the riverside walk and past a temple, then up the walkway past a few little shops to the restaurant we had earlier visited, the *Choti Wala.* I notice that next door to it there's another place to eat, the *Rama Hotel,* but this appears not to be a hotel at all, just another restaurant, and altogether less attractive than its neighbour. So we stride into *Choti Wala,* sit down at one of the many empty tables, and wait to be served.

Menus are soon thrust into our hands, and we check them thoroughly, noting the many interesting sounding dishes, but there's no mention of Yolanda's sought after dish.

'This sounds like it. Peas pilao.' I suggest, *'What do you think?'*

'Yes. Okay. But just look at that picture over there, the picture of the boy!' Yolanda says in a surprised whisper.

I look over at the wall to which she is pointing, at the photograph of a corpulent pink boy wearing nothing but a loincloth and a wide grin on his heavily made up face. And he has a very fancy hairdo, a projection of long hair forming a long spike sticking out from the crown of his bald head.

'S-s-s strange!' I hiss.

Next to this photograph are others, framed hand tinted colour photographs, which appear to be stills from Indian films, and all of the same actor. Perhaps these are of the proprietor when he was a young man, or maybe it's a relative of his? I turn back to Yolanda; she looks relaxed, beautiful even. Her thoughtful brown eyes are particularly alive and shining. For so much of our journey we have travelled side by side, and now, facing her, there stirs a realisation within me, that though we have been together the whole time, we have been paying but scant attention to one another.

Our food arrives.

With a pinch of pepper and a liberal sprinkling of salt, the *pilao* tastes simply delicious, it's piping hot and tasty, and we finish every morsel.

'Mmmmm, that was scrumptious. Almost like vegetable pilao at the Eagle in Delhi,' Yolanda states, a compliment indeed.

The waiter returns to gather up our plates and the steel water goblets.

'You want sweets? Barfi? Jelabi? Gulab jamun?' he asks.

Neither of us know what he means, so instead we opt for a hot drink.

'Hot milk please,' Yolanda asks.

When it arrives Yolanda claps her hands together with glee.

'Lovely, lovely, it's got the thick creamy milk on top. I love it like this,' she enthuses, scooping off the froth with a teaspoon.

Our meal over, we pay up and leave, then slowly we walk back in the direction of the *ashram*. On our way back we halt at an enclosure to the side of the walkway, in which are a charming group of colourful statue figures stood surrounded by a pool of water in which are countless coins having all been donated. Thinking to add a few of our own, we press them through the netting.

Shri Ananta Padmanabha statue

'Do you know meaning of this?' a voice booms. *'It is story of creation. Here the blue skinned Lord Vishnu lies on the many-headed snake, Ananta Shesha, while Mahavishnu's consort, Lakshmi Devi, attends him. From his belly rises lotus flower in which sits god Brahma, god of creation, holding holy Vedas, the most ancient of Holy Scriptures. They are worshipping Mahavishnu. Garuda the eagle.'*

'Those two at the back, who are they?' I ask. *'Why has one got a horse's head?'*

'That one to right that looks to be horse is divine musician, one of Gandarva. The one on left is sage Narada.'

'Thanks a lot for telling us.' I respond politely, though not really understanding much of what he's been saying

'You are English?'

'From London.'

'Very good, where you are staying?'

'The ashram just beyond the path here. We arrived today.'

'I am guide here, Mr. Singh. I can show you many things. I can take you to caves where yogis are. Maybe you come to see very holy Swiss lady, she has been in jungle cave many years. She is very holy person.'

Absorbed with the flow of his words we stand nodding and making appreciative sounds. In point of fact the ideas presented by him are so new to me, so very different, I have no reference point from which to respond.

'I must go now, we shall see each other again,' he says, before promptly disappearing into a building close by.

Resuming our walk it's not long before we are back at the *ashram*.

In a doorway there sits a lad, a European, with long straight corn coloured hair, wearing only a piece of cloth tied around his waist and a generous smile.

'Welcome. My name's John.'

After introducing ourselves, I ask him where he's from and why he's here.

'Southend,' he replies.

Whereas many such coastal destinations, like Bexhill, are coupled with the words 'on-Sea', Southend is sometimes referred to as Southend-on-Mud. At the mention of Southend, which was for our family one of the closest seaside holiday resorts to London, fractured recollections of daytrip outings on steam trains with my grandparents tumble into my mind. *'I used to go to Southend when I was young,'* I remark.

'So you understand why I'm here then?' he says with an air of finality.

'Mmmmm and you're on your own here are you?' I ask

'My friend Rob is around somewhere, you'll meet him some time. You're staying here too aren't you? I caught sight of you earlier.'

'Yes that's right, our room is over there,' says Yolanda pointing, *'Is there such a thing as a toilet about?'*

'There is, but you can always go in the jungle,' he says in all seriousness, pointing

254

out back.

I go with the latter option, and relieve myself squatting amongst the undergrowth; using fresh leaves as a substitute for toilet paper.

This getting back-to-nature feels great. I yearn to explore the jungle further, for the place literally throbs with life, such as insects, birds, and from somewhere not far off comes the screech of monkeys accompanied by the sound of rustling leaves and cracking of twigs.

What other animals lurk deep in the wild undergrowth I wonder? Elephants? Bears? Tigers even?!

I sit down on a tree stump in this enchanting place and recall our visit to the office at the Maharishi's place - Shankaracharya Nagar - and I fish out the pamphlet the German gave me, entitled *'Right and Wrong'*. It's a curious little item, the convoluted message of which could be stated quite simply as: - *By following the rules, we all hope to find happiness, but that is not always the outcome, and sometimes, when we get disappointed, we break the rules, but the outcome of this can also be unhappiness.*

I finish reading the text, slowly fold it and slip it in my pocket.

The ideas presented seem a bit rambling and inconclusive, and I wonder how this philosophy squares with my discovery, that following the 'No Entry' signs gets one out of an underground station quicker than following the 'Exit' signs.

Yolanda's voice rings out, *'Paul are you all right? It's getting dark.'*

I stand, stretch and suddenly realise that I'm actually extraordinarily tired. Following in the direction of her voice I find her standing in the half-light.

She looks relieved to see me.

'Shall we turn in soon?' she asks. *'It's dark and we don't have any proper light in our room.'*

Inside I discover that Yolanda has lighted two candle stubs, which flicker uncertainly.

After a hurried brush of my teeth at the standing pipe outside, I undress and slip into my sleeping bag on the floor, tucking the passport pouch inside the 'pillow' that I make from my clothing, not forgetting to wind my wristwatch.

I kiss Yolanda goodnight and blow out the flickering candles.

'I hope there are no mosquitoes in here,' Yolanda murmurs *'I thought I saw one earlier.'*

'Ah ha,' I yawn, *'Sleep well.'*

'Buono notte.'

Chapter 18

WELL BEYOND THE WORLD

Despite the shutters being tightly closed, thin shards of daylight pierce the darkness of the room.

I have slept well despite lying on the concrete floor. Whilst unbolting the wooden shutters I hear the faint sound of tinkling bells, and linger awhile, taking in the view of the jungle behind our *ashram,* enjoying the sound of birdsong.

After our ablutions we set about making our room as clean and comfortable as we can.

We open all the shutters wide and go outside in search of a broom. The Indian guy in the room next to ours lets us have a brush, a rudimentary handmade straw effort, which we use to clear the floor of sand, then we throw a bucket of water across the floor and scrub it from wall to wall.

The water drains through a conveniently situated vent, which we afterwards block with a stone to prevent entry of any unwelcome scaled or furry visitors.

The sun has already arisen and there's a gentle breeze; the warm airflow soon dries the floor and we then proceed to unpack our rucksack, for the first time in almost three months, and I remember how all so very recently I was tempted to be rid of my possessions, when I'd almost thrust everything into the River Yamuna. I'm so glad I didn't succumb to the temptation.

In the right hand corner of the room, about two-foot off the floor and projecting from the wall, is a concrete shelf, large enough to lie on. But though it's tempting to try sleeping on it, I feel sure we are safer on the floor. A fall from that would be enough to crack one's head open, I reckon.

Two sets of concrete shelves are also built into the walls, and on these we place our spare clothing, our books and our other nick-knacks.

Unpacking done, we now need to get some breakfast in the village, and before leaving I close our door and push the same stick in through the staple and hasp lock.

'Can we go to the shops?' Yolanda asks, sounding unusually enthusiastic and efficient. *'We need candles, fruit, a cooking pot and some potatoes. We can't go eating at restaurants all the time you know.'*

It's a welcome idea.

'We need another one of those paper packets of Surf, oh and some cigarettes and

some shampoo. I could do with a cuppa too,' I chip in.

On the way to the village we meet with John, who obligingly explains that we can get our mail sent to the local Post Office.

'The address is 'Post Restante, Swargashram, Via Rishikesh, Uttar Pradesh, or U.P. for short.' he explains.

'Why "Via Rishikesh"?' I ask.

'Because the post comes via Rishikesh?' he suggests quizzically.

On our walk to the village, we exchange nods and smiles with passers-by, and we see the occasional cow ambling along.

We notice people sitting around on the steps down to the ferry crossing, drying themselves after a dip in the river. We come to a temple near which we find a little hut that functions as the general store here, with all sorts of merchandise spilling out onto the walkway; and here we buy a small packet of washing powder, some *Simla* cigarettes, matches, and a packet of incense sticks. They have potatoes here, but no cooking pan, so we'll have to make an excursion to Rishikesh to find one.

To round off the trip to the village we visit *Choti Wala* for breakfast, and as we sit waiting for our order to arrive, I notice that it's brought from outside the restaurant; a little white pot of sweet milky boiled tea for two, and a plate of toast made from English style bread.

When we return to the *ashram*, we go to pay our rent money to the orange lady, who we find standing about. Instead of taking the money, she leads us to an office, a room full of curiosities, statues and pictures, and points to a large wooden box there marked 'Donations', so I push a blue 1 *rupee* note into the slot and leave.

Remembering our commitment to return to Shankaracharya Nagar, Dhyan Vidya Peeth, the Academy of Meditation, on the hill, we take the path along the shore and climb the steep stairs cut into the hillside. About half way up the climb, I notice that there's a stall there, which seems to be selling tea. There's a man here who seems to hail from far away, perhaps from somewhere high up in the mountains, Tibet even? I make a mental note to return for a cuppa sometime.

We arrive at the academy, and find Andreas working in the office alongside a beaming and hirsute Indian dressed in a spotless white cotton robe.

Andreas smiles expansively and directs for us to go further up the path.

'Just keep walking up there and you will come to some rooms. You want to speak to Bevan Morris, a young Australian. He knows you're coming.'

Once out of his sight Yolanda and I exchange grimaces.

'First a German, now an Australian,' I complain. *'I would much prefer to talk to an Indian, wouldn't you?'*

Yolanda readily agrees.

To one side of the path is a succession of water tanks, one built higher than the next, forming a waterfall of sorts, but at present disused and clogged with silt and twigs. We come to a line of buildings from which a figure draped in white, steps out.

He greets us pressing his palms together, almost religiously. *'Hello, you must be Paul, and you Yolanda. Do step into my room and sit down, my name is Bevan,'* he says, slipping off his flip-flop sandals.

'Pleased to meet you,' I mumble.

I can't take my eyes off him; it's as if I'm having some sort of revelation. All the religious books I'd seen in my childhood have cemented an impression as to how He would look, Jesus, that is. Shoulder length black wavy hair and long beard, white flowing robe and that certain look in his eyes, humble, compassionate, yet strong and dependable.

Yolanda and I listen with interest as Bevan tells us of his beliefs, of which the most compelling idea is that *'Psychology tells us that we use only a small portion of our conscious mind, no more than fifteen per cent. Maharishi shows us how we can harness the full potential of our minds and live in bliss,'* he assures.

I hang on to his every word as he tells us more about his beliefs; his voice is soft and gentle, his words reassuring. When at length he asks if we have any questions, I find it almost impossible to speak. However, I do try. *'You say it is easy, so why aren't more people using their whole minds?'* I ask, stumbling with my words.

'Simply they have not received this teaching. Now, whatever it is that we already enjoy, we will enjoy more. When we listen to music, we hear much, much more. Our enjoyment is maximum.'

All the while Yolanda stays mute, wearing a look of rapt amazement, almost devotion in her eyes. Evidently for her too Bevan seems a truly remarkable person.

A shout from outside followed by a loud knocking at the door interrupts Bevan, who excuses himself and disappears into an adjoining room. After several minutes he returns and gently resumes his position, sitting crossed legged on a rug. I ask him if everything is all right.

'Only a snake in their room,' he answers matter-of-factly.

'I hope you didn't have to kill it,' I respond, Yolanda gives a nod.

'That wasn't necessary. I removed it with a stick and placed it out of the window.'

I am impressed by how he's so calm and collected when most people would get into a state of complete panic in similar circumstances. I'm also curious to find out whom the other Europeans are who are staying here.

'I think we saw some people from here when we were in Hardwar, they were riding on tricycles,' I tell him.

It transpires they are the same couple that are having trouble with the snake; and they are due to leave tomorrow.

When Bevan winds up the chat, he informs us; *'Andreas would like you to see him before you go. I hope we meet again soon,'* he adds, with evident sincerity.

When Andreas catches sight of us on our return, he sidles up and asks what we think. I'm not sure what he means, I'm not clear whether he is referring to what we thought of the monk, or about what he said.

'You can be initiated tomorrow morning. Come at ten o'clock. Be sure to bring some fruit, some flowers and a new white handkerchief'.

'I don't think I know what initiation is,' says Yolanda, breaking her silence.

'Tomorrow all will be explained. Either Bevan or myself will talk to you again. Come here to my cottlage at ten o'clock. Incidentally don't take any breakfast tomorrow,' he tells us.

I puzzle about what we've heard, and about his pronunciation of the word cottage as 'cottlage', wondering if perhaps this is an Indian or German form of the word. I puzzle too as to why we must forgo our breakfast, though for us it's no concern, as we have long since abandoned such routine niceties as regular meals, in fact I can't remember the last time I ate a full breakfast.

On the way back down the hillside we don't hurry ourselves, but walk slowly, taking our time, and at the bottom of the hill we meet with an elderly Indian couple.

'Friends. Hello. Are you dis-sip-pals of Maharishi Ji?'

I have to think a few moments before I realise that he must mean by *'disciples'*.

'Are we? I don't know. Maybe? We must go now, maybe we'll meet again.' I answer vaguely.

We go in search of food, and find ourselves going back to *Choti Wala* - there's a boy there who is painted head to toe with pink makeup, with his head shaven except for a tuft of hair that's been waxed into a spike on top of his head. His face is also painted, and he wears a cotton cloth about his waist. He seems to be the restaurant's mascot.

We pick up a couple of steel goblets and pour ourselves some chilled water before studying the menu, and end up choosing to have another Peas Pilao.

It's a glorious day, and it seems a great opportunity to go down to the river, to the waters' edge and wash ourselves, and our hair. We also do a little handwashing of our clothes, and after applying a bar of soap over the fabrics; we rinse them through in the current of the river, and lay out our clothes to dry in the sun. Sometimes a bird or two comes near and hops about on the sand.

It's lovely to sit and relax here, with no one coming to disturb us, though we are not entirely alone, for at some distance a holyman sits himself down and browses the pages of a book he has open before him.

Our clothes are all dry long before the sun goes down, so we have time to wander into the village and have another cup of tea before turning in for the night.

* * *

There's that unfamiliar jingling sound again, similar to the sound I heard yesterday, and there's also the sound of loud snorting, and the noise of hooves scrunching on gravel.

I lie here just coming-to and puzzling over the sounds.

Getting up I open the shutters and look out between the bars that separate us from the jungle, enjoying the sunshine, feeling the fresh air on my face.

'What was all that noise?' asks a sleepy voice - that of Yolanda.

'I don't know, I didn't see anything, it sounded like an animal didn't it?'

Yolanda agrees and joins me at the window.

'Are we going to Rishikesh today?' she pleads. *'You said we would go yesterday. I'd like to see the shops there. The ones over this side don't sell much in the way of new vegetables.'*

'Sure, I want to go there too.'

After freshening up and tidying our room we set off to catch the ferry over to Rishikesh. The path into Swargashram seems busier than usual this morning and for the first time I notice beggars along the way, to whom I lose a little change. A group of people stand outside one of the big buildings near to the riverfront, the Gita Bhavan, and near them sit vendors selling little pellets of food wrapped in cones of newspaper.

A ferryboat scuds towards us.

Moving as one, the waiting Indians descend the steps to the river and are soon aboard the boat. We move to climb aboard too, and then I stop.

'Yolanda! What about the fruit, the flowers? Andreas Müller?'

Yolanda's hand clasps at her mouth.

'Oh my God. Yes, we'd better hurry. Where can we get flowers here? I don't think they sell them.'

After buying some bananas, I enquire at a stall nearby, which sells jars of honey, peanut butter and medicines, *'Handkerchief? Where to buy handkerchief?'*

I'm directed to a cloth shop but there I am disappointed in that they don't have any handkerchiefs. But sensing my frustration the owner shows me a bale of white cloth and makes as if to tear some off.

'Better than nothing,' I answer him. *'Yes okay. Shoukria,'* I add, a word I picked up in Pakistan meaning 'Thank you'.

As we continue to look for a place where we might buy flowers, Yolanda points out: -

'It's too late to look for flowers now, let's get up there quick or we'll be late.'

So, with a spring in our step we return along the sandy path and make our way up towards the hillock upon which stand the Maharishi's buildings.

The steps, difficult enough to climb at any time, prove even harder today. Miraculously though, we make up it to the 'cottlage' in the gee nick of time, and Andreas responds to our knock at the door, coming out clutching a file of papers.

'I have done no teaching of late, I'm a bit rusty,' he explains with a far away look upon his face. *'Please wait for me, I won't be long.'*

'We have the fruit but we couldn't find any flowers,' I confess.

His brow creases and he stares into the sky.

'Then pick some from this garden. You have handkerchiefs though?' he asks.

We nod obediently.

As we set about gathering a few delicate blooms from the rocky beds, a calm falls on the garden. We are like children in a fairytale wood, butterflies flitting about, birds watching us from the trees. Time stands still.

A footstep behind us suggests to me that Andreas has rejoined us.

'Good, you have the flowers. Would you both come with me? We will go to the bungalow.'

He leads us up a neatly swept hedge-bordered dry soil path, and over a low bridge spanning a lotus pond, to the veranda of a newly constructed, rather grand looking, bungalow, skirted by grassy lawns and well-kept gardens.

'Here are your forms.' Andreas announces, with an air of efficiency. *'I would like you both to fill them in. Do you have pens?'*

I rummage deep in Yolanda's black suede shoulder bag and find us both a usable biro pen. The forms, academy registration forms, ask many questions; names, address, age, and others, concerning health, and surprisingly, what spiritual literature one has read.

Regarding the latter I include *The Bible* for one, and as another, Christian Science's Mary Baker-Eddy's book *'Science and Health with a Key to the Scriptures'*.

When we have completed the forms Andreas talks to us in turn on a one-to-one basis. His patient and interested attention I somehow find flattering.

'Are you sure you wish to learn?' he asks quite suddenly. *'Are you sure you are serious? You know that one prerequisite for learning your technique is to be abstaining from drugs?'*

What a cheek he has! I've spent so much of my time searching for the truth and here's this German doubting my suitability to learn these teachings.

'I have never been more ready. We gave up drugs ages ago, before leaving England,' I answer emphatically.

'In that case, which of you would like to receive their technique first?' he inquires with a smile. *'Incidentally, normally a donation of one week's wages is offered but in your case I think it can wait until your return to England.'*

He slips off his sandals and we follow his example. Courtesy requires that I allow Yolanda to learn her 'technique' ahead of me.

Maharishi Mahesh Yogi's bungalow   © Jonathan Miller

The two of them disappear down a staircase to the basement, and I am left to contemplate alone.

As the minutes pass I begin to wonder if everything is all right with Yolanda.

I can't help but wonder about what is going on? What if this man's intentions are less than pure? Perhaps right at this moment he is making unwelcome advances towards my girlfriend. I control an urge to investigate, and instead force myself to think of something else. I try to relax.

Looking about me and espying some wooden easy chairs with wickerwork backs I decide to sit down, and having done so, something stirs in my memory. Didn't I once see a photograph of this very terrace? The recollected image settles in my mind. Yes, I'm pretty sure I remember seeing a photo of a Beatle, possibly Paul McCartney, sitting somewhere here, by this building.

I strum my fingers on the arm of the chair and nestle back comfortably, losing myself in the hum of nature. No sounds emerge from downstairs, which I take to be a good sign, for I assume that Yolanda would shout out if she found herself in trouble.

So I just sit easily, looking out into the expanse of greenery and the sky beyond.

At length I hear a click, as of a door opening, and then the sight of Yolanda's head rising up from the stairwell.

'He wants you to go down now,' Yolanda remarks solemnly, her manner distant and withdrawn, a slight smirk playing on her lips.

I'm soon downstairs and entering the dimly lit room there, my feet sinking into the deep pile carpet.

After checking that the door is firmly closed, Andreas extends his arms out, inviting me to pass him the fruit and flowers, and the piece of cloth.

'Please, the offerings?' Andreas asks.

He moves to the end of the room and places the 'offerings' on a tabletop.

The table resembles an altar, with candles burning; there are little brass objects and a vase containing fresh-cut flowers, all spread out on a pure white linen cloth. At the back of the table, resting against the wall is an oil painting of a crossed-legged aged Indian with his hands clasped, attired in an orange robe. His austere expression is framed by long grey hair and a bushy white beard; he gazes out benignly.

Andreas busies himself at this table, now lighting a stick of sandalwood incense, now moving his hands slowly about. I watch this strange spectacle as if in a dream.

Dipping a flower in a tureen he sprinkles the droplets of water on the fruit and on the handkerchief. Lighting a dish of camphor he rotates it gently and sings to himself in a deep low voice. Snatches of sound float across the room to me, melodious and strange, though I can't quite catch the words they appear to be in some ancient mystical language. He seems to be performing some sort of religious or magical ritual; the air carries the scents of camphor and sandalwood smoke.

'Sit down if you would. Make yourself comfortable.'

Sat on a foam mattress and leaning against another I observe Andreas as he seats himself opposite me, closes his eyes and becomes motionless. I watch him with increasing interest as his mouth begins to twitch.

He then proceeds to intone something, and repeats some sounds, ever increasing in volume until the sound fairly fills the room. He then opens his eyes and asks me to repeat the words; just two short words; first with my eyes open and then to myself with them closed. I do as I'm asked and sit there, back straight, repeating the sounds within my mind. It's as if this mental repetition is some sort of chant.

'Slowly open the eyes,' a voice says. It is Andreas, of course.

He then asks me to say the sounds out loud again, and then urges me to repeat them.

He seems satisfied, and explains to me that these are special sounds that emanate from a very subtle level of creation, that they can connect me with the very source of sound, of Being, that some call God.

'Now, sitting comfortably, close the eyes,' he directs me.

Though I do as he says, I can't help wondering where all this is leading, I feel tempted to take a peep to see what he is up to. He speaks again:

'Again slowly open the eyes.'

I open my eyes and find him still seated opposite me, looking at me.

'Did you have any thoughts in the silence?' he asks.

'Yes,' I answer simply.

'Did you notice that thoughts come naturally, effortlessly?'

'Yes, I think so,' I answer again.

'This time when you close your eyes, sit easily for about half a minute and then think the sound, your technique, in the same effortless and natural way.'

I do what he tells me. I wonder how long he wishes me to do this and am glad when I hear his voice again, calling upon me to open my eyes again. Raising himself up, he walks to the door and returns accompanied by Yolanda. We exchange looks as she sits down on the sheet-covered mattress a little way from me.

He now instructs us in the use our sounds, or *'mantras'* as he calls them, warning us to avoid pushing other thoughts from of our minds.

'Let the thoughts come and go, take no notice of them. Do not be held by them. Do not concentrate. Effortlessly repeat the mantra but do not hold on to the mantra. Do not mind it getting fainter or disappearing. As we dive we appreciate the mantra at subtler and subtler levels until transcending thought we arrive at pure Being, the source of all creativity.'

He does the bit about 'closing the eye's again, and we both settle down to our first proper experience of meditation.

It seems easy enough, though I'm not sure how I am getting on. Nothing startling happens.

What did he say? What has he been telling us?

A stream of thoughts come to me: *Take it easy, Take it as it comes, When thoughts come just gently return to the mantra,* so I return to the *'mantra'*.

After a time, I can't be sure how long; maybe 10 minutes or so, the sound of an insect, maybe a grasshopper, catches my attention. The sound fascinates me, but I remember to return to my 'thought', the sound Andreas has given me. I begin to wonder what this '*mantra*' means? But, I remember Andreas saying *'The sound has no meaning for us, it is a vehicle to take us to Being'.*

So, I repeat the sound, which becomes ever fainter, when suddenly, from within me there's a rush of activity.

A vertical pillar of light appears within me, containing the images of countless beautiful Indian-looking women bedecked with jewellery and garbed in shimmering coloured robes, spiralling upwards within myself. They appear to be checking me out, some celestial inner world visitation! I watch, eagerly trying to catch the expression on any one of their faces. The one I focus on looks this way and that, looking about within me, not establishing eye contact with my inner gaze.

Then I recall the instructions of Andreas, who stated that when we find ourselves thinking, we let go of the thought and gently return to the *mantra*.

Reluctantly, as per instruction, I return to the *mantra*, and the cosmic inner vision disappears, it's erased entirely.

Inwardly, I sort of blink at the empty space within, and instantly I miss their presence. It was an absolutely wondrous experience to feel linked with such a subtle beautiful mysterious spectacle, and now there's nothing, not even a smidgen of a trace of the divine drama. Nothing.

How did I become the focus of this divine pageant? Why were they drawn to me? Did I do something to summon them from the mysterious 'beyond' within?

I miss the beautiful women, and all the rest of the slow moving 3-dimensional movie within. Nevertheless I continue to meditate as per the guidance I've been given today, and it's pleasant enough, but nothing like the build-up Bevan and Andreas have given it.

Then I remember that I'm being directed towards an experience beyond thought, and it dawns on me that I've been sitting for quite a while without going beyond thought, and though I have had an astonishing inner experience, I'm not convinced that repeating the *mantra* will ever take me beyond thought.

In a flash it occurs to me that it's my responsibility to contribute to my own success; that it's up to me to fill in the missing link in the instruction, that this is my role in this 'initiation', to solve the riddle, which has been set here.

There is a conflict.... Should I attend to the *mantra* or attend to having no thought? Should I let go of the *mantra* or, maybe, should I let go of all thought?

Just as an experiment, I decide to let go of the *mantra*, **and** all thoughts.

Momentarily I'm confused, as I'm not sure what I should do next.

I hear sounds seeping in from outside the room, the chirruping of birds, and I think I can hear insects too, yes, and now I can hear a gardener clipping away at the grass… but I just sit here listening, and make no attempt to push the sounds away, no attempt to do anything, I just sit and be…..

Chapter 19

RENEWED

There is no sound, no feeling, and yet there is something, I am aware of a pulsing eternal NOW, a marvellous tranquil STILLNESS.

I sense a twitch, as a faint thought tries to form.

A little time passes and again a thought attempts to stir, and then nothing.

The moment merges once more into eternity.

A question forms, *what am I?*

I am aware, of lightness, a glow, nothing more.

Then I flex, and gradually I sense a body.. my body, sitting…. sitting in stillness. Flexing some more, I am aware of my crossed legs, and I smile inwardly.

I am delighted to be conscious, to be alive, to discover that I am alive and in this body.

I sit enthralled with the wonder of the stillness, of my own consciousness.

I witness the miracle of being alive.

…………………………..

I hear a voice, it comes from outside of myself; I focus on the words and understand I'm being asked to open my eyes.

The decision to let go, to let go of all instructions about meditation, with the intention of letting my awareness go to a space without thought, has provided me with such utter and complete peace, an extraordinary serenity, an experience of eternity, calm and refreshing. It has been so utterly and completely rewarding for I have become uncluttered and completely at ease within myself.

Totally and completely relaxed I slowly, very slowly, open my eyes and contentedly stare at the man in front of me, the German man, Andreas.

Ah yes, I remember now, he's the one who I came to see, up the hill, who was going to teach me meditation.

I look about me, and notice a young woman sitting across from me. Though I sense I know her I'm not entirely sure who she is. I look at Yolanda and realise that the bonds that have tied us all too tightly have loosened, as though a spell has been lifted.

Andreas asks Yolanda and myself to tell him how long we think we have been sitting here meditating.

It's a difficult question to answer, as personally I haven't a clue, no idea at all, for since hearing the gardener, time went completely out of my mind.

I tell Andreas so, and it seems to me he's surprised.

He continues asking questions about our experience of meditation, but as I attempt to answer his questions, I sense my heart overflowing with happiness and I find it a strain to stifle my merriment.

'...So this is how we shall meditate morning and evening for 15 to 20 minutes,' Andreas continues.

Oh, it seems he expects us to get into a routine of meditating twice a day. This is something of a surprise. I've just had the most profound and cleansing experience of my whole life, and feel reborn. Why do I now need to make a habit of meditating?

Andreas has not finished, he stiffens perceptibly before saying:

'We do not tell anyone else our mantras, they are to be kept secret.' Andreas announces.

'I never agreed to that!' I muse to myself, surprised that he now wants us to be secretive about this meditation.

A knocking at the door takes Andreas's attention. He seems hesitant about getting up and slowly opens the door, and there I see two faces craning their necks to look into the room. It's the Indian couple that we met the day before, the ones who mistook us for being disciples. I beam at them, and as I do I sense my self-control slipping. I laugh long and hard, oh, it has been so long since I laughed as much!

The Indian couple don't stay long, and it becomes apparent the meditation session has come to an end. Andreas invites us to stay for lunch, but before we leave the basement he presents each of us with a flower, a banana and a handkerchief, and then accompanies us back up the path from the bungalow.

'Don't drop the peel. Throw it over the hedge; there it will soon return to the earth,' he states in a schoolmaster tone.

Cheek! I think to myself, I was thinking of saving the banana for later anyway!

We walk back along the path with him, and follow him to a building adjacent the office.

After washing our hands at the small white sink outside the building, we enter inside and sit down at a table, where we are served cooked food in shiny steel dishes. We tuck into a very simple meal of lentil soup, vegetables and small round flat breads. The custom here in India, as elsewhere throughout most of our travels, is to eat with the right hand (the left reserved for dealings in the toilet); but spoons are also laid on for our use.

The food is simple, divinely simple and tasty. I cannot remember enjoying my food so much in a long, long while.

Whilst we are dining, Bevan comes into the dining room and settles himself down to eat. There's no conversation, it's almost monastic here.

Before departing we arrange with Andreas what time we will meet him the next day, and then we are off, set up for the day, gleefully striding down the steep magical footpath that zigzags down the hill.

'I could live on food like that all the time,' I spout eagerly to Yolanda.

The afternoon is spent happily on the foreshore of the river, where we wash a few clothes in the running waters and dry them across the smooth boulders there. The events of the day have put us both in high spirits. It's therefore odd that I begin to review our 'initiation' in the most critical terms. I ask myself if we've been the victims of hypnotism or something? The words of Mary Baker Eddy come to me, *'Let hypnotism, mesmerism and necromancy be denounced'.* No, I don't think the meditation is anything like that, though maybe there's a touch of autosuggestion involved in the teaching?

I turn the subject over and over in my mind until at last I convince myself that I've not been a victim of hocus-pocus brainwashing, I let the subject drop, relieved that all appears to be in order, after all.

Returning to Ved Niketan, to our room, we dutifully sit ourselves down to meditate again, as suggested by Andreas. I can't see what the purpose is, because as far as I'm concerned I don't feel a need to sit down, or to meditate again just yet.

I find myself somewhat oversensitive, acutely aware of sounds seeping in from outside, and find it difficult to settle down. But within a few minutes I am comfortably meditating as per instructions.

After meditation Yolanda and I wander into the village, where we partake of a glass of hot milk and a portion of melt-in-the-mouth fudge, called *'barfi'*, from *Choti Wala,* which rounds the day off very nicely. Good to be alive!

* * *

Hearing the jingling sound again I quickly get up and pull open the shutters, as fast as I can, just in time to see a heavily laden mule accompanied by its stick-wielding driver, and from what I can see the poor beast is heavily burdened, carrying baskets of shingle and stones, and heading in the direction of the village.

After freshening ourselves up and cleaning our teeth at the standing pipe just along the way from our room, we close ourselves inside our room and sit meditating for twenty minutes. From time to time I think of something about meditation I'm puzzled about, and I make a mental note to ask Andreas next time we meet him.

Andreas had indicated that we should return to him for further sessions, at which time he would check our experiences and give us further instruction.

Before going to see him, we visit *Choti Wala* again for tea and toast, and there is our 1 *rupee* rent to pay, so we stop by on the way back, in order to post our donation in the box.

En route to visiting Andreas again, we hear the chatter of monkeys coming from the jungle, so we go to investigate and find a group of monkeys playing in a glade where at least a dozen of them are disporting themselves. A newborn baby clings to its mother's belly.

I watch as others climb up into the branches of nearby trees, chasing one another, and generally cavorting about. An uncle figure dangles and swings the younger ones from his spot on a long branch.

The message of family unity is not lost on me; it's time to write home. I will get down to it just as soon as I can.

Arriving at the academy, there is, as ever, next to no activity going on, and I am surprised we've not been invited to stay, since there are so many vacant rooms.

Our session with Andreas starts by him asking a few questions about my meditations, and I take the opportunity to ask him what we should do if we cannot find the peace and quiet to sit for meditation.

'Whatever sounds we hear, let them come and go, they are just thoughts. We do not try and push them from our minds. Innocently we take up the mantra.'

Mmm... Easier said than done, I think to myself.

This morning when we meditate with him and we come to the moment when he says *'Open the eyes,'* I realise that something has really happened to me. I am literally agog at the sight of my own body. I lift my arm up and lower it once more. What a gift this body is and this mind too. I sit absorbed, enjoying the moment, the fullness of my existence. After all the thrills and experiences in my life I am now discovering the value of 'not doing'.

But I have all sorts of questions about meditation, not least about the *mantra*. I gather from Andreas that the *mantra* he chose for me was picked up at a very subtle level of thought, and that it's the appropriate sound for me to use to meditate. Certainly, the *mantra* is a pleasant sound, and apparently the sound is 'meaningless to us', which suggests that it might be meaningful to someone else. I can't quite understand why, if the goal of meditation is to 'transcend' thought, that one needs to sit and repeat a *mantra*, no matter how pleasant sounding it is. Surely, once one is settled, one can just let go of thinking and be at one with oneself, as I experienced when I did so yesterday?

Before we leave, Andreas presents each of us with a picture of Maharishi Mahesh Yogi - a black and white portrait image. I wonder if there is also one of his master, Swami Brahmananda Saraswati, the monk in the painting.

269

Maharishi Mahesh Yogi

Swami Brahmananda Saraswati

Then we make our way to the gate and are off down the broad steps, and as we descend the path I'm surprised and pleased to find that a tea stall has materialised there again. Eagerly we order ourselves tea and toast from the couple that run the stall, who look more oriental than the other locals hereabouts, so we wonder that they might have come down from much higher in the mountains.

After another glass of tea and another stick of toast each, we set forth again, to make a belated visit to Rishikesh proper.

View of Swargashram from Rishikesh © Jonathan Miller

The ferry is full of people this time, and some are clutching newspaper cones of gram balls for the fish. As we near the middle of the river the boat slows and from all directions come fishes, slithering and sliding over each other, silver and gold, shining and shimmering in the sunlight. The cones of food are broken open and the contents tossed to the fishes that literally leap out of the water to catch the food.

After arriving on the opposite bank, at Sivananda Nagar, we make our way to the road. The pathway is crowded with beggars, amongst whom I note many that display the obvious symptoms of leprosy. Though these people have to bear this terrible disease, some with deformed limbs and open sores, they grin and joke amongst themselves as they beg for alms and cajole us to give them cigarettes.

It seems to me that the people of the East are subject to all too many diseases. So many of those we meet with here have appalling problems, especially diseases of the eyes and teeth. These people know nothing of the concept and benefits of a National Health Service. We all take our health for granted too often.

Walking past the taxi stand near which the horse *tangas* wait, we set forth on foot towards Rishikesh, but after a short while a car slows and stops, and the passenger invites us to share the taxi. Though we at first decline the offer, we soon find ourselves persuaded and seated in the back of the vehicle.

When the driver restarts the car, I begin to regret accepting the lift, for though the taxi chugs along quite slowly, it's not slow enough for me. So, how is it that I baulk at the speed, feeling that we are going too fast, at only ten miles an hour? And us well-seasoned hitchhikers at that!

Seems that in the last few days, what with meditating and being here at this sacred pilgrim spot, we've become rather used to going at a slower pace of life.

A large signboard catches my eye; proclaiming an uncommon message:-

Vegetarian Restaurant

'My father would have liked to see that. He was a vegetarian. Well so was I until a few years ago,' I tell Yolanda, who looks interested.

'We could go there on the way back,' Yolanda suggests.

In Rishikesh we buy ourselves some fruit and vegetables from the market, where the attractive stalls are stacked with fresh produce.

Surprisingly, at the mention of eggs, the stallholder looks about shiftily, and with much gibbering and fuss he finally produces two small eggs and palms them to Yolanda. Though I understand that most people hereabouts seem to be vegetarian, I'd never before thought of eggs as being non-vegetarian. Watching the proceedings I'm agape, for I hardly expected to find that eggs would only be available on the black market here, something for me to think about.

It's so nice to be in Rishikesh, there's such an air of peace and holiness, even though it's quite busy here. There are many *ashrams* and temples too, and as we move about Rishikesh we pass so many buildings housing holymen, young and old, longhaired, shorthaired, many of them in rags.

Strolling about the roads of the bazaar we discover we're attracted to almost everything we lay our eyes upon. We light on some textile shoulder bags, which we see as being very practical for carrying our bags of fruits and vegetables in. We buy one for each of us.

At a metalware shop we find a broad lipped aluminium pan to do our cooking in, and even though it has no handle we convince ourselves it will serve our purpose.

Our shopping done, we make our way back to the vegetarian restaurant, and there ask for some soup, and are provided with bowls of hot steaming *dhal*, which each come with a small plate of round flat breads, some sliced white radishes and a portion of sweet chutney.

A very nice lunch it is too, simple and satisfying.

Filling our glasses from the jug of clear water, we take our time, slaking our thirsts. When we go to pay for our food the manager takes much less money than I offer, accepting just a few small coins.

'But you haven't charged me for the soup,' I tell him.

'Han ji, that is correct. Only chapatti you must pay, no charge dhal is.'

I make an instant decision to come back here again, soon.

The walk back along the road to the ferry point proves most pleasant in every way. To the right of the road we can see, across the river, our own *ashram*. I also catch sight of the clock tower and the rest of Swargashram. It has already become like home to us now; I can't wait to get back there.

As the boat slowly makes its way across the flowing river, I let my hand trail along through the freezing cold water, such a contrast to the heat of the air.

Once across, we return along the lovely peaceful walkway, past the *ashrams* with the images of gods and heroes, past the few traders who sit patiently, smiling and waving to us as we pass on our way back to Ved Niketan (I really must find out what the name means!).

We're becoming very settled in our little room and we enjoy exchanges with our neighbours here, in the rooms immediately next to us. On one side there's the Indian schoolmaster, and on the other side, a newly arrived hippy-couple with a dog. The Indian couple at the end of the row of rooms kindly offers to get us regular *doodh* (milk) delivered from the *doodhwala* (milkman). And of course, in a room in the other direction is John, the chap from Southend, who introduces us to his friend Rob, who generously gives me some back issues of the *Rolling Stone* magazine.

It's great to suddenly have a bunch of 'instant' friends. Sharing a cigarette, a cup of tea, or some food. We all find we have something or other in common as we share our thoughts and our lives together, not least that we all like being here in Swargashram. For me this is a rediscovery of something for too long lost to me, the enjoyment of normal everyday domestic life. I'm so contented here; it's as if I'm living in some sort of Shangri La, a little bit of heaven on earth.

After gathering some firewood from the jungle (a task I discover I relish), I light a fire in the rusty brazier outside and we boil some potatoes.

Having no plates or cutlery, we serve the hot salty vegetables off a plastic bag, picking them up with the penknife and trying hard not to stab ourselves in the process.

After our simple meal we sit for some moments and smoke cigarettes by the light of the candle, watching as our shadows dance about.

How wonderful it is to be here, near the jungle in this holy village next to the River Ganges, in our own room. Our sleeping bags are rolled out awaiting us, and it's not long before we blow out the candle to enjoy an early night's sleep.

Chapter 20

MONKS AND MONKEYS

Clutching toothpaste and brush, I open the door to a bright new day. I notice the morning air carries an unfamiliar scent that I can't immediately place. As I clean my teeth Yolanda sidles up to me with an attitude of extreme confidentiality and whispers; *'Fleas, their dog has fleas.'*

I peer into the room next door to ours just in time to see the hippy couple dousing themselves with a tin of flea powder.

'Want some powder, Man?' my neighbour asks.

I pass up the offer easily.

The situation reminds me that only yesterday I felt guilty for not having befriended the local stray dogs; now, instantly, my conscience clears.

'By the way, Man,' he adds, *'We're moving back to the caves. Drop by sometime, yeah?'*

I conceal my ignorance about my not knowing of any caves hereabouts, by maintaining silence.

Later in the day, Yolanda and I take a walk to meet with Andreas again, and on our way we encounter a young American lad.

'Hari Om,' comes his greeting, *'I'm staying in the caves, why not come and see us?'*

He tells us the location of the caves, which are close by, in the area bordering the river, at the foot of the hill on which the 'academy' stands.

'We learnt to meditate up the hill there,' I tell him.

'You got a mantra you mean?' he asks directly.

'There's more to it than that,' I answer, a touch flustered.

I receive an interested but sceptical look.

'The Maharishi people, are they cool?' he asks.

I make no comment.

'Yes? Well maybe I'll check them out sometime. See you later, Man. Hari Om,' he adds smiling broadly as he wanders off.

Meditating in the basement of the bungalow is becoming a routine for us. We've been getting used to meditating twice a day, once in the morning and again in the

274

evening, and then having this extra session with our 'initiator', in which our meditations are 'checked'. Andreas asks us about our experiences, and repeatedly explains the process to us, and wishes to verify that we're keeping to the method. We assure him we are meditating according to his instructions.

In truth, the meditations are not as profoundly astonishing as I experienced in that first session, with the cosmic visitation or the very total immersion in inner peace that I enjoyed after I felt inspired to add my own instruction of letting go of thought. But that inspiration, to let go of thought entirely, set me free and enabled me to become immersed in timelessness. And emerging from that experience, it was as if my reset button had been pressed, and I was now refreshed and rejuvenated, a once-in-a-lifetime eureka experience, a rebirth.

But, that said, I also enjoy meditating according to the guidance given by my Transcendental Meditation teacher, and during my meditations I experience periods of very profound rest, which seem to result in benefits outside of meditation, such as increased confidence, buoyancy and sense of fun. Indeed, I've never felt healthier or happier in my life. But then I suspect that most of those staying in Swargashram feel this way, as everyone in these parts appears so peaceful and well intentioned.

Whilst chatting with Andreas, he confides that as a young man, he and a friend experimented with thought transference, that whilst the friend was taking an examination Andreas was outside attempting to stay in contact with him. He also mentions something of his background, in that he has worked in medicine, at a pharmacy. In response to a question from Yolanda, he assures us that during the armed conflict between Germany and the Allies he 'only did his duty'.

Before leaving the academy today, I ask Andreas if there's a book available to help me find out more about this meditation. He frowns, as if in some pain, and then warns me not to be unduly influenced by what I might read about what the Maharishi has said, but he agrees to find such a book for me.

The session over, he goes off to find some books, and returns with a large hardback - a commentary on the first few chapters of the *Bhagavad Gita* - and two paperbacks, one being *'The Science of Being and the Art of Living'*, with a photo of Maharishi Mahesh Yogi on the cover, and the other simply titled *'Meditation'*.

I buy two copies of each of the paperbacks, one for myself and the other for Yolanda, and I ask Andreas if we might also have a picture of the old man that we've seen in the portraits of dotted about the academy.

Andreas walks over to a cubbyhole by the office and brings for us two small pictures of the man, Swami Brahmananda Saraswati.

Later, walking to the village we notice a little stall there selling inspirational books. In addition to purchasing some of the booklets we also buy a couple of attractive books of illustrations, depicting traditional religious stories, of mankind and gods and goddesses. Yolanda also chooses for herself a colour litho print of the child Krishna, and I pick up a picture of the goddess of music, who I discover is called

Saraswati, portrayed sitting playing a long necked stringed musical instrument.

At another stall, I buy a book of postcards and a white marble incense holder, with the faces of lions looking out to the four directions.

To my recollection, during my entire upbringing, I have never heard about India's ancient history or about anything of its religious beliefs, but now, as I'm becoming better acquainted with Indian culture, I wonder that I must have overlooked it somehow, for India **must** be mentioned somewhere in the Old Testament of *The Bible*. I make a mental note to check this sometime, as I'd like to have a fuller picture of India's place in world history, and how its beliefs have influenced other religions. Perhaps all religions have a similar message, perhaps the same goal even?

The presence of a local Christian mission run by an Indian monk adds weight to this hope. By appearances alone it's extremely difficult to differentiate the beliefs of the local people, for most of the monks here wear their hair and beards long, the exceptions being the few who shave their heads entirely as if disgusted with hair, rather than proclaiming a particular faith. It's gratifying to see that the various faiths and sects hereabouts apparently live harmony, free from conflict.

Back in our room, I display our acquisitions on one of the concrete shelves.

The incense holder has been hand carved to show four lions heads, each facing a different direction. Looking at an illustration in one of our tourist handouts leads me to think the shape is based on a Buddhist statue, one known as the Ashoka Pillar, the Lion Capital of Emperor Ashoka, which dates back to the 3rd century BC. This image also appears on the reverse side of virtually every Indian coin. The currency here having only recently been decimalised, as formerly there were 16 *annas* to the *rupee* and now it is split into 100 *naya* (new) *paise*.

Actually, I've started collecting mint examples of each of the coins, variously multi-sided, scalloped and round, some of them with images of lotus flowers or some national hero. An Indian neighbour to whom I show my coins seems baffled and bemused to discover that I've placed these in a line along one of my shelves.

'Shops. Money for shops!' comes his response.

The shelves with the pictures and nick-knacks on soon resembles a sort of shrine.

On a summer vacation, long, long ago, our family holidayed in a lovely quaint cottage nestled at the heart of the charming hamlet of Combpyne, in East Devon, in southern England; the buildings there dating back to the 12th century. In the front room of the house where we stayed I discovered an arched niche. Long I had contemplated it, discovering that such attention bestowed unexpected calm and happiness upon me. Such and more is the happiness I feel before these shelves in our whitewashed cell.

Before leaving for this trip to India, I'd thrown a few strings of beads from my hippy days into our rucksack, and now, amongst the holy men in the village I notice many wear necklaces similar to these, so I feel it reasonable to wear mine again.

After some further time spent pottering about our room, we go out and sit in the sun on the sandy foreshore by the river, and there I take the opportunity to start looking through one of my new books, the *'The Science of Being and the Art of Living'*.

There are photographs of the white-robed author, Maharishi Mahesh Yogi, who wears his hair long and is of indeterminate age. There is also a photo of his master, Swami Brahmananda Saraswati, Shankaracharya of Jyotir Math, Badrikashram, whose appearance I am already acquainted with, for it's his stern face I have seen portrayed in the paintings displayed in the basement and the upstairs room of the bungalow.

Whilst the book says nothing about 'how' to meditate, it's a pleasant and relaxing read, a dissertation on how life might be made better by meditating regularly, the Maharishi's claim being that if one percent of mankind were to follow this dictum then world peace would ensue. So, the 'Maharishi' ('Great seer') wants one per cent of the world's populations to try this idea? Mmmm, whilst there must be many millions who desire to find inner peace, I can't imagine so many of them being attracted to this practice, what with the religious looking ceremony, mysterious *mantras*, and the expectation that one will make a contribution of a week's wages.

When Bevan and Andreas introduced Yolanda and myself to this form of meditation, Transcendental Meditation, they led us to believe that, simply by the practise of the technique, anyone could find the 'source of creative intelligence', i.e. God, within. Whilst I was happy to accept the invitation, it was only out of curiosity, and certainly not out of any desire to find a spiritual teacher or *'guru'* (to use a word that I've heard from Yolanda). Whilst it's said that one can learn this meditation without having any faith in Maharishi Mahesh Yogi himself, he does seem to give the impression of knowing all or most of life's answers.

Personally, I've never been particularly attracted to the idea of seeking out a special someone who has all the answers to life's mysteries, and even if such an all-knowing person were found to exist, it would be extremely unlikely that I would surrender my free-will to them and allow myself to become subservient, at least not for long, and definitely not if I could help it.

I suspect that, of the two of us, Yolanda is the more likely to want a *guru* figure in their life, as she has hitherto placed far greater value on the words of famous philosophers and religious leaders than I have. However, that said, I doubt she would unquestioningly accept someone as her living spiritual guide or teacher, as I don't think she would willingly allow her freedom of choice to be compromised, or put herself in a position where her sense of identity was likely to become jeopardised, but then who knows? Actually, as I think we all of us have a spark of specialness, I don't believe I could possibly put my trust in anyone who would put themselves in a position where they were likely to be looked up to as being superior or more important than others, even if some viewed them as such, and most especially if he or she were being seen as an infallible *guru*, a Saviour or Messiah.

Generally, I'm not inclined towards those who hold sway over the masses, as do some famous philosophers, preachers and politicians, no, I'm rather more drawn to unconventional creative types, such as musicians, writers, poets and artists, but if I have the chance, I will surely like out more about Maharishi Mahesh Yogi and his teacher, Swami Brahmananda Saraswati, concerning their relationship with one another and their teachings. I also want to discover what impact the Maharishi has had on the lives of The Beatles, The Beachboys, and Donovan, and his many other followers, but particularly I want to know how the meditation he teaches affects those who take up the practice.

'Let's go into Swargashram again,' says Yolanda, *'I need to buy some rice.'*

On our way to the shops the same kindly person who told us so much about the statue to the side of the walkway, now stands blocking our path. He wants to know what we've been up to, and on hearing of our involvement in meditation he tells us:

'Not everyone is pleased with the Maharishi. They say these mantras are only for monks - I am only telling you their opinion.'

I listen carefully, wondering quite what he means.

'Tell me,' he continues, *'Have you seen the bridge at Lakshman Jhoola yet? No? You must go there. It is beyond the Swargashram village and along the riverbank and through the mango trees, but be careful of the monkeys, the ones with red faces,*

they are most unfriendly. Do you know that in these parts we have no record of crime? Only there was the case of the elephant who strangled a man, we have to be mindful of the animals.'

Thanking him for this information we make our way along the riverside walkway, past the numerous *sadhus* (holy men) and beggars on the way. The old men who sit on the path are mainly clad in orange cloth, and have varied daubed markings on their foreheads. They seem to spend their time peacefully reading religious texts, and sometimes chanting whilst fingering their beads. Many nod and smile as we pass. It's only the beggars who will sometimes open their hands for money, though we give to both beggars and *sadhus* alike.

In the village the little shop that sells basic provisions also sells newspapers, fireworks and cigarettes. Of the many cigarettes they sell, such as *Charminar*, *Gaylord*, *Gold Flake*, *Esquire* and *India Kings*, our favourite brand is *Simla*, which are fairly low-priced cigarettes with a good smooth flavour, in a box, which is printed in green and gold, having a silhouette of the Himalayan mountains on it.

I buy some cigarettes, and some matches too, an Indian variant of the *Ship* brand, in a wooden matchbox with blue paper covering, a blue of such astonishing richness and vibrancy as to beg the question of its source.

Yolanda buys some rice, which is duly weighed and bagged (the bags here are made from recycled newspapers, or else paper from old exercise books). Whilst we're here I thumb through the colourful calendars; I've come to be able to distinguish divines from humans with a very simple rule-of-thumb, that gods and goddesses are usually depicted with more than two arms. I'm okay with the notion that divine beings dwell on higher planes, yes; I'm fairly comfortable with the idea. But I'm still puzzled as to why I saw what appeared to be images of divine beings in my meditation. Dare I speculate that gods and goddesses really exist, and that they were drawn to me after the 'initiation', on account of the intensity of my meditation? Though I see divines on calendars in the village here every day, I haven't seen them in my meditations again. But maybe I created the spectacle myself, a hallucination based on random images I'd seen?

Meanwhile, back on earth, and only a little farther up the pathway, stands the *Choti Wala* restaurant. *'Time for tea,'* I suggest.

Here at *Choti Wala*, like many eateries in India, the place is totally open-plan, so one can watch the food being prepared.

'Namastay,' calls one of the cooks, staring intently at me.

Since I don't know what he means to communicate by this greeting, so I merely smile at him as pleasantly as I can.

Now ordinarily I might order a sweet bun with our *chaay*, but today I'm feeling adventurous, so I order an Indian snack.

'Not too hot,' I say, meaning 'not too spicy'.

The snack soon arrives, a pyramid shaped pastry containing potatoes and peas in a tasty sauce. The waiter has taken me on my word; the *samosa* is not too hot at all, in fact it's stone cold, but very tasty. Really nice!!!

After our tea, having told myself I should settle down to do some writing soon, we make a visit to the local Post Office nearby to buy a couple of aerogrammes. Just a little way up from the Post Office sits a Nepalese woman, or perhaps she's Tibetan, who's selling sweaters. Yolanda guesses her to be Nepalese. Though the days are still very hot, the nights are getting colder, so it will soon be time to wear my homemade jumper, which I brought with me from England.

* * *

Reading the little books I obtained in the village I find that certain words, ancient philosophical words, are used very frequently. One such word is *karma,* which means 'action' or 'actions', *karma* being the notion that every action has its consequences, not least for the doer, which equates to Newton's Third Law of Physics, i.e. 'every action has an equal and opposite reaction'. Another frequently used word is *dharma* - which means 'right action', and refers to those actions which one **should** do, that one **should** abide by a correct code of living. I'd come across this word before, some time back; in a song entitled *'Dharma for One'* by the rock act Jethro Tull.

The guidance is, to live virtuously, by a code of non-violence, non-attachment and truthfulness, and also that one must avoid any temptations that might impede fulfilment of one's destiny. So, it seems, that with the inner confidence and light bestowed by deep meditation, one has an opportunity of living one's *dharma* and of resolving one's *karma*. And beyond that, what else is there to do? Well, certainly not to lean back and expect to be looked after by a teacher, guide or *guru*.

Right now I figure that my *dharma* lies in gathering firewood (or *lakri* as an Indian neighbour calls it), for cooking our evening meal. This task takes me on a walk into the jungle where I scour the leafy floor for kindling and fuel. Such walks lead me to go ever further into this uncharted and magical place.

Pretty soon I have enough firewood for our needs. On my way back to the room I raise my eyes up to the higher reaches of the forested hill and become convinced I see the shape of a tiger in the far, far distance.

Returning to Ved Niketan *ashram* I find Yolanda singing happily as she tidies our room.

* * *

Over the ensuing days, we spend much of our time in our room, or on the sandy shore of the Ganges, and exploring the general area, with the occasional trip to Rishikesh. The days seem incredibly long, with time passing very slowly.

Wandering along eating a banana, I am about to throw the skin down when I feel a nudge from behind me. Turning around I find no frowning Mr. Müller but a cow eager for the peel. A long fleshy tongue winds its way around the offering and the peel is soon on its way to becoming tomorrow's fresh milk.

A little farther on is a group of Indian tourists gathering for a photograph, and when a dog strays into the picture it's dealt a hefty kick. Incensed by the unnecessary brutality delivered to this pathetic creature I decide to give the aggressor a bit of instant *karma*.

Hopping around on one leg this upstart asks why I kicked him.

'Simple,' I answer, *'You kick the dog, I kick you.'*

I'm content here in Swargashram, and for me the hours pass most happily, with few things happening to upset us, but when they do occur I feel surprisingly indignant. I learn that unlike cows, dogs are not considered sacred here, and neither are monkeys, as I discover when a man offers to sell us a baby monkey!

On a trip to nearby Lakshman Jhoola, just up the river by a mile or two, we spot several gingery-brown coloured monkeys prancing about. We've been warned about them so we kept our distance, and this is just as well, as on the elaborate suspension bridge ('*jhoola*' means bridge) over the rushing River Ganges, we witness one such monkey creeping up behind a boy; the monkey grabs the fruit, and bounds away with his prize, leaving the child to cry out in fright.

A notice affixed to the bridge advises:

STOP

VEHICULAR TRAFFIC

ELEPHANTS AND CAMELS ETC.

This announcement is accompanied by a message in an Indian script of flourishing letters capped with lines running horizontally.

The pathway through Lakshman Jhoola village takes us past several institutes of *yoga*, outside which are posted photographs of muscular Indians striking difficult looking poses. *Yoga*, I have read is a Sanskrit (an ancient Indian language) word meaning 'yoke' or 'union', and this form of *yoga* looks much like hard work, like gymnastics or some sort of keep fit routine. Why such exertions are believed to lead one to enlightenment is quite beyond me, but I try to keep an open mind. It's interesting that so far, back at Swargashram, I have yet to see anyone practising these postures.

Whilst in Lakshman Jhoola we are approached by a man who wishes to talk with us, and when he hears we have visited the academy, he tells us, *'Mahesh Yogi, he is making some announcement that at such a time he will walk on Ganga.'*

I ask him what happened, whereupon the man raises his eyebrows and furrows his brow as if puzzled, and says *'but come that hour Mahesh Yogi no one seeing'.*

We don't delay long in Lakshman Jhoola, but return back along the wooded pathway, home to Swargashram.

Lakshman Jhoola   © Jonathan Miller

From time to time, Yolanda and I still visit the academy of meditation up the hill in order to have our meditation 'checked', as the process is known. I go along with this idea, largely on account of getting in an extra meditation, and there is always the chance we might be invited to dine again at the lovely eatery there, but I doubt that there is anything further to learn about meditation, more than we picked up in the first session, the most important thing being that meditation is not about effort but about letting go and relaxing.

I have been pleasantly surprised of late, in that I've been experiencing far greater clarity of thought and fluidity of speech, actually I've find there's so much to talk about that I find it difficult to stop talking! This condition has spurred me into thinking up increasingly difficult questions with which to confound Andreas. These questions he generally deals with disarming ease, however, today he resists the temptation to reply at all, choosing instead to give me a long penetrating look.

Surprised at his response, I then introspect on my question, and very soon discover its answer. Over the next few minutes we continue to converse in this way, in silence, with me looking over at him, and him looking back, and very satisfying it is too, as I get to understand I can access the answers to all my questions.

Indeed, I'm aware that in these days of living in the Rishikesh area, I am experiencing all sorts of positive feelings and perceptions. Whilst sitting on the banks of Ganga (the Indian name for the River Ganges) I witness another phenomenon occurring. It seems to me the accumulated store of music I've ever heard becomes available to me, that there's a personal record collection contained in my mind, and all I have to do is to select and play. This works so efficiently that once actioned I can listen not merely to the words but to any background accompaniment on these records. Of the discs I take to playing, are; Tim Hardin's *'Hang on to a dream'*, the Vanilla Fudge version of *'You Keep Me Hangin' On'* and The Beatles' *'I Am A Walrus'*, which all soon become firm favourites; *'I am you as you are me as we are all together. Sitting in an English garden waiting for the sun..'*

'Can we buy a mosquito net?' comes Yolanda's surprising request.

'What? Are you kidding? Surely only people in films have those don't they?' I laugh.

'Mosquitoes, they carry diseases, I don't want to catch malaria, you can die from that you know? I'm sure we have mosquitoes in our room, I hear them at night.'

I start to take her seriously, as I have open sores on my toes where flies land for feeding (my sandals haven't really worn in yet), though I haven't been particularly concerned about this until now, but malaria, now that sounds decidedly nasty.

It sets me a dilemma. Should I stomp on the mosquitoes? Our lives or theirs?

I stomp on them! One can take this non-violence ideal too far, but I nevertheless give this Hindu teaching a good deal of thought and attention.

On one of my *lakri* (firewood) expeditions to the jungle I start to wonder where my 'destiny' lies. I suspect that it will involve my swift return to England and a rapid re-entry into the hurly-burly of everyday life there. But what does the future hold for me, what work am I to do? Immediately it occurs to me that I will take to writing. I recoil, *but what about my passion for music...?* I wonder.

I find myself in a clearing of the jungle where I stand composing my thoughts, when all of a sudden a very curious spectacle materialises. There in front of me stands a figure playing a black custom Les Paul electric guitar in front of a *Marshall* amplification set-up.

I look long and hard, realising the figure is me!

I study the spectacle before me, carefully, even stooping down to examine the unusual foot pedal being used. Though less than solid this 'vision' proves very enduring, lasting many minutes and surrendering a wealth of detail.

When at length it fades, I make my way back, infused with a glow of exhilaration. However, I think better of telling Yolanda about the incident; instead I tell her that I plan to return to London soon, and I then think to ask whether she wishes to return with me to England or to break company instead.

She looks shocked, and annoyed.

In these moments our relationship seems to hang in the balance.

'But I thought we were going to visit some of the Buddhist holy places. Are you sure you want to go back?' she asks.

I nod decisively.

'But of course, if you're quite sure, I'll go wherever you go,' she adds.

* * *

Ever since leaving England with so little money, I've been concerned about conserving and stretching our finances, so it obviously makes a lot of sense for us to try to live as cheaply as possible. Apart from obvious economies - like cooking for ourselves - I even like to reduce even our normal expenditures, like the price of our cups of tea. Since a pot of tea at *Choti Wala* costs 30 *paise* and at the *chaay* stall a glass of tea cost 25 *paise*, I wonder couldn't we get the cost down further?

Close to the *Choti Wala* we discover a tea stall where we can get tea for 20 *paise*. In fact the Afghan owner of the stall readily agrees to lower the price even further by a couple of *paise* more. On his stall he has the buns and long toasts we generally eat, and to my surprise I find it is he who actually supplies the *Choti Wala* with all their tea. So it seems that here is our chance to cut out the 'middle man'.

The cigarette vendor nearby tells us something about our tea vendor: *'This Chaay Wala, he is muscle man.'*

Confused, I ask another Indian there to explain what is meant by *'muscle man'*.

'This man is Mussalman, or Muslim. All religions are welcome here,' the man informs us with an air of pride.

This particular *chaay* shop soon becomes a regular haunt for us; the tea and hot milk are unequalled locally. The *chaay wala* - originally from Afghanistan - boils fresh water in a pan, adds tealeaves and sugar, and then blends boiling milk in with the hot sweet tea, tipping the resultant concoction to and fro from pan to heatproof glass until it's nice and frothy. He even allows me the use of his open fire cooker, where I hold the long strips of bread over the glowing coals to toast them to perfection before we dunk them in our *chaay*.

* * *

One afternoon we decide to walk along to Lakshman Jhoola again, and on our way there we discover a *sadhu* playing a most peculiar stringed instrument. Under his right arm the *sadhu* holds a hollowed gourd, the centre of which is attached by a button to a solitary string stretched to a piece of wood in his left hand. When the string is tensioned he plucks it with a sliver of ivory held in his right hand, and by varying the tension of the string between the gourd and the piece of wood he is able to strike a sequence of notes. I watch intently until he gestures for me to try it for myself. So, I sit and settle down on the cloth there, putting the drum under my arm, and holding the wood with the end of the wire in my left hand. After some initial difficulty I master the instrument and am soon sitting strumming quite happily.

Then the *sadhu* holds aloft a conical earthenware tube wrapped around with rag, which he holds to my lips.

'*Chillum*,' he murmurs.

The scent of pungent hashish fills the air and soon I am giggling merrily as I resume playing the curious instrument.

As I play, passers-by throw money around where I sit; my very first wages as a busker in fact.

When I get up I leave all the money there, and in gratitude to the *sadhu* for inviting me to play I add a few coins of my own.

On our way back to Swargashram we get into conversation with a man standing using an old-fashioned smoothing iron, who is flattening out some material. I watch with interest when he opens up the iron and blows on the glowing embers within it.

I marvel that whilst ironing he doesn't burn the cloth with this dangerous looking device, and say as much.

In response he smiles and asks me if we would like him to make clothes for us. I am doubtful about the idea so I just smile. He then gestures for us to wait for him whilst he gets something from inside the shop.

He soon returns carrying with him a hard-backed exercise book, on the cover of which is a picture of the Maharishi. He passes it to me for me to look through.

Fanning through the pages I find drawings of shirts, skirts, trousers and the like.

'*Look at these Yolanda. These ones were drawn by Cynthia Lennon, and these here by Donovan. They're good drawings aren't they?*' I marvel. '*I'm sure I remember pictures of Donovan in that shirt!*'

Easily hooked in, we decide to have some clothes made for ourselves. Quickly we come up with designs, which we draw in the book. For me it will be an orange cotton trouser suit and for Yolanda one in turquoise. At a little over £1 per suit we figure we can just about afford them, and the tailor promises they'll be ready within a week or at the most 10 days.

* * *

The following day when I awake I am surprised at feeling a touch gloomy; and I suspect the cause to be my smoke with the *sadhu*. Thankfully the shadowy feeling soon wears off, but I decide again to steer clear of the stuff in future.

We see very little of the 'orange' lady, so it surprises me when she pays us an unexpected visit, and presses a small book into my hands, a copy of *'Bhagavad-Gita'*, the *'The Lord's Song'*, published by the *Gita Press* at Gorakhpur, the record of an alleged conversation between the famed Lord Krishna and Arjuna, his charioteer.

Riffling through the *Gita* I see it contains guidance on the practice of meditation:-

> *'Having firmly set his seat in a spot which is free from dirt and other impurities, with the sacred Kusha grass, a deerskin and a cloth spread thereon, one upon the other, (Kusha below, deerskin in the middle and cloth uppermost), neither very high nor very low.' Gita 6:11*

> *'And occupying that seat, concentrating the mind and controlling the functions of the mind and senses, he should practise Yoga for self-purification' Gita 6:12*

> *'He should through gradual practice, attain tranquillity; and fixing the mind on God through reason controlled by steadfastness, he should not think of anything else.' Gita 6:25*

> *'Drawing back the restless and fidgety mind from all those objects after which it runs, he should repeatedly fix it on God.' Gita 6:26*

> *'For, to the Yogi whose mind is perfectly serene, who is sinless, whose passion is subdued, and who is identified with Brahma, the embodiment of Truth, Knowledge and Bliss, supreme happiness comes as a matter of course.' Gita 6:27*

> *'The sinless Yogi, thus uniting his Self constantly with God, easily enjoys the eternal Bliss of oneness with Brahma.' Gita 6:28*

Otherwise, the text of *Bhagavad Gita* seems to be mainly concerned with Arjuna's indecision about fighting with his family, but Krishna exhorts his friend Arjuna to fight in the coming battle, however Arjuna is far from convinced. He is confused. Me too!

Whatever happened to non-violence I wonder? Actually, I suspect our landlady has somewhat similar confusions, for I chance on her berating a troupe of monkeys that have clambered onto the roof of the *ashram*. Her patience is soon spent, and she picks up a stone and tosses it near them. But they don't budge.

'Haa-reee Raaa-maaa!' she moans.

* * *

It's John who tells us about the room, located above the office on the other side of the *ashram*, that it's soon to be vacated, and as soon as Yolanda hears about it she's very keen to see it, so we wander over there.

286

A staircase leads to the roof on which a solitary room stands, which is surmounted by another much smaller structure, a meditation chamber, I suppose.

The American couple staying in the room are very friendly, and they confirm they're moving out soon, and are eager for us to take the room.

I ask them what they think of our landlady.

'Oh, a personality, definitely,' the girl answers.

When I ask what she means, her partner gives me a grin.

'Well for instance, we have a bowl full of fruit here, right? When we go out, she comes in and helps herself. Hey, we don't mind, she's okay,' he re-assures, laughing.

Though he makes light of her behaviour, it seems the orange lady can act in quite an entitled manner. I reckon that if we take the room, we should treat ourselves to a padlock, if only to keep her out.

After the visit, Yolanda tries hard to persuade and convince me about the merits of the room. It has its advantages for sure, an electric light and an adjoining bathroom with a loo too, but it will cost us an extra *rupee* a day. Besides, I'm happy in our current room, where we have neighbours; it feels like we're in a community where we are. Over there we would be isolated.

So, as it happens, though I don't really want to move I'm tempted to yield to Yolanda, on this occasion, to repay her a little for the unwavering support she gives me. Besides, I don't want an argument over it.

* * *

On the 29th of October, the crack of fireworks sounds from over the river in Rishikesh.

Later, when we go into Swargashram village I hear fireworks being let off, and am horrified to see a young man exploding a particularly explosive firework in our path. It leads to some very heated words with the guy, who turns out to be the servant of the owner of the grocery hut, who comes out and gives some sort of explanation, for evidently tonight is to be a celebration, which is why there are fireworks.

Minutes later and suddenly all the electric lights that illuminate the valley at night are extinguished and from out of the resultant darkness there appears a mass of tiny flickering stars of candlelight. On the riverbank clusters of figures stoop to launch candles upon the waters, I watch as the little flames bob about in the breeze as they float down the river to eventually disappear from view.

We walk back to the *ashram* in near darkness, soaking up the atmosphere. After we return to our room, the wife of our neighbour - whom I once discovered feeding her baby raw chillies - pays us a visit and daubs a fingertip of red dye (containing grains of rice) on our foreheads.

'*Tilak,*' she explains. Then she presses us to accept some sweet puffed rice and sugar coated liquorice sweets. She explains to us that this is the festival of '*Divaali*' and wishes us a Happy New Year.

This is New Year's Day, the first day of the year 2028, of the 'Vikraami' calendar. I see someone carrying a torch; it's Rob coming across to speak with us. It's been a few days since he gave me the *Rolling Stone* magazines, which after a half-hearted attempt to read them, I gave up on and have since wondered how to dispose of them. Since Rob doesn't want them back I make a decision to take them to the jungle to return them to the earth (merit mark from Andreas!).

Rob asks us if we have any hashish, explaining that it seems to him a good time for a smoke. In this I disappoint him. I had stopped using hash and other stimulants because I wanted to find out if I could get high without them. And on the basis of the smoke from the chillum the other day, I would say that not only do I experience greater enjoyment when I don't smoke the stuff, but overall, I actually feel less good when I do. So whilst it's still tempting to smoke hash just to socialise, I don't think it's worth it anymore, at least not for me.

When I next meet the American couple they explain to me they've been asked by the orange lady, that before leaving their room, to remove the lighting cord, and they warn me of this, explaining that the landlady has a 'thing' about it, but thoughtfully they show me how it can be re-connected.

We move into the new room in the partly finished front area of the *ashram*, and it feels quite luxurious, having a bathroom and an outside terrace to sit around on. When I come to check the electricity supply I note the light bulb has disappeared.

Ved Niketan Ashram   © Jonathan Miller

After our afternoon meditation we think to take a trip to Swargashram in order to look for a light bulb, but discover there are none for sale there.

This evening we dine quite lavishly at the *Choti Wala,* trying the house favourite, a *thali*, which is an eat-as-much-as-you-like meal; a stainless steel tray of curried vegetables, *dhal*, salad and yoghurt (*dhaiee*), and a choice of rice, or *chapatti* breads. We still find the idea of eating unsweetened yoghurt rather odd, and though we notice Indians eat their yoghurt with the vegetables and rice, we still prefer instead to eat ours with sugar, as a dessert.

I make a visit to the toilet whilst here and notice a spare light bulb, which virtually begs to be liberated. Only with difficulty do I fight the temptation. Before leaving *Choti Wala,* we stop in front of the shop to buy some *barfi* (melt-in-the-mouth fudge), which is served up on banana leaf plates.

'Namastay,' the cook shouts, his hands placed tightly together.

I reply in confused and inhibited style, still not knowing what he means.

As we return to the *ashram* we get quite a shock, for we all but fall and trip over a herd of slumbering cows lying in the darkness. In consequence we are then very careful climbing the stairs to our room, where we light a couple of candles, and I reassure Yolanda that we'll soon have electric lighting.

A replacement light bulb proves hard to find, evidently it's a luxury item, but, going over to Rishikesh, we eventually track one down at the pricey sum of Rs. 4.

Back in Swargashram, I've seen a *sadhu* wearing a worn silver coin with the image of Queen Victoria on it, dangling on a string around his neck. So when I find a jeweller in Rishikesh I think to look for a similar coin. The man who runs the shop is elderly, wears a white turban, and sits cross-legged on a carpet in front of an open safe. I ask him if he has an old silver coin and he digs about and finds me a silver *rupee.*

On one side it is embellished with an attractive floral pattern (with rose, shamrock, thistle and lotus) around the words 'ONE RUPEE 1913', and on the other side are the words 'GEORGE V KING AND EMPEROR', and the king is depicted in profile with crown and full regalia. At the top edge two clasps have been affixed, so all that is needed is a chain. The old man cuts a length of shiny plaited links, and from silver wire he fashions an 's' shaped fastener. Then I place the *chain* and *rupee* around my neck, a token of my having hitchhiked to India.

Yolanda has her eyes on an antique ring of heavy silver with a deep red stone set across it.

'Hakeek,' the jeweller explains, when asked what sort of stone it is.

Another ring in the shape of a clover also catches her eye.

'This for marriage and good luck,' comes the old man's voice.

Needless to say she buys it, along with two cheap but pretty rings set with reddish brown glass, one for each of us.

I ask him if we can buy some metal polish, he ignores me and instead takes Yolanda's agate ring and energetically rubs it across the carpet rug. The silver band sparkles as good as new. Neat trick that!

Before leaving Rishikesh market we buy ourselves a frying pan, some mustard oil, and a padlock. Whilst in town we also meet up with a young westerner, and when he hears where we're staying he looks horrified; *'But there are wild animals over there,'* he says, grimacing. *'Why don't you stay at the Swiss Cottage, here in Rishikesh?'*

On the road back to Shivanand Nagar, a lady stops us to present us with a little honey. Sublime! I make a mental note to buy some more from her soon. Back at our room we joyfully examine our purchases, we've really pushed the boat out, so to speak.

The flat concrete roof around the new room certainly provides us with space to prepare, cook, and lounge about. Yolanda cuts up the tomatoes and potatoes, which we later intend to fry, whilst I throw together a fruit salad, and add the honey, before leaving to go in search of firewood. Being closer to the river than to the jungle I now go beachcombing for driftwood. Meeting with success I return and climb the stairs that lead to our new room, whereupon I chance upon our landlady's stock of coal. *She's got all the mod-cons!* I think to myself.

The fry-up goes well, and the fruit salad with honey tastes divine. If I have to fault the meal, I would have preferred to be able to get normal cooking oil, rather than the mustard oil.

On another occasion we try to re-create the delectable *dhal* soup that we sampled at the academy, but with depressing results, for we can't even guess the necessary ingredients or the correct method.

We tend to augment our frugal homemade meals with lots of chopped fresh vegetables. Actually, I've made up my mind to resume the vegetarian diet I've strayed from. In fact I'm a third generation vegetarian and I recall that back in my primary school days, when I mentioned I was vegetarian even the adults there didn't know the meaning of the word, thinking it was some sort of religion, like being Presbyterian or Wesleyan, perhaps.....

When I mention to Yolanda that I'm determined to stay with vegetarianism, far from being surprised, she says that she too will not eat meat again.

* * *

Nothing much comes to disturb us up in our ivory tower at Ved Niketan Ashram, though all manner of birds wing their way to our rooftop, sometimes flying straight into our room. Solemn mysterious crows cloaked in shiny black plumage often visit; making their mysterious sonorous calls. Sometimes the sound of the clock chiming on the path to Swargashram is carried on a breeze - it chimes on the quarter hour - and from far off sometimes the barking of a dog can be heard. Otherwise all is still and silent. In ancient Sanskrit the word for heaven is *'swarg'*, as in Swargashram. Yes, this is some sort of heaven here.

Chapter 21

MAD DOGS AND ENGLISHMEN

Yolanda looks a little concerned for me.

'I've got another cold coming on,' I moan.

It feels like being a heavy cold, but I hope for the best that it won't get a grip on me.

After traipsing along to Swargashram to buy a couple of aspirin, I have a brainwave.

'Let's go over to Shivanand Ashram, they have a pharmacy there.'

The ferryboat soon takes us over to the other side of the river. At the pharmacy I search through the *ayurvedic* medicines and find a box of tablets designated for flu and colds. I pay the few *paise* for them, and then turn the tablets over in my hand. These are not the normal bleach white variety, but large pellets of crushed Himalayan herbs, I swallow a couple and hope for the best.

शिवानन्द आयुर्वेदिक फार्मास्युटिकल वर्स, शिवानन्दनगर
The Sivananda Ayurvedic Pharmaceutical Works,
DIVISION OF THE DIVINE LIFE SOCIETY
P.O. Sivanandanagar, (via) Rishikesh, (Himalayas).

Picking up a leaflet titled *'Sivananda's Renowned Himalayan Ayurvedic Products'* I leaf through it and feel most fortunate not to be suffering any of the terrible ailments for which the remedies are intended, foot-fissures, wind-humour, joint pains and the like. But I'm drawn to obtaining a bottle of *Brahmi-Amla Medicated Oil, 'an excellent Himalayan herbal medicated oil. Ensures healthy hair and prevents it's fall. Cools the brain and eyes'*, which turns out to have a distinctly nutty smell. Hair oil seems very popular in the East, used by men and women alike.

I decide to pass up the opportunity of sampling the *Divyamrit Vasanta Kusumakar* with it's gold, pearls and musk for *'body building and new strength'*, and Yolanda and I now decide to return to base camp. I am astonished that by the time we arrive on the other side of the river and go back to our *ashram*, every trace of the cold symptoms are mercifully vanished. It feels like a miracle.

Paying in our donation at the office, I pass a nook I've not noticed before, so I pause and look closely. Within the recessed space is an image of a god reflected in mirrors to either side, leading the viewer to see a whole host of the god's reflected images, a sudden immersion in sacred forms and feelings.

* * *

A local monk befriends us, giving us newly picked flowers every single day; and occasionally I wear one of these fresh blooms, sometimes a bright orange marigold, weaving its stem through the clasps on my silver *rupee*. One time, whilst presenting us with a flower, he looks me straight in the eyes and with an awkward expression murmurs '*chadda*,' without giving the slightest clue as to what this might mean.

I reckon it must be time to take Bevan up on his offer to lend me his copy of *'Hugo's Hindustani in Three Months'*.

When we revisit the academy I discover Andreas in the company of a tall middle-aged American man, who holds a copy of *The Bible* in his hand. He is questioning Andreas concerning the likely whereabouts of his missing son. The calm German listens patiently and suggests various places that the man might try. It transpires that this man has searched far and wide, but has precious little to go on, for he is in possession of only one clue; that the youth decided to go to India! They are well matched these two, with Andreas and his interest in redirecting wanderers to their countries of origin. Recently an English girl appeared on the scene, and got herself 'initiated' by Andreas, who has already dispatched her back to England before you could say '*Hari Om'*.

Talking of '*Hari Om*', our friend Hari Om has by now also found his way up the hill, and has even persuaded his mother to join him in India. After a brief stay at the academy she jets off home together with her son. It seems to me that Andreas has charged himself with the responsibility for all those who are lost and found here.

Today I meditate with him again, and during my sitting I have one of those rare flashes of inner vision. This time within my gaze I discern a line of Buddhas seated and still, statue-like but giving forth a living energy. *Just another thought,* I say to myself, and they are gone.

Later, after our meditation and a brief chat, Andreas goes upstairs and enters the room up there, where he rearranges some flowers. I notice that on a low seat there has been placed a small pair of banded sandals, wooden soled, not dissimilar to the ones Yolanda wears, austere, and no doubt belonging to the absent 'master'.

I find myself trying to imagine what the Maharishi's life is like. From what I gather he teaches that meditation leads to instant wish fulfilment, so I guess that travelling in a car with him must mean getting green lights and no hassles all the way. And at a deep level within me, that feels wrong, as surely we are all in this life together, so how can it be right or fair that someone gets special treatment in all situations. With this great emphasis being placed on wish-fulfilment, rather than on simple spiritual values, I sense that he must exert an enormous influence on those about him; I therefore wonder that I really want a meeting with this Maharishi fellow, after all.

But the teaching is the meditation and since we've already learnt this, I consider that there's little point in being drawn into the power sphere of this man. Besides, from all that I hear here, meditation 'automatically' makes life better, so it shouldn't be necessary to join up and become a devotee of his.

Apart from his self-elected social role at sending wanderers home, Andreas also wages a campaign to tidy the academy, and in that capacity offers us to go through the pile of shoes that people have left behind. Not even the chance of stepping into discarded Beatle boots or shoes induces me to accept his offer. But to my relief he doesn't pressurise me and instead asks if I have seen two longhaired German lads about. As it happens, lately I have seen young guys fitting this description, sitting on boulders by the Ganges wrapped in blankets meditating in the light of the setting sun.

'Would you tell them to come and see me?' he requests.

Instead of walking back down the hill path, today we choose to find out what lies in the other direction, so we make our way up the footpath adjacent to Bevan's lodgings. There we meet briefly with Bevan, who willingly lends me the self-tuition Hindustani language book. Whilst we're with him Yolanda asks Bevan what food is conducive to a spiritual way of life. He answers that the food that does not disturb the meditation is the best food, and this can vary from person to person. Effectively the individual must make his own decisions, which sounds fine and suits me to a tee.

We leave the academy by a different exit, for I've espied a gate and a track that seem to lead off into the jungle. Also making their way towards the gate is a couple of curious looking individuals, a pair of monkeys! Walking so close to one another that they seem to touch hands, these charming and exceedingly gentle spirits shyly glance away and lope off into the undergrowth. Resembling aged monks with bearded faces these beautiful monkeys affect me greatly. Quite unlike the chattering 'red arsed' variety they move with dignity and grace, these are *langur* monkeys.

* * *

Down in Swargashram one morning, on our way to the Afghan *chaay wala*, we pass the stationary figure of a young *yogi* who stands in our path, wearing nothing but a loincloth. He doesn't communicate with us nor indeed does he speak to anyone else, seemingly content just to stand erect and to Be. I've seen him about before, and always he appears impassive and completely withdrawn.

Coming to the teahouse we find another such *yogi*, though clearly his senior by many years, with long knotted greying hair and beard streaked with puffs of pure whiteness, which perhaps reveal a clue as to his age. He smiles at me and nods gently. Like the other *yogi* he is clad scantily in a loincloth, and like the other has a strong muscular body, which exudes health and power. His skin resembles highly polished supple shoe leather. I offer him a tea which he somewhat hesitantly accepts, but declines the offer of a current bun.

He emanates an extraordinary air of sanctity and peace. His personality is magnetic.

Though awe-struck by his presence I nevertheless engage him in conversation. Seated in the *chaay* shop he answers me in a mixture of Hindi and English, explaining that until recently he has been in Kashmir, but has recently come to

Rishikesh, on account of the weather.

'The people are dying of the cold there,' he tells me. *'I must admit it was chill some,'* he adds, smiling.

He seems radiantly fit. So, accordingly, this *yogi* seems to have evolved something of an immunity to outside influences.

On the subject of health, he mentions that a midday meal is all that is required to sustain the body. He speaks with a singsong lilt to his words, at times his words cascade into sheer poetry, especially when explaining spiritual matters. Addressing Yolanda and myself and also addressing his God, he sings, his eyes focused within himself, *'On the altar of my heart, in the temple of my soul, the almighty is with me always.'*

No doubt attracted by the presence of the *yogi*, the teahouse fills with customers and bystanders. As such, our conversation lulls for a while. The onlookers sit mute, as if they recognise they have intruded in on us.

Some months earlier, back in London, I had opened up and unravelled the packaging of the packet of incense, and to my surprise had discovered that the packet was constructed from re-used sheets of printed-paper. Lines of characters of an Indian alphabet danced before my eyes, enticing me to understand them. Perhaps one day, I'd thought, one day I might learn this language.

I mention to the *yogi* my wish to learn Hindi.

Enthusiastically he exhorts me to do just that, *'Come back to my ashram'*, he says, *'There I will teach you the Hindi.'*

I thank him, but as I am so much in awe of him, to expect him to fulfil this offer would be totally out of the question.

Placing my hands together, I bow slightly before him.

With a waggle of his head he returns the gesture, and I leave with Yolanda by my side.

< Photo of this same *yogi*, on the cover of a 1956 book

On our next visit to the Maharishi's academy we meditate together with Andreas again, and during our sitting I have one of those rare flashes of inner vision. On this occasion, sitting in utter silence in the basement room below the bungalow, I am surprised to see no lesser person than Beatle George Harrison sitting opposite me. His hair and beard have grown extremely long. We observe each other in silence for quite some time before I realise that I have my eyes closed and have become distracted in my meditation.

It appears that deep in meditation one is quite open, one might even say susceptible, to experiences of a 'cosmic' nature, whether actual or hallucinatory one cannot say.

From the roof outside our room at Ved Niketan, we have a panoramic view of the surrounding area and can see a very long distance in all directions. Today I notice a group of people walking from the direction of the academy, and in their midst, sun glinting off his bald pate, strides Andreas, garlands of orange marigolds draped around his neck. As he approaches, I note that his expression is one of jubilation, he beams me a radiant smile and pauses to call to me.

'Is there anything you wish to know before I leave?' he asks. *'I go now to Delhi, for I am due to fly back to Germany. But Bevan will be here still.'*

Yolanda and I both wish him a very safe trip. *'All the best,'* I shout down.

'Jai Guru Dev,' he answers, which according to Bevan means *'Glory be to Guru Dev'*, a phrase written up large at the academy with pebbles set in concrete; 'Guru Dev' being a term adopted to refer to the Maharishi's departed *guru*.

Image from Frank Papentin's book, *'Darshan'* [reproduced with permission] >

For many the river Ganges is considered sacred, and it's believed by many that this water has healing properties, that unlike tap water it will not support bacteria even when sealed and kept for a long period. I notice the monks from the academy come daily down to the waters edge to fill black pitchers with the crystal clear refreshing waters of this fast flowing river. Pilgrims also come to collect the precious water, and some visiting devotees of Mother Ganga sing hymns to her in praise, inspiring me to write a few verses myself: -

> *Ganga Ganga, Holy Ganga*
> *Hearing chanting voices*
> *singing, praising you.*
>
> *Ganga Ganga pray thee tell*
> *What it is that makes man get sick*
> *when you can make them well?*
>
> *Ganga Ganga, Holy Ganga*
> *Ganga Ganga Ganges blue*
> *Alone I came to sit with you.*

I notice holymen, whilst ritually bathing, sprinkle water over their shoulders, sing and mutter *mantras*. Bathing in the river is a must for all devout pilgrims. The everyday folk hope to 'purify' themselves. The men take a dip stripped to their shorts, and the women cheerfully submerge themselves, and then re-emerge with their *sarees* (Indian style dresses) soaked and clinging to them in a state of disarray.

The many cows claim the pilgrims' interest too; I even notice that the urine of the calf is collected and eagerly dabbed on the forehead by some. The cow is honoured here, and for good reason, as it provides milk, and in turn *ghee* (butter oil), yoghurt, *paneer* (Indian yoghurt cheese), and even their dung is used, burnt as fuel. Hence the cow's 'holy' status.

We take yet another trip to Rishikesh, which yields another chance to rummage around the marketplace and explore the back street shops more closely.

In the market we meet a kindly old couple who tell us they have chosen to spend their retirement in Rishikesh, and promise Yolanda and myself the pick of their allotment next time we visit town.

Searching the back streets, we are today rewarded in finding a shop selling brightly coloured pictures of gods, *gurus* and saints. To my amazement, amongst these prints, I find two that form the basis of the cover art for the *'Axis: Bold as Love'* LP by The Jimi Hendrix Experience. Although Jimi apparently wanted the music and graphics of this album to reflect his American Indian heritage, somehow these Asian Indian devotional images were used instead.

We buy a good selection of printed-paper pictures, which veritably glow with their bright-saturated coloured inks. And there are some few prints that are less gaudy, survivors of an older subtler style, I suppose, beautifully conceived in pastel shades. These pictures are but a few pence each so we decide to buy ourselves a reasonable amount of them as souvenirs to take back to England.

We also decide to buy a second rucksack to pack away our extra purchases. This we soon find in the market, a khaki number, strong but cheap.

In a Hindi primer I consult in the market, I discover the meaning of *'chadda'*, the word that the *sadhu* had used, which I find means 'bed sheet', so we set about trying to find a stall selling cotton sheets, to get one for our friend to wear. My only concern is that I might not have heard him correctly!

We also visit a branch of the National Bank where we exchange another of our precious £10 notes, almost our last. We really need a cash injection; we have to think of a way to make some money.

Whilst we are in Rishikesh we also take Yolanda's black suede shoulder bag to be mended by one of the many cobblers here. He agrees to mend the bag, which is coming apart at the seams, but to my surprise, instead of using black thread, he uses white string to sew the seam up, and then makes good by staining the string with black boot polish. I'm shocked to see him bodge the sewing like this, but it works, so we have no grounds to complain.

We now walk the road from Rishikesh to the ferry point, which takes us past an *ashram,* outside of which many holy men are congregated. This is the Baba Kali Kamliwala Panchayati Kshettra, a mission that administers free food and lodging to *sadhus* and *swamis*. The facility could be described as a little like an Indian version of an old folks home, though with one major difference, that holy men are meant to travel, so visitors are not supposed to stay longer than three days in such lodgings.

Before taking the ferry back over the river we first buy some honey and a small cut loaf.

* * *

Life ticks away very slowly here in our Swargashram haven.

On our frequent walks, exploring the local byways and footpaths, we familiarise ourselves ever more thoroughly with the area. On these walks we sometimes talk with the *sadhus* and monks, and at other times we just observe them.

The central feature of the lifestyles of people in this area appears to be about obtaining closeness to God and nature, thus we seek to acquaint ourselves with all the practices in use.

For some of the holy men, control of their breath features large amongst their self imposed disciplines. One such practitioner appears bashful, maybe even a little annoyed, at being watched and seats himself in the opposite direction and covers his head with a cloth before resuming his breathing exercises. Yolanda becomes intrigued with the supposed benefits of this technique and encourages me to breathe 'properly', and also she becomes taken with the idea of giving up smoking.

Apart from *hatha yoga* (conventional *yoga* exercises), *pranayama* (breathing control), *dhyana* (meditation), and *bhakti yoga* (union through faithful service) there is also ritual worship and *tapasya* (self control).

In the temples *sadhus* busy themselves prostrating themselves before their favoured deities, and elsewhere many subject themselves to physical endurance in attempts to raise themselves higher. But on all these paths the target appears to be the same; that of becoming spiritually enlivened and enlightened.

Perhaps the least interesting are those practitioners who, after having daubed themselves with ashes, place themselves on public view beside their begging bowls. But perhaps they too are finding an inner glow?

* * *

The need to keep our clothes clean takes us again to the quiet silver-sanded beach close to the Ved Niketan Ashram, where we bathe in the freezing waters and dash our soapy clothes against the smooth black boulders. After stretching them out in the sun to dry, I take the chance to write in my notebook, sometimes trying my hand at crafting songs and poems.

Beside the gurgling eddies of water; I contemplate and sing to myself.

> *Prophets, seers and sages, coming through the ages,*
> *singing of the love, singing life's sweet song.*
>
> *Buddha, Jesus, Krishna, enrapturing the listener,*
> *Swamis, sadhus, saints and rishis,*
> *coming as though guide lights, anchorage in the storm.*
>
> *Cynicism blunts the heart, prevents us from making our new start,*
> *the holy hand that gives, can also take away.*
>
> *'Born in God's reflection', The Bible says of man,*
> *what a vast potential lies dormant here at hand.*

297

Listening to the wise, listening to the holy,
living, giving reminders of the hidden cosmic mind.

* * *

Yolanda and I are both feeling pretty healthy, and as the days pass the constant sunshine deepens our tans. Not since we travelled through Spain have I deliberately set out to get a tan, but one day I decide to venture onto the flat roof outside our room and lie down on the discarded table there. Though the breeze takes away the discomfort of the prolonged exposure to the sun, in time I begin to feel less than comfortable, and sitting up, I realise that my skin feels very sore indeed.

'A little bit longer then I'll go in', I decide. But the sun is now at it's zenith and is grilling my tender flesh, so I sit up again and wonder if perhaps I am overdoing it.

In the distance a dog howls, and all at once I remember the oft spoken but little understood phrase; *'Only mad dogs and Englishmen go out in the midday sun'.*

* * *

Yolanda and I have been on the road for many months, so receiving letters occasion's enormous anticipation and great excitement. The postmaster of the little Post Office in Swargashram becomes very accustomed to our visits, with us buying aerogrammes, sending letters and going to check as to whether or not we have received any 'Post Restante, via Rishikesh' letters. There's a pot of glue on the counter for sticking postage stamps and letters that have no gum on them.

In time both Yolanda and I receive letters, and these communications assume great importance to us.

To me, reading letters from my mother and from my friends Henderson and his brother, Charles, fulfil a need to tie together past and present. Henderson writes saying he observed us from a bus as we straggled in the rain towards Putney station all those months ago. He asks me *'to pass on my regards to Raja the elephant'.*

The thrill of seeing an envelope addressed to us, and poring over the contents is something we eagerly look forward to, to such an extent it borders on the obsessional.

I've come to the realisation that despite being somewhere that to me is heaven on earth, I **really** want to get back to London to re-discover the world I left behind, as I'm convinced that after our trip it will appear changed, more attractive. But I can't see how we can get back to England on the little money we have left. The postal orders that are sent to us certainly help to bolster our funds and make life more manageable, but Yolanda and I both realise that it will take a miracle to scrape together enough money for the airfare, and quite honestly the prospect of hitching back to England holds no appeal whatsoever.

On a visit to the Post Office one day we meet with an elderly English gentleman by the name of Frank Burkhill, who, having reached retirement age, decided to go in search of mystical India, and having made the effort to travel here, is enjoying

298

himself hugely. With his rolled-up black umbrella he strides along the riverfront path at Swargashram with an air of authority and importance, lecturing us on things Indian, telling us tales of his horse riding in the mountains, and his participation in curious fire rituals. His eyes sparkle as he recounts his exploits.

I ask him why locals here paint wounds with a red liquid, as happened to me when my foot got a gash in it.

'Mercuric oxide, standard practice, they do it all the time; they don't seem to realise that mercury is a poison; some people die of the stuff. On that subject, don't make any enemies in India, you might end up having ground glass put in your food!' he states with finality.

Whilst we walk I catch the eye of the man who runs the cigarette stall, the one whose servant almost blew us up with the high explosive firework, and I'm concerned that he might still be upset that I took the young lad to task?

'I see you have silver rupee,' he says smiling, *'you would like other old coin? I find for you, come back soon.'*

What a lovely thought of his!

And whilst outside his shop I look at the newspapers on display, the *Hindustan Times*, and the *Times of India*. I buy one, after all, if I'm to return to the West I'm going to have to get used to its predilection with news.

* * *

We have committed ourselves to staying on in our 'Shangri La' for a month, but with the prospect of returning home looming in my mind I begin to find myself increasingly at odds with my environment. Why, there is even an uninvited guest, who, after taking a dip in the Ganga, takes it into his mind to climb the stairs to our room and join us, presumably in order to enjoy the view from our rooftop. He assails the impenetrable sanctuary of our ivory tower at Ved Niketan Ashram!

Emphatically we tell him that this area of the *ashram* isn't open to visitors, but he ignores us, sits himself down and proceeds to dry his waist length hair, and then, eventually, when his hair is dry, he winds yard upon yard of cloth around his head. His turban finished, he departs as cheerful as when he arrived.

On another occasion our landlady shouts up from downstairs, berating us for dropping a cigarette butt over the edge of the flat roof, I guess it was blown by the breeze that cools us through the heat of the day, and which has now put us in trouble. Though with all sincerity we apologise to the orange lady, the incident definitely puts an additional strain on our relationship with her, and the on-off situation with regard to our water supplies continues, so occasionally words continue to be exchanged with her. Seeing as we usually pay an extra *rupee* for the luxury of the bathroom, I make it clear to her that we will only contribute the extra *rupee* when water is available.

299

'Paani nahin. Paani nahin, do rupee do!' she crows, telling me to give the money even when there is no water.

With the help of Bevan's book (*Hugo's Hindustani*), I give her as good as I get.

But later she finds a way of getting back at me, for some days later when I visit the little meditation chamber above our room, I discover it has now been padlocked.

The problems over the water supply doesn't go away, and next time the water is turned off, I again scale down the rent, and place only 1 *rupee* in the donations box.

Barely a minute later, I hear the orange woman screaming up to me! Really... I hadn't realised until now how closely she watches the flow of contributions.

Next time I see her, and in an attempt to foster good relations with her, I ask her concerning something I've wondered about since arriving here, whether tigers live in the nearby jungle.

'Ji, jangal men ('Yes, in the jungle'),' she confirms.

She goes on to gesture and babble excitedly, explaining that in the rains, all the animals come out of the jungle and go down to the river - elephants, tigers and all the rest of them.

In truth, right now, the closest we are likely to come to a tiger is by looking at the one on the reverse side of the red 2 *rupee* note, which is perhaps just as well.

* * *

We maintain our regular visits to the Post Office, ever hopeful of receiving more letters from home, and one day a typewritten envelope from England awaits me, and after failing to guess the identity of its sender, I at last open it. The mystery typist proves to be none other than my eldest brother, Adrian, who has evidently been informed by my mother of my whereabouts. I digest the contents of the letter, which suggests that I pay a visit the British Consul for help.

* * *

From our rooftop we are in a great position to observe the progress of the building works at the *ashram*, sporadically undertaken and presumably funded by the dribble of *rupees* into the wooden box below. Today they've been working, and when evening comes the labourers are still not finished.

As we sit to meditate there comes an urgent knocking at the door, and opening it brings me face to face with our landlady, who, smiling benignly fairly orders us to loan them our light.

I suggest they come back the next day.

As her voice soars quite unbearably, I relent and drag the cable with the light bulb attached, so as to illuminate their nocturnal labours.

Hopefully this will mean that we'll now be back in favour with our landlady?

* * *

Another visitor to our eerie is John. It's nice to see him again. I have missed the casual fraternisation I'd become accustomed to whilst staying down in the rooms at the back of the *ashram*, so it's good to see John here.

'Do you know where I can find the Psalm about the 'Lord is my shepherd'?' he asks.

'Sure, it's either the 23rd or the 123rd. I've got a Bible here, I'll look it up for you,' I answer confidently.

'Thanks a lot,' he says, sounding surprised and grateful. *'By the way I came to tell you that a friend of yours is staying here, a girl, an Italian I think.'*

The new visitor turns out to be none other than Donna, the Brazilian girl that we encountered in Pakistan, in Islamabad. She's here with a *swami*, an aged fellow who she struck up with on her travels. *Swami* or no *swami* he is very much in tow to this thoroughly modern Miss.

* * *

Thinking that the clothes we ordered must, by now, have been completed we make a visit to Lakshman Jhoola.

The shop is closed so we take a wander about the area, with the intention of returning a little later. As we walk, I notice a group of people ahead of us, but when I take a closer look at them I can't quite believe my eyes, for it's as though I've travelled back in time, as the ladies are holding dark parasols, and they bustle about with ankle length black crinoline dresses, and they're accompanied by a gent with a wide brimmed black hat who is wearing a tight dark overcoat. It's as if I am looking at a scene from the last century.

Then, in the flicker of an eyelid they have all disappeared from my view.

Silently contemplating this strange sighting, I continue my walk with Yolanda, and as I survey the ground before me, I spot a piece of carved marble attached to a piece of string.

'It's a minaret like the one on the Taj Mahal,' volunteers Yolanda. *'Someone's lost it from around their neck. The Taj is one of the Seven Wonders of the World, would you like to see it?'*

I muse on this idea, but not for long, as my attention is taken with the sight of a *sadhu* nursing a cow. The cow has a crooked jaw; and the *sadhu* cuddles the huge animal as though it were a pet.

Returning to the tailors we find the shop now open and our *'suits'* are ready. They've done us proud, for not only have they followed our designs, but they have also included a couple of extra pieces - a bra-like garment for Yolanda and a loincloth for me. I can't wait to get back to our room and try my outfit on!

'Ram Ram. Namastay,' shouts the cook again at the *Choti Wala* as we pass.

He is making *jelabi* sweets, squeezing the mixture into crazy patterns in the cooking oil and producing mounds of brilliantly orange confectionery.

Completing the preparation of another sweetmeat involves throwing some sticky doughy mixture on to a long hook on the wall and stretching it out again and again.

We decide to stop for a meal, as it will save us coming back later. A young lad, daubed with pink body paint, with a little tuft of hair waxed into a long spike atop of his head, parades around the restaurant. It transpires that he is the *'choti wala'*- the 'small person', or the person with the *'choti'*, referring to the pigtail of hair worn in exaggerated imitation of some Hindu monks.

Regd T.M.

On finishing our tasty meal I go to pay the bill, and I tell the owner I've been undercharged, only for him to angrily deny it, as though he has been affronted in some way. With so little money left, it's ironic that I am attempting to persuade a seemingly wealthy man to take our coins. I make a mental note, that henceforth, if I'm undercharged; I shouldn't automatically feel obliged to point it out!

On our way back to the *ashram* a fruit vendor shouts his wares. *'Amrud, amrud,'* he cries.

'I think they're guavas,' Yolanda observes. *'Let's buy some?'*

We do, but immediately regret our decision, as the fruit is sour, the taste strange, and the pips stick uncomfortably between our teeth.

This evening, on our way back to the *ashram*, I observe a lovely young couple on the shore of Ganga, sensuously disporting themselves. The young lovers appear intoxicated with each other's company, and seemingly oblivious to the sanctity of this place. I wonder how long it will be before they too begin questioning? How long it will be before they search for answers to their spiritual dilemmas?

* * *

To make ourselves some money we decide to sell our wristwatches.

Actually, for Yolanda this is an easy decision, as she never wears hers anyway, since she has the peculiar ability of stopping any self-respecting watch stone dead, just by wrapping it around her wrist and wearing it for a few hours. For hers we receive R/s 35 in the Rishikesh market, and to celebrate the sale we visit the vegetarian restaurant there, and afterwards take a taxi back to the ferry crossing.

Mine, a grander item, an *Oris* with a black dial, goes for R/s 110 to a shopkeeper in Swargashram village. But, a few days later, when I see him wearing the watch, I notice the smart broad green suede strap, that I purchased at Kensington Market, has been replaced with a cheap plastic substitute, so I ask him where the strap has gone.

'My mother has told me it is better not to wear that strap, it maybe comes from cow,' he tells me, somewhat accusingly.

'You can take these things too far,' I remark later to Yolanda. *'I remember that he was the one who gave me a funny look when he noticed the feather I was holding the other day. Anyone would think I'd ripped it out of a bird's wing!'*

The sight of Bevan racing along the foreshore, white robe billowing, his long black hair streaking behind him, begs a question. He is obviously pointed in the direction of the village, but what is the urgency that takes him there?

On his return I ask him whether everything is all right. Judging by his expression I detect a hint of guilt, as he holds up a leaf with the remnants of a portion of fudge.

'Maharishi instructed me to buy them,' he states.

I puzzle how this could be so? Did the Maharishi really call Bevan all the way from Canada, or do they have some other method of communication? And if so, what are the options? Telephone? Telegram? Telepathy?

I mention to Bevan that we've sold both our wristwatches and now have difficulty in timing our meditation sessions. He has a ready answer, suggesting that if we burn an incense stick, it should last for approximately the required time.

Before leaving us, he invites us to the academy for lunch, which will most probably be our last chance to savour the delectable bread and soup of the academy's kitchen.

* * *

The following morning, casually smoking our *Simla* cigarettes, we make our way towards the steps up the hill, and there we happen upon a group of *swamis* huddled in the bushes smoking *bidee* cigarettes. We smile at them cheerfully and make our way up to the academy in time for lunch.

After some minutes, the old *swamis* we met on the way also come to eat, and for no apparent reason they give us grudging glances. Is it because they think the food is only for monks, or maybe because Yolanda is here, a lone woman amongst renunciates?

Bevan later explains to us later that the *swamis* have berated him for allowing us to eat at the academy. I stare at him impassively.

We chat to Bevan about many things, and I discover, like us, he can't understand the Indian's attitude towards dogs.

'There is one dog,' he tells us, *'who alone can guide us through the jungle when we*

wish to visit a certain place, I call him St. Peter.'

Yolanda brings up the topic of being a monk, about deciding to be a *brahmachari* (taking a vow of celibacy and monkhood), and Bevan explains to her that it isn't necessary for her to become a monk, that she can simply carry that feeling within. He takes this opportunity also to tell us why he wears his hair long, explaining that this is a part of his training, of the tradition of this Order, rather than it being his personal choice, He also explains how his being a monk does not mean renouncing all worldly associations (hence the presence of his record player I guess).

But I wonder. To my mind I figure that if he wants to grow his hair, and if he wants to listen to sounds, it's up to him. Also, I don't share his passionate unquestioning belief in this particular style of meditation and its attendant beliefs.

When I point out that meditating has rekindled my interest in the Christian Science religion, he gives me a disapproving look; he appears somehow disappointed, and instantly directs me back to thinking and talking about Transcendental Meditation. So it seems to me, that in matters spiritual, he believes that only Maharishi Mahesh Yogi and Transcendental Meditation merit any particular attention, and that all other teachings are of little or lesser value. I discern that the reasoning behind this thinking is that without meditation no real experience of the Supreme is possible, and other teachings don't offer a method of direct realisation. But personally I like to keep an open and questioning mind, though I appreciate his explanation.

The Maharishi speaks of what he calls 'cosmic consciousness', a state where the experience of 'pure consciousness', as experienced in meditation, is lived throughout ones day-to-day life; an all-time state of living in blissful happiness forever more. Certainly, I'm convinced that accessing clear inner awareness, as found in deep meditation, provides a strong basis for a happy and satisfying life.

Living here in Swargashram these last few weeks has given me a strong taste of this higher consciousness, of being totally at one with myself and upbeat too, so I hope that after I leave Rishikesh I'll continue to be able to live such a life wherever I am. I sometimes wonder how much this journey has changed us for the better, and wonder that once Yolanda and I are out of this holy area of Rishikesh, how well we'll cope with life's up's and down's.

I confess I hope to continue living a life similar to that which we've been living here, experiencing that profound peace within, which seems to stick and make our lives lighter and more attractive, but it remains to be seen whether meditation alone is enough to strengthen oneself, enough to withstand the pressures of everyday life. Still, if it's the missing factor in living a fulfilled life, then I have high hopes for the future.

I guess I'll have my work cut out in dealing with my past *karma*, viz. getting back to England, finding a job, and getting enough money to find a place to live etc, but I'll do my best to continue to live in a state of clarity, making sure I renew and refresh my state of consciousness by setting aside time for inward meditation.

Chapter 22

YOGA MEDITATION

I recall as if it were yesterday the memorable occasion, when I was sitting comfortably with my eyes closed and was tempted to find out what would happen if I abandoned the all-too-familiar mechanical process of thinking.

That experience left a marked impression on me, leaving me refreshed and re-invigorated, and in addition it also restored my feelings of self worth and made me feel that I could look forward to a bright and fulfilling future.

Interestingly, I discover in the teachings of various respected Indian spiritual teachers and Scriptures, repeated references to the stopping of thought during meditation, confirming my belief that this is the correct, and authentic, way to meditate.

'Raja Yoga is the king of Yogas. It concerns directly with the mind. In this Yoga there is no struggling with Prana or physical body. There are no Hatha Yogic Kriyas. The Yogi sits at ease, watches his mind and silences the bubbling thoughts. He stills the mind, restrains the thought-waves and enters into the thoughtless state or Asamprajnata Samadhi, Hence the name Raja Yoga.'

'ASAMPRAJNATA: Highest superconscious state where the mind is completely annihilated and Reality experienced.'

Swami Sivananda Saraswati (1887-1963)
Raja Yoga, Divine Life Society, Rishikesh, 1937

'In samadhi, there is only the feeling 'I am' and no thoughts. The experience 'I am' is being still'

'When these thoughts are dispelled, you remain in the state of meditation (aware of awareness), free from thoughts. When the practise becomes firm, your real nature (awareness of awareness) shows itself as true meditation.'

'The limited and multifarious thoughts having disappeared, there shines in the Heart a kind of wordless illumination of 'I - I' which is pure consciousness (Being-ness).'

'What is meditation? It is the suspension of thoughts.'

Ramana Maharshi (1879-1950)

'According to Upasana Khand of the Vedas we are told:-
'"yoga" is stopping the fluctuations of consciousness'.
The ultimate aim is this, that by the practice of having stopped the fluctuations of
the inner self, to experience the Supreme form of the Self. Calm without a ripple
in any part of the pool of water, that manner a person can see his own face. That
really is the method, stopping the fluctuations of the consciousness is really
giving a clear reflection of the imperishable self in the instrument of inner vision.
This indeed is "darshan" (sight) of the "atma" (self or soul).'

Swami Brahmananda Saraswati (1871-1953)
Shankaracharya of Jyotirmath
Shri Shankaracharya Vaaksudhaa, p86, published 1947

* * *

Indeed, in the ancient Sanskrit treatise on *yoga*, variously known as *'Yoga Darshanam'*, *'Patanjali's Yoga Sutras'*, or simply *'Yoga Sutras'*, - the very meaning of the word *'yoga'* is declared as being the *'halting of mental activity'*:

अथ योगानुशासनम् ॥ १ ॥

योगश्चित्तवृत्तिनिरोधः ॥ २ ॥

तदा द्रष्टुः स्वरूपेऽवस्थानम् ॥ ३ ॥

वृत्तिसारूप्यम् इतरत्र ॥ ४ ॥

'Now, the teaching of "yoga"... 1:1

"Yoga" is "nirodha" (restraint, stopping, halting) *of the "vritti"* (whirling, thought-waves, mental activity) *of the "chitta"* (consciousness, memory, subconscious). 1:2

Then the seer rests in his own self. 1:3

At other times he is identified with the whirling [of the mind].' 1:4

Yogadarshanam - Patanjali's Yoga Sutras

* * *

I am curious to find out whether I can revisit and rediscover the experience of being without thought in meditation, so after closing the door to ensure that I am unlikely to be disturbed, and checking that I am wearing reasonably loose clothing, I sit myself down on a cushion with my back reasonably straight and supported, and I then compose myself for a couple of minutes making sure I am comfortable, and after allowing my breathing to normalise and settle, I close my eyes.

I'm aware that I'm thinking, and I remember it's my intention to let go of my thoughts and attain an experience of no thought. Therefore I watch and witness any mental activity, hopeful that I don't become absorbed in some distraction.

This feels progressively calmer and pleasant, but the thought process is still there, and subtly active, so, though I am now much more relaxed, I think to move the process on a little, and begin to focus my attention on my body, and in so doing I detect an area of warmth and light within.

I notice that though there has been thought occurring, it is, by now, as it were suspended, inactive.

I continue to observe, and before long I find that my inner space is now completely silent, motionless, there is no thought and I am only slightly aware of my breathing.

Actually, I find myself in a pleasant state of inner alertness, nothing is happening and I even wonder if I am actually breathing at all. I suddenly take a short breath, after which all is still again. I sit long in this state, not thinking but aware. Aware of inner happiness, a profound immersion in eternity, with nothing stirring, nothing, no activity within, until a vague thought arises. *'How long?'*

* * *

And in the *Upanishads* - the earliest Scriptures known to have detailed the practice of *yoga* meditation - this practice is spoken of:

यदा पञ्चावतिष्ठन्ते   ज्ञानानि   मनसा सह।
बुद्धिश्च   न विचेष्टते   तामाहुः परमां गतिम्॥ २-३-१०॥

'When the five senses are settled
and the mind has ceased to think
and the intellect does not stir
That is the highest state, they say.'

Katha Upanishad 2-III-10 / 6.10

तां योगमिति मन्यन्ते स्थिरामिन्द्रियधारणाम् ।
अप्रमत्तस्तदा भवति योगो हि प्रभवाप्ययौ ॥ २-३-११

'Thus "yoga" is considered to be holding still the senses.
Then one should be alert,
for "yoga" comes and goes.'

Katha Upanishad 2-III-11 / 6.11

* * *

Another Indian Scripture, revered by many, is the *Vigyana Bhairava Tantra*, which details some 112 practices aimed at stilling the mind, with one such practice being *dharana* (attention):

यत्र यत्र मनो याति तत्तत्तेनैव तत्क्षणम् ।

परित्यज्यानवस्थित्या निस्तरङ्गस्ततो भवेत् ॥

'The very moment that the mind goes wandering,
that inattentiveness is to be abandoned - stillness should follow.'

Vigyana Bhairava Tantra, verse 129

* * *

And here is a surprisingly simple quote from an Indian Buddhist monk: one who adhered to the *tantric* school of *yoga*, his words preserved in Tibetan;

མི་མནོ་ མི་བསམ་ མི་སེམས་ མི་དཔྱོད་ མི་སྒོམ་ རང་སར་བཞག

'mi-mno - Don't recall,
mi-bsam - Don't imagine,
mi-sems - Don't think,
mi-dpyod - Don't examine,
mi-sgom - Don't control,
rang-sar-bzhag - Gather oneself anew.'

- Tilopa - an Indian *tantric* (988-1069)

* * *

308

It's a relief to find that one can actually put oneself on pause, that one can, at least for a while, withdraw one's attention from involvement in day-to-day activities, thoughts, and distractions, and totally refresh oneself.

In this method of meditation I practice, it appears I've re-discovered the *'chittavrittinirodha'* mentioned in the *Yoga Sutras*, the art of stilling the motions of the mind and becoming established in *yoga*, experiencing *samadhi* (immersion in calmness), and I am therefore very curious to know of others who have this knowledge. I search through the teachings of numerous teachers.

Whilst researching, I wonder what else, other than attaining a state of deep relaxation, is to be derived from this *yoga* meditation? Already I notice that my senses are sharpened, that I am seeing much more vividly, and that I'm hearing more acutely, even to the point where I now find myself asking others not to speak so **loudly**! But by tuning into the inner silence of the universe, what other benefits are likely to arise from such practise?

The oldest known text on *Hatha Yoga* exercise is the *Hatha Yoga Pradipika*, which also refers to this same practice:

'.. when the mind becomes devoid of all the activities, and remains changeless, then the "yogi" attains to the "laya" stage. ' 4-31
'When all the thoughts and activities are destroyed, then the "laya" stage is produced to describe which is beyond the power of speech, being known by self-experience alone. ' 4-32
'They often speak of "laya", "laya"; but what is meant by "laya"? "laya" is simply the forgetting of the objects of senses when the "vasanas" (desires) do not rise into existence again' 4-33

Hatha Yoga Pradipika
(translation by Pancham Sinh)

* * *

When I sit for another period of stillness, I notice there is soon no thought; just awareness, awareness of awareness, and that afterwards it occurs to me the experience of deep meditation might be likened to restful suspended motion.

And when eventually, after what seems an infinity spent absorbed in silence, there is another thought, and I notice it very subtly forming, I pay attention to the message of that thought, which is, *'I think I've been sitting long enough now'*. So I slowly open my eyes, blinking for a moment, and then close them again before I lay myself down. I rest awhile, a long while, during which time I hardly think, and when I check the clock I find that three-quarters of an hour has passed. Yet, apart from those first few thoughts, and my response, which was just to observe, well, nothing else has happened. It's as though I've been in a state of wakeful suspended animation. Very relaxing and reassuring, and there is no urgency, no hurry to do anything, I just rest awhile longer before getting up and getting busy again.

Of course, the *Bhagavad Gita* – *'The Lord's Song'* - contains at its heart, instructions for meditation, which, in light of experience, appear to be none other than this practice of going within and being without thought, *chittavrittinirodha*:

'In a clean spot, having set a firm seat (cushion) *of his own, neither too high nor too low, made of cloth, a deerskin and kusha-grass, one upon the other.* Gita 6:11
'There, having made the mind one-pointed, with the activities of the mind and the senses controlled, let him seated on the seat, practice "yoga" for self-purification.
Gita 6:12
'Let him steadily hold his body, keeping head and neck erect and still, directing the gaze towards the tip of the nose, without looking in any direction. Gita 6:13
'Abandoning without reserve all desires born of thought and imagination, and completely restraining the whole group of senses by the mind from all sides.
Gita 6:24
'Gradually, gradually let him attain to quietude by firmly holding the intellect; establishing the mind in the Self; let him not think even of anything. Gita 6:25
'From whatever cause the restless and unsteady mind wanders away, from that let him restrain it and bring it under the control of the Self alone. Gita 6:26
'For supreme happiness comes to the yogi whose mind is quite peaceful, whose passion is quieted...' Gita 6:27

- Bhagavad Gita

* * *

I'm not sure how often I should sit to meditate. Maybe once a day, twice a day, or just whenever I feel like it? I am minded to observe that since this is, to me, a special activity, I should make sure I am fully awake before sitting.

I get into a habit of lighting a short stick of incense beforehand. I love the relaxing fragrance of some brands of incense.

* * *

Valmiki is best known as the poet, who is thought to have composed the epic Sanskrit poem known as the *Ramayana*, but it is also said he composed the *Yoga Vasistha*, a large work that includes guidance with regards meditation:

'.. by self-effort and self-knowledge make the mind no-mind. Let the infinite consciousness swallow, as it were, the finite mind and then go beyond everything. With your intelligence united with the supreme, hold on to the self which is imperishable.' YV 3.111

'If you give up all thoughts you will here and now attain to the realisation of oneness with all.' YV 3.17

- Yoga Vasistha Maharamayana
translation by Venkatesananda - SUNY, 1993

310

I notice that each time I sit to meditate; it's as if it's the first time. Each time I sit I must learn anew just how to proceed, and on each occasion the process of settling down is slightly different. In fact I make a point of observing my meditations in the hope of witnessing how the process works, so I might remember and be able tell others. Not to form a set of instructions, but to gain an understanding of the process.

Instead of trying not to think, which would be a strain, be counter productive and probably give me a headache, I instead choose just to remain watchful for any thoughts, and by doing so I usually find myself naturally detached from the content of a thought, an observer, uninvolved.

Another thing to understand is that the purpose of the meditation is not merely to be without thought - it's not a fight against thoughts, but a wish to settle and replenish, and to discover and revisit a crystal clear feeling of oneself. Always, the realm of the mind beyond thought is serenity, which appears to be the nature of the mind.

It seems a good idea only to meditate when you want to! There are no rules, so if you want to skip meditation because you don't feel like it - fine - or if you are tired or stressed, don't force it. Not a good idea to sit for this meditation if one is feeling needy. Also, it's not a good thing to meditate just after a meal or after strenuous exercise. So whilst there are few 'do nots', I still reckon it's not a good idea to sit to meditate if one is in a stressed out state of stress, especially if one has just received bad news, just had an argument, experienced something that has unsettled you particularly. Or else you are likely to try to force yourself not to think about the cause of your anxiety, in which case it's unlikely you will be at peace with yourself.

Above all, this meditation is not a challenge or a competition, one is not challenging the mind, nor is one competing with others.

* * *

Meditation is an age-old practice described in ancient texts of various cultures across the world, some from more than 2000 years ago. Meditation is variously referred to as *'dhyana'* in Sanskrit, *'ch'an'* in Chinese, *'zen'* in Japanese, *'jhana'* in Pali and *'sgom'* in Tibetan.

Here is a random selection of references to this practice from Scriptures of various traditions:

Nirodha-samapatti
The Buddha is said to have rediscovered a state of consciousness that is beyond the dimension of perception or non-perception, a state referred to as *'nirodha samapatti'*. This is sometimes called the "ninth *jhana*" of nine *jhanas* (*jhana* = *dhyana* = meditation). The word *'nirodha'* means 'cessation', whilst *'samapatti'* means 'attainment' (and it's also a synonym of *'samadhi'*, which is the state of 'profound meditation'), so *nirodha-samapatti* is both the 'attainment of cessation' and the *'samadhi* of cessation'.

- Theravada Buddhism

zazen

'When no thought arises in the mind it is called za (sitting) *and to look at one's own nature inwardly is called zen* (meditation).*'*

wu nien

[about *zen* (meditation) & *wu nien* (no thought)]
'Have your mind like unto space and yet entertain in it no thought of emptiness.'

- Platform Sutra
Hui-Neng (638-713)
Chinese Ch'an Buddhist

* * *

'Question: A little while ago you spoke of refraining from thinking (nien), but you did not finish your explanation.

Answer: It means not fixing your mind upon anything any-where, but totally withdrawing it from the phenomena surrounding you, so that even the thought (szu) of seeking for something does not remain; it means that your mind, confronted by all the forms composing your environment, remains placid and motionless. This abstaining from all thought whatever is called real thought...'

- Zen Teaching of Instantaneous Awakening, IA 36.1
Dazhu HuiHai ('the Great Pearl')
Chinese Ch'an Buddhist - 9th century

* * *

312

'Think the unthinkable.
How to think the unthinkable?
Be without thoughts - this is the secret of meditation.'

- Fukan Zazen-Gi
Do-gen Zenji
Japanese Zen Buddhist - 13th century

* * *

致虛極
守靜篤

zhì xū jí
shŏu jìng dŭ

'Empty yourself of everything.
Let the mind rest at peace.'

Tao Te Ching v16
(translation by Gia-fu Feng and Jane English)
Lao Tzu
Chinese Taoist - c. 6th century BC

* * *

'Be still, and know that I am God.'   *- Psalms* 46:10

'But seek ye first the kingdom of heaven of God
and all these things will be added unto you.' *- Matthew* 6:33

'.. the kingdom of God is within you.'   *- Luke* 17:21

- The Bible

* * *

In 16th century Europe, the Spanish mystic, Saint John of the Cross, asserted that *'God's first language is silence,'* and centuries later, Fr. Thomas Keating, an American Trappist monk, commented: *'Everything else is a poor translation. In order to understand this language, we must learn to be silent and to rest in God.'*

* * *

313

Sometimes, after meditating, I feel inspired to write down some fresh personal observation about the meditation process:

'Each meditation is as if one has never meditated before, and one rediscovers its simplicity anew.'

'Stilling thought, yet watchful and listening.'

'Gentle tidying of the mind with clear intent, and good-humoured patience.'

'Wave of intent, washing the shore, erasing, clearing seeds of thoughts away.'

'And then, occasionally, meditation seems to be a mixture of some faint thinking interwoven with flashes of stillness and delicious silence.'

'A settling - such as changes the perspective - one sees the thought as detached - with choice as to giving it attention or paying attention to stillness.'

'It's as if breath has altogether *ceased or is so imperceptible that it appears so.'*

'Observe, observation - when there is no thought, there is still awareness.'

'Total Immersion, the sea of Being.'

'A deactivated thought, abandoned; not a puff of breeze to blow it away, not a flicker in the stillness.'

'I wonder, that by sitting in the vast silence, if we are ever isolated, alone or separate? Or else, paradoxically, that one is actually at one with everyone and unified with everything. Again, in the silence, is one really hearing nothing, or else hearing everything, from everywhere? For isn't this tuning into the infinite what intuition really is?'

'A day comes when the air carries the sound of strong winds, and when I sit to meditate I wonder if it's possible to meditate with so much sound around.
I sit witnessing the sounds, and witnessing my thoughts, about the sounds, and gently I let my thoughts subside. Yet, even when the thoughts have blown themselves out, I hear the sound of the wind.
And I realise that in meditation awareness of airborne sound can occur whilst being totally at one with oneself, settled in inner blissful inner energy. Awareness of sounds can dip and rise, even when one is in a hallowed inner state of meditation.'

'To be within, in meditation, without thought, is not to be without awareness!'

'Breath and attention, light as a feather.'

'Removed from stimuli yet nestled in a vast sea of reassuring blissful silence, & with a sense of serenity and peace, then one is just simply being.'

॥ नमस्ते ॥

Namasté, I bow to you

Lightning Source UK Ltd.
Milton Keynes UK
UKHW020707130622
404345UK00006B/587